Discourses and Strategies:

The Role of the Vienna School
in Shaping Central European Approaches
to Art History & Related Discourses

Slowakische Akademie der Wissenschaften
Slovak Academy of Sciences

Schriftenreihe der Slowakischen Akademie der Wissenschaften
Series of the Slovak Academy of Sciences
Band / Volume 5

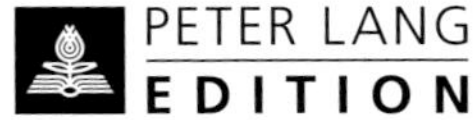

Ján Bakoš

Discourses and Strategies:

The Role of the Vienna School in Shaping Central European Approaches to Art History & Related Discourses

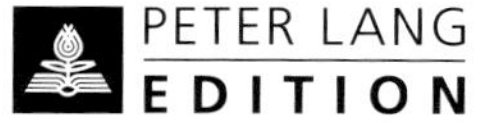

Bibliographic Information published by the Deutsche Nationalbibliothek
The Deutsche Nationalbibliothek lists this publication in the Deutsche Nationalbibliografie; detailed bibliographic data is available in the internet at http://dnb.d-nb.de.

Library of Congress Cataloging-in-Publication Data

Bakoš, Ján, 1943 – author.
  [Essays. Selections]
  Discourses and strategies : the role of the Vienna school in shaping Central European approaches to art history and related discourses / Ján Bakoš. – 1 [edition].
    pages cm. – (Series of the Slovak Academy of Sciences ; vol. 5)
  Essays collected in this book were drafted and written during the previous decade and published in their original form, without correction.
  Includes bibliographical references and index.
  ISBN 978-3-631-64452-2
1. Art – Historiography. 2. Universität Wien. Kunsthistorisches Institut – Influence. 3. Europe, Central – Intellectual life – 19th century. 4. Europe, Central – Intellectual life – 20th century. I. Title.
  N7480.B35 2014
  707.2′2 – dc23
                                                                2013016173

Frontispiece: *Spiral VII*, 1995, by Milan Paštéka. Courtesy of Milan Paštéka, Jr.
Cover design: *Jana Sapáková*
Layout: *Jana Janíková*
Printing: VEDA, Publishing House of the Slovak Academy of Sciences

ISSN 1612-149X
ISBN 978-3-631-64452-2 (Print)
E-ISBN 978-3-653-03167-6 (E-Book)
DOI 10.3726/978-3-653-03167-6

CONTENTS

PREFACE & ACKNOWLEDGEMENT

The essays collected in this book were drafted and written during the previous decade. Many were delivered as papers at international conferences and appeared in various journals or conference proceedings. Here they are published in their original form, without correction.

All share a common denominator: concern with the trajectories of art historical ideas and their ideological instrumentality. Seen thus, the history of art history appears not simply as a history of theoretical constructs but as a story of concealed political interests and implicit ideological strategies. Nonetheless, the author is also more than aware that the zenith of research into the relationship between epistemology and ideology is almost over and that searching for the hidden ideological dimension of art historical research is, therefore, no longer on the main agenda of present day art history. However, it must also be said that the author's aim in analysing the premises and intentions of art historical discourse in its many forms, together with his reconstruction of their historical paths, is not to undermine the credibility of art history by reducing it to total epistemological relativism. The historiography of art historical theories and critical reflection on their ideological background is understood by the author as an auxiliary art historical subdiscipline. Therefore his chief ambition has been to demonstrate that ideological involvement is an unavoidable part of art historical research, from which it must follow that art historians, to be worthy of their salt, must always be extra vigilant when it comes to this aspect of their work.

It is not the ambition of the present book to map the full spectrum of theories and methods that have shaped the paths of modern art history. Inevitably, the personal perspective of any researcher affects the choice of their object of investigation, which, in this author's case, is evidently that of a Central European art historian. That is why the Vienna School of Art History and its impact is put at the centre of the investigations presented in this book.

Without research grants awarded by the Österreichische Akademie der Wissenschaften, the Landis & Gyr Foundation, the Fritz Thyssen Stiftung, the British Academy, the Getty Thrust, the Geisteswissenschaftliches Zentrum Geschichte und Kultur Ostmitteleuropas an der Universität Leipzig (GWZO) and grant agency of the Slovak Academy of Sciences VEGA, and without research carried out at the Swiss Institute for Art Research in Zürich, the Zentralinstitut für Kunstgeschichte in München, the Getty Research Institute in Los Angeles, the Courtaud Institute of Art in London or the GWZO in Leipzig, the present essays might not have seen the light of day. That is why the author would like to express a deep gratitude to Stephen Bann, Gottfried Böhm, Albert Boime, Thomas Crow, Heinrich Dilly, Jiří Fajt, Clair Farago, Eric Fernie, Hans Joerg Heusser, Stefan Muthesius, Donald Preziosi and Artur Rosenauer for their faith in his research and broad-minded support of his projects. The author's thanks go also to Wojciech Bałus (Jagiellonian University Kraków), Horst Bredekamp (Humboldt University Berlin), Kornelia Imesch (Swiss Institute for Art Research Zürich), Thomas DaCosta Kaufmann (Princeton University), Jiří Kuthan (Charles University Prague), Adam S. Labuda (Humboldt University Berlin), Michaela Marek (University Leipzig), Sergiusz Michalski (University Tübingen), John Onians (University of East Anglia Norwich), Piotr Piotrowski (Adam Miczkiewicz University Poznań), Charles Salas (Getty Research Institute Los Angeles) and Michael Viktor Schwarz (University Vienna) for invitations to conferences or lectures which gave him the opportunity to present the results of his research to a larger art historical comunity. For their generous assistance and valuable suggestions and comments on English version of the papers the author is greatly indebted to Robert Gibbs, Matthew Rampley and Paul Stirton. A particular gratitude is directed to Nick McAdoo, for improving the final text immensurably and making it more comprehensible and readable. Important stimulus was also given by the interest taken in his research on diferent occasions by Robert Born, Marina Dmitrieva, James Elkins, Jaś Elsner, Jaromír Homolka, Jiří Kroupa, Marian Kutzner, Steven Mansbach, Branko Mitrović, Keith Moxey, Piotr Skubiszewski and Christopher Wood, among others. They all have the author's gratitude.

Finally, the author is no less indebted to Robert Suckale and Ingrid Ciulisová for encouragement to publish these collected essays in book form and to Jan Michl and Oliver Bakoš for their massive support for this project. The author knows how lucky he has been to have had the benefit of the support from all these people.

And last but not least, the author would like to express his gratitude to the Slovak Academy of Sciences for the financial support of the book and the publishing houses VEDA and Peter LANG GmbH, for including the book among their projects.

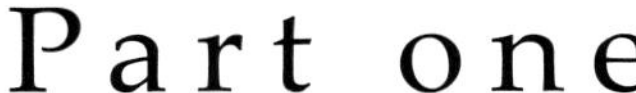

Part one

I. "HUMANISTS" VERSUS "RELATIVISTS": METHODOLOGICAL VISIONS AND REVISIONS WITHIN THE VIENNA SCHOOL

The Common Denominator

Irrespective of whether the Vienna School can be regarded as a dialectical system within a bipolar structure or as a merely pluralistic succession of methodological discourses,[1] and despite all the deep differences concerning the nature of art, the historical process and art historical research, there were at least three common characteristics shared by all art historians trained at Vienna University from Moritz Thausing to Ernst H. Gombrich. They are as follows: 1. the idea of art history as a science; 2. the notion of the historical basis of art history, and 3. belief in the method as a methodological credo or doctrine.[2]

Summary or a Foreshadowing of Revisions to Orthodoxy?

It is well known that Hans Tietze, in his *Methode der Kunstgeschichte*, published in 1913, attempted to summarize the basic principles of the evolution-

---

[1] See HOFMANN, Werner: Was bleibt von der "Wiener Schule"? in *Kunsthistoriker*, 1-2, 1984 – 1985, No. 1, pp. 4-8, here p. 4; ZAUNSCHIRM, Thomas: Kunstgeschichte als Geistesgeschichte. Eine andere Wiener Schule, in *Das grössere Österreich*. Ed. Kristian SOTRIFFER. Wien 1982, pp. 162-164, here p. 162; POCHAT, Götz – SCHMIDT, Gerhard – VASOLD, Georg: Der Beitrag der Kunstgeschichte zur Ausformung der Humanwissenschaften, in *Geschichte der österreichischen Humanwissenschaften*. Vol. 5. Ed. Karl ACHAM. Wien 2003, pp. 403-444; AURENHAMMER, Hans: Zäsur oder Kontinuität? Das Wiener Kunsthistorische Institut im Ständestaat und im Nationalsozialismus, in *Wiener Schule. Erinnerung und Perspektiven* (=Wiener Jahrbuch für Kunstgeschichte, 53). Wien – Köln – Weimar 2004, pp. 11-54, here p. 53.

[2] On this issue, see FREY, Dagobert: Bemerkungen zur "Wiener Schule der Kunstwissenschaft", in FREY, Dagobert: *Eine Erinnerungsschrift*. Kiel 1962, pp. 6-7; GOMBRICH, Ernst H.: *Topics of Our Time. Twentieth-Century Issues in Learning and in Art*. London 1991, p. 64; LACHNIT, Edwin: Ansätze methodischer Evolution in der Wiener Schule der Kunstgeschichte, in *L'Art et les révolutions, 5. Révolution et évolution de l'Histoire de l'Art de Warburg á nos jours. Actes du XXVIIème congrès international d'histoire de l'art, Strasbourg, 1 – 7 septembre 1989*. Strasbourg 1992, pp. 43-52, here p. 43; SEILER, Martin: Empirische Motive im Denken und Forschen der Wiener Schule der Kunstgeschichte, in *Kunst, Kunsttheorie und Kunstforschung im wissenschaftlichen Diskurs. In memoriam Kurt Blaukopf*. Eds. Martin SEILER – Friedrich STADLER. Wien 2000, pp. 49-86.

ist methodological project developed by Franz Wickhoff and Alois Riegl and articulated explicitly by Max Dvořák.[3] In "Das Rätsel der Kunst der Brüder van Eyck" (published in 1903),[4] Dvořák had expressed the credo of a *"genetic approach"* as follows: *"... die moderne Wissenschaft hat uns gelehrt... die Tatsachen in einzelne... Kausalverbindung zwingende Entwicklungsketten umzusetzen. Unter dem Einflusse der exakten Forschungsmethoden haben wir... gelernt... eine Tatsache nie als eine vereinzelte Erscheinung, sondern stets als ein Glied in einer bestimmten Aufeinanderfolge von Tatsachen derselben oder verwandten Art zu betrachten."*[5] In Tietze's reconstruction of the genetic method of the Vienna School, the first rifts in this doctrine occurred.[6] Arguing against the idea of a work of art as part of an immanent evolution[7] and anticipating Schlosser's nominalism, Tietze claimed that the work of art is an isolated phenomenon.[8] Inspired by neo-Kantian philosophy, he even started to conceive of evolution as a scientific construct.[9] His characterization of the key idea of Viennese orthodoxy, the belief in *"the immanent evolution of art"* as *"a reduction and abstraction"*[10] foreshadowed the revision of the formalist-evolutionist model and the first steps towards a new heteronymous and expressionist notion of art history. The idea of art history as the history of ideas or worldviews was, however, not explicitly or fully articulated by Hans Tietze but rather by Max Dvořák.[11]

Unfolding Revision

It is well known that the new approach articulated in Dvořák's "Idealismus und Naturalismus in der gotischen Malerei und Plastik" (1918) resulted

---

[3]   TIETZE, Hans: *Die Methode der Kunstgeschichte*. Leipzig 1913.

[4]   DVOŘÁK, Max: Das Rätsel der Kunst der Brüder van Eyck, in *Jahrbuch der Kunstsammlungen des allerhöchsten Kaiserhauses*, 24, 1903, pp. 161-319 (2nd ed. 1924. Eds. Johannes WILDE – Karl M. SWOBODA; 3rd ed. 1999. Ed. Artur ROSENAUER).

[5]   DVOŘÁK 1999 (see note 4), p. 12.

[6]   TIETZE 1913 (see note 3), pp. 41-46.

[7]   In Dvořák's words: *"Jede geschichtliche Bildung ist ein Glied einer bestimmten geschichtlichen Entwicklungskette und bedingt durch die vorangehenden Bildungen derselben Materie." "Das eigentliche und wichtigste Substrat der Geschichte der Kunst, wenn sie mehr sein soll als Künstlergeschichte, ist die Entwicklung der formalen Darstellungsprobleme."* – DVOŘÁK 1999 (see note 4), p. 13.

[8]   *"Jedes Kunstwerk ist seinem Wesen nach etwas völlig Isoliertes."* – TIETZE 1913 (see note 3), p. 2.

[9]   *"Gruppierung in genetischen Zusammenhang... [ist] eine wissenschaftliche Rationalisierung."* – Ibid., p. 45.

[10]   *"Reduzierung... auf eine immanente Entwicklung is eine Abstraktion."* – Ibid., p. 44.

[11]   DVOŘÁK, Max: *Kunstgeschichte als Geistesgeschichte. Studien zur abendländischen Kunstentwicklung*. Eds. Johannes WILDE – Karl M. SWOBODA. München 1924.

in a fundamental revision of the orthodox genetic-autonomous model.[12] Seeing art in terms of the solution of formal problems was replaced by the idea of art as an expression of ideas; the notion of history as a continuous process, by the idea of turns, ruptures or revolutionary breaks, and the notion of art historical research as a rational explanation (*"Erklärung"*) unveiling causal connections, by the concept of art history as a grasping and interpretation of unique and even irrational historical phenomena.[13] Despite that, the notion of art history as the history of ideas represented no revolutionary rupture.[14] It was an organic result of the consistent development of Riegl's late ideas about the puzzling parallelism between the history of style and the history of worldviews.[15] The new paradigm still shared with the old orthodox one not only a belief in historical relativism but also a conviction that the history of art had an impersonal nature, despite the independent and active (if not autonomous) role played by art itself. Riegl's antinormativity still implied the notion of *"ars una"*[16] or at least a belief in the lasting essence of all art, identified either as a *"Wettschaffen mit der Natur"*[17] or as a sensuous common denominator and the core of the art work, i.e. *"das eigentlich Bildkünstlerische im Kunstwerk… Form und Farbe in Ebene oder Raum"*.[18] He regarded the historical changes of *"Kunstwollen"* as variations on a common core oscillating between two alternative poles of human perception (resulting in "haptic" or "optic" artistic rendering). Dvořák, by contrast, arrived at a radical historical relativism. He

---

[12] DVOŘÁK, Max: Idealismus und Naturalismus in der gotischen Malerei und Plastik, in *Historische Zeitschrift*, 119, 1918, pp. 1-62, 185-246; reprinted in DVOŘÁK 1924 (see note 11), pp. 41-147.

[13] DVOŘÁK, Max: Kunstbetrachtung.Vortrag gehalten am Denkmalpflegetag in Bregenz im 1920, in *Mitteilungen des Bundesdenkmalamtes*, 2, 1920 – 1923, pp. 93-97: *"Die Kunst besteht nicht nur in der Lösung und Entwicklung formaler Aufgaben und Probleme; sie ist auch immer und in erster Linie Ausdruck der die Menschheit beherrschenden Ideen… ein Teil der allgemeinen Geistesgeschichte."* Quoted according to Johannes WILDE – Karl M. SWOBODA: Vorwort der Herausgeber, in DVOŘÁK 1924 (see note 11), p. X.

[14] See TIETZE, Hans: Geisteswissenschaftliche Kunstgeschichte, in *Die Kunstwissenschaft der Gegenwart in Selbstdarstellungen*. Ed. Johannes JAHN. Lepzig 1924, pp. 183-198, here p. 185: *"Diese geisteswissenschaftliche Einstellung ist nicht Absage an die entwicklungsgeschichtliche Auffassung… sondern ihre notwendige und folgerichtige Fortbildung."*

[15] Riegl spoke of *"die Parallele zwischen bildender Kunst und Weltanschauung"* in the last chapter of his *Spätrömische Kunstindustrie*, published 1901, entitled "Die Grundzüge der spätrömischen Kunstwollens". – RIEGL, Alois: *Spätrömische Kunstindustrie*. Wien 1927 (2nd ed.), pp. 401-405.

[16] BELTING, Hans: *Das Ende der Kunstgeschichte?* München 1984, p. 15, attributed *"das Axiom einer ars una"* to the whole Vienna School.

[17] RIEGL, Alois: *Historische Grammatik der bildenden Künste*. Eds. Karl M. SWOBODA – Otto PÄCHT. Graz – Köln 1966, p. 2.

[18] See DITTMANN, Lorenz: Der Begriff des Kunstwerks in der deutschen Kunstgeschichte, in *Kategorien und Methoden der deutschen Kunstgeschichte, 1900 – 1930*. Ed. Lorenz DITTMANN. Stuttgart 1985, pp. 51-88, here p. 55.

developed the idea of the history of art as the history of the concept of "art". According to Dvořák, *"der Begriff des Kunstwerkes und des Künstlerischen hat im Laufe der historischen Entwicklung, und zwar bis auf die Grundlinien, die mannigfaltigsten Wandlungen erfahren und war stets ein zeitlich und kulturell begrenztes und variables Ergebnis der allgemeinen Evolution der Menschheit"*.[19] Consequently, the view of art history conceived of as changes to the identity of art itself, opened the door to later sociological interpretations of art.

However, the impersonal determinism and relativism of Dvořák's history of worldviews inherited from Riegl, provoked criticism. Even Dvořák's close adherents, Otto Benesch and Hans Tietze realized very early the dangers implied in Geistesgeschichte, as follows: that of turning art history into history without works of art[20] and of neglecting the active nature of art, this being the consequence of treating works of art as mere documents of intellectual history.[21]

The Turn to Individuality

Dvořák himself escaped both perils mentioned above in his late lectures and papers. Leaning upon a neo-Kantian belief in the unique nature of historical phenomena combined with the idea of the irrational nature of the historical process, Dvořák abandoned his old belief in historical causality. This he replaced with the idea of great artists as the initiators of the history of art and creators of the worldviews of their age.[22] As a consequence, radical histori-

---

[19] DVOŘÁK 1918 (see note 12) in DVOŘÁK 1924 (see note 11), p. 125. On this issue, see BAKOŠ, Ján: Max Dvořák – a Neglected Re-Visionist, in *Wiener Schule. Erinnerung und Perspektiven* (see note 1), pp. 55-71.

[20] See BENESCH, Otto: Max Dvořák. Ein Versuch zur Geschichte der historischen Geisteswissenschaften (1922), in *Repertorium für Kunstwissenschaft*, 44, 1924; reprinted in BENESCH, Otto: *Collected Writings*. Vol. 4. London 1973, pp. 267-303, here p. 285: *"… man könnte jetzt von einer Kunstgeschichte ohne Kunstwerke reden, deren Inhalt nur mehr die Geschichte der künstlerischen Ideen ist."*

[21] According to TIETZE 1924 (see note 14), p. 194: *"Die geistesgeschichtliche Auffassung erbt aber auch von ihrer Vorgängerin die Gefahr, sich in eine blosse Abstraktion zu verlieren... das Kunstwerk läuft Gefahr, aus einem organischen Ganzen zum blossen Träger von Ideen zu werden."*

[22] According to BENESCH 1973 (see note 20), p. 290, Dvořák's appreciation of the important historical role of the great masters (*"die neue Bedeutung der großen Einzelpersönlichkeiten"*) was the consequence on his new view of the irrational nature of the historical process: *"Dvořák hat in letzter Zeit den tiefsten Grund alles geistigen Fortschrittes in den schöpferischen Wirken einzelner großer Geister gesehen. Die Geschichte ist... das schöpferische Resultat des Wirkens jener Großen, die zum Schicksal ihres Zeitalters geworden sind."* TIETZE 1924 (see note 14), pp. 196-197, also observed Dvořák's resort to the history of artists. On this issue, see MICHALSKI, Sergiusz: Zur methodologischen Stellung der Wiener Schule in den zwanziger und dreißiger Jahren,

cal relativism started to evolve into transhistoricism. Dvořák articulated the belief that the history of art resulted in eternal artistic values.[23] Seen thus, the consequence was that art historical research itself transformed its character: no longer the mere reconstruction and interpretation of the past, it took on rather a new role, moralizing about the present and prophesying the future.[24] Thus, Dvořák's late essays about great masters like Tintoretto, El Greco, Dürer or Pieter Brueghel the Elder can be regarded as anticipating the explicit critical revision of Vienna School orthodoxy carried out and declared by Julius von Schlosser in 1924. Riegl's and Dvořák's "realism" was replaced by the extreme "nominalism" of Schlosser. In place of formal evolution or collective worldviews, the singular work of art and the artist were established as the basic elements of the history of art and the genuine objects of art historical research.[25]

Insularist Turn

Even if Schloser's turn to insular theory,[26] conceiving of the work of art as a monad,[27] represented an open revolt against Riegl's hegemony, having the character of a revolutionary break, it came into existence more as a metamorphosis of previous notions. His long museum practice necessarily focused on singular works of art and his intensive study of the history of writing on art[28] contained the seeds of nominalism on the one hand, and of individualism on the other. Moreover, an indication of an implicit revolt against Riegl's deductionist approach, abstract *"Grammar"*[29] and immanent and impersonal

---

    in *Wien und die Entwicklung der kunsthistorischen Methode. Akten des XXV. Internationalen Kongresses für Kunstgeschichte*. Wien – Köln – Graz 1984, p. 86.

[23]   BENESCH 1973 (see note 20), p. 303: *"Dvořák trug in sich den Glauben an die unsterblichen Ideen."*

[24]   Ibid., pp. 294-295. Benesch speaks of the later Dvořák's understanding of science as *"Lebensgestaltung"*.

[25]   See SCHLOSSER, Julius von: Ein Lebenskommentar, in *Die Kunstwissenschaft der Gegenwart...* (see note 14), pp. 95-134.

[26]   Schlosser adopted Croce's term *"Inselhaftigkeit"*. See Ibid., p. 129.

[27]   Schlosser speaks of *"Das Monadische des Kunstwerks"*. Nevertheless, Schlosser also attributed the status of monad to great artists: *"Jedes echte Kunstwerk trägt, wie die ideale Künstlerpersönlichkeit... einen Massstab in, nicht ausser sich... als Monade."* – Ibid., p. 130.

[28]   The result was his monumental book *Die Kunstliteratur. Ein Handbuch zur Quellenkunde der neueren Kunstgeschichte* (Wien 1924).

[29]   Riegl's *"historische Grammatik"*, i.e. the search for styles (*"Zeitstil"* or *"objective style"*) and general historical patterns, also referred to as *"die Grammatik der Kunstsprache"*, was denounced by Schlosser as *"die Generalisierung, eine Abstraktion, vielmehr 'Fiktion'"*, or as a *"historisch-logische Konstruktion"*. See SCHLOSSER 1924 (see note 25), pp. 102-103, 108-109, 117.

determinism can already be detected in Schlosser's "open" idea of the art-work[30] as a cultural/historical phenomenon and in his attempt to replace Riegl's "*Kunstwollen*" with the idea of "*Kunstanschauung*".[31] Schlosser himself dated the implicit start of his nominalist turn as early as between 1901 – 1903.[32] As is known, the role of catalyst for the insular and individualist theory of art was played by Schlosser's friend Benedetto Croce.[33] But Croce not only inspired Schlosser to conceive of art history as the history of great artists, but expelled history from art *per se*.[34] As a consequence, Schlosser, as a member of an historical school *par excellence*, was faced with a dilemma. His extreme atomist historicism, which regarded works of art as utterly unique phenomena ("*monads*") threatened to lead towards an ahistorical transcendentalism. Consequently, the history of art was transformed into the reconstruction of timeless masterworks or into a transhistorical communion of genii.[35] Croce prompted Schlosser to replace Riegl's impersonal determinism with individualist activism, the abstract "*Kunstwollen*" with the individual artist. He also substituted an aristocratic individualism, appreciating only great artists and their masterworks for Riegl's democratic idea of removing the gap between high and low art.[36] Croce's work also stimulated him to reject Riegl's relativism. In order to overcome Riegl's indifference to aesthetic value, Schlosser

---

[30] HOFMANN, Werner: Stil- und Sprachgeschichte: Julius von Schlosser's offenes System, in *Merkur*, 46, 1992, No. 3, pp. 255-262, here p. 260, interpreted Schlosser's "*open concept of art*" ("*offener Kunstbegriff*") as communication ("*Mitteilung*").

[31] This can be regarded as a transformation of Rumohr's concept of "*Kunstauffassung*". Schlosser re-edited and introduced Rumohr's *Italienische Forschungen* in 1920. See RUMOHR, Carl Friedrich von: *Italienische Forschungen*. Ed. Julius von SCHLOSSER. Frankfurt am Main 1920. See also SCHLOSSER 1924 (see note 25), p. 106.

[32] Schlosser referred it to his contribution to Wickhoff's Festschrift "Randglossen zu einer Stelle Montaignes" (1903). – SCHLOSSER 1924 (see note 25), p. 121. Nevertheless, it also relates to Schlosser's distinction between "*grammar*" ("*Grammatik*") and "*language*" ("*Kunstsprache*") and to the discovery of the role of tradition as articulated in his papers "Zur Genesis der mitelalterlichen Kunstanschauung" (1901) and "Zur Kenntnis der künstlerischen Überlieferung im späten Mittelalter" (1903).

[33] Schlosser acknowledged his indebtedness to Croce in his "Lebenskommentar": "*Meine Bekanntschaft mit ihm* [i.e. Benedetto Croce] *ist das eigentliche Ereignis meines Lebens geworden, mir eine völlige Erneuerung, eine zweite Jugend gebracht hat.*" – SCHLOSSER 1924 (see note 25), pp. 121-122.

[34] On Benedetto Croce, see GANTNER, Joseph: *Schönheit und Grenzen klassischer Form*. Wien 1949, pp. 43-94.

[35] Later, Hans Sedlmayr also shared this idea. See SEDLMAYR, Hans: Kunstgeschichte als Geistesgeschichte, in *Wort und Wahrheit*, 4, 1949, pp. 264-277; reprinted in SEDLMAYR, Hans: *Kunst und Wahrheit. Zur Theorie und Methode der Kunstgeschichte*. Hamburg 1958, pp. 71-86, here p. 81: "*So gesehen aber sind die großen Kunstwerke... untereinander verwandter als die Werke gleichen Stils. Es gibt über Raum und Zeit hinweg eine geistige Kommunion der wahren Künstler...*"

[36] According to SCHLOSSER 1924 (see note 25), p. 125: "*... es gibt keine 'Kunst', nur 'Künstler'.*"

appropriated Croce's idea of art history as art criticism. According to Schlosser, art history must be anchored in an axiology that distinguishes between creative and non-creative art, between genii and epigones. Furthermore, following Croce's belief in art as expression, Schlosser held up for contrast expression and communication, together with style and language. Style, for Schlosser, was the product of individual artists and the embodiment of their creative expression and not, as Riegl claimed, the result of an anonymous artistic intention (*"Kunstwollen"*). As a consequence, the dilemma mentioned above that resulted from Croce's antinomy of *"art criticism versus history"*, was overcome by means of a dualist theory. In 1935, Schlosser, following Karl Vossler[37] but contradicting Croce's ahistorical model in a sense, distinguished *"Stilgeschichte"* from *"Sprachgeschichte"*, the history of style from the history of language, individual expression from collective communication, and creation (by great artists) from imitation (by epigones).[38] In this way, Schlosser counterpoised Croce's belief in creative expression with the Viennese idea of style and its history. The true history of art was regarded by Schlosser as the production of styles, but styles were themselves conceived of as individual expressions executed exclusively by great artists.[39] Consequently, neither Riegl's history of grammar nor the history of language could be regarded as true art history, according to Schlosser. They represented only an empty abstract construction or inferior cultural and historical aspect of true art history.[40] In this way, Schlosser aimed to preserve the historicity of art without losing artistic creation's unique, individual and transcendental nature, and to reconcile Vienna School historicism with Croce's expressionist transcen-

---

[37]   Schlosser was attracted by Vossler's synthesis of language as expressive creation with language regarded as history (*"Sprache als 'Schöpfung' und 'Evolution'"*) and adopted Vossler's distinction between *"Literaturgeschichte"* und *"Sprachgeschichte"*. – SCHLOSSER 1924 (see note 25), pp. 122, 126. On Croce's and Schlosser's concept of language, see BAKOŠ, Ján: Prague Linguistic Circle's Contribution to Art History, in *Human Affairs*, 15, 2005, June, pp. 22-34; WYSS, Beat: "Stil" und "Sprache" der Kunst: Julius Schlosser, in *Wiener Schule. Erinnerung und Perspektiven* (see note 1), pp. 235-246, links Schlosser's notion of language to Ferdinad de Saussure's structuralist conception.

[38]   See SCHLOSSER, Julius von: Über "Stilgeschichte" und "Sprachgschichte" der bildenden Kunst, in *Sitzungsbericht der Bayerischen Akademie der Wissenschaften*, 1. München 1935, 39 pp.

[39]   On Schlosser's inverse use of the term *"style history"* and *"language history"*, see SEDLMAYR, Hans: Geschichte und Kunstgeschichte, in *Mitteilungen des Österreichischen Instituts für Geschichtsforschung*, 50, 1936, pp. 185-199, here p. 190: *"… das, was bei J. von Schlosser 'Sprachgeschichte' genannt wird, wir mit dem gebräuchlichen Namen der 'Stilgeschichte' benennen, den J. von Schlosser mit bewusster Absicht gerade für die echte Kunstgeschichte vorbehalten möchte."*

[40]   SCHLOSSER 1924 (see note 25), pp. 129-131. According to Schlosser: *"'Kunstgeschichte' im eigentlichen Sinn kann niemals und nirgends Sprachgeschichte sein."* – Ibid., p. 129. *"Auch sind es die originalen schöpferischen Gestalten, um die es sich handelt, nicht die Nachahmer und Verwässerer, die keinen Ausdruck haben und… nicht in die Kunstgeschichte gehören."* – Ibid., p. 130.

dentalism. However, it was a new nominalist model that gave material expression to the critical revision of the orthodox paradigm and shattered its hegemony.

Counter-Paradigm

In 1924, at the same time that Benesch and Tietze were casting doubt on *"Geistesgeschichte"* and the radical revision of Riegl's orthodoxy by Schlosser, Josef Strzygowski the most intransigent critic of the Vienna School, equated the crisis of the *"Geisteswissenschaften"* in general with the methods of the Vienna School.[41] In contrast to Schlosser and Tietze or Benesch, Strzygowski's criticism was an external and negative one. Not only rejecting the diachronic and linear idea of history, he also dismissed the Eurocentric and humanist concept of the history of art as hegemonic, and the immanent conception of art history as entirely mistaken.[42] He suggested instead that it be replaced with a geography of art, focusing on a pluralist notion of world art history. This was to be conceived as a plurality of simultaneous, constant and interacting artistic territorial circles anchored in different nations, peoples or races. In addition, Strzygowski insisted on replacing the philological, formalist and monistic method of inquiry characteristic of the Vienna School with a systematic science of art (*"Kunstwissenschaft"*). This should consist of factual art historical study on the one hand and study of artistic reception on the other.[43] Because of its vicious and negative intention, Strzygowski's project only affected the development of the Vienna School indirectly, through the mediation of students who had attended Dvořák's, Schlosser's and Strzygowski's lectures simultaneously, despite the interdictions of each side, being at war with the other.[44]

The Inductionist "Revolution"

The group of art historians entering the scene in the second half of the 1920s and known as the "Viennese Structuralists", also regarded the situ-

---

[41]   See STRZYGOWSKI, Josef: *Die Krisis der Geisteswissenschaften. Vorgeführt am Beispiele der Forschung über bildende Kunst.* Wien 1923.

[42]   See FRODL-KRAFT, Eva: Eine Aporie und der Versuch ihrer Deutung. Josef Strzygowski – Julius v. Schlosser, in *Wiener Jahrbuch für Kunstgeschichte*, 42, 1989, pp. 7-50.

[43]   See STRZYGOWSKI, Josef: Grundsätzliches und Tatsächliches, in *Die Kunstwissenschaft der Gegenwart...* (see note 14), pp. 157-181.

[44]   Dagobert Frey and Hans Sedlmayr were counted among such students.

ation in post-war art history as a crisis in its scientific status. For this reason, they launched a project of art history as a rigorous and exact science ("*strenge Kunstwissenschaft*").[45] Even if the group, consisting, above all, of Schlosser's graduates also targeted Riegl's evolutionary version of the history of style,[46] their criticism was directed primarily against Geistesgeschichte, its deductive procedure and its spiritual character.[47] Following in the footsteps of Schlosser's criticism of Riegl's abstractions, the members of this group regarded deductive generalizations as unverifiable abstract constructions.[48] Consequently, they introduced a strictly inductive "bottom up" procedure, focusing on the analysis of a single work of art.[49] In addition, interpretation by means of analogies was replaced with "*Sachforschung*", the empirical analysis of the structure of the work of art based on objective perception.[50] It was felt that such analysis should uncover the inner organization and function of the work and grasp its aesthetic status and message. The representatives of the group,

---

[45] The structuralist-inductionist project was proclaimed by "*the doctrinaires of the school*" (to use Meyer Schapiro's words), i.e. Hans Sedlmayr in his paper "Zu einer strengen Kunstwissenschaft" in *Kunstwissenschaftliche Forschungen*, 1, 1931, pp. 7-32; reprinted in SEDLMAYR 1958 (see note 35), pp. 35-70, re-named significantly as "*Kunstgeschichte als Kunstgeschichte*" ("*art history as the history of art*"). On this issue, see ROSENAUER, Artur: Zur neuen Wiener Schule der Kunstgeschichte, in *L´Art et les révolutions* (see note 2), pp. 73-83; *The Vienna School Reader. Politics and Art Historical Method in the 1930s*. Ed. Christopher S. WOOD. New York 2003, pp. 9-81; POCHAT – SCHMIDT – VASOLD (see note 1), pp. 423-432.

[46] Riegl's history of style was blamed for seeing the work of art solely as an instrument of something else, as an element in an evolutionary chain, instead of as an immanent "world". In evolutionist theory, "*Das Kunstwerk wird nicht als eine 'Welt' angesehen, sondern als ein Medium, in dem etwas anderes sich 'äussert.' Es wird nicht als Kunstwerk angesehen,*" according to SEDLMAYR, Hans: Zum Begriff der "Stukturanalyse", in *Kritische Berichte zur kunstgeschichtlichen Literatur*, 3-4, 1930 – 1932, pp. 146-160.

[47] Dvořák was blamed for neglecting concrete works of art regarding them as mere expressions of world views. According to KASCHNITZ-WEINBERG, Guido von: Alois Riegl, Die Spätrömische Kunstindustrie, in *Gnomon*, 4-5, 1929, pp. 195-213; reprinted in *Die Neue Wiener Schule*. Ed. Artur ROSENAUER. Wien 1986, pp. 92-101, here p. 99: "*Dvořák's Hauptwerk 'Idealismus und Naturalismus'... ist einen ausgesprochenen Rückschritt. Hier geht Dvořák nicht mehr von den Denkmälern aus, sondern er versucht die ganze mittelalterliche Kunst aus einer an sich überzeugend konstruierten Weltanschauugstheorien zu erklären. [...] Hier [wurde] ein Versuch gemacht, die Kunst zum blossen Ausdruck einer... a priori gegebenen Weltanschuung zu machen.*"

[48] SCHLOSSER 1924 (see note 25), pp. 127-129.

[49] SEDLMAYR 1931 (see note 45) in SEDLMAYR 1958 (see note 35), pp. 51-55: "*Nichts ist im gegenwärtigen Stadium so wichtig wie eine verbesserte Erkenntnis des einzelnen Kunstwerks... das einzelne Kunstwerk [tritt] in den Vordergrund der Forschung... das einzelne Kunstwerk [wird] als eine eigene, noch unbewältigte Aufgabe der Kunstwissenschaft.*"

[50] According to Guido von Kaschnitz-Weinberg: "*Das Kunstwerk soll von sich selbst aus beurteilt werden... nicht subjektiv vom Beschauer.*" Analysis should concentrate on "*das Gegebene*", "*das Kunstwerk selbst*". – KASCHNITZ-WEINBERG 1929 (see note 47) in *Die Neue Wiener Schule* (see note 47), pp. 96-97.

above all Hans Sedlmayr, viewed their initiative as a methodological revolution, overestimating it as a *"new epoch in art history"*.[51] However, rather than being an original innovation or radical turn, it was more an attempt at synthesis of diverse stimuli taken from their predecessors. Croce's and Schlosser's insular notion of the artwork as a monad,[52] now characterized as an independent world or microcosm,[53] was combined with Riegl's analysis of formal structure[54] and the idea of a centrally organized functional whole, taken over from *"Gestalt Psychology"*. Drawing on a synthesis of Croce-Schlosser's axiological dualism and Strzygowski's idea of a systematic science of art (*"Kunstwissenschaft"*) that strictly separated case studies from the study of artistic reception, or the immanent history of art from the social history of art,[55] Sedlmayr thus attempted to overcome the gap between art history and aesthetics, between *"Kunstgeschichte"* and *"Kunstwissenschaft"*.

This project resulted in an hierarchical theory of two art histories.[56] The first art history, regarded as a craft (concentrated on dating, attribution or iconographic identification), was delimited from the second and higher science of art, which he regarded as the investigation and observation of art's aesthetic nature and artistic quality. Moreover, following *"Gestalpsychologie"*, Sedl-

---

[51] SEDLMAYR, Hans: Nekrolog "Julius Ritter von Schlosser", in *Mitteilungen des Österreichischen Instituts für Geschichtsforschung*, 52, 1938, No. 1, pp. 513-516, here p. 516.

[52] SEDLMAYR 1936 (see note 39), p. 190: *"Es ist das unvergleichliche Verdienst Julius von Schlosser mit Benedetto Croce... immer wieder auf die Einzigkeit des Kunstwerks hingewiesen zu haben, immer wieder ausgesprochen zu haben, daß 'Kunst' aktuel nur in einzelnen Kunstwerken ihre Existenz habe und... in den Künstlern."* See also SEDLMAYR 1958 (see note 35), p. 196.

[53] SEDLMAYR 1931 (see note 45) in SEDLMAYR 1958 (see note 35), p. 53: *"Das Kunstwerk... erscheint jetzt als eine in sich ruhende kleine Welt."* (*"The work of art now appears as a self-contained small world or microcosm."*)

[54] According to Guido von Kaschnitz-Weinberg, Riegl was *"der eigentliche Begründer der Strukturanalyse"*. See KASCHNITZ-WEINBERG, Guido von: Bemerkungen zur Struktur der ägyptischen Plastik, in *Kunstwissenschaftliche Forschungen*, 2, 1933, pp. 7-24, here p. 8. Compare with SEDLMAYR 1936 (see note 39), p. 186.

[55] See STRZYGOWSKI 1924 (see note 43), p. 159, who speaks of the *"Trennung von Sach- und Beschauerforschung"*. Similarly, Kaschnitz-Weinberg demanded the clear separation of the analysis of the work of art itself from the beholder's subjective sensation, with a preference for the analysis of the work. See KASCHNITZ-WEINBERG 1929 (see note 47) in *Die Neue Wiener Schule* (see note 47), p. 97. Also according to SEDLMAYR 1936 (see note 39), p. 191: *"Der Betrachter ist später als das Werk."* At the same time, Strzygowski differed from the Viennese structuralists in regarding both *"Sachforschung"* and *"Beschauerforschung"* as equal parts of a complex system of art science. On the other hand, if the Viennese structuralists shared with Riegl a preference for the work itself, the strict isolation of the work of art from its recipient distinguished them unequivocally from Riegl as the predecessor of reception theory. See *Der Betrachter ist im Bild. Kunstwissenschaft und Rezeptionsästhetik*. Ed. Wolfgang KEMP. Köln 1985, pp. 17-20.

[56] SEDLMAYR 1931 (see note 45) in SEDLMAYR 1958 (see note 35), pp. 35-43.

mayr developed the concept of *"gestaltetes Sehen"*,[57] i.e. the *"right"* sensuous approach to the work of art enabling the beholder to grasp simultaneously its organization, aesthetic status and inner content[58] without preconceptions and *a priori* knowledge.[59] Sedlmayr thereby implicitly reintroduced normativism into art history.[60] Consequently, his notion of structural analysis assumed a contradictory nature: in the sense that an impartial, empirical and rational analysis, insofar as it adopted the *"correct"*, i.e. centralized sensuous approach, was supposed to guarantee a grasp of the aesthetic quality of a work of art. Consequently, an immanent, decontextualized analysis of an artwork's structure was expected to discover its inner spiritual content. No wonder that Sedlmayr's colleague Otto Pächt warned, in his paper "Das Ende der Abbildtheorie",[61] against the danger of slipping from scientific analysis into poetry.[62]

The Reverse of "Rigorous Science"

In 1936, the year Sedlmayr took over the chair of art history at Vienna University from Schlosser, a fundamental critique of "The New Vienna School"

---

[57] See SEDLMAYR, Hans: Gestaltetes Sehen, in *Belvedere*, 40, 1925, pp. 65-73.

[58] SEDLMAYR 1931 (see note 45) in SEDLMAYR 1958 (see note 35), p. 63, called it *"die 'Sinnschichten' des Kunstwerkes"*.

[59] The principle of *"gestaltetes Sehen"* can be regarded as a predecessor of Sedlmayr's future belief in the direct, mystical understanding of the concealed spiritual meanings of the work of art. See SEDLMAYR, Hans: Probleme der Interpretation, in SEDLMAYR 1958 (see note 35), pp. 87-127. On this issue, see *The Vienna School Reader* (see note 45), p. 34: "Strukturanalyse *rests on the intuitive, nondiscursive, holistic apprehension of meaning. At the moment of interpretation... the art historian simply recognizes the world concretized in the work."*

[60] Due to the view that the central organization of a work of art is identical with its aesthetic quality, an historically limited and very particular formal characteristic was raised by Sedlmayr to the level of a lasting criterion for all art.

[61] PÄCHT, Otto: Das Ende der Abbildtheorie, in *Kritische Berichte zur kunstgeschichtlichen Literatur*, 3-4, 1930 – 1931, pp. 1-9; reprinted in PÄCHT, Otto: *Methodisches zur kunsthistorischen Praxis. Ausgewählte Schriften.* München 1977 (2nd ed. 1995), pp. 121-128.

[62] WOOD, Christopher S.: Introduction, in PÄCHT, Otto: *The Practice of Art History. Reflections on Method.* London 1999, pp. 9-18, here p. 13, states that Pächt *"deplored poeticizing, belletristic attempts to transpose intuitive, subjective responses to works of art into language"*. According to HALBERTSMA, Marlite: *Wilhelm Pinder und die deutsche Kunstgeschichte.* Worms 1992, p. 95, Pächt's essay on "The End of the Image Theory" represets *"eine wichtige Kritik an Sedlmayrs 'richtige Einstellung'"*. According to ROSENAUER, Artur: Otto Pächt – Bemerkungen zu seinen frühen Schriften, in *„am Anfang war das Auge", Otto Pächt. Symposion anlässlich seines 100. Geburtstages.* Eds. Michael PÄCHT – Artur ROSENAUER. Wien 2006, p. 60, Pächt's critique targeted expressionist art history, particularly that of Otto Benesch.

was published in *The Art Bulletin*.[63] Its author, Meyer Schapiro, unmasked the metaphysical core of the structuralist project of *"rigorous science of art"* as it had been articulated in two volumes of the journal *Kunstwissenschaftliche Forschungen*, 1931 – 1933. According to him, the Viennese Structuralists *"neglect the social, economic, political and ideological factors in art"* and *"isolate forms from the historical conditions of their development"* explaining *"art as an independent variable... which has an immanent goal"*.[64] He also argued that they substituted *"in an animistic manner... mythical, racial-psychological constants... entities like race, spirit, will, and idea... for a real analysis of historical factors... giving them an independent self-evolving career"*.[65] As a consequence, *"theological deductions"* were preferred by Viennese art historians *"to an empirical study"* and *"a mysterious racial and animistic language"* was offered *"in the name of a higher science of art"*.[66]

There is no doubt that Schapiro's criticism concerning the lack of methodological self-reflection[67] and the notion of art as autonomous with an immanent history, was well-founded.[68] However, as far as the reproach of the *"mythical constants"* or *"mysterious entities"* was concerned, the situation was a little more complicated. In his paper on Riegl, Sedlmayr explicitly kept aloof from any abstract, racist explanation of the history of art.[69] According to him: *"Ebensowenig kommen als Träger des Kunstwollens die Völker in rasenmässigen Sinn in Betracht; die Verteilung der Stile und ihre Grenzen decken sich nicht mit Grenzen und Verteilung der Volkstümer."*[70] Sedlmayr pleaded instead for a more concrete, sociological approach: *"Der Träger des Kunstwollens ist vielmehr immer eine bestimmte Gruppe von Menschen, die sehr verschieden groß sein kann."*[71] On the other hand, in the "manifesto" of Viennese Structuralism, Sedlmayr, in his essay "Towards a Rigorous Study of Art", published in 1931,[72] refers explicitly to Otto Pächt, acknowledging *"attempts to work out historical constants or invariants*

---

[63] SCHAPIRO, Meyer: The New Viennese School, in *The Art Bulletin*, 18, 1936, pp. 258-266.

[64] Ibid., pp. 259-260.

[65] Ibid., p. 259.

[66] Ibid., p. 260.

[67] According to Schapiro: *"The doctrinaires of the school have not investigated their own method of approach... They assumed that it is a purely 'scentific' approach without pressupositions and a set of values which operate in the choice of objects and aspects."* – Ibid.

[68] Schapiro expressed it as follows: *"... 'the structure' or 'principle' of the work as a whole seems to create its own parts... The nature of the individual work is grasped more and more as something strictly internal in its origin... dependent on a logical working out of structural principles... a self-regulating aesthetic machine... deduced from the autonomous whole or center."* – Ibid.

[69] SEDLMAYR, Hans: Die Quintessenz der Lehren Riegls (1927), in RIEGL, Alois: *Gesammelte Aufsätze*. Augsburg – Wien 1929 (2nd ed. 1996), pp. XII-XXXIII.

[70] Ibid., p. XVIII.

[71] Ibid.

[72] See *The Vienna School Reader* (see note 45), p. 132.

(of a national or regional type, for example)" as legitimate objects of art history.[73] Then, in 1936, Sedlmayr started to turn away from the immanent structuralist conception of art.[74] In his paper "Geschichte und Kunstgeschichte",[75] written when he was already head of the Institute of Art History at Vienna University, Sedlmayr dissociated himself from Pächt's isolationist approach and pleaded for an equilibrium between autonomous and heteronymous art history,[76] for a synthesis of the structural analysis of a single artwork and its wider historical interpretation. In no time, he then adopted the racist mythical theory, conceiving of the work of art as *"eine Monade, in der die kunstwirkenden Kräfte eines Volks und einer Epoche sich verdichten".*[77] Despite that, Sedlmayr continued to try and reconcile his original belief in the individualist nature of art as the product of great masters with the collectivist metaphysical notion of art as an expression of anonymous collective subjects.[78] As a result, he articulated a theory of the *"circulation"* or *"an exchange between high and low"* art, claiming that: *"Die Geschichte der hohen Kunst wird ein Bündnis mit der Geschichte der Volkskunst eingehen."*[79]

The Turn to Invariants or Biological Revision

As is known today, Sedlmayr's methodological turn was the consequence of his ideological conviction shifting from Austrian Catholic monarchism to pan-German hegemonic nationalism.[80] At the same time, in the middle of

---

[73] SEDLMAYR 1931 (see note 45) in SEDLMAYR 1958 (see note 35), p. 64. See also the English translation in *The Vienna School Reader* (see note 45), p. 168.

[74] AURENHAMMER, Hans: Hans Sedlmayr und die Kunstgeschichte an der Universität Wien 1938 – 1945, in *Kunst und Politik*, 5, 2003, pp. 161-194, here p. 175.

[75] SEDLMAYR 1936 (see note 39), pp. 185-199.

[76] *"… ein Gleichgewicht zwischen 'innerer' and 'äusserer' Kunstgeschichte".* – Ibid., pp. 196-197.

[77] SEDLMAYR, Hans: Nekrolog "Julius Ritter von Schlosser", in *Miteilungen des Österreichischen Instituts für Geschichtsforschung*, 52, 1938, No. 1, pp. 513-516, here p. 516. According to AURENHAMMER 2003 (see note 74), p. 184: *"Die Bedetung der Volkskunst für die Kunstgeschichte hatte Sedlmayr schon in seiner Antrittsvorlesung als Wiener Ordinarius unterstrichen."* In spite of that, biological racialism was absent in Sedlmayr's writings. See Ibid., p. 175: *"Ein… biologischer Rassismus fehlt in den Schriften Sedlmayrs fast gänzlich."* See also AURENHAMMER 2004 (see note 1), p. 43.

[78] *"Echte Kunstwerke gibt es in jeder Schicht des völkischen Schaffens, in jedem seiner Bezirke sind sie… das Werk individueller Meister."* Quotation from SEDLMAYR, Hans: Österreichs bildende Kunst (1936), in SEDLMAYR, Hans: *Epochen und Werke.* Vol. 2. Wien – München 1960, pp. 266-286, here p. 283.

[79] Ibid. See also BAKOŠ, Ján: Vienna School Disciples and "The New Tasks" of Art History, in *Ars*, 40, 2007, No. 2, pp. 145-155, here pp. 150-151.

[80] See AURENHAMMER 2003 (see note 74); AURENHAMMER 2004 (see note 1). See also

1930s, another pupil of the Vienna School and a former assistant of Dvořák, Karl Maria Swoboda, noted a similar methodological change becoming a part of the main trend of German art history at that time. In his inaugural address at German University in Prague in 1934, he drew up *"the new tasks of art history"*.[81] Owing to the deep changes in art after World War I and the self-consciousness of nations as well as a large expansion in the field of art historical research, the discipline was faced with new problems, according to Swoboda. As a consequence, new concepts and methods and a new theory of art history (*"Theorie der Kunstgeschichte"*) were urgently needed.[82] Referring to Viennese Structuralism Swoboda specified that the first task of art history should be an exact analysis of a single work of art and its artistic structure.[83] Implicitly criticizing Riegl's and Dvořák's evolutionist project, Swoboda contraposed *"the new tasks"* with the schematic constructions of genetic chains that had dominated art history during the previous period. The second task was defined by him as the study of *"the real historical relations"*(*"reale historische Zusammenhänge"*) of art to all fields of culture, i.e. to the economy, society and religion.[84] As a consequence, art history had to become part of *"a new science of Man"* based on close cooperation with history, ethnology, philology and anthropology.[85] Needless to say, the anthropological dimension of art was understood by the adherents of *"Neue Aufgaben"* of art history as a biological or racial one.[86]

Three years later, Swoboda's critique of the orthodox Vienna School became more explicit and negative.[87] Riegl and Dvořák were directly blamed for

---

OTTENBACHER, Albert: Kunstgeschichte in ihrer Zeit. Zur Hans Sedlmayrs "abendländischer Sendung", in *Kritische Berichte*, 29, 2001, No. 3, pp. 71-86.

[81] SWOBODA, Karl M.: *Neue Aufgaben der Kunstgeschichte*. Brünn – Prag – Leipzig – Wien 1935, pp. 9-24. On the issue of the "new tasks" for German art history in the 1930s, see DILLY, Heinrich: *Deutsche Kunsthistoriker, 1933 – 1945*. München – Berlin 1988, pp. 43-54; BAKOŠ 2007 (see note 79).

[82] SWOBODA 1935 (see note 81), p. 17.

[83] *"Heute... geht es um ein adäquates Erfassen und Beschreiben des einzelnen Kunstwerk als eines künstlerischen Gebilde eigener Art... Organismus... die Struktur des künstlerischen Gebildes, die sie bestimmende Prinzipien."* – Ibid., p. 20.

[84] *"An Stelle von schematischen Entwicklungsreihen... soll eine Darstellung der realen historischen Zusammenhänge treten... die zu den anderen Kultursektoren hinüberführen, wie Wirtschaft, Gesellschaft, Religion..."* – Ibid., pp. 20-21.

[85] *„... eine neue Wissenschaft vom Menschen."* – Ibid., pp. 21-22.

[86] See FREY, Dagobert: Zur wissenschaftlichen Lage der Kunstgeschichte, in *Kunstwissenschaftliche Grundfragen. Prolegomena zu einer Kunstphilosophie*. Darmstadt 1972 (1st ed. 1946), pp. 23-79, here p. 60. Frey mentions three points of view concerning the "new tasks": *"den soziologischen, den anthropologisch-biologischen und den kulturell-ethnischen"*.

[87] In SWOBODA, Karl M.: *Zum deutschen Anteil an der Kunst der Sudetenländer. Beiträge zur Geschichte der Kunst im Sudeten- und Karpathenraum 1*. Brünn – Leipzig 1938.

the immanent and idealistic approach to art history.[88] In addition, the relationship of art to politics was emphasized. Swoboda spoke of the dependence of the history of art on the history of politics.[89] The third new task of art history was the most topical, according to Swoboda. This was regarded as the study of the *"second dimension"* of art history in addition to the first, diachronic dimension. Swoboda characterized it as the investigation of art historical constants.[90] It consisted in searching for the *"constant character of the art of a people, region, or a town"* that *"resisted historical changes"*.[91] The focus of art historical research had accordingly to transfer from the diachronic dimension to the second one. Despite the fact that the geography of art based on belief in territorial constants and racial collective subjects was Strzygowski's domain, Swoboda mentioned Riegl and Wölfflin or Dvořák and Pinder as the true initiators of this kind of research. Their more or less *"intuitive"* research devoid of any theoretical reflection, had to be transformed into a systematic exploration of *"the constant and specific character"* of the art of particular nations. Swoboda's papers published at that time, such as "Kunst und Nation"[92] or "Zum deutschen Anteil and der Kunst der Sudetenländer",[93] illustrated just what the theoretical completion of Dvořák's legacy *de facto* meant: Dvořák's spiritual approach was transformed into a biological (or racial) theory, and his cosmopolitanism into nationalism.[94] Art historical constants (*"künstlerische Konstante"*) were conceived of as national and regional stylistic constants.[95] Thus, constant artistic style was regarded as an embodiment and expression of the lasting spiritual character of a collective subject – a race, a tribe, a nation.[96]

---

[88] *"Die Kunstgeschichte hat da... sehr viel nachzuholen... als sie allen künstlerischen Wandel nur als immanenten Ablauf sah oder als man... Verwandschaften des Geschehens auf verschiedenen kulturellen Ebenen bloss mit dem sehr unrealen Begriff der Weltanschauung zu erklären versuchte."* – Ibid., p. 26.

[89] *"... die kunstgeschichtliche Einheit... beruht... auf der Annahme einer weitgehenden Abhängigkeit der Geschichte der Kunst von der politischen Geschichte."* – Ibid., p. 25.

[90] *"Erst die allerjüngste Kunstgeschichte sucht nach Arbeitsverfahren, die imstande sind, das örtlich, landschaftlich usw. im historischen Wandel der Stile sich Gleichbleibende, die 'künstlerische Konstante' eines Ortes, einer Landschaft zu erfahren und zu beschreiben... Erforschen der sogenannten kunsthistorischen Konstanten."* – SWOBODA 1935 (see note 81), p. 21.

[91] According to Swoboda, the most urgent question was: *"Die Fragestellung dazu lautet: Welches ist trotz allem geschichtlichen Wandel der sich gleichbleibende Charakter der Kunst eines Volkes, einer Landschaft, einer Stadt?"* – Ibid.

[92] SWOBODA, Karl M.: Kunst und Nation, in *Nation und Staat*, 9, 1936, pp. 439-452.

[93] SWOBODA 1938 (see note 87).

[94] *"Die Kunstwissenschaft ist wie alle Kulturwissenschaften heute im Begriffe, sich einer übergreifenden Wissenschaft von den Nationen, ihren Lebensgesetzen unterzuordnen."* – Ibid., p. 7.

[95] See SWOBODA 1936 (see note 92), pp. 439-440: *"nationale Charaktere"*; *"die künstlerische Konstante eines Ortes, einer Landschaft"*.

[96] For more on Swoboda's standpoint in the 1930s and 1940s, see BAKOŠ 2007 (see note 79), pp. 151-152.

Syncretism as Justification of Expansionism

Another disciple of Dvořák, Dagobert Frey, professor at Wrocław University since 1931, joined the project of *"the new tasks"* of art history and participated in its *"fascist turn"*. In order to reach that goal, Frey synthesized Dvořák's legacy with Strzygowski's. In his essay "Die Entwicklung nationaler Stile in der mittelalterlichen Kunst des Abendlandes", published in 1938,[97] he developed a syncretic, theoretical system combining the diachronic conception of art history with a synchronic one, the idea of history as an universal linear process with the notion of a plurality of constant territorial wholes,[98] and the notion of art as the expression of the worldview of an age with the idea of the expression of the psyche of a collective subject (*"Nation, Volk, Stamm"*). Like Sedlmayr, he maintained that art is, on the one hand, the product of individual artists,[99] but on the other, he adopted the idea of *"national art"* and conceded the existence of collective standard bearers of art history such as the *"Nation"* or the *"Volk"*. At the same time, he stressed the relative nature of *"constants"*, the changing character of nations, their lack of homogeneity, their coming into existence at a concrete historical moment and the difference between nation and state.[100] In addition, he not only emphasized the creative role of art as far as its relation to the nation was concerned,[101] but also regarded national styles as aspects of a European artistic unity.[102] Consequently, he resolutely refused to hypostatize collectivities (nations) *a priori*, insisting on a strictly inductive way of researching them.[103] Thus, Frey on the one hand defended the independent scientific status of art

---

[97] FREY, Dagobert: Die Entwicklung nationaler Stile in der mittelalterlichen Kunst des Abendlandes, in *Deutsche Vierteljahrsschrift für Literaturwissenschaft und Geistesgeschichte*, 1938, pp. 1-74; reprinted in Darmstadt 1970.

[98] *"... eine übernationale, entwicklungsgeschichtliche Betrachtung"* and *"eine überzeitlich nationale Betrachtung"*. – Ibid., p. 6.

[99] *"Die Kunst ist... an die schöpferische Persönlichkeit gebunden und in der personalen Einmaligkeit und Einzigartigkeit des Individuums begründet."* – Ibid., p. 9.

[100] Ibid., pp. 7-12.

[101] According to Dagobert Frey: *"Kunst ist nicht Ausfluss der Nation, sondern Gestaltungsform der Nation, durch die erst die Nation mitbestimmt wird."* – Ibid., p. 13.

[102] *"Eine Untersuchung der Entwicklung nationaler Stile... darf nicht die einzelnen Nationen für sich betrachten, sondern sie muss ebenso hinabsteigen zu den kleineren landschaftlichen und stammlichen Einheiten, aus deren Gefüge sich die Nationen bilden, wie aufsteigen zu der höheren, umfassenderen Einheit, aus der sie sich aussondern. Europa ist nicht nur ein geographischer Begriff... ein Raum, in dem bestimmte Völker nebeneinander wohnen, sondern auch ein kultureller Begriff... Gerade die Kunstgeschichte zeigt diese Einheit eines Kulturorganismus... In dieser Kultureinheit ist auch die Berechtigung einer übernationalen, europäischen Stilgeschichte begründet."* – Ibid., pp. 22-23.

[103] Ibid., p. 13.

historical research, while, on the other, tacitly and deliberately adopting the instrumental, political commitments of art history. In a very sophisticated way, he combined impartial and unbiased theoretical writing with a politically engaged and partial practice. It was precisely the nationalist theory of the identity of an artistic style (regarded as the expression of a collective psyche) with a nation (a people or a tribe) and a region ("*Kunstlandschaft*") that was intended to help justify expansionist territorial demands.[104] Nevertheless, there was a difference between Karl Maria Swoboda and Dagobert Frey as far as the legitimation of expansionism was concerned.[105] As is well known, Frey provided invaluable services to the Nazi regime by assisting as an expert in the robbery of Polish art collections.[106] In contrast, Swoboda's explicitly racial and nationalist notion of art (as an expression of the unchanging mentality of a tribe, e.g. the "*Sudetenländischer Stamm*"), which helped to legitimize ideologically the annexation of Bohemia, did not prevent him from maintaining a sympathetic relationship with Czech art historians and a protective approach to Czech cultural heritage.[107]

Thus Riegl's original project of art history as an objective and impartial discipline, modified by Franz Wickhoff's idea of art historical investigation as involving the projection of contemporary artistic values onto the past (thereby opening up a vista on the past by means of contemporary art) or Max Dvořák's notion of art history as a prophesying of the future by means of

---

[104] SWOBODA 1938 (see note 87), p. 11, expressed it as follows: "*... künstlerisch einheitliche Gebiete stimmen stark mit den geographischen Einheiten der politischen Geschichte überein.*"

[105] According to AURENHAMMER 2004 (see note 1), p. 44: "*Im Unterschied zu... anderen Vertretern der Wiener Schule wie Swoboda und Frey wirkte Sedlmayr nur selten im Sinne der 'Kulturboden- -Ideologie' an der kunsthistorischen Legitimation deutscher Eroberungs- und Germanisierungspolitik mit.*"

[106] See STÖRKUHL, Beate: Paradigmen und Methoden der kunstgeschichtlichen "Ostforschung" – der "Fall" Dagobert Frey, in *Die Kunsthistoriographien in Ostmitteleuropa und der nationale Diskurs*. Eds. Robert BORN – Alena JANATKOVÁ – Adam S. LABUDA. Berlin 2004, pp. 155-172; MUTHESIUS, Stefan: *Kunst in Polen/Polnische Kunst, 966 – 1990. Eine Einführung.* Königstein im Taunus 1994, p.12. See also BAKOŠ 2007 (see note 79), pp. 152-154.

[107] See CANZ, Sigrid: Karl Maria Swoboda (1889 – 1977). Kunsthistoriker: Wissenschaftler zwischen Wien und Prag, in *Prager Professoren, 1938 – 1948. Zwischen Wissenschaft und Politik*. Eds. Monika GLETTER – Alena MIŠÍKOVÁ. Essen 2001, pp. 175-195, here pp. 187-188. On Swoboda's activity in Bohemia between 1938 – 1945, see also VLNAS, Vít: Diplomacie viržinky a koňaku [Diplomacy of Cigars and Cognac], in *Vita nostra revue*, 9, 2000, No. 2, pp. 32-38, here p. 37; BARTLOVÁ, Milena: Německé dějiny umění středověku v Čechách do roku 1945 [German Art History of the Middle Ages in Bohemia until 1945], in *Německá medievistika v českých zemích do roku 1945* (=Práce z dějin vědy, 18). Eds. Pavel SOUKUP – František ŠMAHEL. Praha 2004, pp. 74-76.

projecting the past onto the future, resulted in Swoboda's and Frey's conception of art history as a direct political instrument.

Marxist Revision

As can be seen, Dvořák's students, contrary to those of Schlosser, did not negatively revise Dvořák's legacy but rather modified it in an affirmative way. Irrespective of how they transformed Dvořák's spiritual perspective, they attempted to specify the standard bearer (*"Träger"*) of art history and shared the belief in anonymous collective subjects. This was confirmed by Frederick Antal, a Hungarian disciple of Dvořák.[108] In the second half of the 1940s, while an émigré in London, Antal definitively transformed *"Geistesgeschichte"* into a Marxist social history of art.[109] He even attempted to synthesize a Marxist version of the history of ideas with Warburg's social and cultural history. On the one hand, Antal followed Dvořák in regarding art as the expression of a worldview. On the other, conceiving of society in Marxist fashion as a class structure, he replaced the idea of art as the expression of an age with the idea of artistic style as the expression of a class outlook on life, or ideology.[110] According to Antal, the simultaneous existence of different social classes in one social organism resulted in a diversity of artistic styles, each expressing the world outlook of the class in point.[111] Though adopting Dvořák's impersonal concept of expression, Antal did not regard artistic style as the embodiment of the worldview of the individual artist or as the expression of the ideology of the class from which he came. Antal adopted Warburg's idea of the active participation of patrons in the production of art and combined it with the idea of art as an intellectual expression.[112] Accordingly, he conceived of artistic style

---

[108] See WESSELY, Anna: Die Aufhebung des Stilbegriffs: Frederick Antals Rekonstruktion künstlerischer Entwicklungen auf marxistischer Grundlage, in *Kritische Berichte*, 4, 1976, No. 2-3, pp. 16-34, here pp. 17-20; STIRTON, Paul: Frederick Antal and "The Social History of Art" in Britain, in *Britain and Hungary. Contacts in Architecture, Design, Art and Theory during the 19th and 20th Centuries*. Ed. Gyula ERNYEY. Budapest 2003, pp. 236-253; KÓKAI, Károly: Impulse der Wiener Schule der Kunstgeschichte im Werk von Frederick Antal, in *Wiener Schule. Erinnerung und Perspektiven* (see note 1), pp.109-120; BAKOŠ, Ján: From the Ideological Critique to the *Apologia* for the Market, in *Artwork through the Market. The Past and the Present*. Ed. Ján BAKOŠ. Bratislava 2004, pp. 13-51, here pp. 21-22; in this volume pp. 69-106.

[109] ANTAL, Frederick: *Florentine Painting and Its Social Background. The Bourgeois Republic before Cosimo De Medici's Advent to Power: XIV and Early XV Centuries*. London 1947.

[110] Ibid., p. 4: *"... the public is by no means unanimous in its outlook on life, and this divergence of outlook among its various sections explains the coexistence of different styles in the same period."*

[111] Ibid.: *"... we can understand the origins and nature of co-existent styles only if we study the various sections of society..."*

[112] A little later a very similar notion of style was articulated by SCHAPIRO, Meyer: Style, in

as the expression of its commissioner's class ideology, i.e. the mentality of the class of the patron.[113] As a consequence, the metaphysical theory of expression of Hegelian origin was relativized by Marxist as well as non-Marxist sociological theories. Moreover, the idea of art as an expression of truth, inherited from Romanticism, clashed with the craft concept of art as the execution of a commission.[114] Nevertheless, Antal was convinced that Dvořák's legacy could easily be synthesized with Warburg's and that the future of art history depended on that synthesis: *"The severely historical spirit of the school of Vienna and the resolutely anti-art for art's sake attitude of Warburg together paved the way for a deeper, richer, and less nebulous study of art history."*[115]

Theophanic Revision

If Schlosser's revision of Riegl's *"realist" "historical Grammar"* by means of the *"nominalist"* model can be regarded as the first immanent critique of Vienna School orthodoxy, and if the dismissal of Dvořák's history of art without artworks by Structuralists can be conceived of as the second one, then Sedlmayr's essay "Kunstgeschichte als Geistesgeschichte", published in 1949, represented the second revision of Dvořák and the third revision of the Vienna School.[116] This time, Sedlmayr's criticism was not aimed at Dvořák's spiritual approach but at his understanding of history. In contrast to his paper "Geschichte und Kunstgeschichte" (1936), which had called for the close study of the relation between art and history,[117] Sedlmayr now reproached Dvořák's in-

---

Anthropology Today. An Encyclopedic Inventory. Ed. Alfred L. KROEBER. Chicago 1953, pp. 287-312; reprinted in *Aesthetics Today.* Ed. Morris PHILIPSON. Cleveland – New York 1961, p. 81: *"But style is, above all, a system of forms with a quality and a meaningful expression through which the personality of the artists and the broad outlook of a group are visible. It is also a vehicle of expression within the group, communicating and fixing certain values of religious, social, and moral life through the emotional suggestiveness of forms."*

[113] According to ANTAL 1947 (see note 109), p. 6: *"... the art of the period under discussion expresses mainly the outlook of the patrons of art, it is this that has been emphasised throughout rather than the view of the artists..."*

[114] Ibid., p. 7: *"... stylistic divergences between various works of art are due not only to individual differences between the various artists but also to the fact that these works were intended for different sections of the public or satisfied different artistic needs."*

[115] ANTAL, Frederick: Remarks on the Method of Art History, in *The Burlington Magazine*, 91, 1949, pp. 49-52, here p. 50.

[116] SEDLMAYR 1949 (see note 35) in SEDLMAYR 1958 (see note 35), pp. 71-86.

[117] SEDLMAYR 1936 (see note 39), p. 197: *"Diese... Forderung, 'historisch' zu denken, hat ihre einfache Begründung in der Tatsache, daß das Kunstwerk nicht als Projektion der Ideen seines Schöpfers in den luftleeren geistigen Raum entsteht, sondern als eine Auseinandersetzung des geistigen Schaffens mit den verschiedensten Gegebenheiten der konkreten historischen Situation..."*

terpretative emphasis on the relationship of art to the real history of ideas. Dvořák's interpretation of art as the expression and materialization of the worldview of an age was regarded as limiting its focus to the transient dimension of the history of art, thereby neglecting art's transcendent essence.[118] According to Sedlmayr, art history should be a *"metahistory of art"*, the history of the eternal values created by art,[119] *"the history of the epiphany of absolute spirit"*.[120] Nevertheless, Sedlmayr's critique was not intended as a total dismissal of Dvořák's model. On the contrary, drawing on Dvořák's late call for art history to pay attention to *"the correlation between human soul and God"*,[121] Sedlmayr regarded his critique of *"Geistesgeschichte"* as the true development of Dvořák's legacy.[122] As a consequence, art history should be transformed from a documenting of the past into a kind of theology revealing the hidden meanings of a work of art,[123] and vivifying the eternal values of artworks by means of a re-creative interpretation.[124] If Dvořák's post-war attempt at promoting a spiritual approach could be regarded as a critique of materialism, the promotion of transcendentalism by Sedlmayr after 1945 functioned rather like an escape from the collapse of the ideology in which he had been deeply involved. In contrast to Swoboda and Frey's post-war recourse to an anthropological approach and their attempt to transform the expansionist geography of art into a universal art history or world comparatistics,[125] Sedlmayr re-

---

[118] SEDLMAYR 1949 (see note 35) in SEDLMAYR 1958 (see note 35), p. 85: *"... die Kunstgeschichte als Geistesgeschichte in ihrer ersten Phase [ist] fast immer zu einer Stilgeschichte als Geschichte der Weltanschauung geworden... während sie... Kunstgeschichte als Geschichte der Epiphanie des absoluten Geistes in den Brechungen des zeitabhängigen menschlichen Geistes sein könnte und sollte..."*

[119] Ibid., p. 81: *"So gesehen aber sind die großen Kunstwerke... untereinander verwandter als die Werke gleichen Stils. Es gibt über Raum und Zeit hinweg eine geistige Kommunion der wahren Künstler."*

[120] Ibid.: *"Und Kunstgeschichte als Geistesgeschichte wird so, den ästhetischen Relativismus überwindend, zur Geschichte der Kunsthöhe als Geschichte der geistigen Höhe der Menschheit in ihrem Werden."*

[121] The idea was expressed by Max Dvořák in his lecture "Kunstbetrachtung" at the Bregenz Denkmalpflegetag in 1920. See DVOŘÁK, Max: Kunstbetrachtung.Vortrag gehalten am Denkmalpflegetag in Bregenz im 1920, in *Mitteilungen des Bundesdenkmalamtes*, 2, 1920 – 1923, pp. 93-97. On this issue, see SEDLMAYR 1949 (see note 35) in SEDLMAYR 1958 (see note 35), p. 86.

[122] Ibid., pp. 81-82: *"Auf dieser höchsten denkbaren Ebene wandelt sich Kunstgeschichte als Geistesgeschichte in Kunstgeschichte als Pneumatologie und Dämonologie."* Similarly BENESCH 1973 (see note 20), p. 303, claimed that *"beim späten Dvořák ahnt man eine neue Gläubigkeit an das Jenseits"*.

[123] Sedlmayr distinguished between three and four meanings of an image, i.e. *"der 'wörtliche', der allegorische, der mystische oder anagogische Bildsinn"*. See SEDLMAYR, Hans: Der Ruhm der Malkunst: Jan Vermeer "De schilderconst", in *Festschrift Hans Jantzen*. Berlin 1951, pp. 169-177; reprinted in SEDLMAYR 1958 (see note 35), pp. 161-172.

[124] SEDLMAYR, Hans: Probleme der Interpretation, in SEDLMAYR 1958 (see note 35), pp. 87-127.

[125] In *Metzler Kunsthistoriker Lexikon. Zweihundert Portäts deutschsprachiger Autoren aus vier Jahrhunderten.* Eds. Peter BETTHAUSEN – Peter H. FEIST – Christiane FORK. Stuttgart – Weimar 1999, p. 409, Swoboda's post-war project is characterized as *"universelle Kunstgeschichte"*

sponded to ideological collapse by means of an aggressive counterattack. His transformation of art history into a theological iconology and his conservative attack against modern art were two sides of the same coin.[126] Paradoxically, Sedlmayr's post-war transcendentalism can, in a sense, be regarded as a metaphysical variation of Schlosser's humanist individualism. Intended as a radical revision of the historical relativism of the Vienna School, it aimed after all at the condemnation of the relativist nature of Modernism.[127] Sedlmayr's anxiety to blame Modernism for all the crises of the 19th and 20th centuries was a sophisticated attempt to escape complicity in and readdress responsibility for the cataclysm of World War II.

Expressionism in the Dock

However, Vienna School relativism and impersonal expressionism were also severely criticized by the last graduate of the Vienna School of the "archhumanist" Schlosser, Ernst Hans Gombrich.[128] In comparison with Sedlmayr, Gombrich's revisionism was conducted from an entirely opposite point of

---

looking for *"übernationale und epochenübergreifende Zusammenhänge"*. On Swoboda's methodological position after 1945, see AURENHAMMER 2004 (see note 1), pp. 52-53; CANZ 2001 (see note 107), pp. 188-190. The pluralist idea as implied in the comparative approach was introduced in order to replace the hegemonic concept of the former nationalist *"Kunstgeographie"*. See FREY, Dagobert: Geschichte und Probleme der Kultur- und Kunstgeographie, in *Archaelogia Geographica*, 4, 1955, pp. 90-105; reprinted in FREY, Dagobert: *Bausteine zu einer Philosophie der Kunst*. Darmstadt 1976, pp. 260-319; FREY, Dagobert: *Grundlegung zu einer vergleichenden Kunstwissenschaft. Raum und Zeit in der Kunst der afrikanisch-eurasischen Hochkulturen*. Innsbruck 1949. With regard to Frey's post-war methodological work, see also GENSBAUR-BENDLER, Ulrike: Dagobert Frey – Lebensphilosophische Grundlagen seiner Kunsttheorie, in *Wiener Jahrbuch für Kunstgeschichte*, 42, 1989, pp. 51-79.

[126] See SEDLMAYR, Hans: *Verlust der Mitte. Die bildende Kunst des 19. und 20. Jahrhunderts als Symptom und Symbol der Zeit*. Salzburg 1948; SEDLMAYR, Hans: *Die Entstehung der Kathedrale*. Zürich 1950. On Sedlmayr, see SCHNEIDER, Norbert: Hans Sedlmayr (1896 – 1984), in *Altmeister moderner Kunstgeschichte*. Ed. Heinrich DILLY. Berlin 1990, pp. 266-288; SAUERLÄNDER, Willibald: Hans Sedlmayrs "Verlust der Mitte", in SAUERLANDER, Willibald: *Geschichte der Kunst/Gegenwart der Kritik*. Ed. Werner BUSCH. Köln 1999, pp. 229-238; HOFMANN, Werner: *Die gespaltene Moderne*. München 2004, pp. 101-109; AURENHAMMER 2003 (see note 74).

[127] SEDLMAYR 1949 (see note 35) in SEDLMAYR 1958 (see note 35), p. 81: *"Aber nicht nur auf der Seite der Kunst, auch auf der Seite des Geistes muss Relativismus überwunden werden."* Ibid., p. 84: *"Denn es ist möglich und es ist heute an der Zeit, den Relativismus zu relativieren…"*

[128] See the list of Vienna School graduates in HAHNLOSER, Hans R.: Chronologisches Verzeichnis der aus der "Wiener Schule" hervorgegangenen oder ihr affiliierten Kunsthistoriker, in *Mitteilungen des Österreichischen Instituts für Geschichtsforschung*, 13, 1934, No. 2, p. 226. See also BAKOŠ, Ján: The Vienna School's Hundred and Sixty-Eighth Graduate: The Vienna School's Ideas Revised by E. H. Gombrich, in *Gombrich on Art and Psychology*. Ed. Richard WOODFIELD. Manchester – New York 1996, pp. 234-261, here pp. 234-257.

view this time, i.e. from an anti-metaphysical position. According to Gombrich, relativism and metaphysical determinism were responsible for all the anti-humanist totalitarianisms of the 20th century. For him: *"By inculcating the habit of talking in terms of collectives, of 'mankind', 'races', or 'ages', it weakens resistance to totalitarian habit of mind."*[129] Indeed, Gombrich had already launched a fundamental criticism of Vienna School orthodoxy shortly before leaving Vienna for exile in London in 1937, one year after Schapiro's review of the *Kunstwissenschaftliche Forschungen.*[130] Reviewing Dvořák's pupil, Ernst von Garger's attempt to overcome Riegl's historical relativism,[131] Gombrich critiqued the metaphysical expressionist idea of style, resolutely refusing to conceive of *"the style as a whole expressive system... set over against a hypostasized collective personality – either of a people or a period – of which it is held to be the expression".*[132] Later, in *The Story of Art*, published in 1950, he referred to Schlosser's nominalist individualism claiming that *"there really is no such thing as Art. There are only artists."*[133] Nevertheless, he still combined this with Dvořák's historical relativism, i.e. with his belief in art as an historically changing concept[134] when he states that *"a word (i.e. art) may mean very different things in different times and places".*[135] This criticism of expressionist and physiognomic theories of art, which he characterized as *"the physiognomic fallacy"*, was elaborated further in his essay "Meditation on a Hobby Horse, or the Roots of Artistic Form" (1951).[136] Rejecting the notion of art as imitation and expression or abstraction, he came to a proto-semiotic substitution idea of art claiming that *"all art is 'image-making' and all image-making is rooted in the creation of substitutes".*[137] At that time, he was also following and elaborating on Schlosser's notion of art

---

[129] GOMBRICH, Ernst H.: *Art and Illusion. A Study in the Psychology of Pictorial Representation.* London 2002, pp. 16-17.

[130] See GOMBRICH, Ernst H.: Wertprobleme und mittelalterliche Kunst, in *Kritische Berichte zur kunstgeschichtlichen Literatur*, 6, 1937, pp. 109-116; English version: Achievement in Mediaeval Art, in GOMBRICH, Ernst H.: *Meditations on a Hobby Horse and Other Essays on the Theory of Art.* London 1963, pp. XI, 70-77.

[131] GARGER, Ernst von: Über Wertungsschwierigkeiten bei mittelalterlicher Kunst, in *Kritische Berichte zur kunstgeschichtlichen Literatur*, 5, 1932 – 1933, pp. 97-125.

[132] GOMBRICH 1963 (see note 130), p. 75.

[133] Quoted after GOMBRICH, Ernst H.: *The Story of Art.* Englewood Cliffs 1985 (14th ed.), p. 4.

[134] DVOŘÁK 1918 (see note 12) in DVOŘÁK 1924 (see note 11), p. 125.

[135] GOMBRICH 1985 (see note 133), p. 4.

[136] Originally published as GOMBRICH, Ernst H.: Meditation on a Hobby Horse, or the Roots of Artistic Form, in *Aspects of Form: a Symposium on Form in Nature and Art.* Ed. Lancelot L. WHYTE. London 1951, pp. 209-228; reprinted in GOMBRICH 1963 (see note 130), pp. 1-11. Concerning the term *"physiognomic fallacy"*, see GOMBRICH, Ernst H.: Art and Scholarship (1957), in GOMBRICH 1963 (see note 130), pp. 106-119, here p. 108.

[137] GOMBRICH 1963 (see note 130), p. 9. Gombrich here adopted the iconological idea of art as a world of images, combining this with the formalist idea of art as shaping.

as a (social) conception[138] that determines artistic practice, in his paper "The Renaissance Conception of Artistic Progress and Its Consequences", read at the CIHA Congress at Amsterdam in 1952.[139] Even before his later articulation of the theory of art as social communication, Gombrich drafted a new conception of the status of art historical research in his inaugural lecture *Art and Scholarship* at University College, London in 1957, casting doubt on the Vienna School's belief in art history as a science, and formulating the idea of art history as scholarship.[140] He combined the figure of the art historian as scholar with the iconological idea of *"the guardian of memories"*.[141] Despite his scepticism concerning the scientific nature of art history, Gombrich still insisted on a scientific ethic in art historical research, and on art history's obligation to proceed self-reflexively and critically. Gombrich appealed for resistance to all kinds of *"irrational myths"*, irrespective of whether they concerned the myth *"of the life cycle of art"*, " an *"exaggerated emphasis on the belief in progress"*,[142] the notion of style as *"an utterance of the collective, in which a nation or an age speaks to us"*,[143] the *"'physiognomic fallacy'... the illusion that mankind changed as dramatically and thoroughly as did art"*,[144] or *"the pitfalls of circular interpretations of images"*.[145] In his magnum opus *Art and Illusion. A Study in the Psychology of Pictorial Representation* (1960), Gombrich adopted Schlosser's idea of language, but transformed his teacher's axiological dualism into a monist theory of communication. According to Gombrich, art as a whole and not only the productions of minor artists, must be regarded as a language, as communication.[146] Consequently, style cannot be understood only as the expression and

---

[138] SCHLOSSER 1924 (see note 25), pp. 103, 118, spoke of *"das Verhalten der Zeit zu ihrer Kunst"* or of *"Kunstanschauung"*.

[139] GOMBRICH, Ernst H.: The Renaissance Conception of Artistic Progress and Its Consequences, in *Actes du XVIIe congrès international d'histoire de l'art, Amsterdam, 1952*. Den Haag 1955, pp. 291-307; reprinted in GOMBRICH, Ernst H.: *Norm and Form. Studies in the Art of the Renaissance*. London – New York 1966 (3rd ed. 1978), pp. 1-10.

[140] GOMBRICH 1963 (see note 130), pp. 106-119. The idea was then elaborated in his lecture *Art History and the Social Sciences. The Romanes Lecture for 1973* (Oxford 1975); reprinted in GOMBRICH, Ernst H.: *Ideals and Idols. Essays on Values in History and in Art*. Oxford 1979, pp. 131-166.

[141] GOMBRICH 1957 (see note 136), in GOMBRICH 1963 (see note 130), p. 107.

[142] Ibid., p. 109.

[143] Ibid., p. 112.

[144] Ibid., p. 108.

[145] Ibid., p. 117.

[146] Karl Bühler and Roman Jakobson played an important role as catalysts in the transformation of Schlosser's Crocean idea of language as an expression into Saussure's socio-functional notion of language as a system of communication. See GOMBRICH, Ernst H.: Kunstwissenschaft und Psychologie vor fünfzig Jahren, in *Akten des XXV. Internationalen Kongresses für Kunstgeschichte, Wien, 4. – 10. September 1983*. Vols. 1-9. Eds. Hermann FILLITZ – Martina PIPPAL. Wien – Köln – Graz 1984 – 1986, Vol. 1: Wien und die Entwicklung der kunsthis-

product of great masters, but also as a system of conventions. Not only the *"Kleinmeisters"* but also the great masters were working within the frames of a system of artistic tradition and social conventions. Genii too, were bound to the principle of *"scheme and correction"*, according to Gombrich. That is why masterworks could not be regarded as absolutely original products transcending all borders. On the contrary, they must be conceived of as only relatively innovative solutions, as variations of previous schemes. Consequently, Gombrich not only revised Schlosser's aristocratic individualism but also silently transformed Riegl's and Dvořák's impersonalism. The idea of the superiority of impersonal evolutionary chains over individual artists and the notion of genius regarded as a mere executor of style was transmuted into the idea of art as governed by a system of conventions. And the notion of the history of art as an autonomous formal evolution (Riegl) or spiritual expression (Dvořák) was replaced with the sociological idea of the persistence of tradition and the notion of historical changes regarded as the results of slow experimental alterations of artistic conventions adjusted to the social functions demanded of art.[147] For this reason, the Romantic notion of artistic production as a transcendental creation was replaced with the notion of art regarded as skill-based craft. Inspired by Thomas Kuhn's distinction between normal and revolutionary science,[148] Gombrich also transformed Schlosser's axiological dualism of *"style versus language"* into a diachronic one. Normal periods of art history were dominated by the principle of *"scheme and correction"*, whereas artistic revolutions deeply changed the paradigm owing to the changing social functions of art.[149]

Relativism Condemned

Although compiling and transforming Schlosser's and Riegl's ideas, Gom-

---

torischen Methode (1984), pp. 99-104, here pp. 101-103. See also GOMBRICH, Ernst H.: Wenn's euch Ernst ist, was zu sagen – Wandlungen in der Kunstbetrachtung, in *Kunsthistoriker in eigener Sache. Zehn autobiographische Skizzen.* Ed. Martina SITT. Berlin 1990, pp. 62-101, here p. 69; GOMBRICH, Ernst H. – ERIBON, Didier: *Looking for Answers. Conversations on Art and Science.* New York 1993, pp. 114, 129.

[147] For more on Gombrich's concept of the art historical process, see BAKOŠ, Ján: Der tschechoslowakische Strukturalismus und die Kunstgeschichtsschreibung, in *Zeitschrift für Ästhetik und Allgemeine Kunstwissenschaft*, 36, 1991, pp. 53-103, here pp. 92-99.

[148] KUHN, Thomas: *The Structure of Scientific Revolutions.* Chicago 1962.

[149] See WOOD 1999 (see note 62), pp. 9-18. Pächt himself regarded Gombrich's simultaneous emphasis on the power of conventions and on the creative independence of great masters as a contradiction. See PÄCHT 1977 (see note 61), p. 285.

brich dismissed the historical relativism of the Vienna School and its anonymous collectivist determinism or its *"mythological explanations"* as he called them.[150] He resolutely refused to surrender *"the belief in the unity and immutability of human nature and human reason"*, no less than the idea that *"nature remains the same and is only 'represented' in different modes"*, and he also refused *"to renounce causal analysis of history"*.[151] Moreover, in 1964, Gombrich criticized Sedlmayr's pupils for recycling their teacher's *"metaphysics of essences"*, i.e. the belief in *"'the structure' of a work of art as a kind of hidden essence"*[152] and for maintaining Sedlmayr's *"mumbo-jumbo"* epistemological relativism (i.e. the conviction that *"reason is a variable that changes with history"*[153]), according to which *"art* [is] *being both everything and nothing"*.[154] Gombrich believed that through all deep historical changes there had been only one single form of rationality enabling scientific research, and also, only one common core to art, rooted in anthropological constants.[155] According to him, historical relativism could be overcome by anthropological humanism when synthesized with sociological conventionalism.[156] Despite the contradictory nature of such a synthesis,[157] he assumed that historical changes of style could be explained by means of the notion of tradition and *"the idea of skill"* or *"the theory of alternatives"* without resorting to axiological and epistemological relativism.[158] Gombrich's idea of the art historian as a guardian of memories and lasting values has leaned on that synthesis. Nevertheless, the polemic against relativism and the relationship to

---

[150] GOMBRICH 2002 (see note 129), p. 16.

[151] Ibid., p. 17: *"I happen to be a passionate believer in all those outmoded ideas which Sedlmayr… asked… to discard… the idea that 'only individual human beings are real, while groups and spiritual collectives are mere names'… the belief in the unity and immutability of human nature and human reason no less than the idea that 'nature remains the same and is only 'represented' in different modes'… the causal analysis of history 'which conceives of historical changes merely as a result of blind and isolated chains of causation'."*

[152] GOMBRICH, Ernst H.: [Review of] Kunstgeschichte und Kunsttheorie im 19. Jahrhundert. Probleme der Kunstwissenschaft I. Berlin 1963, in *The Art Bulletin*, 46, 1964, pp. 418-420, here p. 418.

[153] Ibid., p. 419.

[154] Ibid.

[155] Gombrich's idea of the *"minimal image"*, to be found in the specific nature of the human species, was already articulated in GOMBRICH 1951 (see note 136) in GOMBRICH 1963 (see note 130), and developed in GOMBRICH, Ernst H.: Image and Code: Scope and Limits of Conventionalism in Pictorial Representation, in *Image and Code*. Ed. Wendy STEINER. Ann Arbor 1981, pp. 11-42.

[156] Thus Gombrich subscribed to Panofsky's iconological notion of humanism as a system of lastingly valid norms, i.e. the ideology of humanism.

[157] That is to say that emphasis on the social basis of art runs against an interest in its psychological nature in one sense, and that the focus on historical and socially determined changes contradicts the anthropological concern with the lasting core of art.

[158] GOMBRICH 2002 (see note 129), pp. 17-18.

Riegl can be regarded as a constant refrain or the burden of Gombrich's life work.[159] In a sense, Gombrich's critique of relativism rounded off the polemic of the humanists against the anti-normativists launched by his teacher Schlosser. Gombrich, as the faithful adherent to humanism, repeatedly cast doubt on Riegl and Dvořák's idea of the history of art as the history of changes in intentions or values, replacing it with a revived classical idea of art history conceived of as the process of perfecting skill motivated by social competition. Thus, *"a preference for the primitive"* need not necessarily be the consequence of *"a new conception of art characteristic of the Middle Ages"*, as Dvořák had believed, but could *"refer to the factor of competition"* because: *"The idea of the primitive... implies the possibility of technical progress, and this in its turn may depend on the kind of competition we encountered in Pliny's chapters on ancient art."*[160]

Revived Orthodoxy in Counterattack

If Gombrich represents the most radical criticism of the historical relativism of Riegl's Vienna School, which extended to a rejection of epistemological and value relativism in general, Otto Pächt represents his polar opposite.[161] In contrast to the majority of Schlosser's pupils, he became *"a consistent relativist"*.[162] Despite fundamental criticisms by Schapiro and Gombrich, he

---

[159] Gombrich's relationship to Riegl has been interpreted as an obsession dictated by Gombrich's permanent emulation of the "father" of the Vienna School. See BAKOŠ 1996 (see note 128), pp. 234-257. Nevertheless, Gombrich's polemic against Riegl can also be regarded as a substitute for the virtual duel between Schlosser and Riegl that had never taken place. On the Gombrich-Riegl relationship, see also PODRO, Michael: Responding to Gombrich's Response to Riegl, in *Wiener Schule. Erinnerung und Perspektiven* (see note 1), pp. 153-160. Compare also PODRO, Michael: Risposta alla risposta di Gombrich a Riegl, in *L'arte e i linguaggi della percezione. L'eredità di Sir Ernst H. Gombrich*. Eds. Richard BOSEL – Maria G. Di MONTE – Michele Di MONTE – Sybille EBERT-SCHIFFERER. Milano 2004, pp. 121-130; ROSENAUER, Artur: Gombrich e la Scuola Viennese di Storia dell'Arte, ibid., pp. 131-140.

[160] GOMBRICH, Ernst H.: *The Preference for the Primitive. Episodes in the History of Western Taste and Art*. London 2002, pp. 37, 40. It is symptomatic of Gombrich's humanist normativism that he regards the revivals of *"the primitive"* as mere *"episodes"* in comparison with the Renaissances or renascences of the classical canon.

[161] See GOMBRICH, Ernst H.: Relativism in the Humanities: The Debate about Human Nature; Relativism in the History of Ideas; Relativism in the Appreciation of Art, in GOMBRICH 1991 (see note 2), pp. 36-61.

[162] See WOOD 1999 (see note 62), p. 13. In Wood's words, *"Pächt was a more consistent relativist than Panofsky or Gombrich"*. Wood juxtaposes Pächt's relativism to Panofsky's and Gombrich's inconsequential kind. According to Wood, *"both Panofsky and Gombrich backed off from the full implications of their own insights into the relativity and incommensurability of representational systems... Both scholars built normative models of the history of art."* – Ibid.

maintained that national collective subjects could be regarded as the standard bearers of the history of art,[163] insisting on this belief from his early paper "Gestaltungsprinzipien der westlichen Malerei des 15. Jahrhunderts"[164] through to his late methodological writings, as represented by his *Methodisches zur kunsthistorischen Praxis.*[165] Moreover, Pächt truly followed and developed Riegl and Dvořák's legacy. After a twenty-six-year exile in England, he accepted the offer to take over the chair of art history at Vienna University from Swoboda in 1963. The following year, he was strongly critical of Panofsky's iconology at the CIHA Congress in Bonn.[166] Pächt reproached the iconological method for its neglect of artistic originality and for missing out on the essence of art as a consequence of focusing on iconography alone.[167] Pächt's plea for the recognition of originality did, of course, imply that the paradigm of modern art was generally valid.[168]

Pächt's intention of reviving Rieglian orthodoxy was expressed unequivocally in 1966 when, together with Swoboda, he edited Riegl's unpublished lectures held at Vienna University in 1897 – 1899 entitled the *Historische Grammatik der bildenden Kunste.*[169] Five years later, Pächt summarized his methodological credo in the lecture course held at Vienna University in 1970/1971, published under the title *Methodisches zur kunsthistorischen Praxis.*[170] Conceived of as a summary of the basic principles of art history in order to give practical instructions on research, the paper coped with the main methodological trends of art history and drew up a sophisticated, even if not very original,

---

[163] PÄCHT 1977 (see note 61), p. 272. Pächt speaks about *"Kollektivpersönlichkeiten"* as *"Träger der Entwicklung"*.

[164] PÄCHT, Otto: Gestaltungsprinzipien der westlichen Malerei des 15. Jahrhunderts, in *Kunstwissenschaftliche Forschungen*, 2, 1933, pp. 75-100.

[165] PÄCHT 1977 (see note 61), p. 299. Even if admitting that *"Das sind... höchst umstrittene Konzeptionen,"* and that *"Im Sinne solcher mit eigenen Bewegungsenergien ausgestatteten charakterologischen Einheiten sprechen wir also von historischen Konstanten... als ob es sich um die Entfaltung organischer Lebewesen, zielbewusst schaffender aktiver Personen handelte,"* Pächt was convinced that *"Man muss die Definition der Konstanten aus den Kunstwerken und den genetischen Reihen, die sie bilden, herausholen, nicht in sie aus anderen Gebieten hineintragen."*

[166] PÄCHT, Otto: Künstlerische Originalität und ikonographische Erneuerung; reprinted in PÄCHT 1977 (see note 61), pp. 153-164.

[167] Pächt had already taken a strong line over Panofsky's iconological approach in his review of Panofsky's *Early Netherlandish Painting* published in *The Burlington Magazine*, 98, 1956, pp. 110-115, 267-277.

[168] On this subject, see BAKOŠ, Ján: Kritiky ikonológie a Albert Kutal [Critiques of Iconology and Albert Kutal], in *Sborník prací filosofické fakulty brněnské university*, 23-24, 1979 – 1980, pp. 9-18.

[169] RIEGL 1966 (see note 17).

[170] See note 163.

methodological project.[171] Accusing iconology of laying claim to methodological hegemony, Pächt charged it with neglecting the specific nature of visual art.[172] According to him, iconological interpretation resulted in a total intellectualization of the work of art, regarding it merely as a kind of *"hieroglyph"* or *"secret writing"*,[173] accessible exclusively to an elite.[174] At the same time, Pächt equally rejected Croce's and Schlosser's belief in *"creatio ex nihilo"* and the idea of genius regarded as the absolutely unconditioned and free creator.[175] Moreover, Pächt also resolutely rejected Gombrich's ideas of the determining role of tradition and the power of *"form conventions"*. According to him, such a theory neglected the creative basis of art and transformed art history into a mere history of copying.[176]

He contrasted iconology, transhistoricism and conventionalism with the orthodox Vienna School belief in historical evolution. He reintroduced Riegl and Dvořák's genetic theory,[177] which he regarded as the most reliable and effective of methodologies.[178] According to Pächt, the evolutionary method and its idea of genetic connections between works of art, respected not only the

---

[171] Pächt expressed his intention as follows: *"Mir geht es um Fragen der Arbeitshygiene in der praktischen Ausübung unserer Handwerks als Kunsthistoriker."* – PÄCHT 1977 (see note 61), p. 187.

[172] Ibid., p. 374: *"… das Spezifische der künstlerischen Ausdrucksphäre… daß die bildende Kunst… Dinge sagen kann, die in keinem anderen Ausdrucksbereich gesagt werden können…"*

[173] *"Geheimsprache".* – Ibid., pp. 354, 364.

[174] Ibid., p. 264: *"Die ikonologische Forschung… [ist]… die totale Intellektualisierung des Kunstwerks, die das Bild für eine Bilderschrift nimmt."*

[175] *"Die These von der absoluten Unabhängigkeit wahrhaft schöpferischer Gestaltung in der Kunstgeschichte."* – Ibid., p. 282. According to Pächt, *"der Versuch, das Kunstschaffen der Genies von der Allgemeinentwicklung zu sondern ist zum Scheitern verurteilt… die genialen Leistungen sind nicht minder ableitbar als die kleinen Vorwärtsbewegungen der Durchschnittskünstler."*

[176] *"Nach Gombrich… als Sprecher der Antievolutionisten… [ist] ein Künstler, und sei es auch der größte… gebunden, sich… der Formeln, Schablonen, Muster, Klischees zu bedienen, die ihm seine Zeit, sein Milieu, seine Tradition… anbietet… [es] beruht die Möglichkeit einer historischen Ableitung von Kunstwerken darauf, daß einer vom anderen abschreibt… wir als Historiker müssen uns wirklich damit begnügen, eine Geschichte des Kopierens zu erarbeiten…"* – Ibid., pp. 284-285.

[177] Symptomatically, in 1974, Pächt re-edited DVOŘÁK, Max: Über die dringendsten methodischen Erfordernisse der Erziehung zur kunstgeschichtlichen Forschung, in *Die Geisteswissenschaften*, 1, 1913 – 1914, pp. 932-936, 958-961; reprinted in *Wiener Jahrbuch für Kunstgeschichte*, 27, 1974, pp. 7-19. As far as method was concerned, the essay represented a compromise between the formalist genetic approach and the cultural/historical approach developed by Dvořák just before his conversion to art history as the history of world views. According to Pächt, *"erscheint uns… dieser vor 60 Jahren geschriebene Artikel von großer Aktualität und programmatischer Bedeutung gerade heute, wo, nach ehe die Gefahr der Monopolisierung der Interpretation von Kunstwerken durch Ikonologie gebannt ist, die Kunstgeschichte einer neuen schweren Belastungsprobe ausgesetzt wird, indem man versucht, sie… in das Schlepptau der Soziologie zu bringen."* – Ibid., p. 7.

[178] *"Genealogieforschung, gewöhnlich genetische Ableitung genannt, wird zu einem der dringendsten Anliegen unserer Disziplin."* – PÄCHT 1977 (see note 61), p. 272.

specifically non-verbal nature of the visual arts[179] together with the creative and unique nature of art production, but also the innovative and immanent character of its history and, at the same time, viewed the history of art as a causal and thus rationally explicable process. As a consequence, the genetic approach could be regarded as the best verifiable art historical method despite the fact that it was nothing more than a hypothetical explanation.[180]

Nevertheless, Pächt argued that in order to develop a complex explanation of the history of art, the genetic approach had to be combined with the structural analysis of the single work of art based on its central organizing formal principle. He was convinced that combining an evolutionary approach, focused on reconstructing genetic links, with a structural analysis, concentrated on the single artwork, was possible and represented the best available model of art historical research.

Conclusion: An Epistemological or Ideological Struggle?

The revival of Riegl's and Dvořák's orthodoxy by Otto Pächt seems to conclude the story of the Vienna School. Pächt's return to the evolutionary project gives the story a cyclical nature. It started with Riegl and the young Dvořák's optimistic model of art historical research as a neutral, rational and objective science. This was transformed, first, into the later Dvořák's hermeneutic project. It was then revised by Sedlmayr's first optimistic model of a *"rigorous science"*, only to be replaced later with his mystical but still optimistic idea of interpretation conceived of as re-creation. This was followed by Gombrich's skeptical idea of art history as *"scholarship"*, and ended, finally, with Pächt's revival of a modest version of Riegl's epistemological model that regarded art history as an exercise in relativism, whose "objectivity" was purely hypothetical in nature. The story of the Vienna School represented an

---

[179] According to Pächt: *"Am Anfang war das Auge, nicht das Wort."* See PÄCHT, Otto: Am Anfang war das Auge, in *Kunsthistoriker in eigener Sache* (see note 146), pp. 25-61, here p. 25.

[180] According to PÄCHT 1977 (see note 61), pp. 202-203: *"Ich sagte vorhin, daß jede wissenschaftliche These, also auch jede Stilerklärung oder Bildinterpretation, zunächst nur eine Hypothese ist und auf ihre wissenschaftliche Haltbarkeit überprüft werden muss."* Ibid., p. 225: *"Wir suchen in der entwicklungsgeschichtlichen Betrachtung Hilfe und Stütze für unsere Interpretation und Beurteilung des Einzelobjektes. Gelingt die Einordnung in eine genetische Reihe, d.h. werden die von uns festgestellten Eigenschaften ableitbar, dann können wir unseren Befund mit gutem Gewissen als verifiziert angesehen."* Ibid., p. 226: *"In theoretischen Erörterungen ist einerseits meistens von der genetischen Ableitung als dem entscheidenden Verifizierungsverfahren die Rede, in der Praxis wird jedoch der umgekehrte Weg, der Weg von Später zu Früher, gar nicht so selten begangen wie die Literatur zu diesem Problem uns glauben machen könnte."*

immanent dialogue between two camps, between adherents of Riegl's impersonalism on the one hand, and the followers of Schlosser's humanistic individualism on the other. Dvořák's followers concentrated on modifying or transforming their teacher's model (mostly by means of synthesizing diverse impulses including Strzygowski's ones), while Schlosser and his pupils liked to attack and critically revise the orthodoxy of the opposite camp. Naturally, there were some exceptions to that "rule": Sedlmayr's flirtation with Riegl and Dvořák for example, or Pächt's transfer of allegiance to the Riegl-Dvořák camp and his counterattack against the "humanist" Ernst Gombrich. However, this story of the methodological visions and revisions of the Vienna School was only on the surface a purely epistemological issue or introverted art historical dispute. As is well known, members of the Vienna School of Art History were deeply immersed in debates concerning modern art,[181] and these methodological disputes also had a clear ideological dimension, being a part of the struggle that has continued till the present, i.e. the struggle between normativists and relativists.[182]

---

[181] On the relationship between the Vienna School and modern art, see in particular LACHNIT, Edwin: *Die Wiener Schule der Kunstgeschichte und die Kunst ihrer Zeit. Zum Verhältnis von Methode und Forschungsgegenstand am Beginn der Moderne.* Wien – Köln – Weimar 2005; HOFMANN 2004 (see note 126).

[182] On this issue, see also MITROVIĆ, Branko: Humanist Art History and Its Enemies: Erwin Panofsky on the Individualism – Holism Debate, in *Konsthistorik tidskritt – Journal of Art History*, 78, 2009, No. 2, pp. 57-76.

II. THE DEPTH OF THE HISTORICITY OF ART AND WALTER BENJAMIN

Benjamin and "Will of Art" (Walter Benjamin and Alois Riegl)

The close relationship of Walter Benjamin to the Vienna School of Art History, and especially to Alois Riegl, is well known.[1] According to the testimony of Werner Kraft, Benjamin got already to know Riegl's epoch making work, *Spätrömische Kunstindustrie* (The Late Roman Art Industry, 1901) during his university studies in the period 1916 – 1919.[2] Michael Jennings found confirmation of this in the expressions which Benjamin took from Riegl and used in his early essays "Über das Mittelalter" (On the Middle Ages) and "Die Bedeutung der Sprache im Trauerspiel und Tragödie" (The Meaning of Language in Tragic Drama).[3] Perhaps the article "Bücher, die lebendig geblieben sind" (Books That Have Remained Alive, published in *Literarische Welt* in 1929) testifies most eloquently to the deep respect Benjamin felt for Riegl.[4] In it, Benjamin mentioned *The Late Roman Art Industry* among four permanently inspiring books. The others were Georg Lukács's Marxist work *Geschichte und Klassenbewusstsein* (History and Class Consciousness, 1923), Franz Rosenzweig's book *Stern der Erlösung* (Star of Salvation, 1911) on Jewish theology

---

[1] See KEMP, Wolfgang: Walter Benjamin und die Kunstwissenschaft 1. Benjamins Beziehung zur Wiener Schule, in *Kritische Berichte*, 1, 1973, pp. 30-50; KEMP, Wolfgang: Fernbilder. Benjamin und Kunstwissenschaft, in *"Links hatte noch alles sich zu enträtseln..." Walter Benjamin im Kontext*. Ed. Burkhardt LINDNER. Frankfurt am Main 1978, pp. 224-240; JENNINGS, Michael W.: Walter Benjamin and the Theory of Art History, in *Walter Benjamin, 1892 – 1940. Zum 100. Geburtstag*. Ed. Uwe STEINER. Bern 1992, pp. 77-102; LEVIN, Thomas Y.: Walter Benjamin and the Theory of Art History, in *October*, 47, Winter 1988, pp. 77-83; PEAKER, Giles: Works that Have Lasted... Walter Benjamin Reading Alois Riegl, in *Framing Formalism, Riegl's Work*. Ed. Richard WOODFIELD. Amsterdam 2001, pp. 291-309.

[2] KRAFT, Werner: Über Benjamin, in *Zur Aktualität Walter Benjamins. Aus Anlass des 80. Geburtstags*. Ed. Siegfried UNSELD. Frankfurt am Main 1972, pp. 60, 62. See also LEVIN 1988 (see note 1), p. 78, n. 6.

[3] JENNINGS, Michael W.: *Dialectical Images. Walter Benjamin's Theory of Literary Criticism*. Ithaca – London 1987, p. 154; LEVIN 1988 (see note 1), p. 78.

[4] BENJAMIN, Walter: Bücher, die lebendig geblieben sind, in BENJAMIN, Walter: *Gesammelte Schriften*. Eds. Rolf TIEDEMANN – Hermann SCHWEPPENHÄUSER. Frankfurt am Main 1972 – 1989, Vol. III: Kritiken und Rezensionen, p. 170; KEMP 1978 (see note 1), p. 225; LEVIN 1988 (see note 1), p. 80; JENNINGS 1992 (see note 1), p. 82.

and Alfred G. Meyers' analysis of the architecture and technology of the 19th century, *Eisenbauten* (Iron Buildings,1907). However, Benjamin expressed his view of Riegl and the Viennnese School in most detail, in the essay "Strenge Kunstwissenschaft" (The Rigorous Study of Art),[5] the first version of which was published in the *Frankfurter Zeitung* on 30th July 1933.[6] He also gave a detailed review here of the first volume of the annual *Kunstwissenschaftliche Forschungen* (1931) published by the so-called Viennese "Structuralists" headed by Hans Sedlmayr and Otto Pächt, who declared allegiance to the heritage of Alois Riegl. In complete contrast to Meyer Schapiro, who later subjected the so-called New Vienna School to severe criticism and unmasked it as metaphysics hiding behind rationalism,[7] Benjamin proclaimed unambiguous support for the methodological position of the Vienna School and Riegl's principles. He also explicitly confirmed this in his posthumously published biography "Drei Lebensläufe", in which he wrote about the *"decisive influence"* of Riegl and especially of his concept of *"Kunstwollen"* (*"will of art"*) on his early writings.[8] The fact that Riegl was a permanent source of inspiration for Benjamin is also confirmed by his familiarity with Riegl's selected articles published in 1929 under the title *Gesammelte Aufsätze*, especially with his essay "Der moderne Denkmalskultus, sein Wesen, seine Entstehung" (The Modern Cult of the Monument, Its Essence, Its Origin, 1903), which was reflected in Benjamin's central concept of *"aura"* as well as elsewhere.[9]

The points of agreement which Benjamin found in Riegl can be summarized as follows:[10]

1. Historical pluralism: the conviction of the equality of all epochs, the non-existence of declines in the history of art and appreciation of transitional and late periods such as the Baroque.

2. A democratic understanding of art: rejection of the dualism of *"high"* versus *"low"* art, acceptance of industrial art and mass production as a phenomenon equal to high art.

---

[5] BENJAMIN, Walter: Strenge Kunstwissenschaft, in BENJAMIN 1972 – 1989 (see note 4), Vol. III: Kritiken und Rezensionen, pp. 363-374; English translation in LEVIN, Thomas Y.: The Rigorous Study of Art, in *October*, 47, Winter 1988.

[6] On this LEVIN 1988 (see note 1), p. 82.

[7] SCHAPIRO, Meyer: The New Viennese School, in *Art Bulletin*, 18, 1936, pp. 258-266.

[8] BENJAMIN, Walter: Drei Lebensläufe, in *Zur Aktualität Walter Benjamins* (see note 2), p. 51.

[9] According to PEAKER 2001 (see note 1), p. 306: *"There can be no doubt that Riegl's influence on Benjamin was profound and enduring."* On the other hand, *"Benjamin's reading of Riegl has more of the character of a selective appropriation, or a transformation perhaps"*.

[10] KEMP 1978 (see note 1), pp. 225-227; LEVIN 1988 (see note 1), p. 78; JENNINGS 1992 (see note 1), pp. 81-89.

3. A rejection of romantic subjectivism, that is the identification of the individual artists as the creators and true authors of the history of art, and its replacement with the idea of collective experience[11] and the impersonal determination of the art historical process, expressed by the term *"Kunstwollen"* (*"will of art"*).

4. An overcoming of mechanistic determinism with the help of the category of expression, with an activist expressive model, in which the superstructure, including art, is not a passive reflection, but an active expression of the economic base.[12]

5. An inter-disciplinary understanding starting from Hegel, that is an understanding of the work of art *"as an integral expression of the religious, metaphysical, political and economic tendencies of the time, so that it cannot be limited to one discipline"*.[13]

6. Inductionism: replacement of research into developmental connections of universal history with the analysis of the individual solitary work of art, in harmony with the programme of Hans Sedlmayr,[14] or even with research into details, in the footsteps of Riegl.

7. *"Physiognomism"* associated with *"symptomatology"*:[15] namely, the analysis of the form or *"physiognomic character"* of the work as something representative of the whole culture of the period[16] on the basis of the conviction of the meaningfulness of form, the connection of the material aspect of the work (*"Sachgehalt"*) with its meaning (*"Bedeutungsgehalt"*),[17] or in other words, on the basis of the understanding of the history of form as the history of expression.[18]

8. In agreement with Aby Warburg, honoring *the detail* as the throne of God: i.e. acknowledging the unimportant element (*"Unbedeutenden"*), insignificant detail (*"Unscheinbaren"*), accidental fragment (*"Zufälligen"*) or curious and marginal element (*"Grenzfall"*) as a meaningful document, symptom

---

[11] Ibid., p. 85.

[12] KEMP 1978 (see note 1), pp. 227-228.

[13] Walter BENJAMIN in *Zur Aktualität Walter Benjamins* (see note 2), p. 46: *"… die Analyse des Kunstwerks…, die in ihm einen integralen… Ausdruck der religiösen, metaphysischen, politischen, wirtschaftlichen Tendenzen einer Epoche erkennt."*

[14] SEDLMAYR, Hans: Zu einer strengen Kunstwissenschaft, in *Kunstwissenschaftliche Forschungen*, 1, 1931, pp. 7-32; reprinted in SEDLMAYR, Hans: *Kunst und Wahrheit. Zur Theorie und Methode der Kunstgeschichte*. Hamburg 1958, pp. 35-70 (chapter "Kunstgeschichte als Kunstgeschichte"); BENJAMIN 1972 – 1989 (see note 5), p. 374; JENNINGS 1992 (see note 1), p. 80.

[15] LEVIN 1988 (see note 1), p. 78.

[16] BENJAMIN 1972 – 1989 (see note 5), p. 367; LEVIN 1988 (see note 1), p. 80.

[17] BENJAMIN 1972 – 1989 (see note 5), p. 367.

[18] KEMP 1978 (see note 1), p. 227.

or nucleus containing the whole culture of the time and the whole historical process.[19]

The Depth of the Historicity of Art
(Walter Benjamin and Max Dvořák)

Finally, Benjamin and Riegl were connected by their radical historicism or
historical relativism: the view that the history of art is the history of changes
in the actual core of art, its essence, its identity. Benjamin found this idea in
Riegl's understanding of the history of art as made up of changes in artistic
intention. He valued Riegl's view that changes in *"Kunstwollen"* were deep
changes, that changes in artistic form or artistic representation also meant
a change in the actual intentions of art and its perception of reality.[20]

Benjamin understood Riegl's identification of the connection between
"Kunstwollen" and contemporary worldview, as that of direct causality.[21]
However, Riegl was more cautious: in order to preserve the autonomy of art,
he described the relationship between *"Kunstwollen"* and *"Weltanschauung"*
more as a parallel or analogy.[22] It was only Riegl's pupil and successor at Vienna University, Max Dvořák, who returned to Hegel and connected changes
in art with changes in worldview. It was Dvořák, in the essay "Idealismus und
Naturalismus in der gotischen Skulptur und Malerei" (Idealism and Naturalism in Gothic Sculpture and Painting, 1918), who derived from this premise
the radical conclusion that the history of art is not only the history of forms
and contents, but of actual historic changes in the conception of art.[23] However, Benjamin did not mention Dvořák in his works. Therefore, it is probable
that, although with some delay, he derived a very similar conclusion from
Riegl's understanding of the deep historicity of art: that the actual identity

---

[19]　BENJAMIN 1972 – 1989 (see note 5), pp. 366-367. On Benjamin-Warburg relationship, see
　　　KEMP, Wolfgang: Walter Benjamin und die Kunstwissenschaft 2. Walter Benjamin und Aby
　　　Warburg, in *Kritische Berichte*, 3, 1975, pp. 5-25; DIDI-HUBERMAN, Georges: *Devant le temps.*
　　　Histoire de l'art et anachronisme des images. Paris 2000, pp. 90 f.
[20]　KEMP 1973 (see note 1), p. 39; JENNINGS 1992 (see note 1), p. 84.
[21]　Ibid., p. 84; RIEGL, Alois: *Spätrömische Kunstindustrie.* Wien 1927, p. 401.
[22]　Ibid., p. 405; KEMP 1978 (see note 1), p. 226.
[23]　DVOŘÁK, Max: Idealismus und Naturalismus in der gotischen Skulptur und Malerei, in
　　　Historische Zeitschrift, 119, 1918, pp. 1-62, 185-246; reprinted in DVOŘÁK, Max: *Kunstgeschich-*
　　　te als Geistesgeschichte. Studien zur abendländischen Kunstentwicklung. Eds. Johannes WILDE
　　　– Karl M. SWOBODA. München 1924, pp. 41-147, here p. 120. On Dvořák's historical relati-
　　　vism, see BAKOŠ, Ján: Max Dvořák – a Neglected Re-Visionist, in *Wiener Schule. Erinnerung*
　　　und Perspektiven (=Wiener Jahrbuch für Kunstgeschichte, 53). Wien – Köln – Weimar 2004,
　　　pp. 55-72.

of art changes in history. Riegl did not entirely free himself from the premise of *"ars una"*, since he regarded *"competition with nature"* (*"Wettschaffen mit der Natur"*), meaning sensuous depiction, as the basic characteristic of art,[24] and for him historicity, understood as changes of perception, occurred on the basis of this unchanged core of art as variations of *"Kunstwollen"*. However, for Dvořák and Benjamin, changes in the identity of art involved not only ontological but also sociological changes: historic changes in the actual nature of art began to appear as a history of the social conception of art, and as the history of the social status of art.

As Wolfgang Kemp stated,[25] Benjamin was not only a successor but also a competitor of Riegl. However, he only explicitly criticized Riegl once, reproaching him for continuing to register the perceptual and formal changes in art whilst ignoring the social changes on which they were based: *"However far reaching their insight, these scholars* [Wickhoff and Riegl] *limited themselves to showing the significant, formal hallmark which characterized perception in late Roman times. They did not attempt – and perhaps, saw no way – to show the social transformations expressed by these changes of perception."*[26] At the same time, Benjamin's materialistic criticism is paradoxical because Riegl actually used the term *"Kunstwollen"* to deliberately and critically revise Semper's materialist interpretation of art history.[27] Demanding that this term be understood in a materialist way actually meant revising its basic meaning.

---

[24] DITTMANN, Lorenz: Der Begriff des Kunstwerkes in der deutschen Kunstgeschichte, in *Kategorien und Methoden der deutschen Kunstgeschichte 1900 – 1930.* Ed. Lorenz DITTMANN. Stuttgart 1985, pp. 52-56. On the notion *"ars una"* in relation to the Vienna School of Art History, see HOFMANN, Werner: Was bleibt von der "Wiener Schule", in *Kunsthistoriker,* 1-2, 1984 – 1985, No. 1, pp. 4-8. See also, the enlarged version in *Jahrbuch des Zentralinstituts für Kunstgeschichte,* I/2, 1986, pp. 273 -290. On this, see also BELTING, Hans: *Das Ende der Kunstgeschichte?* München 1984, p. 15.

[25] KEMP 1978 (see note 1), p. 226.

[26] BENJAMIN 1972 – 1989 (see note 4), Vol. I-2: Abhandlungen, p. 478 f.: *"So weitgehend ihre* [sc. Wickhoff's und Riegl's] *Erkenntnisse waren, so hatte ihre Grenzen darin, daß sich diese Forscher begnügten, die formale Signatur aufzuweisen, die der Wahrnehmung in der spätrömischen Zeit eigen war. Sie haben nicht versucht... die gesellschaftlichen Umwälzungen zu zeigen, die in diesen Veränderungen der Wahrnehmung ihren Ausdruck fanden."* English translation by Harry Zohn in BENJAMIN, Walter: *Illuminations. Essays and Reflections.* Ed. Hannah ARENDT. New York 1969, p. 222. On this, see KEMP 1978 (see note 1), p. 226.

[27] Ibid., p. 226.

The Ahistorical Historicity of Art
(Walter Benjamin, Benedetto Croce, Hans Sedlmayr)

However, Benjamin only definitively accepted radical historicism in the explanation of art and its materialistic-sociological version in the thirties. In 1923, he still fully accepted (a)historical transcendentalism. In a letter to Florens Christian Rang, he expressed the conviction that the work of art has no history: *"The work of art... is in terms of its essence ahistorical."* (*"Kunstwerk...ist seinem Wesentlichen nach geschichtslos."*)[28] – so that according to Benjamin's view at the time, *"there is no such thing as the history of art"*.[29] In his view, contemporary historiography of art was ignoring this timeless character of works of art and perceiving only their external history of material (*"Stoff-Geschichte"*) and form (*"Form-Geschichte"*). In this framework, works of art were degraded into mere examples. *"The history of works of art as such is out of consideration."* (*"Eine Geschichte der Kunstwerke selbst kommt dabei gar nicht in Frage."*)[30] However, according to Benjamin, the ahistoricity of works of art does not mean they are outside history, but that they have a *"specific historicity"* (*"die spezifische Geschichtlichkeit von Kunstwerken"*). It involves establishing intensive mutual relations between works of art, and, so to speak, the creation of an autonomous, metahistorical world of art (*"die wesentliche Verbindung unter Kunstwerken bleibt intensiv"*). These internal artistic relations transcend time (they are *"Zeitlos"*) forming a timeless context of works of art, but they are not without historical importance (*"Zusammenhänge von Kunstwerken untereinander... welche zeitlos und dennoch nicht ohne historischen Belang sind."*).[31] They can be called history-making. However, according to Benjamin, this specific historicity of the work of art cannot be grasped by the historiography of art, but only by a creative or *"intensive"* interpretation.

If Benjamin in a sense anticipated Heidegger's conception of art as constitutive of the truth of history, with his idea of the time-transcending significance of works of art, there is also an obvious affinity with the position of Benedetto Croce and his Viennese followers, Julius von Schlosser and Hans

---

[28] BENJAMIN, Walter: *Briefe.* Vol. 1. Eds. Gershom SCHOLEM – Theodor W. ADORNO. Frankfurt am Main 1966, p. 322; English ed. *The Correspondence of Walter Benjamin.* Eds. Gershom SCHOLEM – Theodor W. ADORNO. Chicago 1994, p. 223. On this, see SCHWARTZ, Frederic J.: Walter Benjamin's Essay on Eduard Fuchs: An Art-Historical Perspective, in *Marxism and the History of Art: From William Morris to the New Left.* Ed. Andrew HEMINGWAY. London – Ann Arbor 2006, p. 109.
[29] BENJAMIN 1966 (see note 28), p. 322.
[30] Ibid.
[31] Ibid. On Benjamin's idea of *"specific historicity"* of art, see DIDI-HUBERMAN 2000 (see note 19), pp. 87-89.

Sedlmayr.[32] He agreed with their conviction that art consists of individual works of art, that the work of art transcends history, despite its ahistoricity being a special form of historicity, and that this specific transhistorical nature of the work of art cannot be grasped by the traditional historiography of art, but only by creative interpretation. The premise of the transcendental historicity of works of art led Benjamin at this time to the threshold of dividing the study of art into two parts: *"historiography"* and *"interpretation"*. It not only recalls Croce's dualism: *"history – criticism"*, but also anticipates Sedlmayr's later distinction between two art histories (*"zwei Kunstwissenschaften"*: positivist, based on external rational reconstruction, and hermeneutic, based on intuitive understanding),[33] and his post-war conception of interpretation as a recreation of the work of art.[34] However, as we already mentioned, Benjamin rejected Sedlmayr's methodological dualism at the beginning of the thirties.[35] The reason was that he replaced this transcendentalist, individualist, creationist, essentially autonomist idea of art with the sociological and materialist version of radical historicism, at precisely this time.

"Will of Art" Versus the Work of Art
(Walter Benjamin and Julius von Schlosser)

However, Benjamin had already, in the mid twenties, interpreted Riegl's historical relativism from a normative point of view, in spite of his fascination

---

[32]　Julius von Schlosser articulated the *"insularist theory of art"*, conceiving the work of art as a monad, in his curriculum vitae published in 1924. See *Die Kunstwissenschaft der Gegenwart in Selbstdarstellungen*. Ed. Johannes JAHN. Leipzig 1924, p. 130. On Benedetto Croce's impact on Viennese art historians, see HALBERTSMA, Marlite: *Wilhelm Pinder und die Deutsche Kunstgeschichte*. Worms 1992 (1st ed. Groningen 1985), pp. 91-95; BEYER, Andreas: "Pfadfindung einer zukünftigen Kunsthistoriographie". Julius von Schlosser, Benedetto Croce und Roberto Longhi, in *Kritische Berichte*, 16, 1988, No. 4, pp. 24-28; LACHNIT, Edwin: Julius von Schlosser (1866 – 1938), in *Altmeister moderner Kunstgeschichte*. Ed. Heinrich DILLY. Berlin 1990, pp. 156-157; De MAMBRO SANTOS, Ricardo: *Viatico viennese: la storiografia critica di Julius von Schlosser e la metodologia filosofica di Benedetto Croce*. Sant'Oreste 1998. On Croce's criticism of art historical formalism, see MORPURGO-TAGLIABUE, Guido: *L'esthétique contemporaine*. Milan 1960, s. 144-147. According to DIDI-HUBERMAN 2000 (see note 19), p. 86, Benjamin's relationship to Croce was rather dismissive: *"On se souvient avec quelle sévérité Benjamin aura pu… balayer le 'subjectivisme inductif' d'un Johannes Volkelt et bousculer les conceptions d'un Konrad Burdach, voire d'un Benedetto Croce."* On this, see also COQUIO, Catherine: Benjamin et Panofsky devant l'image, in *Présence(s) de Walter Benjamin*. Ed. Jean-Marie LACHAUD. Bordeaux 1992, p. 26.

[33]　SEDLMAYR 1958 (see note 14), pp. 35-43.

[34]　Ibid., pp. 87-127 (chapter "Probleme der Interpretation").

[35]　BENJAMIN 1972 – 1989 (see note 5), p. 367.

with the expressive or symptomatological potency of Riegl's *"Kunstwollen"*. Although in 1929 Benjamin already unambiguously emphasized Riegl's rejection of *"the theory of declining periods and that in what had been regarded as decline into barbarism, he discovered a new understanding of space, a new artistic intention"*,[36] in his "Habilitationsarbeit" *Ursprung des deutschen Trauerspiels* (Origin of the German Tragic Drama, written in 1925 and published, 1928),[37] he declared: *"Since like Expressionism, the Baroque is not so much an age of genuine artistic achievement as an age possessed of an unremitting will-to-art. This is true of all periods of so-called decadence. The supreme reality in art is the isolated, self-contained work. But there are times when the well-wrought work is only within reach of the epigone. These are the periods of 'decadence' in the arts, the periods of will-to-art. [...] The form as such is within the reach of this will, a well-made individual work is not."*[38] As we see, Benjamin distinguishes those periods in which the anonymous *"Kunstwollen"* prevails from periods in which the isolated self-sufficient work of art is decisive. He describes the first as periods of decline, and regards the creation of individual works of art as true art, free from decline. A decade later, Julius von Schlosser made a similar distinction following in the footsteps of Croce. In the essay "Stilgeschichte und Sprachgeschichte der bildenden Kunst" (The History of Style and the History of Language), he distinguished the true art of the great personalities who shape artistic styles, from the works of epigones, who only produce the *"language"* of art.[39] By distinguishing periods of anonymous will of art as periods of decline from periods of individual works of art, Benjamin clearly placed himself in the opposite position to Riegl: that of undemocratic, aristocratic, creationist individualism. According to Riegl, the anonymous *"Kunstwollen"* is decisive in all periods, the individual work being only an expression of it. Only the character of this will of art varies historically. Periods of flowering and decline do not exist in history, because there are various *"Kunstwollen"* and so no single criterion

---

[36] BENJAMIN 1972 – 1989 (see note 4), Vol. III: Kritiken und Rezensionen, p. 170.

[37] BENJAMIN, Walter: *Dílo a jeho zdroj* [Work and Its Source]. Praha 1979, p. 429. According to KORTA, Tobias F.: Walter Benjamin (1892 – 1940). Der Engel im "Grand Hotel Abgrund", in *Culture Club. Klassiker der Kulturtheorie.* Eds. Martin L. HOFMANN – Tobias F. KORTA – Sibylle NIEKISCH. Frankfurt am Main 2004, p. 93: *"Ab März 1923 arbeitete Benjamin intensiv an seinem Habilitationsprojekt Ursprung des deutschen Trauerspiels."*

[38] BENJAMIN 1972 – 1989 (see note 4), Vol. I-1: Abhandlungen, p. 235; English translation: BENJAMIN, Walter: *The Origin of German Tragic Drama.* London 1998, p. 55. The view of the work of art as a monad had already been articulated by Julius von Schlosser in 1924 (see note 32). According to SCHWARTZ 2006 (see note 28), p. 19, Benjamin's *"monadological conception of the work of art"* already articulated in 1923 – in the letter to F. CH. Rang, see BENJAMIN 1966 (see note 28) – refers to Benjamin's whole work.

[39] SCHLOSSER, Julius von: Über "Stilgeschichte" und "Sprachgeschichte" der bildenden Kunst, in *Sitzungsbericht der Bayerischen Akademie der Wissenschaften, 1.* München 1935.

for true art. There is no such thing as a self-sufficient individual work of art since its orientation can only be an expression of an historically specific artistic intention. Against this background, Benjamin's normativity, based on appreciation of individualism as the true non-decadent position of art, is evident, although only nostalgic. His sympathies are on the side of the decadent impersonal periods, among which he includes his own time as well as the Baroque and the 19th century.

The Functional and Receptive Depth of the Historicity of Art

We mentioned that it was Max Dvořák who had already radicalized Riegl's historical relativism in the second decade of the 20th century, and understood the history of art as meaning change in the actual idea of art. He found the source of this deep change in the spiritual or intellectual sphere, in changes of worldview. But since he understood the deep historicity of art as meaning changes in the concept of art, he placed himself on the threshold of the sociological understanding of historicity, with the idea that changes in the identity of art are anchored in a social concept. Thus the ontological conception of art began to change into a sociological conception, and the doors were opened to an understanding of the identity of art as a fundamentally social concept.

In the mid thirties, Walter Benjamin completed this transformation of radical historical relativism into sociological historicism with the epoch-making essay "Das Kunstwerk im Zeitalter seiner technischen Reproduzierbarkeit" (The Work of Art in the Age of Mechanical Reproduction, 1935 – 1936).[40] He reinterpreted Riegl's historicism here in a consistently sociological way: transformations of autonomous *"Kunstwollen"* (*"will of art"*), which Dvořák had transformed into changes in the idea of art, were now understood by Benjamin as changes in the social status of the work of art. He conceived changes in visual perception as not only changes in collective perception, but also

---

[40] Originally published as "L'œuvre d'art à l'epoque de sa reproduction mécaniseé, in *Zeitschrift für Sozialforschung*, 5, 1936, pp. 40-66. See TIEDEMANN, Rolf: Bibliographie der Erstdrücke von Benjamins Schriften, in *Zur Aktualität Walter Benjamins* (see note 2), p. 270; EBERLEIN, Johann K.: Zur Grundlage von Benjamins Aura-Begriff, in *Zeitenspiegelung. Zur Bedeutung von Traditionen in Kunst und Kunstwissenschaft. Festschrift für Konrad Hofmann*. Berlin 1998, p. 298, n. 7. BÜRGER, Peter: Benjamins Kunsttheorie. Möglichkeiten und Grenzen ihrer Aktualisierbarkeit, in *Schrift – Bilder – Denken. Walter Benjamin und die Künste*. Ed. Detlev SCHÖTTKER. Berlin 2004, pp. 174-174, speaks about Benjamin's *"radikaler Historisierung des Kunstbegriffes"*. According to him, Benjamin *"hofft die Vorstellung vom 'Ewigkeitswert' der Kunst destruieren zu können"*.

in social reception. He identified changes in the form and medium of art as changes in its social function. Here, Benjamin not only detached himself from an historical transcendentalism and normativism, which had identified alternating periods of non-decline and decline, but replaced them with a radical historical relativism, above all, connecting it with materialistic sociology. He began to see the history of art as meaning changes in the social identity of the work of art, i.e. as the historical transformation of its social function and its social reception. Thus, the work of art lost its metaphysical nature and definitively gained a social identity in terms of the function and concept given to it by society. Moreover, historic changes in the identity of art, involving its social function and reception, were placed in relation to material determinants, especially the history of technology.

As is well known, Benjamin regarded the shift from the solitary individual work to mass production as a decisive change in the history of art. Under the influence of Riegl's respect for the receptive side of art, he perceived that the shift from individual work to mass production was accompanied by a change in the reception of art, with a shift from contemplation to a distracted form of vision (*"zerstreute Rezeption"*). On one side, Benjamin explained this shift in the ontological nature of the work and its collective perception as a result of changing media and use of technical inventions in the form of reproductive technology.[41] The history of art gained a new dimension, becoming, as it already had for Hegel, the history of media. On the other hand, Benjamin placed this transformation in relation to changes in the social status of art and the function of the work of art in society. The history of art, understood as the metamorphosis of the unique cult object into the unique and autonomous aesthetic object, which was finally replaced by the reproducible instruments of mass consumption, was placed by Benjamin in relation to the transformations of functions: the history of art was presented as the shift from the magic/ ritual or religious function and cult value of the work of art to the exhibition or museum function of the artwork and its aesthetic value, finally retreating before mass entertainment and political propaganda, these being the main functions of art in the age of mass culture.[42]

---

[41]   PEAKER 2001 (see note 1), p. 297, rejects the generally accepted belief that Benjamin's conception of the work of art articulated in his essay "The Work of Art in the Age of Mechanical Reproduction" can be regarded as an example of *"technological determinism"*.

[42]   According to HABERMAS, Jürgen: Bewusstmachende oder rettende Kritik – die Aktualität Walter Benjamins, in *Zur Aktualität Walter Benjamins* (see note 2), pp. 179-181, changes in the *"organization of reception"* of art correspond to changes of the *"inner structure"* of the work of art. Transformations of the *"status of the work of art"* and of its *"mode of reception"* result into the *"changes of the function of art"*: *"An die Stelle ihrer Fundierung aufs Ritual tritt ihre Fundierung*

It appears that Benjamin had no interest in the exact untangling of the causal relations between the changes in the identity of the work of art, its function, social status, collective reception, chosen artistic medium and social class to which it was addressed. What he emphasized was mainly their complex mutual interaction and dynamics. It is possible to agree with the view that *"Benjamin does not provide a full scale socio-historical account of the reason for a shift in perception"*.[43] He probably considered it too trivial to state that the new reproductive technology, which caused such deep change in the identity of the work of art and its reception, was deliberately chosen and used as an artistic medium. It required deep social changes, new needs and social interests, namely the rise of the mass public as a result of industrialization, its free time, need for entertainment, need for political control and so on.[44] However, in his own biography, Benjamin especially underlined the functional determination of the historical metamorphoses of the work of art. He described his essay "The Work of Art in the Age of Mechanical Reproduction " as a *"contribution to the sociology of the visual arts, which tries to understand particular artistic forms in terms of the changes of function, that art generally had to undergo in the course of social development"*.[45] Benjamin's understanding of the connection between art and society can be reconstructed as follows: changes in social structure produce a need for a new function of art, which seeks an adequate artistic medium. The corresponding medium uses all the technical resources including new technical inventions so that it can fulfil the new function. The change of media is finally projected into the changed structure of the work, its new status and the new way in which it is received. Thus Riegl's sensuous-vitalist

---

auf eine andere Praxis: nämlich ihre Fundierung auf Politik." PEAKER 2001 (see note 1), pp. 299-300, speaks about *"Benjamin's attention to the social role of art... The broad shifts that Benjamin narrates, from magical ritual value to secular cult value to exhibition value, are not just changes in mode of perception but changes in the relationship to the object and the social significance and functions with which it is invested."* According to Peaker: *"The poles of Benjamin's axis are cult value and exhibition value. Cult value is based in ritual, which can still be recognized in the secular cult of beauty which replaces the magical and religious use of art. Exhibition value has its ground in another kind of use value, for which the best name might be politics."* See also KORTA 2004 (see note 37), pp. 98-99.

[43] PEAKER 2001 (see note 1), p. 297.

[44] According to PEAKER 2001 (see note 1), pp. 298, 300: *"The relation of non-auratic perception to the rise of the mass is at the heart of the essay as a whole"* but, on the other hand, *"the relation of artworks and the mode of existence of a society"* was *"described very loosely by Benjamin."*

[45] *"Beitrag zur Soziologie der bildenden Kunst"* that *"sucht bestimmte Kunstformen... aus dem Funktionswechsel zu verstehen, dem die Kunst insgesamt im Zuge der gesellschaftlichen Entwicklung unterworfen ist."* English translation by Martin Styan. See *Zur Aktualität Walter Benjamins* (see note 2), p. 54. See also HABERMAS 1972 (see note 42), p. 181; PEAKER 2001 (see note 1), p. 299.

or sensuous-spiritualist connection was reinterpreted by Benjamin in a materialist-sociological way: the changes to *"Kunstwollen"* became instruments of *"materielles Wollen"*.

The History of Art as the Fading of "Aura"

To express the complex crossing of the ontic and social identity of the work of art, the overlapping of form, medium, function and reception, Benjamin introduced the term *"aura"*. With it, he attempted to capture the unity of the form of existence, social status and collective reception of the unique work of art, which has a cult function. According to Benjamin, a work gradually loses this synthesis of individuality, uniqueness, magic and nostalgia in the course of history. It is initially the result of commodification, aestheticization and museumization. Later, under the influence of the new media and the introduction of reproductive technology into art, in the interest of mass effect, art finally lost its aura completely. Analysts agree that Benjamin derived his concept of *"aura"* from Riegl's concept of *"Alterswert"*, transforming Riegl's idea of *"age-value"*.[46] They are also similar in being relational terms, neither purely ontological nor purely receptive. Benjamin does not mean by it just the unique object or specific collective perception of its uniqueness, but the specific relationship between the work and the perceiver.[47] *"Aura"* aims to express the specific ontological and sociological status of a work, a status that arises from the relation between the unique work as an object and its social reception. In other words, it aims to articulate the conviction, which Benjamin shared with the artistic Avant-garde of the first half of the 20th century, that art has a social identity, involving both function and reception, but this is achieved only through the artistic structure, through the special nature of works of art.

---

[46] On this, see ZERNER, Henri: Alois Riegl: Art, Value, and Historicism, in *Daedalus*, 105, 1976, No. 1, pp. 186-187; KEMP 1978 (see note 1), pp. 236-240; KEMP, W.: Benjamin e il culto dei monumenti di Riegl, in *Alois Riegl: teoria e prassi della conservazione dei monumenti. Antologia di scriti, discorsi, raporti 1898 – 1905, con una scelta di saggi critici.* Ed. Sandro SCARROCCHIA. Bologna 1995, pp. 417-419; LANG, Karen: *Chaos and Cosmos. On the Image in Aesthetics and Art History.* Ithaca – London 2006, pp. 136-178 (chapter "The Experience of Time and the Time of History: Riegl's Age Value and Benjamin's Aura").

[47] BÜRGER, Peter: Kunstsoziologische Aspekte der Brecht-Benjamin-Adorno-Debatte der 30er Jahre, in *Seminar: Literatur- und Kunstsoziologie.* Ed. Peter BÜRGER. Frankfurt am Main 1978, p. 15: *"Benjamin gelingt es mit dem Begriff der Aura den Typus der Beziehung zwischen Werk und Rezipient zu fassen, der der Vorstellung vom autonomen Kunstwerk entspricht... Der Begriff der Aura ist ein Relationsbegriff."*

Benjamin's term *"aura"*, which is applied to the unique, individual work of art, also includes nostalgia for the distant, the remote and the inaccessible.[48] However, if Riegl regarded the *"age-value"* as the most topical value that the present day attributed to old works of art, the nostalgia of Benjamin's *"aura"* is melancholic and retrospective, turned to the past. It is not only a sentiment for the signs of age, but also a resigned sense of unavoidable loss. Benjamin's interpretation of the history of art is similarly melancholic. It appears to him as the irresistible process of gradual loss of aura, a process in which the original magic *"aura"* of the cult object changes under the influence of the commodification of art into a secularized *"museum"* or *"exhibition aura"*. The true cult *"aura"* of uniqueness is replaced by the false aura, by aesthetic authenticity, which is only a kind of secular reactivation of aura. But in reality, it is nothing other than a fetishized commodity.[49] However, this nostalgic interpretation of the history of art as the history of the transformation or loss of aura contains residues of Benjamin's older ahistorical normativism. History is not divided into periods of decline, where anonymous will of art prevails, producing artistic industry or reproducible art for the masses, and periods of non-decline, in which individual works dominate as expressions of true art, whether as religious cult objects of veneration or as luxury objects. However, history is understood as an irreversible process of gradual, but unavoidable loss of the original magic of art. Hegel's prophecy of the end of art is heard here, but now interpreted as a loss of the original nature of art as a result of capitalist commodification, technological progress and the mass character of society. The increase of the mass effect of art or of mass artistic communication is compensation for the loss of uniqueness and magic.

Although Benjamin thought that the definitive suppression of individualist art by mass production was unavoidable, it seems that he could not decide on which side his sympathies lay. He looked with nostalgia at the magic of uniqueness getting lost in the depths of the past, but he was equally fascinated by the new riches brought to the perception of reality and artistic communica-

---

[48]   BENJAMIN 1972 – 1989 (see note 4), Vol. I-2: Abhandlungen, p. 479: *"Was ist eigentlich Aura? Ein sonderbares Gespinst aus Raum und Zeit: einmalige Erscheinung einer Ferne, so nah sie sein mag."* On Benjamin's notion *"aura"*, see TIEDEMANN, Rolf: Aura, in *Historisches Wörterbuch der Philosophie*. Vol. 1. Basel 1971; KEMP 1978 (see note 1), pp. 228-235 (part "Benjamin's Aura-Begriff und das Problem der ästhetischen Distanz"); JAUSS, Hans R.: *Studien zum Epochenwandel der ästhetischen Moderne*. Frankfurt am Main 1989, pp. 189-215; NOMURA, Osamu: Der Begriff der Aura bei Walter Benjamin, in *Global Benjamin. Internationaler Walter-Benjamin-Kongress 1992*. Vol. 1. Eds. Klaus GARBER – Ludger REHM. München 1992, pp. 391-402; EBERLEIN 1998 (see note 40), pp. 291-299.

[49]   For more on this, see RAMPLEY, Matthew: *The Remembrance of Things Past. On Aby M. Warburg and Walter Benjamin*. Wiesbaden 2000, pp. 73-100 (chapter "Aura and Memory").

tion by the aura-less reproductive media such as photography and film, for example focusing on detail or mosaic-style capturing of reality by means of montage. However, from his position as empathetic observer with an understanding of both sides – the vanishing individualism of objects and the rising collectivism in communication – Benjamin defended the historical pluralism that he had appropriated from the Vienna School of Art History.

The Construction of History

But this was not Benjamin's final word concerning history. Three years after publication of "The Work of Art in the Age of Mechanical Reproduction", in a commentary on Paul Klee's picture "Angelus Novus" in his "Theses on the Philosophy of History" (1939 – 1940), he unmasked liberal faith in progress as an illusion and metaphorically outlined a catastrophic vision of history.[50] Moreover, from the historical-materialist position, he vehemently distanced himself from objective and retrospective historicism: *"Historicism offers a 'permanent' image of the past, but the historical materialist offers a certain experience with it which is unique... He remains master of his forces: he is manly enough to break the continuum of history."*[51] Moreover, according to Benjamin, the historical materialist should maintain a critical position in relation to the past. He considers it his role: *"... to comb history against its obvious direction."*[52] Thus, he unambiguously occupied a position of avant-garde presentism, of critical evaluation and a view of the shaping of history from the perspective of the present and its needs.[53] He added his voice to the protagonists of the avant-garde revolutionaries, according to whom *"the past is only valid as long as it expresses the present, as long as it lets us forget that it is historic"*.[54] Therefore,

---

[50] BENJAMIN, Walter: *Illuminationen. Ausgewählte Schriften.* Vol. I. Ed. Siegfried UNSELD. Frankfurt am Main 1961, pp. 268-281; BENJAMIN Walter: Über den Begriff der Geschichte, in BENJAMIN 1972 – 1989 (see note 4), Vol. I-2: Abhandlungen, pp. 693-704; English ed. "On the Concept of History" in BENJAMIN, Walter: *Selected Writings.* Ed. Michael W. JENNINGS. Cambridge – London 1996 – 2003, Vol. 4, pp. 389-400. On this, see KORTA 2004 (see note 37), pp. 89-90.

[51] BENJAMIN 1972 – 1989 (see note 50), p. 701.

[52] Ibid., p. 697: *"Geschichte gegen den Strich zu bürsten."*

[53] JENNINGS 1992 (see note 1), p. 99: *"The importance of history [according to Benjamin]... lies primarily in its relation to the immediate present."* PEAKER 2001 (see note 1), p. 301: *"... it is the present which is the motivation of the historian and... the focus of the historical investigation."* See on this also GUBSER, Michael: *Time's Visible Surface: Alois Riegl and the Discourse on History and Temporality in Fin-de-Siècle Vienna.* Detroit 2006, p. 212.

[54] TIETZE Hans: *Lebendige Kunstwissenschaft. Zur Krise der Kunst und Kunstwissenschaft.* Wien 1925, p. 72.

the past had to be *"critically mastered and reworked... for the purpose of practical solution of contemporary problems".*[55] According to Benjamin: *"History is subject to construction"* and *"its place does not consist of homogeneous and empty time, but of time filled with the contemporary."*[56] At first sight, this resembles the post-modern concept of history as a construct. However, Benjamin's avant-garde constructivism still differs substantially from the agnostic post-modern conception of construction as an arbitrary structure: for him, construction meant an heroic instrument for shaping the present. Thus, Benjamin's conception of the historicity of art can be characterized as a trajectory from transhistorical individualism through socio-historical relativism to Messianic[57] constructivism.

---

[55] TEIGE, Karel: Sovětská kulturní tvorba a otázky kulturního dědictví [Soviet Cultural Production and the Question of Cultural Heritage] (1936), in TEIGE, Karel: *Jarmark umění* [Art Fair]. Praha 1964, pp. 99,101.

[56] BENJAMIN 1972 – 1989 (see note 50), p. 701. English translation by Martin Styan. See on this KORTA, Tobias F.: *Geschichte als Projekt und Projektion.* Frankfurt am Main 2001.

[57] EAGLETON, Terry: *The Ideology of the Aesthetic.* Oxford 1990, p. 325, speaks of Benjamin's *"Messianic reading of history".* SCHWARTZ 2006 (see note 28), p. 119, characterizes Benjamin's approach to history as *"politicised Messianism".*

III. BETWEEN TASK AND FUNCTION: METAMORPHOSESOFJACOBBURCKHARDT'SLEGACY

Art History as the History of Tasks

Thanks to Heinrich Wölfflin we know that Jacob Burckhardt, on his 75th birthday in 1893, conveyed his legacy in the following terms, to the next generation of art historians: the history of art was to be understood as the history of tasks (*"die Kunstgeschichte nach Aufgaben behandeln, das ist mein Vermächtnis"*).[1] Nonetheless, in keeping with his distrust of philosophy, Burckhardt bequeathed no definition of *"tasks"*. He did, however, display very vividly his notion of *"Aufgaben"* in the *Beiträge zur Kunstgeschichte von Italien*, a book consisting of three essays – "Das Porträt", "Das Altarbild", "Die Sammler" – only published posthumously in 1898.[2] According to Norbert Huse, Burckhardt *"verstand unter Aufgaben weder... die Aufträge... noch die Lösung von 'Kunstproblemen'"*.[3] In contrast to this, Nicolaus Meier thinks that Burckhardt used the notion *"Aufgabe"* in three different but clearly-defined ways: *"Zuerst... als formale Aufgabe... Zweitens... als Funktionsbegriff... er weist auf kausale Zusammenhänge von Kunst und Auftraggebern... Und zuletzt... eine 'Aufgabe' [als] ein von allen Bedigtheiten unabhängiges... Phänomen... eine Art unbedingter Autorität."*[4] Consequently, Burckhardt's model represents *"ein offenes System..., in dem bald einmal der Stil, dann wieder eine Aufgabe... die größere Wirkung auf die Entwicklung der Kunst hat"*.[5]

---

[1] WÖLFFLIN, Heinrich: Jakob Burckhardt, in *Repertorium für Kunstwissenschaft*, 20, 1897, p. 344.

[2] See the latest edition of BURCKHARDT, Jacob: *Werke* (=Kritische Gesamtausgabe, 6). München 1998.

[3] HUSE, Norbert: Anmerkungen zu Burckhardts "Kunstgeschichte nach Aufgaben", in *Festschrift Wolfgang Braunfels*. Tübingen 1977, p. 162; reprinted in *Umgang mit Jacob Burckhardt. Zwölf Studien*. Vol. 1. Ed. Hans R. GUGGISBERG. Basel – München, 1994, pp. 245-261.

[4] MEIER, Nikolaus: Kunstgeschichte und Kulturgeschichte oder Kunstgeschichte nach Aufgaben, in *Kunst und Kunsttheorie 1400 – 1900* (=Wolfenbütteler Forschungen, 48). Eds. Peter GANZ – Martin GOSEBRUCH – Nikolaus MEIER – Martin WARNKE. Wiesbaden 1991, p. 426.

[5] Ibid.

Norbert Huse pointed out that from the 1870s onwards a gap between cultural history and art history entered Burckhardt's thinking.[6] The idea of *"Aufgaben"* could therefore be regarded as an attempt to escape Hegelian determinism whereby art is considered to be the direct product of the spirit of the age. As a result, according to Huse, Burckhardt's *"Beiträge"* came to anticipate the future social history of art.[7] On the other hand, Nikolaus Meier[8] and Irmgard Siebert[9] came to the conclusion that Burckhardt began to develop the notion of *"Aufgaben"* as early as his *Einleitung in die Ästhetik der bildenden Kunst* (1863). By employing the notion of *"Kunstgeschichte nach Aufgaben"*, Burckhardt not only attempted to overcome the old paradigm of *"the history of art as the history of artists"*,[10] but also *"wollte Kunstgeschichte und Kulturgeschichte verbinden"*.[11] In spite of the fact that the notion of *"Aufgaben"* had to show the bonds between art and society,[12] Burckhardt overcame *"die parellele Organisation"*[13] and already, in his *Die Geschichte der Renaissance in Italien* (1867), launched the development *"towards an autonomous history of art"*.[14]

Between Renaissance Revival and Modernism

Irrespective of whether Burckhardt's idea of the history of art as the history of tasks is regarded as anticipating the social history of art or as the immediate preparation for an autonomous history of styles, its dualistic nature is obvious.[15] On the one hand, Burckhardt worshipped art as a mystery, on

---

6   HUSE 1977 (see note 3), p. 162.

7   Ibid.

8   MEIER 1991 (see note 4), pp. 424-425.

9   SIEBERT, Irmgard: *Jacob Burckhardt. Studien zur Kunst- und Kulturgeschichtsschreibung.* Basel 1991, pp. 154-156.

10   WÖLFFLIN, Heinrich: *Gedanken zur Kunstgeschichte.* Basel 1941, p. 150; SIEBERT 1991 (see note 9), p. 154. See also Irmgard Siebert, in BURCKHARDT, Jacob: *Ästhetik der bildenden Kunst. Der Text der Vorlesung "Zur Einleitung in die Ästhetik der bildenden Kunst".* Darmstadt 1992, p. 28.

11   MEIER 1991 (see note 4), p. 419.

12   Ibid., p. 425: *"… die 'Aufgabe' soll den Zusammenhang zwischen Auftraggeber und Künstler herstellen."*

13   Ibid., p. 426.

14   GOSSMAN, Lionel: *Basel in the Age of Burckhardt. A Study in Unseasonable Ideas.* Chicago – London 2000, p. 364; MEIER 1991 (see note 4), p. 437; SIEBERT 1991 (see note 9), p. 154.

15   I.e. BOEHM, Gottfried: Genese und Geltung: Jacob Burckhardts Kritik des Historismus, in *Umgang mit Jacob Burckhardt* (see note 3), pp. 84-85, speaks about *"Autonomie des Ausdrucks"* on the one hand, and *"… dem historischen Kontext… Auftraggeberinteressen… ikonographischer Problematik etc."* on the other.

the other, he stressed its social purpose (*"Dienst"*).[16] In order to escape Hegelian spiritual and expressionist interpretation, he emphasised the social tasks of art, while at the same time not ignoring the relative autonomy of art. In addition, Burckhardt's dualism was explicit and privileged as a central theme. Burckhardt regarded the relationship between cultural history and the history of art, between the social tasks of art and artistic autonomy as being an interaction and interdependence. Admittedly, artistic styles do not exist in a vacuum but *"entwickeln sich an und in den Aufgaben"*. However, at the same time *"Aufgaben werden durch die Macht eines einmal seiner selbst bewust gewordenen Styles hoch über ihr ursprungliches Wesen hinaufgehoben"*.[17] In other words, the fulfilment of a social task by art results in an autonomous artistic solution – the establishment of an artistic genre that responds to the social demand. Burckhardt's reluctance to publish his *"Beiträge"* during his lifetime can be seen as a consequence of the dilemma posed by his dualist interpretation of art - cultural history versus art history, heteronomous versus autonomous. Moreover, the very fact that he was unable to harmonize this can even be regarded as a projection of his ambiguous position between Renaissance revival and anticipated Modernism.

"Aufgaben" as Fundamental Stylistic Problems

It was precisely the modernist point of view that enabled Burckhardt's pupil Heinrich Wölfflin to transform his mentor's dualistic conception into a monist one.[18] Wölfflin based his book *Klassische Kunst* (1899) on the scheme of art history *"nach Sachen und Gattungen"* and dedicated it to Burckhardt, deeply convinced that he was following in his admired teacher's footsteps.[19] Throughout his life, Wölfflin believed that *"Kunstgeschichte nach Aufgaben"* could be regarded as a preparatory step, not only towards his idea of a systematic search for the autonomous *"Grundprinzipien"* and *"Grundbegriffe"* of art history, but also towards his idea of an impersonal *"Kunstgeschichte ohne*

---

[16] See BURCKHARDT, Jacob: *Die Kunst der Betrachtung. Aufsätze und Vorträge*. Köln 1997, pp. 188, 191-199.

[17] BURCKHARDT 1992 (see note 10), quoted by MEIER 1991 (see note 4), p. 424; SIEBERT 1992 (see note 10), p. 27.

[18] See GANTNER, Joseph: Heinrich Wölfflin und die moderne Kunst, in *Merkur*, 13, 1959, pp. 937-945; SCHMITZ, Norbert: *Kunst und Wissenschaft im Zeichen der Moderne. Hoelzel, Wölfflin, Kandinsky, Dvořák*. Wuppertal 1993; WYSS, Beat: *Der Wille zur Kunst. Zur ästhetischen Mentalität der Moderne*. Köln 1997, pp. 103-119.

[19] LURZ, Meinhold: *Heinrich Wölfflin. Biographie einer Kunsttheorie*. Worms 1981, p. 155.

Namen".[20] As a consequence, he misinterpreted Burckhardt's model, viewing *"Aufgaben"* in much the same way as had Alois Riegel, that is, as offering a solution to formal problems.[21] Or, to quote Arnold Hauser, Wölfflin turned *"die Geschichte der künstlerischen Aufgaben und Motive in eine reine Formen- und Problemgeschichte".*[22] In this way, Burckhardt's dual, or even dialectical heteronomy/autonomy model was simplified into a pure, autonomous history of art, *"reine Behandlung nach Form und Stil".*[23] Nevertheless, Wölfflin's interpretation of *"Kunstgeschichte nach Aufgaben"* can be regarded as more than merely a projection of the modernist idea of autonomy of form. It also projected into the notion of *"Aufgaben"* the modernist ideal of a scientism that sought impersonal and hidden laws.[24]

"Aufgaben" as Arising from the Commissioned Side of Art

In 1902, Burckhardt's legacy was cited from yet another point of view. Aby Warburg, in his paper "Bildniskunst und florentinisches Bürgertum", refers to Burckhardt's *Beiträge zur Kunstgeschichte von Italien* as an example *"eine[s] dritten empirischen Weg[s]"* worth following.[25] Nonetheless, Warburg also turned Burckhardt's dualism into a kind of monism. In contrast to Wölfflin's stress on artistic autonomy, Warburg emphasised another element of Burckhardt's dual model – art's social link. Warburg came to the conclusion that Renaissance portraiture was shaped not only by the artist alone but also, and even to a considerable extent, by patrons. He was convinced that art should be regarded as the result of *"Zusammenwirken zwischen Auftraggebern und Künstlern",*[26] attributing, at the same time, an important role to the psychological motives of clients. Consequently, Burckhardt's notion of *"Aufgaben"* was interpreted by Warburg in terms either of very practical social demands (*"praktische Aufforderungen des*

---

[20] WÖLFFLIN, Heinrich: Jacob Burckhardt und die systematische Kunstgeschichte, in WÖLFFLIN 1941 (see note 10), pp. 147-155.

[21] GOSSMAN 2000 (see note 14), p. 365.

[22] HAUSER, Arnold: *Methoden moderner Kunstbetrachtung.* München 1970, p. 130.

[23] WÖLFFLIN 1941 (see note 10), p. 151.

[24] Ibid., p. 153. See also HART, Joan: *Heinrich Wölfflin. An Intellectual Biography.* Berkeley (CA) 1981; HART, Joan: Reinterpreting Wölfflin. Neo-Kantianism and Hermeneutics, in *Art Journal,* 42, 1982, No. 4, pp. 292-300; HART, Joan: Une vision fictive. La trajectoire intellectuelle de Wölfflin, in *Relire Wölfflin.* Paris 1995, pp. 61-92.

[25] WARBURG, Aby: Bildniskunst und florentinisches Bürgertum, in WARBURG, Aby: *Gesammelte Schriften.* Berlin 1998, pp. 93-94.

[26] Ibid., p. 95.

wirklichen Lebens")[27] or of social commissions (*"Aufträge"*). Warburg's stress on the social dimension of art should be seen in the context of an avant-garde critique of Modernism.[28] Art was conceived of as a means of social communication rather than as an autonomous phenomenon.[29] Warburg developed the idea in his iconological interpretation of individual works of art.

The Historical Nature of the Concept of "Art"

Nevertheless, the Avant-garde not only articulated a new notion of art as social communication (or even as instrument of social reconstruction) but also problematised the concept of "art" itself by questioning its very identity.[30] Simultaneously, Max Dvořák in his famous "Idealismus und Naturalismus in der gotischen Skulptur und Malerei" (1918)[31] arrived at the conclusion that it is not only artistic form and content that are changing throughout history but also the very concept of "art" itself.[32] Irrespective of whether Dvořák's discovery was a logical consequence of following Riegl's relativism and the Hegelian legacy or rather a result of the impact of the Avant-garde, he arrived at the very threshold of understanding the history of art as the history of social models of art. Unfortunately, an early death was to prevent Dvořák from articulating art history either as the history of changing social ideas of "art" or as the history of the social functions of art.

---

[27]   Ibid., p. 94.

[28]   See BÜRGER, Peter: *Theorie der Avantgarde*. Frankfurt am Main 1974, pp. 63-75.

[29]   About the *"Kongruenz"* between Warburg and and avant-garde art, see FORSTER, Kurt W.: Warburgs Versunkenheit, in *Aby M. Warburg. Ekstatische Nympfe… trauernder Flussgott. Portrait eines Gelehrten*. Eds. Robert GALITZ – Brita REIMERS. Hamburg 1995, pp. 190-196. See also FORSTER, Kurt W.: Die Hamburg-Amerika-Linie, oder: Warburgs Kulturwissenschaft zwischen den Kontinenten, in *Aby Warburg. Akten des internationalen Symposiums*. Hamburg – Weinheim 1991, pp. 11-37.

[30]   BÜRGER 1974 (see note 28), pp. 26-34.

[31]   DVOŘÁK, Max: *Kunstgeschichte als Geistesgeschichte. Studien zur abendländischen Kunstentwicklung*. Eds. Karl M. SWOBODA – Johannes WILDE. München 1924, pp. 41-147.

[32]   HOFMANN, Werner: *Grundlagen der modernen Kunst*. Stuttgart 1966, pp. 28-29; RADNÓTI, Sándor: Die Historisierung des Kunstbegriffs: Max Dvořák, in *Acta Historiae Artium*, 26, 1980, No. 1-2, pp. 125-142; LACHNIT, Edwin: Ansätze methodischer Evolution in der Wiener Schule der Kunstgeschichte, in *L'Art et les révolutions, 5. Révolution et évolution de l'Histoire de l'Art de Warburg á nos jours. Actes du XXVIIème congrès international d'histoire de l'art, Strasbourg, 1 – 7 septembre 1989*. Strasbourg 1992, pp. 43-52.

The History of Functions as the History of Social Roles

In Russia during the 1920s, Marxist historicism combined with the impact of the Avant-garde resulted in the articulation of art history as the history of the changing social functions of art. Applying Marxist economic determinism, V. M. Fritche in his *Sociology of Art* (1926) regarded the history of art as a sequence of magical, religious, moral and hedonistic functions played by art within different social structures.[33] Combining Formalism with a sociological approach, I. I. Ioffe in his *Culture and Style* (1917) interpreted the history of art as the history of the changing identity of "art" caused by the alteration in its practical functions in society. Ioffe's view was that the concept of "art" regarded as decoration in feudal society came to be replaced by "art" conceived of as knowledge in capitalist society which was in turn to be replaced by "art" as a construction of life in post-capitalist society.[34] In harmony with the Hegelian legacy and despite their sociological view of art, both Fritche and Ioffe viewed the functions of art in terms of its general social roles or abstract missions; this was in contrast to Burckhardt's and Warburg's very particular and practical conceptions of the social tasks of art.

"Aesthetic Function" as Anthropological Constant

Avant-garde art, and more particularly functionalist architecture on one side, and, on the other, Cassirer's distinction between *"function"* and *"substance"*,[35] along with Bühler's functionalist *"Organon-Modell"* of language,[36] can all be regarded as sources of Mukařovský's introduction of the idea of the social function to art in the mid-1930s.[37] In his "Aesthetic Function, Norm and Value as Social Facts" (1936), he attempted to harmonize the

---

[33] See NOVOZHILOVA, Larisa I.: *Sociologija iskusstva. Iz istorii sovietskoj estetiky 20-tych godov* [Sociology of Art. From the History of Soviet Aesthetics in the 1920s]. Leningrad 1968, pp. 97-115; BAKOŠ, Ján: *Štyri trasy metodológie dejín umenia: Viedenská škola dejín umenia – Česko-slovenský štrukturalizmus – Ruská historiografia umenia – Ikonológia a semiotika* [Four Routes for the Methodology of Art History: Vienna School of Art History – Czecho-Slovak Structuralism – Russian Historiography of Art – Iconology & Semiotics]. Bratislava 2000, pp. 236-240.

[34] BAKOŠ 2000 (see note 33), pp. 115-128.

[35] CASSIRER, Ernst: *Substanzbegriff und Funktionsbegriff*. Berlin 1910.

[36] VELTRUSKÝ, Jiří: Bühlers Organon-Modell und die Semotik der Kunst, in *Bühler-Studien*. Vol. 1. Ed. Achim ESCHBACH. Frankfurt am Main 1984, pp. 161-204; GALAN, Frantisek W.: *Historic Structures. The Prague School Project, 1928 – 1946*. Austin 1985, pp. 70-71.

[37] CHVATÍK, Květoslav: *Tschechoslowakischer Strukturalismus. Theorie und Geschichte*. München 1981, pp. 133-141. See also GALAN 1985 (see note 36), pp. 176-179.

modernist idea of autonomy with the avant-garde idea of social communication by means of the notion of the function of aesthetic autonomy.[38] Synthesizing inspirations drawn from Kant and from Hegel, he combined the notion of *"aesthetic function"* with the idea of the historical polyfunctionality of art.[39] Despite this, anthropological Functionalism was more dominant than was its historical counterpart in Mukařovský's conception: autonomous *"aesthetic function"* being regarded as the primary function and enduring core of art. In addition, Mukařovský's functionalist view can be characterised as socially affirmative rather than ideological and critical: by means of its aesthetic function, art helped to maintain or improve the *status quo* of the social organism.

Functions as Social Services

Unlike Mukařovský, Walter Benjamin in his essay "Das Kunstwerk im Zeitalter seiner technischen Reproduzierbarkeit" (1936) articulated an ideological critique and an explicit historicism.[40] In accordance with the Avant-garde's rejection of the modernist concept of a "work of art" as a unique and autonomous commodity and its questioning of the identity of "art", Benjamin emphasised not only the social, instrumental nature of works of art but also the on-going historical changes in their social status. As is well known, Max Dvořák derived the idea of historical changes in the concept of "art" from different worldviews. By contrast, Walter Benjamin subscribed to true Marxist historicism. According to him, historical changes in the status of "art" should be regarded as consequences of material practice and, in particular, technological discoveries. In addition, he stressed the dialectical interrelationship between technological developments, the social reception of art and changes in the social concept of "art". Due to advances in technology, the reception and conception of the "work of art" and thus the social functions of art undergo radical modifications throughout history. The original ritual function of art (first conceived of as magical and then as religious) was replaced by the political function which in turn gave way to an *"exhibition function"*. Based on the notion of worshipping art for its own sake or, as he called it, a *"theology of*

---

38   ZIMA, Petr V.: *Literarische Ästhetik.* Tübingen – Basel 1985; ZIMA, Petr V.: Formalismus und Strukturalismus zwischen Autonomie und Engagement, in *Prager Schule. Kontinuität und Wandel.* Ed. Wolfgang F. SCHWARZ. Frankfurt am Main 1997, pp. 305-315.

39   On Mukařovský's notion of function, see GRYGAR, Mojmír: *Terminologický slovník českého strukturalismu* [Terminological Dictionary of Czech Structuralism]. Brno 1999, pp. 74-112.

40   See e.g. LIESSMANN, Konrad: *Philosophie der modernen Kunst.* Wien 1998, pp. 115-127.

art", entertainment became, in Benjamin's view, the primary role of art.[41] As was also the case for Ioffe, art history is here regarded as being the history of social functions of art. Nevertheless, in contrast to the utopian messianism of Russian theorists and in keeping with the debt he owed to Marxism, a determinist approach dominated Benjamin's view: in his conception of *"function"* he replaced the idea of *"mission"* with that of a social service (*"Dienst"*).[42]

Function as a Means of Communication

Before Ernst Gombrich brought into play the old rhetorical idea, *"form follows function"*,[43] Rudolf Wittkower pleaded for a functional approach to the history of art.[44] He appealed for a greater emphasis on the study of the meanings of works of art and on the purpose or function of visual symbols. On the other hand, Gombrich's stress on the role of function did not aim at the historicist and relativist idea of the history of art understood as concerned with the historical changes of the social identity of art. Just as Mukařovský had done, Gombrich presupposed an unchanging anthropological constant of art as the true basis of change in its social functions.[45] Nevertheless, Gombrich's belief in the predominance of social function over form cannot be regarded as a revision of Wölfflin's belief in the autonomy of art. He used it above all as a means of criticising the Hegelian metaphysical or spiritual tradition. Consequently, he replaced the idea of *"expression"* with that of functioning as a means of communication.[46]

---

41 BENJAMIN, Walter: *Das Kunstwerk im Zeitalter seiner technischen Reproduzierbarkeit*. Frankfurt am Main 1975, pp. 19-26.

42 Ibid., p. 20.

43 GOMBRICH, Ernst H.: *Art and Illusion. A Study in the Psychology of Pictorial Representation*. London 1960; GOMBRICH, Ernst H.: *Meditations on a Hobby Horse and Other Essays on the Theory of Art*. London 1963, p. 91.

44 WITTKOWER, Rudolf: Interpretation of Visual Symbols in the Arts, in *Studies in Communications*, 1, 1955, pp. 123-124; German translation in *Ikonographie und Ikonologie. Theorien – Entwicklung – Probleme. Bildende Kunst als Zeichensystem*. Vol. 1. Ed. Ekkehard KAEMMERLING. Köln 1979, pp. 253-255.

45 On Gombrich's notion of function, see LEPSKY, Klaus: *Ernst H. Gombrich. Theorie und Methode*. Wien – Köln 1991, pp. 188-229; BAKOŠ, Ján: Der tschecho-slowakische Strukturalismus und die Kunstgeschichtsschreibung, in *Zeitschrift für Ästhetik und Allgemeine Kunstwissenschaft*, 36, 1991, pp. 96-99.

46 BAKOŠ, Ján: Od ikonológie k semiotike [From Iconology to Semiotics], in *Ars*, 31, 1998, No. 1-3, pp. 16-18.

From Utilitarian to Autonomous Functions

In the early 1970s, two Polish art historians joined the Functionalist school of the interpretation of the history of art. Leaning on Gregor Paulsson's theory of *"symbolic milieu"* and the function of art as consisting in the social construction of values,[47] Białostocki regarded art as a polyfunctional phenomenon and its history as made up of changes in the primary social role of art embodied in the main tasks and particular genres of art. Consequently, the history of art was seen to represent a process which began with the dominance of practical or utilitarian functions and then led to their falling away. The notion of art as a practical instrument and later primarily as a carrier of information was replaced first, by the dominance of art's representational function (either through imitation or symbolisation) and then, by the dominance of its decorative or aesthetic function. The production of works of art as autonomous objects could be regarded as the main function of contemporary art, according to Białostocki.[48]

Semiotic Polyfunctionalism

By applying Roman Jakobson's polyfunctional model of linguistic communication[49] to Renaissance art, Lech Kalinowski distinguished six functions operating simultaneously in a work of art: the *"referential"*, the *"expressive"*, the *"conative"*, the *"aesthetic"*, the *"phatic"* and the *"metavisual"*.[50] This use of semiotic Structuralism allowed Kalinowski to replace historical and relativist pluralism with an anthropologically-based simultaneous polyfunctionalism.

---

[47] PAULSSON, Gregor: *Die Soziale Dimension der Kunst.* Bern 1955. See also Paul O. Rave, in *Kunstchronik,* 7, 1954, p. 355.

[48] BIAŁOSTOCKI, Jan: A Broad Humanistic Outlook, in *The American Art Journal,* 3, 1971, pp. 95-100; BIAŁOSTOCKI, Jan: *Spätmittelalter und beginnende Neuzeit. Propyläen Kunstgeschichte,* 7. Frankfurt am Main – Berlin 1972, pp. 21-24 (parts "Kunstfunktionen und Kunstaufgaben", "Die ästhetische Rolle des Kunstwerks").

[49] JAKOBSON, Roman: Linguistics und Poetics, in *Style in Language.* Ed. Thomas A. SEBEOK. Cambridge (Mass.) 1960, pp. 350-377.

[50] KALINOWSKI, Lech: Model funkcjonalny przekazu wizualnego na przykładzie renesansowego dzieła sztuki [Functional Model of the Visual Message Illustrated by Example of the Renaissance Work of Art], in *Renesans. Sztuka i ideologia* [Renaissance. Art and Ideology]. Warszawa 1976, pp. 165-177.

A Plea for Contextual Function

Gombrich's Functionalism mentioned above was not only propagated but also developed by Leopold Ettlinger.[51] At the XIIth Congress of German art historians, held in Cologne in 1970, he called for the study of *"the original function of works of art"* as *"the true task of art historians"*;[52] stressing the historical and contextual nature of art as opposed to its many transcendental interpretations.

From Ideological Critique to the History of Functions

Ettlinger's appeal coincided with a polemic against the German idealistic tradition of art history, launched at the same Congress, by the so-called Ulmer Kreis, a group of young German art historians. Referring to Aby Warburg and Walter Benjamin, the group, led by Martin Warnke, rejected autonomous and spiritual interpretations of art,[53] replacing them with a sociological neo-Marxist approach that regarded "art" as a *"medium of social conflicts"*.[54] Under the impact of the second questioning of the nature of "art" by neo-Avant-gardism in the 1960s, the Warnke group connected the idea of art as a tool of ideological critique with the theme of art's identity.[55] This programme of ideological critique was gradually transformed into an affirmative version of a sociological approach to art history, as the representatives of the movement became established in the main German universities. They developed, on the one hand, the concept of the history of *"reception"* as an active participation by the public in shaping art, and on the other hand, the idea of art history as the history of functions (i.e. of the changing identity of art as a consequence of its changing social roles).[56]

---

[51] ETTLINGER, Leopold: *Art History Today*. London 1961.

[52] ETTLINGER, Leopold: Kunstgeschichte als Geschichte, in *Jahrbuch der Hamburger Kunstsammlungen*, 16, 1971, pp. 7-19.

[53] *Das Kunstwerk zwischen Wissenschaft und Weltanschauung*. Ed. Martin WARNKE. Gütersloh 1970; MITTING, Hans-Ernst: Ein Residuum der Unzufriedenheit. Kunstwissenschaft der 1960er Jahre in der Bundesrepublik Deutschland und Berlin-West, in *L'Art et les révolutions* 1992 (see note 32), pp. 177-195.

[54] Of significance for the first period was the book by BREDEKAMP, Horst: *Kunst als Medium sozialer Konflikte. Bilderkämpfe von der Spätantike bis zur Hussitenrevolution*. Frankfurt am Main 1975.

[55] The book, *Bildersturm. Die Zerstörung des Kunstwerks*. Ed. Martin WARNKE. München 1973, can be regarded as a projection of the neo-avant-garde attack on commodified abstract art onto the history of art.

[56] *Der Betrachter ist im Bild. Kunstwissenschaft und Rezeptionsästhetik*. Ed. Wolfgang KEMP. Köln 1985; BELTING, Hans: *Das Bild und sein Publikum im Mittelalter. Form und Funktion früher Bildtafeln der Passion*. Berlin 1981.

"Existenzformen" und "Funktionsformen"

Hans Belting[57] transformed the idea that *"form follows function"* into that of *"Existenzformen* follow *Funktionsformen"*. As we can see, Belting attempted to synthesise the ontological approach to art history with a sociological one: according to him, not only the form of art, but also its ontological status, change under the impact of varying social functions. As a result, the history of functions is regarded as the history of the changing identity of "art" itself rather than just the history of different tasks taken on by a conception of "art" whose essence is unchanging.

Aesthetic Autonomy as an Historical Function

When, a little later, the concept of the history of art as the history of functions was canonised and became the dominant programme,[58] it was neither Burckhardt nor Gombrich who were acknowledged as having paved the way, but Mukařovský. What probably contributed to this was not only his attempt to synthesise Hegel with Kant (or heteronomy with the idea of "art" as autonomous) but also his affirmative version of a sociological approach to art – i.e. art as the maintenance of the social organism.[59] Nevertheless, it is characteristic of the Funkkolleg conception that Mukařovský's meta-historical constant in art has been historically relativized here. The autonomy of art has been conceived of as a particular historical concept, limited to the modern period.[60]

Function and Genre

Simultaneously with the German functional approach, the notion of function began to play a central role in the so-called *"new social history of art"* as developed in Anglo-American art history since the 1970s.[61] One of its initiators,

---

[57] BELTING 1981 (see note 56), pp. 25-52.
[58] *Funkkolleg Kunst. Eine Geschichte der Kunst im Wandel ihrer Funktionen.* Ed. Werner BUSCH. München – Zürich 1987. The four basic functions of art in the history of art are distinguished as follows: the religious, the aesthetic, the political, and the representative.
[59] BAKOŠ 1991 (see note 45), pp. 99-103.
[60] Nevertheless, the idea had already been expressed by DVOŘÁK 1924 (see note 31). See HOF-MANN 1966 (see note 32), p. 29. See also BELTING, Hans – KRUSE, Christiane: *Die Erfindung des Gemäldes. Das erste Jahrhundert der niederländischen Malerei.* München 1994.
[61] ALPERS, Svetlana: Is Art History, in *Daedalus*, 1, Summer 1977, p. 2; reprinted in *Explanation and Values in the Arts.* Eds. Salim KEMAL – Ivan GASKELL. Cambridge 1993, p. 100.

Michael Baxandall, not only transformed Wölfflin's relativist idea of autonomous history of vision into a sociologically-determined *"period eye"*,[62] but also distinguished between *"manifest and latent functions"*.[63] The first was conceived of as *"effect"*, the second as *"intention"*. In this way, Burckhardt's problem of the relationship between *"Aufgaben"* and *"Gattungen"* was revived. With no knowledge of Burckhardt's having originated the problem, Baxandall solved it in an avant-garde way. By contrast with Burckhardt's modernist solution (stressing, as has been seen, the autonomous role of a genre), Baxandall saw genre as transforming both latent and manifest functions into social convention. Nevertheless, convention (leaving innovation aside) represents only one part of the history of art, a challenge *"to question the genre"*.[64]

Return to Burckhardt

In the *Gerson Lecture* at University of Groningen on October 2, 1981,[65] H. W. Janson became the first to realise just how much the functional approach was indebted to Burckhardt, explicitly calling for a Burckhardt revival. In a sense, the Burchhardt-Wölfflin wheel has here turned full circle: rejecting autonomous Formalism and following Burckhardt's programme for the history of the practical tasks of individual works of art, Janson subscribed to the idea that *"in the history of art form follows function"* (without mentioning Gombrich!). As a consequence, in his opinion, the history of art needed to be reintegrated *"with social and cultural history"*.[66]

"Uses" and "Demands"

Having denounced Burckhardt as a Hegelian for years,[67] Gombrich vindicated him in his most recent essays.[68] Through an analysis of different genres,

---

[62]   BAXANDALL, Michael: *Painting and Experience in Fifteenth Century Italy. A Primer in the Social History of Pictorial Style*. London 1972, pp. 29-108.

[63]   BAXANDALL, Michael: *The Limewood Sculptors of Renaissance Germany*. New Haven – London 1980, p. 50.

[64]   Ibid.

[65]   JANSON, Horst W.: *Form Follows Function, or Does It? Modernist Design Theory and the History of Art*. Maarssen 1982, pp. 3-38.

[66]   Ibid., p. 12.

[67]   GOMBRICH, Ernst H.: *In Search of Cultural History*. Oxford 1969, pp. 14-25.

[68]   GOMBRICH, Ernst H.: *The Uses of Images. Studies in the Social Function of Art and Visual Communication*. London 1999.

Gombrich followed Burckhardt's programme for the history of practical tasks. Stressing the practical or even utilitarian nature of art (regarding works of art as a means to an end), he understood Burckhardt's *"Aufgaben"* as *"uses"* for very practical purposes. To balance his emphasis on the utilitarian potentiality of images and to point out their creativity, he modifies the idea of *"form follows function"*, laying stress on the interaction between form and function.[69] Nevertheless, Gombrich's studies of the practical uses of works of art bear witness to a new trend in art history seen from the commercial point of view. The social functions of art, instead of being seen as ideological tools, are conceived in large measure by Gombrich as responses to very egotistical material demands. Can this then be regarded as a fulfilment of Burckhardt's legacy?

---

[69]   Ibid., p. 7.

IV. FROM THE IDEOLOGICAL CRITIQUE TO THE APOLOGIA FOR THE MARKET

I.

It is well known that art history as an academic discipline was established in the second third of the 19th century: the first permanent chair of art history being established at Berlin University in 1844 (Waagen), at Vienna University in 1852 (Eitelberger), and at Bonn in 1860 (Springer), followed by chairs in Strasbourg, Leipzig, Prague.[1] The institutionalisation of art history in 19th century Germany was launched by a new state ideology – nationalism. University chairs of art history followed the creation of those temples of the new nationalist religion – the public art museums. Art was regarded as an expression of the spirit of a nation and the work of art, as a visualisation of an impersonal spiritual message. As a result, the main task of institutionalised art history was to develop experts for public (state) museums and to reconstruct and promote national historical myths.

Nevertheless, the situation changed significantly in the second half of the 19th century. As international economic competition came into the foreground, romantic nationalism had to be replaced by pragmatic liberalism. This also had serious consequences for art history. The first universal exhibition, the "Great Exhibition" in London of 1851, conceived of as a symbolic international competition, launched a wave of art & industry museums all over the Europe. Art began to be regarded as an efficient means of industrial competition. As a consequence, the study of the history of art was also introduced to polytechnics and academies of fine art. Jacob Burckhardt became professor of art history at the Zürich Polytechnic in 1850 and Hypollite Taine professor of art history at École des Beaux Arts in Paris in 1863.[2] As a consequence, the idea of the history of art as concerned with the spirit of the age as developed by Hegel and his followers, was rejected and replaced by materialist inter-

---

[1] See BEYRODT, Wolfgang: Kunstgeschichte als Universitätsfach, in *Kunst und Kunsttheorie 1400 – 1900* (=Wolfenbütteler Forschungen, 48). Eds. Peter GANZ – Martin GOSEBRUCH – Nikolaus MEIER – Martin WARNKE. Wiesbaden 1991, pp. 313-333; DILLY, Heinrich: *Kunstgeschichte als Institution. Studien zur Geschichte einer Disziplin.* Frankfurt am Main 1979, pp. 173-174.

[2] BEYRODT 1991 (see note 1), pp. 323-324.

pretations. Jacob Burckhardt conceived of the history of art as a part of cultural history and called for art history to become the history of social *"tasks"*, (*"Aufgaben"*).[3] H. Taine stressed the dependence of art upon race, time and milieu and developed a determinist, even fatalist, view of the history of art. According to Philip Watchkiss Walsh, despite the determinist nature of his ideas, Taine promoted *"utilitarian and liberal capitalist values"*, particularly *"the autonomy of the individual, henceforth liberated from the constraints of received values and beholden only to the market"*.[4]

At the same time, the art market started to develop very quickly. This not only presupposed the artist's freedom and the autonomy of art but also intensified it. Commodification of art and the continuing concentration of art on form in the last third of the 19th century – or in other words commercialisation of art on the one hand and artistic formalism (art for art's sake) on the other – were interdependent. The art market therefore called for a new type of art historian: not the art historian as state ideologue but as market expert. The art market needed first of all a connoisseur, specializing in artistic forms and styles. To quote Steve Edwards's words: *"One of the driving forces behind the development of art history as an academic discipline was the necessity to provide the trained personel who could supply the 'productive apparatus' of the salesroom with the intelligence required to pursue its business. Art history was shaped... by its role in the art market: the catalogue raisonneé, the monograph, the one-person show, as well as many of the basic working concepts – provenance... authentication... are all geared to establishing a 'clean bill of health' for the artistic commodity."*[5] No surprise that Burckhardt's idea of the history of art as a history of the tasks that art had to perform, was transformed into the notion of finding a solution for artistic, i.e. formal, problems, by his pupil Heinrich Wölfflin.

If Giovanni Morelli's connoiseurship had still been in the service of Italian patriotism, his follower Bernard Berenson represented a cosmopolitan art market expert *par excellence*. Typically, he was not aware of being in the service of the market rather than of art, nor that the formalist equalization of all art production[6] served market exchange (and profit after all) rather than the

---

[3]   See BAKOŠ, Ján: Metamorphoses of Jacob Burckhardt's Legacy, in *Horizons. Essays on Art and Art Research. 50 Years Swiss Institute for Art Research*. Eds. Juerg ALBRECHT – Kornelia IMESCH. Ostfildern-Ruit 2001, pp. 345-352; in this volume pp. 56-68.

[4]   WALSH, Philip Hotchkiss: Viollet-le-Duc and Taine at the École des Beaux-Arts: on the First Professorship of Art History in France, in *Art History and Its Institutions. Foundations of a Discipline*. Ed. Elisabeth MANSFIELD. London – New York 2002, pp. 96- 94.

[5]   EDWARDS, Steve: *Art and Its Histories. A Reader*. New Haven – London 1999, p. 10.

[6]   About the dehistorisization of art as a consequence of connoiseurship referring to museums as well as the art market, see SCHWARZ, Gary: Connoisseurship: the Penalty of Ahistoricism, in *The International Journal of Museum Management and Curatorship*, 7, 1988, No. 3, pp. 261-268.

evaluation of artistic quality and creativity. We can agree with Jaynie Anderson, however, that *"rather than seeing connoisseurship as the result of egotistical individuals, such as Giovanni Morelli and Bernard Berenson, who wished to dramatize the act of attribution and imprint their authority on the paintings they classified, it should also be seen as being socially and culturally determined, a consequence of the new museums and the activity of an international art market"*.[7]

II.

In this connection, it is worth mentioning that in the market-oriented societies such as those of the USA or Great Britain, art history had been pursued mostly outside universities in the form of connoisseurship for a very long time. And later when it came to be included in the university curriculum, it was introduced in its formalist version. In Michael Podro's words: *"It was to formal values which English writers, Roger Fry and later Herbert Read and Kenneth Clark, gave emphasis."*[8] Consequently, art historical formalism can be regarded not only as a projection of Modernism, but also as a concealed agent of the global art market, as an instrument of the limitless commodification of art.[9]

Nevertheless, art historical formalism had already become the target of a severe critique before World War I. The notion of the artwork as an autonomous form was rejected and replaced by the idea of art as a social phenomenon *par excellence*. Such a sociological critique came simultaneously from three directions: from cultural history, Marxism, and the Avant-garde. Following the legacy of Burckhardt, Aby Warburg focused on the active role of patrons, developing the idea of art as a collective memory of images and calling for multidisciplinary cultural history research.[10] All the same, his appeal found no direct echo. By contrast, Marxism offered four alternatives to the sociological interpretation of art: seeing art either as a mirror of the economic basis

---

[7]   ANDERSON, Jaynie: National Museum, the Art Market and Old Master Paintings, in *Kunst und Kunsttheorie 1400 – 1900* (see note 1), p. 377.

[8]   PODRO, Michael: Art History and the Emigré Scholars, in *The European Challenge. Britain and Germany in Europe*. München – London – New York – Oxford – Paris 1987, p. 85.

[9]   FORSTER, Kurt W.: Critical History of Art, or Transfiguration of Values, in *New Literary History*, 3, 1972, No. 3, pp. 461-464, recognized the role of art history in turning *"works of art into a highly privileged class of consumer... goods"* as a consequence of *"the radical isolation of artifacts from their socio-historical context"*. He attributed it before all to *"a formalist view of art"* and its product, i.e. *"the museum without walls"*.

[10]   See HECKSCHER, William S.: The Genesis of Iconology, in *Stil und Überlieferung in der Kunst des Abendlandes. Akten des 22. Internationalen Kongresses für Kunstgeschichte in Bonn 1964*. Berlin 1967, Vol. 3: Theorien und Probleme, pp. 239-261.

(mode of production), as a reduplication of social (class) structure, as an expression of superstructure (i.e. ideology, masking and cementing status quo), or as an active ideological instrument (i.e. the advancing of class interests). As we can see, Marxism generated both deterministic as well as activist models for the sociology of art. Nevertheless, it excluded one social dimension *a priori*: the role of exchange, commerce and trade. Following and transforming the fundamentalist Christian repudiation of business, Marxism denied any contribution of value by commerce within the transaction from use to exchange value, regarding the market as a parasite *par excellence* (parasitic on the surplus value attributed by Marx solely to material production). Consequently, the commodification of art was regarded as contradicting the creative nature of art and rejected as a form of fetishism. In his polemics against sociological determinism, the Russian philosopher Georgij Valentinovič Plekhanov[11] limited the direct effect of material production on art to primitive classless societies. Conceiving of ideology as a matter of collective psychology, he stressed the active ideological nature of art. Nevertheless, his call to look for a *"sociological equivalent"* to the aesthetic dimension of the work of art shows that he was not able to abandon a dualist view of art. Confronted with Modernism, he regarded art as an aesthetic phenomenon on the one hand and a sociological one on the other.[12] Similarly, the German art historian Wilhelm Hausenstein[13] rejecting materialist determinism (particularly Muther's theory of "milieu"), appealed for the ideological interpretation of artistic forms and historical changes in style.[14]

Adherents to the aesthetics of the Avant-garde attempted to harmonize the idea of the autonomy of art with the belief in art as an instrument of social change. That was why they often joined the Marxist critique of capitalism and the comodification of art. The radical version of avant-garde critique aimed not only at the changing of art market rules but at the abolition of the market society as a whole. On the other hand, they did not accept the Marxist idea of art as a mere ideological tool. Theorists of Russian "productivism"

---

[11] PLEKHANOV, Georgij V.: *Sobranije sochinenij v 24-ch tomach* [Collected Writings in 24 Volumes]. Moskva – Leningrad 1923 – 1927. See particularly his "Letters without Address" (1899 – 1900), "Proletarian Movement and Bourgeois Art" (1905) or "Art and Social Life" (1912 – 1913).

[12] See *Lekciji po istorii estetiki. Kniga 4.* Leningrad 1980; Slovak translation: *Dejiny marxistickej estetiky* [History of Marxist Aesthetics]. Bratislava 1985, pp. 62-66.

[13] HAUSENSTEIN, Wilhelm: Versuch einer Soziologie der bildenden Kunst, in *Archiv für Sozialwissenschaft und Sozialpolitik*, 36, 1913, p. 738 ff.

[14] See SCHNEIDER, Norbert: Kunst und Gesellschaft. Der sozialgeschichtliche Ansatz, in *Kunstgeschichte. Eine Einführung.* Eds. Hans BELTING – Heinrich DILLY – Wolfgang KEMP – Willibald SAUERLÄNDER – Martin WARNKE. Berlin 1986, pp. 246-247.

and "constructivism"[15] rejected easel painting as exemplary of commodified art. Leaning on the Marxist belief in material production as the basis of art, they developed the idea of art as the direct material construction of a new classless society.[16] In contrast to that, Plekhanov's followers V. M. Fritche and F. Schmit[17] dealing with the relationship between social structures and artistic styles formulated a typological history of art. Their belief in the congruity of social structures with historical styles was an evident token of Marxist determinism and teleology. Another Russian sociologist of art of the time, I. I. Ioffe[18] attempted to avoid both extremes of the Marxist approach, i.e. "*vulgar materialism*" as well as "*psycho-ideology*", and in addition tried to overcome historical determinism by means of functional interpretation. He regarded the history of art as the history of the social functions of art. Nevertheless, the functional interpretation of the social nature of art can be regarded as evidence of a shift of approach to art in Russia in the thirties: ideological criticism starting to be replaced by an affirmative relation to the social status quo. Simultaneously with the introduction of the doctrine of socialist realism, the gnoseological dimension of art (and not solely its ideological dimension) started receiving emphasis in Russian Marxist art theory. Alongside Mikhail Lifshits, the Hungarian philosopher Georg Lukács played a leading role in the process of rehabilitating the lasting gnoseological value (and transhistori-

---

[15] ARVATOV, Boris: *Iskusstvo i proizvodstvo* [Art and Industry]. Moskva 1926; ARVATOV, Boris: *Sotsiologicheskaja poetika* [Sociological Poetics]. Moskva 1928; TARABUKIN, Mikhail: *Ot molberta k mashine* [From Easel to Machine]. Moskva 1923.

[16] For more about that, see MIKHAILOV, B. B.: O nekotorych metodologicheskich poiskach sovetskogo iskusstvovedenija [On Some Methodological Findings of Soviet Art Studies], in *Sovetskoje iskusstvoznanije '75* [Soviet Art Science '75]. Moskva 1976, pp. 294- 298; LODDER, Christina: *Russian Constructivism*. New Haven – London 1983, pp. 101-108; *Dejiny marxistickej estetiky* (see note 12), p. 116; BAKOŠ, Ján: *Štyri trasy metodológie dejín umenia: Viedenská škola dejín umenia – Česko-slovenský štrukturalizmus – Ruská historiografia umenia – Ikonológia a semiotika* [Four Routes for the Methodology of Art History: Vienna School of Art History – Czecho-Slovak Structuralism – Russian Historiography of Art – Iconology & Semiotics]. Bratislava 2000, pp. 238-240.

[17] FRITCHE, V. M.: *Sotsiologija iskusstva* [Sociology of Art]. Moskva – Leningrad 1930; SCHMIT, F.: *Predmet i granici sotsiologicheskogo iskusstvovedenija* [Subject and Borders of Sociological Art Studies]. Leningrad 1928. For more about that, see POSPIELOV, G. N.: Dějiny metodologie sovětské literární vědy [History of the Methodology of Soviet Literary Studies], in *Východiska a cíle. Metodologické problémy sovětské literární vědy* [Basis and Goals. Methodological Problems of Soviet Literary Studies]. Praha 1974, pp. 81-85; BAKOŠ 2000 (see note 16), pp. 236-238.

[18] IOFFE, I. I.: *Kultura i stil. Systema i printsipi sotsiologiji iskusstva* [Culture and Style. Systems and Principles of the Sociology of Art]. Leningrad 1927. For more about that, see NOVOZHILOVA, Larisa I.: *Sotsiologija iskusstva. Iz istorii sovietskoj estetiky 20-tych godov* [Sociology of Art. From the History of Soviet Aesthetics in the 1920s]. Leningrad 1968; MIKHAILOV 1976 (see note 16), pp. 295-296; BAKOŠ 2000 (see note 16), pp. 238-240.

cal nature) of art[19] that dominated Marxist discourse on art in Russia in the thirties and fourties.

III.

We have already mentioned that the Marxist concept of commerce as a parasitic activity resulted in the contraposing of art against the market. Art was regarded as a sphere of freedom and creativity, the market, as a realm of appropriation, fraud, exploitation and triviality. Many avant-garde art theorists adopted the idea. Consequently, they regarded the commercialisation of art and commodification of artworks in capitalist society as a token of the degeneration of art, a deformation of its true creative nature. The market, therefore, was conceived of as a new tyranny (a tyranny of greed and trivial taste) enslaving artists, robbing them of their freedom and corrupting them.[20] In the words of one of the leading theorists of the Czech Avant-garde Karel Teige: *"In bourgeois freedom, art was subjected to another bondage... the dictate of the market. It ceased to be a service to become a commodity."*[21] *"Commercialisation of artistic life degraded works of art into commodities; it transformed art critics into agents or organizers of advertisment and artists into hired labourers. Capitalism succeeded in transforming artistic creativity into 'productive labour' and a machine for money."*[22] *"On the art market not only works of art but also artists are for sale... Business success corrupted many Avant-garde artists... they became 'aesthetic courtesans'."*[23] *"Through the market art which was intended to be an art for art's sake changed into art for money."*[24]

No surprise then, that another adherent to avant-garde art, Meyer Shapiro, following up a dialectical model of the art and commerce relationship (*"art versus commerce"*), expressed very similar ideas twenty six years later, in 1960:

---

[19] As a consequence, Mikhail A. Lifshits and Georg Lukács were accused of *"vulgar humanism"*. See POSPIELOV 1974 (see note 17), p. 130; BAKOŠ, Ján: Zrod a cesty sovietskej umeleckohistorickej metodológie [Origin and Paths of Soviet Art Historical Methodology], in *Ars*, 16, 1982, No. 1, p. 18. On Lifshits, see MITCHELL, Stanley: Mikhail Lifshits: A Marxist Conservative, in *Marxism and the History of Art: From William Morris to the New Left*. Ed. Andrew HEMINGWAY. London – Ann Arbor 2006, pp. 28-44.

[20] It is worth noting that already, according to Bernini, business corrupts artistic judgement: *"... commerce qui leur abaisse le jugement."* See WARNKE, Martin: *Hofkünstler. Zur Vorgeschichte des modernen Künstlers*. Köln 1985, pp. 109, 346.

[21] TEIGE, Karel: *Jarmark umění* [The Art Fair]. Praha 1936, quoted according to the 2nd edition in 1964, p. 24.

[22] Ibid., p. 33.

[23] Ibid., pp. 36-37.

[24] Ibid., p. 40.

"The market was never innocent in its judgment of art, but this new awareness of art as a precious speculative commodity now corrupts all awareness of art."[25] And Schapiro continues: *"The knowledge of prices and possible gain through art enters into common perception of art. It also makes artists keenly aware of sales price as a measure of value. Attached now to the speculative market in increasing dependence, art becomes also an object of intense publicity... There is a new and distasteful aesthetic of art propaganda."*[26] As a consequence of the notion of an art and market relationship conceived in terms of an antinomy, Schapiro's pessimistic diagnosis goes on: *"What is disturbing is not that people profit by the rise in prices of art, but the effect this knowledge has on the attitude to art everywhere. Art becomes even more of a commodity than ever before; the relation to art is infected with all the diseases of business enterprise... In art we see in an acute form the effect of commodity psychology and profit attitude on the whole of society today."*[27]

Despite these very depressing diagnoses, avant-garde theorists were no pessimists concerning the future of art. As a matter of fact they stuck to the romantic belief in the artist's freedom and art's autonomy. They were willing to accept the Marxist notion of superstructure as determined by economic basis only in its dialectically softened version. They projected the idea of two simultaneously running arts, i.e. academic art and avant-garde art (or kitsch versus true art), and the notion of art as a transcendental creativity, upon the whole history of art. By this means, they anchored their activity on the Marxist belief in the law of historical necessity. As a consequence, they were able to resist all tempations of the market society.

At the same time (in the thirties), Theodor Adorno came to a very similar conclusion in his polemics against Bertold Brecht and Walter Benjamin. According to Brecht,[28] there was no autonomy of art in capitalist society at all. Autonomy was a pure illusion. In addition, not only new media, but art as a whole and all works of art were without exception, transformed into commodities, according to Brecht.[29] Nevertheless, just this definitive loss of au-

---

[25] SCHAPIRO, Meyer: On the Art Market, in SCHAPIRO, Meyer: *Worldview in Painting. Art and Society.* New York 1999, p. 202.

[26] Ibid., p. 202.

[27] Ibid., p. 204. On Schapiro, see HEMINGWAY, Andrew: Meyer Schapiro: Marxism, Science and Art, in HEMINGWAY 2006 (see note 19), pp. 123-142.

[28] BRECHT, Bertolt: Der Dreigroschenprozess. Ein soziologisches Experiment (1931), in BRECHT, Bertolt: *Schriften zur Literatur und Kunst.* Frankfurt am Main 1967, Vol. 1, pp. 143-234. See BÜRGER, Peter: Kunstsoziologische Aspekte der Brecht-Benjamin-Adorno-Debatte der 30er Jahre, in *Seminar: Literatur- und Kunstsoziologie.* Ed. Peter BÜRGER. Frankfurt am Main 1978, p. 12.

[29] BRECHT 1931 (see note 28), p. 168; BÜRGER 1978 (see note 28), p. 12: *"...'die ganze Kunst ohne Ausnahme' wird zur Ware."*

tonomy could be regarded as a guarantee of art's future: *"Zur-Ware-Werden der Kunst [ist] ein fortschritliches Prozess"*, for Brecht.[30] He was convinced that the abolition of art's autonomy is a prerequisite for the coming into existence of a new art replacing works of art regarded as *"Genussmittel"* (means of enjoyment or pleasure) with art as *"eine pädagogische Disciplin"*, i.e. art conceived of as an instrument of education or propaganda.[31]

Benjamin also articulated a materialist and determinist notion of art.[32] According to him, art was not shaped by capitalist commerce, but primarily by technique. Due to technological discoveries (techniques of reproduction – photography and film), the nature of art changed substantially: works of art lost their "aura", i.e. their uniqueness. As a consequence, the social reception of art was also fundamentally transformed and adjusted to capitalist society's mass culture. Owing to the new techniques of reproduction (new media), the *"auratic reception"* (*"auratische Rezeption"*),[33] i.e. contemplation of the uniqueness of the work of art, was replaced by a *"dispersed reception"* (*"zerstreute Rezeption"*)[34] characteristic of mass consumption.

In contrast to that, Adorno criticizing Benjamin,[35] rejected the idea of the total dependence of art on society and emphasized the dialectical nature of art in capitalism. According to him, there simultaneously existed two different kinds of art in capitalist society: entertaining art for masses on the one hand, and esoteric art for intellectuals on the other: *"Beide tragen die Wundmale des Kapitalismus, beide enthalten Elemente der Veränderung... beide sind die auseinandergerissenen Hälften der ganzen Freiheit, die doch aus ihnen sich nicht zusammenaddieren lässt."*[36] It was the elitist art that was characterized by the ability to transcend all social determinants. Thanks to the implicit autonomy and explicit criticism found in true art, it could become an active social instrument.[37]

---

[30] Ibid., p. 12.

[31] BRECHT 1931 (see note 28), p. 167; BÜRGER 1978 (see note 28), p. 12.

[32] BENJAMIN, Walter: Das Kunstwerk im Zeitalter seiner technischen Reproduzierbarkeit (originally published in 1936); reprinted in BENJAMIN, Walter: *Drei Studien zur Kunstsoziologie*. Frankfurt am Main 1963, pp. 7-63; BENJAMIN, Walter: Der Autor als Produzent (originally published in 1934); reprinted in BENJAMIN, Walter: *Versuche über Brecht*. Ed. Rolf TIEDEMANN. Frankfurt am Main 1966, pp. 95-116; English translation in *Art After Modernism. Rethinking Representation*. Ed. Brian WALLIS. New York – Boston 1984, pp. 297-309.

[33] BÜRGER 1978 (see note 28), p. 14.

[34] Ibid., p. 15.

[35] ADORNO, Theodor W.: Brief an Walter Benjamin vom 18. März 1936; reprinted in ADORNO, Theodor W.: *Über Walter Benjamin*. Ed. Rolf TIEDEMANN. Frankfurt am Main 1970, pp. 126-134. See BÜRGER 1978 (see note 28), pp. 16-19.

[36] ADORNO 1936 (see note 35), p. 129; BÜRGER 1978 (see note 28), p. 19.

[37] Ibid., pp. 16-19.

IV.

Another center of sociological thinking influenced by Marxism came into existence in Budapest. Between 1915 and 1917 the so-called Sunday Circle, consisting of young philosophers, sociologists, theorists of art and art historians (G. Lukács, K. Mannheim, B. Balász, L. Fülep, F. Antal, A. Hauser, J. Wilde or Ch. de Tolnay among them)[38] together developed ideas that later engendered not only a sociology of knowledge but also a social history of art. Frederick Antal who emigrated to Great Britain in the late thirties applied the Marxist idea of class stratification of society to the explanation of simultaneously existing different styles in his book *Florentine Painting and Its Social Background* published in London in 1948.[39] In contrast to materialist determinism, and transforming his teacher, Max Dvořák's homogenous model of the history of art as the history of ideas in a Marxist way, Antal interpreted stylistic diversity as a result of the different worldviews of particular social strata. According to him, class ideology (*"outlook on life"* of a social stratum) determines social practice.[40] Referring to the Middle Ages for example, it means that *"any practical activity or trend of thought was dissociated from... religious sentiment"*,[41] i.e. the medieval *"outlook on life"*.[42] Or, in other words, *"ideologies are reflected in practical*

---

[38] For more about the Budapest Sunday Circle, see WESSELY, Anna: Die Aufhebung des Stilbegriffs: Frederick Antals Rekonstruktion künstlerischer Entwicklungen auf marxistischer Grundlage, in *Kritische Berichte*, 4, 1976, No. 2-3, pp. 17-20; WESSELY, Anna: Antal Frigyes, in *Ars Hungarica*, 6, 1978, pp. 369-375; WESSELY, Anna: Antal and Lukács. A Marxist Approach to Art History, in *The New Hungarian Quarterly*, 1976, No. 73, pp. 114-125; HAUSER, Arnold: *Im Gespräch mit Georg Lukács*. München 1978, p. 48 ff.; KARÁDI, Eva – VEZÉR, Erzsébet: *Georg Lukács, Karl Mannheim und der Sonntagskreis*. Frankfurt am Main 1985, pp. 7-27; WESSELY, Anna: Der Diskurs über die Kunst im Sonntagskreis, in *Wechsel-Wirkungen. Ungarische Avantgarde in der Weimarer Republik*. Ed. Hubertus GAßNER. Marburg 1985, pp. 541-553; WITTEVEEN, Frans J.: Eine Brille gegen den arglosen Blick. Marxismus und Kunstgeschichte, in *Gesichtspunkten. Kunstgeschichte Heute*. Eds. Marlite HALBERTSMA – Kitty ZIJLMANS. Berlin 1995, pp. 148-150; originally published in Dutch in 1993. BORN, Robert: Budapest und die Entwicklung des sozialgeschichtlichen Ansatzes in der Kunstgeschichte, in *Überbringen – Überformen – Überblenden. Theorietransfer im 20. Jahrhundert*. Eds. Dietlind HÜCHTKER – Alfrun KLIEMS. Köln – Weimar – Wien 2011, pp. 93-123.

[39] ANTAL, Frederick: *Florentine Painting and Its Social Background. The Bourgeois Republic before Cosimo De Medici's Advent to Power: XIV and Early XV Centuries*. London 1947.

[40] Antal's anti-materialist emphasis on the ideological dimension of art can be regarded not only as a Marxist transformation of Dvořák's history of ideas but also as a metamorphosis of the original idealist philosophical attitude of the Sunday Circle. About its spiritual concerns or even mysticism, see WESSELY 1976 (see note 38), pp. 18-19; KARÁDI – VEZÉR 1985 (see note 38), pp. 7- 18; WITTEVEEN 1995 (see note 38), pp. 148-149.

[41] ANTAL 1947 (see note 39), p. 5.

[42] In Witteveen words: *"Antal [erklärt] Kunst nicht ausschließlich von ihrem ökonomischen Hintergrund her, sondern... auch aus der religiösen Überzeugung der Künstler... betrachtet... formale Ele-*

life". As a consequence, art in its complexity, i.e. the *"thematic elements"*as well as the *"formal elements"*, *"show... how completely the picture as a whole is but a part of the outlook, the ideas, of the public"*.[43] Thus, according to Antal, art *"expresses mainly the outlook of the patrons... rather than the views of the artists, who were generally much inferior to their patrons in the social scale"*.[44] In addition, *"the public is by no means unanimous in its outlook on life... due to the fact that what we call the public is not a homogenous body, but is split up into various often antagonistic groupings"*.[45] As a consequence, *"this divergence of outlook among its various sections explains the coexistence of different styles in the same period"*, according to Antal.[46] Or, in other words, *"stylistic divergencies between various works of art are due not only to individual differences between the various artists but also to the fact that these works were intended for different sections of the public or satisfied different artistic needs"*.[47] Thus the social commision and not individual artistic expression determines the history of art, in Antal's view. And works of art conceived of as *"dependent on the philosophies of the day"*[48] or *"habits of thinking"*[49] are regarded by Antal as expressions of ideologies (*"outlooks on life"*) of antagonistic social groupings and therefore, as ideological weapons in the class struggle.[50]

Another former member of Budapest Sunday Circle Arnold Hauser, also a refugee to Great Britain, published his two volumes *The Social History of Art* in London in 1951.[51] Aiming at the sociological and Marxist materialist explanation of historical styles, he interpreted them as determined by the material conditions and intellectual life (or psychology) of the dominant classes. According to him, *"all factors, material and intellectual, economic and ideological, are bound up*

---

  mente als Niederschlag der Weltanschauung einer bestimmten gesellschaftlichen Gruppe." – WITTEVEEN 1995 (see note 38), p. 149.

[43] ANTAL 1947 (see note 39), p. 4.

[44] Ibid., pp. 6-7.

[45] Ibid., p. 4.

[46] Ibid.

[47] Ibid., p. 7. In Witteveen's words: *"Die jeweilige Koexistenz verschiedener Stile lasse sich nur durch die Analyse der verschiedenen gesellschaftlichen Schichten und ihrer sozialen, ökonomischen und politischen Denkbilder verständlich machen."* – WITTEVEEN 1995 (see note 38), p. 150.

[48] ANTAL 1947 (see note 39), p. 4.

[49] Ibid., p. 5.

[50] About critique of Antal's Marxist interpretation, see WESSELY 1976 (see note 38), pp. 16-17; WITTEVEEN 1995 (see note 38), p. 150; KROHN, Deborah L.: Antal and His Critics. A Forgotten Chapter in the Historiography of the Italian Renaissance in the Twentieth Century, in *Memory & Oblivion. Proceedings of the XXIXth International Congress of the History of Art, Amsterdam, 1 – 7 September 1996*. Dordrecht 1999, pp. 95-99; STIRTON, Paul: Frederick Antal and "The Social History of Art" in Britain, in *Britain and Hungary. Contacts in Architecture, Design, Art and Theory during the 19th and 20th Centuries*. Ed. Gyula ERNYEY. Budapest 2003, p. 251; STIRTON, Paul: Frederick Antal, in HEMINGWAY 2006 (see note 19), pp. 45-66.

[51] HAUSER, Arnold: *The Social History of Art*. London 1951.

together in a state of indissoluble interdependence".[52] Nevertheless Hauser's Marxist preconceptions *"bubble to the surface"*[53] as far as the relationship between art and the market is concerned.[54] He is convinced that the art market, in degenerating *"into a state of fierce competition"*[55] not only changed the work of art into an *"impersonal commodity as any other"* and *"led the artist to become estranged from the public"*,[56] but also inflicted financial difficulties on many artists. *"The financial troubles... are concomitant of... economic freedom and anarchy in the realm of art, which... controls the art market"*,[57] according to Hauser. As J. M. Montias stated, Hauser *"is convinced that the market economy... provided less security"* to artists,[58] and, in addition, *"that the market was unable to recognize the true artistic qualities"*.[59]

A little later, in his *Philosophie der Kunstgeschichte*,[60] he withdrew from subscribing to a total sociological explanation of art. Despite regarding art as an economically determined ideological phenomenon and the work of art as an ideological message (Hauser speaks about *"die ideologische Beschaffenheit des Kunstwerkes... daß heisst..., daß die Kunst bewusst oder unbewusst stets einen praktischen Zweck verfolgt und manifeste oder verschleierte Propaganda ist"*.[61]), he admitted that social history of art has its limits.[62] Even if it is capable of explain-

---

[52] Ibid., p. 661.

[53] MONTIAS, John M.: Socio-Economic Aspects of Netherlandish Art from the Fifteenth to the Seventeenth Century: A Survey, in *The Art Bulletin*, 72, 1990, No. 3, p. 365.

[54] A. Hauser deals with the art market in the chapter "Baroque of Protestant Bourgeoisie". – HAUSER 1951 (see note 51), pp. 456-475.

[55] Ibid., p. 467.

[56] Ibid., p. 469.

[57] Ibid., p. 467.

[58] MONTIAS 1990 (see note 53), p. 365.

[59] Ibid., p. 366.

[60] HAUSER, Arnold: *Philosophie der Kunstgeschichte*. München 1958; English edition: *The Philosophy of Art History*. London 1959.

[61] HAUSER 1958 (see note 60), p. 5. The opposite interpretation is expressed by BARLOW, Paul: Arnold Hauser, in *Key Writers on Art: The Twentieth Century*. Ed. Chris MURRAY. London – New York 2003, p. 156. For Barlow, Hauser *"does not interpret art primarily in terms of social ideologies. He is not very interested in explaining what interests art has served, or what social messages it has conveyed"* in spite of the fact that *"he acknowledges this, especially in The Philosophy of Art History"*. According to Barlow, even if Hauser favoured *"the view that art is ideological... he takes this to mean that it encodes a world view"*. – Ibid., p. 159. About A. Hauser, see also KLEIN, Peter K.: Arnold Hausers Theorie der Kunst, in *Kritische Berichte*, 6, 1978, No. 3, pp. 18-27; HARAP, Louis: Arnold Hauser: Philosopher of the Arts, in *Science and Society*, 49, 1985, No. 1, pp. 84-90; WITKIN, Robert W.: *Art & Social Structure*. Cambridge 1995, pp. 17-137; HOHENDAHL, Peter Uwe: Das Projekt Sozialgeschichte der Kunst und Literatur, in *Kulturwissenschaftler des 20. Jahrhunderts*. Ed. Klaus GARBER. München 2002, pp. 245-262.

[62] See particularly HAUSER, Arnold: Introduction: The Scope and Limitations of a Sociology of Art, in HAUSER, Arnold: *The Philosophy of Art History*. Evanston 1985, pp. 3-17; German original: Einleitung: Ziele und Grenzen der Soziologie der Kunst, in HAUSER 1958 (see note 60), pp. 1-18.

ing the particular nature and historical changes of style, the sociology of art is unable to account for the uniqueness of art and especially for artistic quality: *"All art is socially conditioned"*, according to Hauser, *"but not everything in art is definable in sociological terms. Above all, artistic excellence is not so definable; it has no sociological equivalent."*[63] Thus: *"Die Soziologie kann höchstens die weltanschaulichen Elemente, die ein Kunstwerk enthält, auf ihren seinsmässigen Ursprung zurückzuführen, wenn es sich jedoch um die Qualität einer künstlerischen Leistung handelt, kommt alles auf die Gestaltung und die gegenseitige Beziehung dieser Elemente an. Die weltanschaulichen Motive können bei den verschiedensten Qualitäten, so wie die qualitativen Merkmale bei den verschiedensten Weltanschauungen die gleiche sein."*[64] As a consequence, the social history of art cannot replace art history, and vice versa: *"Die Sozialgeschichte der Kunst ersetzt oder entkräftet die Kunstgeschichte ebensowenig, wie sie durch die Kunstgeschichte ersetzt oder entkräftet werden kann."*[65]

As is well known, in the development of materialist social history of art, another German emigré also took part, Francis D. Klingender.[66] In his book *Art and the Industrial Revolution,*[67] Klingender analyzed the influence of industrial technologies on art in order to demonstrate the interdependence of art and industry. According to Klingender, technological progress can be regarded as a catalyst for social and economic change. Concerning art, it plays an important role as a source of values produced in the process of social change.[68]

Despite all efforts to advance this Marxist approach, the social history of art was strongly criticized for its impersonal determinism, lack of concreteness and application of *a priori* theses and was consequently marginalized for a relatively long time.[69] Ernst Gombrich's comment on Hauser's *The So-*

---

[63] HAUSER 1985 (see note 62), p. 8; HAUSER 1958 (see note 60), p. 6: *"Alle Kunst is sozial bedingt, doch nicht alles in der Kunst ist soziologisch definierbar. So vor allem die künstlerische Qualität nicht, diese hat kein soziologisches Equivalent."*

[64] HAUSER 1958 (see note 60), p. 7.

[65] Ibid., p. 10.

[66] See ROBERTS, John: Art Has No History! Reflections on Art History and Historical Materialism, in *Art Has No History! The Making and Unmaking of Modern Art.* Ed. John ROBERTS. London – New York 1994, p. 6; DOY, Gen: *Materializing Art History.* Oxford – New York 1998, p. 45; WITTEVEEN 1995 (see note 38), pp. 150-151. On Klingender, see BINDMAN, David: Art as Social Consciousness. Francis Klingender and British Art, in HEMINGWAY 2006 (see note 19), pp. 67-88.

[67] KLINGENDER, Francis D.: *Art and the Industrial Revolution.* London 1947. See also KLINGENDER, Francis D.: *Marxism and Modern Art.* London 1942; and KLINGENDER, Francis D.: Revolutionary Art Criticism, in *Left Review*, 2, 1935, No. 1, pp. 38-40. According to OVERY, Paul: The New Art History and Art Criticism, in *The New Art History.* Eds. Alan L. REES – Frances BORZELLO. London 1986, p. 134, the second edition of *Art and the Industrial Revolution*, published by Arthur Elton in 1968, *"bastardized"* Klingender's original project.

[68] See WITTEVEEN 1995 (see note 38), p. 151.

[69] In N. Schneider's words: *"Der materialistische Ansatz von Hauser, Antal u.a. wurde in der Nach-*

cial History of Art typifies this kind of critique.[70] Due to *"his preoccupation with generalities"*,[71] *"impersonal forces"* or *"factors"* rather than people, and *"the curious lack of concreteness"*,[72] Hauser *"bypasses the social history of art"*,[73] according to Gombrich, since *"the social history of art simply cannot be treated by relying on secondary authorities"*.[74]

In contrast to that, Francis Haskell's *Patrons and Painters*[75] as well as his *Rediscoveries in Art*[76] was very well received[77] and highly appreciated for its enormous historical erudition, sense of detail and intentionally inductive approach, free of any *a priori* generalization,[78] as expressed in the following example: *"Inevitably I have been forced to think again and again about the relations between art and society, but nothing in my researches has convinced me of the existence of underlying laws which will be valid in all circumstances. At times the connections between economic or political conditions and a certain style have seemed particularly close; at other times I have been unable to detect anything more than the internal logic of artistic development, personal whim, or the working of chance."*[79] Following Burckhardt's and Warburg's cultural model of the social history of art, Haskell

---

kriegszeit geflissentlich ignoriert." – SCHNEIDER 1986 (see note 14), p. 248. WITTEVEEN 1995 (see note 38), p. 151, expressed it as follows: *"Die bisher genannten Veröffentlichungen* [i.e. publications by Antal, Hauser, or Klingender; J. B.] *fielen angesichts des konservativen kunsthistorischen Klimas kurz nach dem Zweiten Weltkrieg in ein Vakuum."* According to OS, Henk van: Art History and Social History, in OS, Henk van: *Studies in Early Tuscan Painting.* London 1992, p. 7: *"Art historians of the fifties saw 'their' works of art endangered by Marxists."* For ROBERTS 1994 (see note 66), pp. 8-9, *"the reception of Hauser's work in Britain... was scant"* as a consequence of *"the cultural reaction of the Cold War period"*. See also ORWICZ, Michael: Critical Discourse in the Formation of a Social History of Art: Anglo-American Response to Arnold Hauser, in *The Oxford Art Journal*, 8, 1985, No. 2, pp. 52-62.

[70] E. H. Gombrich's review in *The Art Bulletin*, 35, 1953, pp. 79-84; reprinted as "The Social History of Art" in GOMBRICH, Ernst H.: *Meditations on a Hobby Horse and Other Essays on the Theory of Art.* London 1963, pp. 86-94.

[71] Ibid., p. 92.

[72] Ibid., pp. 93-94.

[73] Ibid., p. 91.

[74] Ibid., p. 93.

[75] HASKELL, Francis: *Patrons and Painters. A Study in the Relations between Italian Art and Society in the Age of the Baroque.* London 1963.

[76] HASKELL, Francis: *Rediscoveries in Art. Some Aspects of Taste, Fashion, and Collecting in England and France.* Oxford 1976.

[77] See GOMBRICH, Ernst H.: A Golden Age of Patronage, in *The Observer*, 23 June 1963; and GOMBRICH, Ernst H.: The Tides of Taste, in *Times Literary Supplement*, 27 February 1976. Republished in GOMBRICH, Ernst H.: *Reflections on the History of Art.* Oxford 1987, pp. 106-108, 160-167.

[78] HASKELL 1963 (see note 75), p. XVIII: *"I have also fought shy of generalisations and have tried to be severely empirical – even at the cost of shirking certain problems which have deeply interested me and which I know to be vital."*

[79] Ibid.

introduced a vast field in looking at the history of collecting, patronage and the history of taste, demonstrating the organic role of commissioners and art dealers in that system.

V.

Nevertheless, the intellectual standing of Marxist social history of art changed radically in the early seventies. Young British art critics and historians started to subject academic art history to a strong critique at that time.[80] The formalism and conservatism of academic art history was unmasked not only as an idealisation but also as a concealed vehicle for the commercialisation of art. Following Walter Benjamin, John Berger, in his *Ways of Seeing*,[81] unveiled the ideological mystifications and power manipulations of art in bougeois society. Leaning on the idea of art as the materialization of *"humanity's creative potential"*,[82] Berger regarded *"the relation between art and property"* as *"the disastrous"* one.[83] Creativity/production and humanity/ownership represent antitheses, according to him.[84] As a consequence, works of art defined as commodities in bourgeois society are unable to express *"a total view of reality"*. Instead, they are used *"to glorify the present social system"*.[85] Only exceptional artworks expressing *"the alienationn of bourgeois society"*[86] are able to transcend the frame of false consciousness,[87] according to Berger.[88]

---

[80] More about that HARRIS, Jonathan: *The New Art History. A Critical Introduction.* London 2001; BRYL, Mariusz: New Art History: nauka, polityka, obyczaj [New Art History: Science, Politics, Habits], in *Artium Questiones*, 7, 1995, pp. 185-218. See also BRYL, Mariusz: Między wspólnota, inspiracji a odrębnościa, tradycji. Niemiecko- i Anglojęzyczna historia sztuki u progu trzech ostatnich dekad [German and Anglo-American Art History Writing at the Beginning of the Last Three Decades], in *Rocznik Historii Sztuki*, 24, 1999, p. 226 ff.; BRYL, Mariusz: *Suwerenność dyscypliny. Polemiczna historia historii sztuki od 1970 roku* [Sovereignty of the Discipline. Polemical History of Art History Since 1970]. Poznań 2008, p. 258 ff.

[81] BERGER, John: *Ways of Seeing. Based on the BBC Television Series.* London 1972.

[82] According to WALLACH, Alan: John Berger, in *Key Writers on Art* (see note 61), p. 50.

[83] Ibid.

[84] Ibid.

[85] Ibid., p. 54.

[86] BERGER, John: *Permanent Red. Essays in Seeing.* London 1979; quoted according to WALLACH 2003 (see note 82), p. 50.

[87] As we can see, Berger faithfully follows Marx's notion of ideology. The contradictions between Berger's interpretation of artworks as the mirrors or reflections of bourgeois ideology on the one hand and as universal visions transcending all social determination, on the other (see WITKIN 1995 (see note 61), p. 90), can be regarded as a logical consequence of his belief in the Marxist model.

[88] Concerning critiques of Berger, see *Art-Language*, 4, 1978, No. 3; OVERY 1986 (see note 67), p. 136; WITKIN 1995 (see note 61), pp. 89-91. See also BRYL 1999 (see note 80), pp. 227-232.

Keeping aloof from Antal's and Hauser's *a priori* models of social history of art and rejecting the abstract paralleling of worldviews with styles, Timothy Clark in his *Image of the People*[89] launched a project for the new social history of art.[90] The political dimension of art, the direct engagement of the artist and his works in particular political events was the main focus of his study.[91] Nevertheless, Clark's inductionist programme[92] was based on an explicit theoretical model.[93] For Clark, art is a sociological phenomenon *par excellence*. That is why *"facts about patronage, about art dealing, about the status of the artist, the structure of artistic production"*[94] should be studied properly. Nevertheless, not only "facts" but new concepts and new questions must be raised. The fundamental question to be studied is *"the relation between the work of art and its ideology"*, according to Clark.[95] Consequently, vulgar materialist or economic determinist interpretation is rejected by Clark as not adequate to the social history of art. For him, *"economic life... is in itself a realm of representations"*,[96] i.e. the realm of ideology. Nevertheless, the concept of ideology *"seems... to be indelibly plural"*.[97] It has a class nature but *"all ideologies share the same function"*.[98] *"Ideologies"*, i.e. *"bodies of beliefs, images, values and techniques of representations"* are means *"by which social classes, in conflict with each other, attempt to 'naturalize' their particular histories"*, *"to generalize the repressions, imagine the contradictions solved"*,[99] in other words to legitimize their particular interests as inevitable and natural.

---

[89]   CLARK, Timothy J.: *Image of the People. Gustave Courbet and the 1848 Revolution*. London 1973; and CLARK, Timothy J.: *The Absolute Bourgeois. Artists and Politics in France 1848 – 1851*. London 1973.

[90]   See OVERY 1986 (see note 67), pp. 134-145; ROBERTS 1994 (see note 66), pp. 11-19; HARRIS 2001 (see note 80), pp. 64-74; HARRIS, Jonathan: T. J. Clark, in *Key Writers on Art* (see note 61), pp. 68-74; DOY 1998 (see note 66), pp. 75-87.

[91]   In 1973 in a letter to Wayne Andersen, Clark defined the aim of his *"scrupulous form of social history of art"* among other things, in the following way: "... *to discover the concrete links between the social and political history of the time, the imagery and visual style of certain painters, and the reaction of the public to them.*" See HARRIS 2001 (see note 80), pp. 88-89.

[92]   *"Conjunctural analysis"* in J. Harris's words, i.e. Clark's concentration on *"relatively short slices of history – in which the relations between artists, art practices, artworks, institutions, and the broader political and historical circumstances... [were] examined in detail."* – HARRIS 2001 (see note 80), p. 65.

[93]   In J. Harris's words: *"This empirical analysis, however, is necessarily based on theoretical assumptions and values relating to Marxist analysis of capitalist society..."* – Ibid., p. 87.

[94]   CLARK, Timothy J.: The Conditions of Artistic Creation, in *Times Literary Supplement*, 24 May 1974, pp. 561-562; reprinted in FERNIE, Eric: *Art History and Its Methods. A Critical Anthology*. London 1995, p. 251.

[95]   Ibid.

[96]   CLARK, Timothy J.: *The Painting of Modern Life. Paris in the Art of Manet and his Followers*. London 1985 (revised ed. 1996), p. 6.

[97]   CLARK 1974 (see note 94) in FERNIE 1995 (see note 94), p. 251.

[98]   Ibid.

[99]   Ibid.

Thus works of art in their figurative specificity are ideological phenomena too (*"'style' is the form of ideology"*, according to Clark),[100] instruments of ideological struggle between classes, *"the tools with which to alter ideology – to transcribe it, to represent it"*.[101] On the other hand, due to *"the fact that any ideology is by its nature incoherent"*,[102] *"ideology is what the picture is, and what the picture is not"*.[103] In other words, Clark seeks to rescue not only the specific (not discursive) nature of artworks but also their creative participation in shaping ideology. Due to *"the unstable essence of ideology"*,[104] the work of art can participate in shaping ideology without loosing its particular and independent nature (i.e. *"the fact that the work is done"*).[105] In that way, T. Clark harmonized the avant-garde idea of autonomy of art with the Marxist notion of its ideological nature.

In spite of T. Clark's later adoption of the semiotic idea of ideologies as *"constructs"* and *"systems of signs"*,[106] his project of the social history of art was mercilessly criticized not only by Marxists and adherents to feminist art history[107] but also by adherents to poststructural semiotics.[108] He was criticized, not only for maintaining traditional canons and ignoring the feminist dimension of art but also for *"operating with a naive and untheorized notion of history"* (by Norman Bryson),[109] logocentrism and an *"ahistorical"* approach (by

---

[100] Ibid. There is a close affinity between Clark's emphasis on the figurative nature of ideology manifested by art and Nicos Hadjinicolaou notion of *"idéologie imagée"*. See note 119. It has its common origin in Louis Althusser's view that *"Kunst offenbart die Ideologie, der sie entstammt"* (*"art reveals the ideology from which it originates"*), see WITTEVEEN 1995 (see note 38), p. 162.

[101] CLARK 1974 (see note 94) in FERNIE 1995 (see note 94), p. 251.

[102] Ibid., p. 252.

[103] Ibid., p. 251.

[104] Ibid., p. 253.

[105] Ibid., p. 251.

[106] CLARK 1985 (see note 96), pp. 6, 8.

[107] RIFKIN, Adrian: Marx's Clarkism, in *Art History*, 8, 1985, pp. 488-495; TAGG, John: Art History and Difference, in *Block*, 10, 1985, pp. 45-47; reprinted in *The New Art History* (see note 67), pp. 164-171; OVERY 1986 (see note 67), pp. 133-145. According to WITKIN 1995 (see note 61), p. 102: *"Clark sets himself critically against modernist art, preferring to see it as a quintessential form of bourgeois ideology and to see artists… as the product of that ideology."* About criticism on T. J. Clark, see ROBERTS 1994 (see note 66), pp. 14-20; DOY 1998 (see note 66), pp. 87, 101; BRYL 1999 (see note 80), p. 234.

[108] CLUNAS, Craig: Social History of Art, in *Critical Terms for Art History. Second edition.* Eds. Robert S. NELSON – Richard SHIFF. Chicago 2003, p. 472, speaks about a current *"binary opposition of 'social history of art v. visual culture' "*. The difference between the two viewpoints are defined by Clunas as follows: *"The social history of art is seen as still having an investment in Art that visual culture/cultural history paradigms do not have."*

[109] MOXEY, Keith: The Social History of Art in the Age of Deconstruction, in *History of the Human Sciences*, 5, 1992, No. 1, p. 37; BRYSON, Norman: Art in Context, in *Studies in Historical Change.* Ed. Ralph COHEN. Charlottesville 1992, pp. 18-42.

Donald Preziosi),[110] subscribing to the correspondence theory of truth,[111] and maintaining a metaphysical notion of immanent aesthetic value[112] while neglecting the fact that aesthetic value is an ideological or cultural construct.[113] Nevertheless, the ideological dimension of art remained the focus of Anglo-American art history during subsequent decades.[114] It can be interpreted as a critical response to the dominance of commodified art parallel to the criticism by conceptual art, and body art, or land art.

VI.

Simultaneously with the launching of revisionist art history in Britain, academic art history was also cross-examined in terms of ideological critique on the continent. In France, Nicos Hadjinicolaou in his *Histoire de l'art et lutte de classes*[115] attempted to unmask the ideological prejudices and class indebtedness of bourgeois art history.[116] Leaning upon Louis Althusser's notion of ideology[117] as *"an allusion to reality which is always accompanied by an illusion,*

---

[110] PREZIOSI, Donald: *Rethinking Art History. Meditations on a Coy Science.* New Haven 1989, pp. 159-168; MOXEY 1992 (see note 109), p. 38.

[111] Ibid., p. 41.

[112] MOXEY, Keith: Semiotics and the Social History of Art, in *New Literary History*, 22, 1991, p. 985; MOXEY, Keith: *The Practice of Persuasion. Paradox & Power in Art History.* Ithaca – London 2001, p. 83.

[113] MOXEY 1991 (see note 112), p. 986.

[114] According to LOCHER, Hubert: "New Art History" und "Visual Studies". Zur kunsthistorischen Methodendiskussion in England und den USA, in *Kunsthistorische Arbeitsblätter*, 2004, No. 5, pp. 5-12, there is a common denominator to be found in all branches of New Art History, i.e. *"the question of art as an instrument of shaping ideology"*: *"Die verschiedenen Ansätze der 'New Art History', deren Vertreter gelegentlich je nach Ausrichtung auch von 'radical art history', 'social art history' oder 'critical art history' sprechen, lassen sich denn auch in ihrem Interesse an einer einheitlichen theoretischen Leitidee zusammenfassen: Dies ist die Frage nach Kunst als Instrument der Ideologiebildung, nach der Art und Weise wie im Medium der Kunst ideologische 'Representation' stattfindet."*

[115] HADJINICOLAOU, Nicos: *Histoire de l'art et lutte des classes.* Paris 1973; English translation: *Art History and Class Struggle.* London 1978.

[116] Hadjinicolaou's book met a strong criticism. See ROBERTS 1994 (see note 66), pp. 9-10; DOY 1998 (see note 66), pp. 69-70; WITTEVEEN 1995 (see note 38), pp. 160-161.

[117] See HARRIS 2001 (see note 80), p. 23. ROBERTS 1994 (see note 66), p. 9, speaks about Hadjinicolaou's *"fairly crude"* application of Althusser's "structuralism". More about Althusser's notion of ideology, see EAGLETON, Terry: *Ideology. An Introduction.* London – New York 1991, pp. 89, 148-150; or ZIMA, Peter V.: *Ideologie und Theorie. Eine Diskurskritik.* Tübingen 1989, p. 153 ff. MOXEY, Keith: *The Practice of Theory. Poststructuralism, Cultural Politics, and Art History.* Ithaca – London 1994, p. 45, speaks about Althusser's *"equation of ideology and signification"*. According to WITTEVEEN 1995 (see note 38), p. 161: *"Für Althusser war Ideologie ein organischer Bestandteil der sozialen Totalität, als der Gesamtheit von Denkgewöhnheiten und Wirklichkeitserfahrungen einer Gesellschaft."*

a comprehension accompanied by a misapprehension",[118] Hadjinicolaou introduced the concept *"visual ideology"* (*"idéologie imagée"*).[119] Refusing to regard ideology as the illustration of *a priori* political ideas or *"as a pure and simple transcription of the political and social ideology of a class into domain of art"*,[120] he conceived of *"visual ideology"* as synonymous with style.[121] Thus, the figurative specificity of visual art itself i.e. style, has also an ideological nature, according to Hadjinicolaou (*"a particular style is synonymous to... 'visual ideology'"*).[122] That is why the concept of *"visual ideology"* can even be substituted for that of style.[123] Moreover, art regarded as *"visual ideology"* has a class nature: *"... the concept of visual ideology corresponds essentially to that of 'the style of a social group'."*[124] Or in other words: *"Visual ideology is a specific combination of the formal and thematic elements of a picture through which people express the way they relate their lives to the conditions of their existence, a combination which constitutes a particular form of the overall ideology of a social class."*[125] Even if Hadjinicolaou does not deny the importance of the economic dimension of art (the role of art dealers *"in an artists's success"* or the status of *"paintings as merchandise"* *"on the capitalist market"*), *"the art historian's principal tasks remains the analysis"* (of the *"visual ideology"*) *"of the paintings themselves"*, according to him.[126] Artistic styles are to be regarded above all as a means of ideological struggle between social classes. As a consequence, the history of art is conceived of as *"the history of visual ideologies"*.[127]

Nevertheless, the materialist revision of traditional art history was first launched within German art history. A group of young Marxist-oriented art historians united in the so-called "Ulmer Kreis" had already attempted a palace *coup* at XIIth Congress of German art historians in Cologne on 6 – 10 April 1970:[128] during the congress section devoted to "Artwork between Science and Worldview",[129] when they argued that the status of German academic art

---

[118]   I quote according to HADJINICOLAOU 1978 (see note 115), p. 100.

[119]   Ibid., p. 95.

[120]   Ibid., p. 96.

[121]   There is a close affinity between Hadjinicolaou's notion of *"idéologie imagée"* and T. J. Clark's idea of *"style as a form of ideology"*.

[122]   HADJINICOLAOU 1978 (see note 115), p. 95.

[123]   Ibid., p. 97.

[124]   Ibid., p. 98.

[125]   Ibid., pp. 95-96.

[126]   Ibid., p. 195.

[127]   Ibid., p. 98.

[128]   See about that SCHNEIDER 1986 (see note 14), pp. 251-254; *Kritische Berichte*, 18, 1990, No. 3: Zwanzig Jahre danach. Kritische Kunstwissenschaft heute; BRYL 1999, (see note 80), pp. 220-225.

[129]   See *Das Kunstwerk zwischen Wissenschaft und Weltanschauung*. Ed. Martin WARNKE. Gütersloh 1970.

history as a nonpartial objective science, was an ideological self-deception.[130] Combining W. Benjamin's critical theory with A. Warburg's iconology[131] and challenging the idea of the autonomy of art,[132] the group led by Martin Warnke took pains to develop a Marxist notion of art as part of a superstructure and the work of art as an instrument of ideological struggle.[133] Nevertheless, the stress on the ideological nature of art was complementary to the critique of commodification of art in late capitalist society.[134] According to Hans Heinz Holz,[135] the evident transformation of artwork into commodity (*"die... offenbar gewordene Tatsache, daß das Kunstwerk zur Ware geworden ist"*) can be regarded as a distortion of the work of art (*"die Depravierung des Kunstwerks"*).[136] Consequently, aesthetic value was changed into use value and finally into ex-

---

[130] SCHNEIDER 1986 (see note 14), pp. 251-252; WITTEVEEN 1995 (see note 38), pp. 155-156; BRYL 1999 (see note 80), pp. 220-225. Nevertheless, it is worth noticing that as early as in 1975, Heinrich Lützeler, one of the representatives of German traditional art history, already acknowledged that artworks have a true commodity nature and the connection between art and money was a legitimate one: *"... trotz aller dieser Bedenken und Auswüchse* [i.e. against commodification of art; J. B.] *bleibt festzuhalten, daß Kunstwerke echten Warencharakter haben und daß es eine überaus einseitige, idealisierende Sicht wäre, den legitimen Zusammenhang von Kunst und Geschäft nicht wahrhaben zu wollen."* See LÜTZELER, Heinrich: *Kunsterfahrung und Kunstwissenschaft. Systematische und entwicklungsgeschichtliche Darstellung und Dokumentation des Umgangs mit der bildenden Kunst.* Vol. 2. Freiburg – München 1975, p. 1265.

[131] DIERS, Michael: Von der Ideologie- zur Ikonologiekritik, in *Frankfurter Schule und Kunstgeschichte.* Berlin 1992, pp. 26-29.

[132] According to MÜLLER, Michael: Künstlerische und materielle Produktion. Zur Autonomie der Kunst in der italienischen Renaissance, in *Autonomie der Kunst. Zur Genese und Kritik einer bürgerlichen Kategorie.* Frankfurt am Main 1972, p. 84: *"Schliesslich war von einer autonomen Funktion der Kunst... erst dort die Rede, wo bereits Geld in Kapital übergangen war, sich in der Ware Gebrauchs- und Tauschwert spalteten und der Tauschwert im Zuge der allgemeinen Kapitalisierung der sogenannten Erwerbswert an Dominanz gewann."* As we see, the autonomy of art is regarded by Müller as a relatively young historical phenomenon (given that there is no generally valid essence of art) that resulted from the dominance of exchange value in modern Capitalism.

[133] SCHNEIDER 1986 (see note 14), p. 252, speaks about *"Kunst als Form des gesellschaftlichen Bewusstseins... und als Kampffeld antagonistischer Klasseninteressen"* (*"art as a form of social consciousness... and battlefield of class interests"*). Collective books *Autonomie der Kunst. Zur Genese und Kritik einer bürgerlichen Kategorie.* Eds. Michael MÜLLER – Horst BREDEKAMP – Berthold HINZ – Franz-Joachim VERSPOHL – Jürgen FREDEL – Ursula APITZSCH. Frankfurt am Main 1972; and *Bildersturm. Die Zerstörung des Kunstwerkes.* Ed. Martin WARNKE. München 1973; or BREDEKAMP, Horst: *Kunst als Medium sozialer Konflikte. Bilderkämpfe von der Spätantike bis zur Hussitenrevolution.* Frankfurt am Main 1975; and WARNKE, Martin: *Bau und Überbau. Soziologie der mittelalterlichen Architektur nach den Schriftquellen.* Frankfurt am Main 1976, can be mentioned as exempificatory publications of that initiative.

[134] See Jutta Held's papers on American Minimal Art, Pop Art or Photo-Realism, quoted in SCHNEIDER 1986 (see note 14), pp. 253, 261.

[135] HOLZ, Hans Heinz: *Vom Kunstwerk zur Ware. Studien zur Funktion des ästhetischen Gegenstandes im Spätkapitalismus.* Berlin – Neuwied 1972, pp. 37-38.

[136] Ibid., p. 37.

change value. In so doing marketing art resulted from the late capitalist need to increase the exchange value of all goods by means of their *"aestheticizing"* (*"Die Vermarktung des Kunstwerks... entspringt das Bedürfnis... nach einer Ästhetisierung der Konsumgüter... Ästhetisierung der Ware als Mittel zur Erhöhung ihres Tauschwertes."*).[137]

Referring to H. H. Holz's analysis and following the idea of the primacy of ideology, Klaus Herding and Hans-Ernst Mittig[138] even reinterpreted W. Benjamin's legacy. According to them, the market was not the opposite of ritual.[139] As a consequence, marketing art in the period of late capitalism meant no loss of the social function of art: *"Aus dem engeblich restlosen 'Vermarktung' auf 'Funktionslosigkeit'... der Kunst zu schliessen... ist... nicht einleuchtend."*[140] That is why it is necessary to distinguish between an *"ideological use value"* and an *"ideological exchange value"* of the work of art, both participating in the struggle of interest (*"die Unterscheidung von 'ideologischem Gebrauchswert' und 'ideologischem Tauschwert' ermöglicht es, den Antagonismus der an ein Kunstwerk geknüpften Interessen zu erkennen"*).[141]

As a matter of fact, the concept of art as a sociological phenomenon was gradually but substantially transformed in the following years. In the eighties, the original programme of ideological critique was replaced by a politically affirmative idea of the history of art as the history of social functions[142] and the *"aesthetics of reception"*[143] project.

VII.

Ernst Gombrich's essay "A Plea for Pluralism" written in 1971 as *"a reply to a question on The State of Art History"*[144] can be regarded as the first declara-

---

[137] Ibid.

[138] HERDING, Klaus – MITTIG, Hans-Ernst: Ästhetik im Spätkapitalismus, in *Kritische Berichte*, 1, 1973, No. 3, pp. 51-170.

[139] Ibid., p. 130.

[140] Ibid., p. 131.

[141] Ibid., p. 141.

[142] See BELTING, Hans: *Das Bild und sein Publikum im Mittelalter. Form und Funktion früher Bildtafeln der Passion.* Berlin 1981; and particularly *Funkkolleg Kunst. Eine Geschichte der Kunst im Wandel ihrer Funktionen.* Ed. Werner BUSCH. München – Zürich 1987. See also BRYL 2008 (see note 80), pp. 219-231.

[143] *Der Betrachter ist im Bild. Kunstwissenschaft und Rezeptionsästhetik.* Ed. Wolfgang KEMP. Köln 1985. About the polemics between W. Kemp and N. Hadjinicolaou, see BRYL 1999 (see note 80), p. 219. See also BRYL 2008 (see note 80), pp. 240-249.

[144] First published in *The American Art Journal*, Spring 1971; reprinted in GOMBRICH, Ernst H.: *Ideals and Idols. Essays on Values in History and in Art.* Oxford 1979, pp. 184-188.

tion of Post-modernism in art history. Rejecting (avant-garde) methodological purism, he pleaded for methodological pluralism in art historical research. Despite his severe critique of Hauser's social determinism in 1953, Gombrich did not deny that *"if by 'the social history' of art we mean an account of the changing material conditions under which art was commissioned and created in the past, such a history is one of the desiderata of our field"*.[145] Twenty years later, still agreeing that *"the organization of production with its attendant social consequences will be part of the situation within which the work of art takes place"*[146] and, therefore, *"social elements play their part in the coming into being of styles"*,[147] Gombrich made the decisive step towards a post-modernist interpretation of art history. In 1974 in his "The Logic of Vanity Fair",[148] implicitly rehabilitating art's indebtedness to the market, Gombrich presented capitalist competition and market strategies as principles ruling modern society, its art not excluded. He conceived of the *"rarity game"*[149] i.e. *"departure from the norm... in order to attract attention"*[150] and *"assimilating art to fashion"*[151] as the *"logic of situation"* of the history of art. According to Gombrich, *"there is a competitive element in art which aims at drawing attention to the artist or his patron"*. Nevertheless, *"competition in art is not necessarily a 'bad thing'"*,[152] he concluded. Consequently, involvement in market strategies results neither in the loss of art's creative autonomy nor in its total commodification.

At the same time, Gombrich's adherent Michael Baxandall, in his book *Painting and Experience in Fifteenth Century Italy*[153] did not merely follow up Gombrich's pattern in claiming *"that the painters are seen very much as individuals in competiton"*.[154] Suppressing *"the ideological element"*,[155] Baxandall radi-

---

[145]   GOMBRICH 1963 (see note 70), p. 86.

[146]   GOMBRICH, Ernst H.: *Art History and the Social Sciences. The Romanes Lecture for 1973*. Oxford 1975, p. 21; reprinted in GOMBRICH 1979 (see note 144), pp. 131-166.

[147]   Ibid., p. 24.

[148]   GOMBRICH, Ernst H.: The Logic of Vanity Fair. Alternatives to Historicism in the Study of Fashions, Style and Taste, in *The Philosophy of Karl Popper*. Ed. Paul A. SCHILPP. La Salle (IL) 1974, pp. 925-957; reprinted in GOMBRICH 1979 (see note 144), pp. 60-92.

[149]   Ibid., p. 928.

[150]   Ibid.

[151]   Ibid., p. 927.

[152]   Ibid., p. 929.

[153]   BAXANDALL, Michael: *Painting and Experience in Fifteenth Century Italy. A Primer in the Social History of Pictorial Style*. London 1972.

[154]   Ibid., p. 26.

[155]   LANGDALE, Allan: Aspects of the Critical Reception and Intellectual History of Baxandall's Concept of the Period Eye, in *About Michael Baxandall*. Ed. Adrian RIFKIN. Oxford 1999, p. 28. *"For circumventing any discussion of ideology"*, Baxandall was strongly criticized by *"the art-historical Left"*. More about that ibid., pp. 28-30.

cally reinterpreted the materialist conception of the history of art. For him, art was determined neither by economic basis nor social structure directly. Everyday working practice and particular practical experience (skills) moulded the concepts of a period as well as did a *"period eye"* , and mediated between society and art. For Baxandall, visual perception on the one hand and commercial transactions, the economic practice of *"gauging"* in particular, on the other, correlated with each other.[156] As a consequence, a way of seeing considered to be characteristic of a period was projected onto and materialized in, the particular shape of works of art of the period. In that internalized way,[157] artworks are seen to be social phenomena *par excellence*: *"painting is the deposit of a social relationship"* or *"paintings are among other things fossils of economic life"*, according to Baxandall.[158] Nevertheless, not only material production but also trade[159] played a very important role within period practice: *"…the relationship of which the painting is the deposit was among other things a commercial relationship, and some of the economic practices of the period are quite concretely embodied in the paintings."*[160] As a consequence, the Romantic or Marxist art versus commerce paradigm was unequivocally replaced here by a new affirmative credo: *"Money is very important in the history of art"*, according to Baxandall.[161]

In *The Limewood Sculptors of Renaissance Germany*,[162] Baxandall explicitly challenged the notion of the art market as providing an external context or *ex post facto* frame for art. In spite of Baxandall's interpretion of the market as providing an organic context for art, he did not regard it as a prison. Rejecting the Marxist negative dialectic *"art versus market"* – *"either freedom or enslavement"*, Baxandall replaced it with the idea of the market as a space for the artist's options. *"To direct attention to the artist's market invites misunderstanding. There are those who resent any suggestion that the artist is not an absolute spirit pursuing his aesthetical way like a bird: they will read any proposition about the relation between artist and market as a coarse innuendo about artists following a style because*

---

[156] See ADAMS, Laurie S.: *The Methodologies of Art. An Introduction.* New York 1996, p. 70.

[157] LANGDALE 1999 (see note 155), p. 20, speaks about Baxandall's *"geological rhetoric"* by means of which *"a solid – virtually petrified – directly imprinting connection between a culture's economic practices and paintings"* came into being.

[158] BAXANDALL 1972 (see note 153), p. 2.

[159] As LANGDALE 1999 (see note 155), pp. 20-21, states: *"Baxandall's elaboration of the structures of the art market, the social relationships between artists and client, the intermediary functions of guilds, workshop practice... presents one with a number of fairly determinable kinds of social things which are 'concretely embodied' in paintings, partially because they operate and circulate so closely to the orbit of the production of painting itself."*

[160] BAXANDALL 1972 (see note 153), p. 1.

[161] Ibid.

[162] BAXANDALL, Michael: *The Limewood Sculptors of Renaissance Germany.* New Haven – London 1980.

it is profitable. On the other hand there are those who will expect the economic to play its full determining role, shaping in the last analysis everything from people's ways of working together and thus their consciousness (and thus the forms of their art), to the function of art and attitudes to artistic tradition.

A market is seen here simply as one medium through which a society can translate both general facts about itself and such preoccupations about art as it possesses into a brief the artist can understand. Because most societies are complex there is usually a plurality of markets embodying diverse briefs. The artist need never become a creature of the market: he may choose which of the briefs he will take up, and he responds to some of its suggestions, ignores others, and sometimes turns yet others on their heads in a pointed way. Artists who get along in a market... manifest their brief and in it general social fact, as well as current ideas about art."[163]

Following Baxandall, another of Gombrich's pupils, Svetlana Alpers in her *Rembrandt's Enterprise,*[164] even internalized the art market as a part of artistic production. She interpreted the particular nature of Rembrandt's art as a consequence of his sophisticated and intentional market strategies.[165] According to Alpers, Rembrandt's *"works are commodities distinguished from others by being identified as his, and in making them, he in turn commodifies himself... was an entrepreneur of the self".*[166] To use Laurie Schneider Adams' comment, Rembrandt commodified his paintings, changed them into a kind of currency, painted so to say his own money[167] in order to free himself from dependence on the patron and to increase his own profit: *"He was not only a man of studio but also a man of market... he made himself a free individual, not beholden to patrons... Rembrandt was in fact refusing to cater to the patronage system... But he was beholden instead to the market – or more specifically to the identification that he made between two representations of value, art and money."*[168] As a consequence, he revolutionized the art market by trying to replace the traditional commision based on the direct patron/artist relationship with an impersonal, anonymous market transaction: *"While he turned against the patronage system, he did not embrace the*

---

[163] Ibid., p. 95.

[164] ALPERS, Svetlana: *Rembrandt's Enterprise. The Studio and the Market.* Chicago 1988.

[165] Leaning upon Georg Simmel's notion of value as a result of judgment, Alpers shares the view that *"the value of a painting is a function of exchange".* – ALPERS 1988 (see note 164), p. 98. About G. Simmel's notion of value, see APPADURAI, Arjun: Introduction: Commodities and the Politics of Value, in APPADURAI, Arjun: *The Social Life of Things. Commodities in Cultural Perspective.* Cambridge 1986. *"Value, for Simmel, is never an inherent property of objects, but is a judgement made about them by subjects."* – Ibid., p. 3. *"Simmel's view that exchange is the source of value and not vice versa."* – Ibid., p. 56.

[166] ALPERS 1988 (see note 164), p. 118.

[167] ADAMS 1996 (see note 156), p. 73.

[168] ALPERS 1988 (see note 164), pp. 88-89.

market in its traditional form but rather felt his way towards finding a place for art in the operations of the developing capitalist marketplace."[169] *"Rembrandt himself circulated art in the marketplace system of exchange*[170]*... he treated it as an alternative to the patronage system"* replacing *"a craftsman selling his products... by an enterpreneur".*[171] Moreover, *"he internalized into his practice this system"*[172] the *"merging of invention with execution",*[173] making use of *"authenticity as a marketing feature"*[174] and developing *"the work of art as a commodity distinguished among others by not being factory produced, but produced in limited numbers and creating its market, whose special claim to the aura of individuality and to high market value bind it to basic aspects of an entrepreneurial (capitalist) enterprise".*[175]

VIII.

Nevertheless, some radical neo-Marxist art historians also began to revise their original belief in the primacy of ideology. Martin Warnke in his *Hofkünstler*[176] unfolding his materialist belief in art as determined by society (*"die Künste haben sich im Bezugsfeld gesellschaftlicher Kräfte bewegt und entwickelt"*),[177] came to the conclusion that the birth of the modern artist seen as a free and misunderstood hero (*"Aussenseiter der Gesellschaft"*)[178] can be conceived of as a byproduct of the collapse of feudal courts.[179] Even the idea of *"incalculable artistic good"*[180] cannot be explained solely by the role of art theory on the one hand, and the introduction of a bourgeois *"market mechanism"* on the other,[181] according to Warnke: *"Doch auch dann, wenn nachgewiesen werden könnte, daß der städtische Kunstmarkt die Preise für Kunstwerke freisetzte, bliebe noch immer unerklärlich, wie die künstlerische Ware, wenn sie neben andere Waren trat, jenen*

---

[169] Ibid., p. 96.

[170] Ibid., p. 98.

[171] Ibid., p. 101.

[172] Ibid., p. 106.

[173] Ibid., p. 102.

[174] Ibid., p. 121.

[175] Ibid., p. 102.

[176] WARNKE, Martin: *Hofkünstler. Zur Vorgeschichte des modernen Künstlers.* Köln 1985; English translation: *Court Artist. On the Ancestry of the Modern Artist.* Cambridge – London 1993.

[177] WARNKE 1985 (see note 176), p. 12.

[178] Ibid.

[179] Ibid., pp. 9-14.

[180] Ibid., p. 201 (or the impossibility of *"pricing the priceless"*, to paraphrase William D. Grampp's expression, see GRAMPP, William D.: *Pricing the Priceless. Art, Artists and Economics.* New York 1989).

[181] WARNKE 1985 (see note 176), p. 200.

Status gewonnen haben könnte, der sie dem handwerklichen Preisreglement, das Arbeitszeit und Materialkosten summierte, entzog."[182] In Warnke's view, the status of artworks as a particular kind of commodity i.e. "*as exotic commodity*"[183] has its origins "*in the sphere of court*",[184] because the market alone was not able to establish it: "*Der Markt hatte kaum die Fähigkeit, von sich aus das Kunstwerk mit jenen Qualitäten zu begaben, die es als geistiges Produkt eines schöpferischen Individuums definierte und honorierte.*"[185] As we have seen, even if the decisive role has not been attributed to the economic dimension of art, the role played by the market has been taken into consideration.

And Otto Karl Werckmeister, a co-founder of "Caucus for Marxism and Art" within the College Art Association of America[186] went a step further. In his *Versuch über Paul Klee*,[187] focusing on the artist's career instead of on his artworks, Werckmeister interpreted Klee's paintings as vehicles for his financial and social success. According to him, "*Klee's cereer itself* [can be approached] *as a historical process enacted between the artist and his public, a process in which the works were not ends but functions*".[188] He critically challenged "*the myth of his* [Klee's] *art*"[189] and demonstrated that the image of an avant-garde artist as rebel targeting the abolition of the capitalist market can simply be a mask hiding a very sophisticated profit-driven businessman. Even if it can be regarded as a logical and necessary step, the persistant ideological critique's demystification of the artist as a free creator by unmasking his commercial strategies, represented itself a kind of market turn within radical art history.

Nevertheless, the rehabilitation of the market provoked critical response very quickly. Jutta Held characterized the abandonment of ideological analysis as a projection of contemporary capitalist market strategies onto history.[190] According to her, the replacement of the idea of art as participating in collective ideological struggles by the notion of art as an aid towards the "*struggle for life*" of an individual artist (covering his egotistic existential needs only) can be regarded as a "*cipher of the market*" ("*Chiffre eines Marktes*").[191] The origi-

---

[182] Ibid., pp. 200-201.

[183] Ibid., p. 201.

[184] Ibid., p. 200.

[185] Ibid., p. 201.

[186] BRYL 1999 (see note 80), p. 227.

[187] WERCKMEISTER, Otto Karl: *Versuch über Paul Klee*. Frankfurt am Main 1981; translated into English under the symptomatic title, *The Making of Paul Klee's Career 1914 – 1920*. Chicago 1989.

[188] WERCKMEISTER 1989 (see note 187), p. 9.

[189] Ibid.

[190] HELD, Jutta: Von der Ideologiekritik zur Akklamation der freien Marktwirtschaft, in *Kritische Berichte*, 18, 1990, No. 3, pp. 21-26.

[191] Ibid., p. 25.

nal Marxist concept of art as a commodity (in other words the Marxist disclosure of capitalism's transformation of art into commodity) was cleaned of the notion of *"alienation"*, according to Jutta Held.[192] As a consequence, the critique of the commodification of art was transformed into its apology.

The Marxist challenge has not been left unanswered. The advocates of the *"new topos"* as Walter Grasskamp called the rehabilitation of commodity nature of art[193] and *"the new interest in the art economy"*[194] not only delimited their position from *"a Marxist idée fixe to theorise over the correlation of art and economics"*,[195] or – we can add – from the obsession with the critical analysis of the art-economy relationship. They also strictly rejected the idea of *"a religion of art"* (*"Kunstreligion"*),[196] i.e. *"the illusion of art as something distant from, and free of the market"*,[197] as well as *"the view... of the artist, unmotivated by economic necessity, working to fulfil a higher, ultimately inexplicable, creative urge"*.[198] This ignoring of, or even condemning, the market dimension of art can be regarded as a survival of the anti-bourgeois campaign, expressing a contempt for commerce by all its traditional enemies – the aristocracy, antisemites, communists, Avant-gardists and the Catholic Church –, according to W. Grasskamp: *"The contempt for the commercial in culture, still the norm today, owes... to Christian tradition... the medieval rejection of commerce [that] still operates"*, to the *"disdain of bourgeois industriousness"* by the aristocracy, and the communist *"attempt to subjugate a flexible economy to a static ideology."*[199] As a consequence, *"the economy has remained unrecognized as an independent domain"* and, consequently, *"the standing of economy has... not emerged from the shadows of religious, aristocratic and socialist stigmatisation"*.[200] According to Grasskamp, it was *"academic art specialists"* who *"contributed in no small measure to suppressing the increasing commodity character of art... [to] the persistent... repression of the fact*[201] *that it was only with bourgeois society, which dreamed of a pure, autonomous art, that art increasingly be-*

---

[192] Ibid.

[193] GRASSKAMP, Walter: Art and Money. Scenes from a Mixed Marriage, in *Artists – Dealers – Consumers. On the Social World of Art*. Ed. Ton BEVERS. Rotterdam 1994, pp. 41-55; German edition: GRASSKAMP, Walter: *Kunst und Geld. Szenen einer Mischehe*. München 1998, pp. 15-22.

[194] GRASSKAMP 1994 (see note 193), p. 46.

[195] GRASSKAMP 1994 (see note 193), p. 46; GRASSKAMP 1998 (see note 193), p. 22.

[196] GRASSKAMP 1998 (see note 193), p. 20; GRASSKAMP 1994 (see note 193), p. 45: the notion of art as *"the successor to religion"* owing to which *"art has taken over the economic taboo"*.

[197] GRASSKAMP 1994 (see note 193), p. 45; GRASSKAMP 1998 (see note 193), p. 20.

[198] Ibid.: *"der Künstler ist ein Schöpfer..., der ohne Gewinnabsichten... aus höherem und letzlich unerklärlichem Schaffensdrang seine Werke herstelle."*

[199] GRASSKAMP 1994 (see note 193), p. 44.

[200] Ibid., p. 45.

[201] GRASSKAMP 1998 (see note 193), p. 20, speaks about *"der paradoxen Erkenntnis"* (*"the paradoxical insight"*).

came a commercial product".[202] For Grasskamp, the *"denial of economic influence in art"*, that *"may be termed The Aesthetic Syndrome"*[203] is an unrealistic illusion or *"the sweet dream of an art free of the market"* that *"could no longer be sustained".*[204]

IX.

Alongside the dispute in art history about ideology and the market, the shift from the ideologically focused social history of art to the economic history of art began to come under the intense focus of sociologists and economic historians.[205] In the words of one of the pioneers of the research into the art trade Michael Montias, *"it is the interplay between supply and demand factors that*

---

[202] GRASSKAMP 1994 (see note 193), p. 45.

[203] Ibid.

[204] Ibid., p. 46.

[205] See MOULIN, Raymonde: *Le marché de la peinture en France.* Paris 1967; MOULIN, Raymonde: *L'artist, l'institution et le marché.* Paris 1992; MONTIAS, John M.: *Artists and Artisans in Delft. A Socio-Economic Study of the 17th Century.* Princeton 1982; MONTIAS, John M.: *Vermeer and his Milieu. A Web in Social History.* Princeton 1988; PARET, Peter: *The Berlin Secession. Modernism and Its Enemies in Imperial Germany.* Harward 1980; NORTH, Michael: *Kunst und Kommerz im Goldenen Zeitalter. Zur Sozialgeschichte der niederländischen Malerei des 17. Jahrhunderts.* Köln 1992; English translation: *Art and Commerce in the Dutch Golden Age.* New Haven – London 1997; *Economic History and the Arts.* Ed. Michael NORTH. Köln – Weimar – Wien 1996; *Art and its Markets in Europe, 1400 – 1800.* Eds. Michael NORTH – David ORMROD. Aldershot 1998; GOLDTHWAITE, Richard A.: *The Building of Renaissance Florence. An Economic and Social History.* Baltimore – London 1980; GOLDTHWAITE, Richard A.: *Wealth and the Demand for Art in Italy, 1300 – 1600.* Baltimore 1993; REITLINGER, Gerald: *The Economics of Taste. The Rise and Fall of Picture Prices, 1760 – 1960.* Vols. 1-3. New York 1982; GREEN, Nicolas: Dealing in Temperaments: Economic Transformations of the Artistic Field in France during the Second Half of the Nineteenth Century, in *Art History,* 10, 1987, No. 1, p. 59 ff.; GREEN, Nicolas: Circuits of Production, Circuits of Consumption: The Case of Mid-Nineteenth-Century French Art Dealing. In *Art Journal,* 48, 1989, No. 1, pp. 29-34; De MARCHI, Neil – Van MIEGROET, Hans J.: Art, Value, and Market Practices in the Netherlands in the Seventeenth Century, in *The Art Bulletin,* 76, 1994, No. 3, pp. 451-464; LENMAN, Robin: *Die Kunst, die Macht und das Geld. Zur Kulturgeschichte des kaiserlichen Deutschland 1871 – 1918.* Franfurt am Main – New York 1994; DRECHSLER, Maximiliane: *Zwischen Kunst und Kommerz. Zur Geschichte des Ausstellungswesens zwischen 1775 und 1905.* München 1996; *Economics of the Arts.* Eds. Victor A. GINSBURGH – Pierre-Michel MENGER. Amsterdam 1996; *Kunst voor de Markt/Art for the Market, 1500 – 1700* (=Nederlands Kunsthistorisch Jaarboek, 50, 1999). Eds. Reindert FALKENBURG – Jan De JONG – Dulcia MEIJERS – Bart RAMAKERS – Mariët WESTERMANN. Zwolle 2000; VERMEYLEN, Filip: *Painting for the Market. Commercialization of Art in Antwerp's Golden Age.* Turnhout 2003; *The Art Market in Italy, 15th – 17th Centuries.* Eds. Marcello FANTONI – Louisa Chevalier MATTHEW – Sara F. MATTHEWS-GRIECO. Modena 2003; De MARCHI, Neil – Van MIEGROET, Hans J.: The History of Art Markets, in *Handbook of the Economics of Art and Culture.* Vol. 1. Eds. Victor A. GINSBURGH – David THORSBY. Amsterdam 2006, pp. 69-122; BAYER, Thomas M. – PAGE, John R.: *The Development of the Art Market in England: Money as Muse, 1730 – 1900.* London 2011.

is of central concern to the art historian".[206] The entry of economic historians and sociologists into the territory of art history has been welcomed by art historians and integrated into art historical discourse, since it corresponded with art history's current trend towards a contextual approach. The shift from the social history to the economic history of art can also be regarded as a token of the withdrawal from large-scale historical generalizations together with the abstract paralleling of art with social structure characteristic of the old social history of art. In Michael North's words: "*...the possible interactions between art and the economy are easier to examine than, for example, the influence of bourgeois society on artistic development.*"[207] Despite that, the shift of focus from art/ideology to the art/economy relationship did not entail a revival of the old materialist determinism: the inquiry has been focused no longer on the conditioning of art by the base (modes of production before all) but on art and commerce, trade and market interrelationship. Nevertheless, the new approach "*attempting to situate... art in its socioeconomic context*" has also its Achilles' heel, namely, to disconnect the market from "*the ideas and mentalities with what men and women do in the marketplace*".[208]

Returning in a sense to Burckhardt's successors like Hans Floerke[209] and Martin Wackernagel,[210] cultural and economic historians or sociologists launched an approach based on archival research and statistics that unequivocally falsified the avant-garde moralizing idea of commerce as a "necessary

---

[206] MONTIAS, John M.: The Souvereign Consumer. The Adaptation of Works of Art to Demand in the Netherlands in the Early Modern Period, in *Artists – Dealers – Consumers* (see note 193), p. 74.

[207] NORTH 1997 (see note 205), p. 133.

[208] De MARCHI – Van MIEGROET 1994 (see note 205), p. 451. The authors' goal is "*to create and illustrate possibilities for reuniting ideas and practices*". – Ibid., p. 452. Nevertheless, "*ideas and mentalities*" are not regarded by De Marchi and Van Miegroet as ideologies or world views but as "*notions... influencing what art was made, how it was produced and marketed*". – Ibid., p. 463. According to WITTEVEEN 1995 (see note 38), p. 166, there are the following weak points concerning archival studies: "*... daß diese Dokumente nicht notwendigerweise von Bedeutung für die Kunstproduktion... sind*", that "*beim Umgang mit dem Quellenmaterial... die Gefahr einer Rückkehr des romantischen Künstlerbildes des 19. Jahrhunderts (Kunst und Leben sind eins) oder der vulgärmarxistischen Auffassung (das Kunstwerk als Niederschlag der Produktionsverhältnisse) [besteht]*".

[209] FLOERKE, Hans: *Studien zur niederländischen Kunst- und Kulturgeschichte. Die Formen des Kunsthandelns, das Atelier und die Sammler in den Niederlanden vom 15. – 18. Jahrhudert.* München – Leipzig 1905. Still in 1991, Gary Schwarz claimed that "*the libraries of art history groan under catalogues and monographs, while no one has tried to improve upon Hans Floerke's study of 1905... – on the trade, production and collecting of art in Holland*" and called for "*the historical study of art... a history of the activity and its products*". – SCHWARZ, Gary: Art in History, in *Art in History/History in Art.* Eds. David FREEDBERG – Jan de VRIES. Santa Monica 1991, pp. 12-13.

[210] WACKERNAGEL, Martin: *Der Lebensraum des Künstlers in der florentinischen Renaissance. Aufgaben und Auftraggeber, Werkstatt und Kunstmarkt.* Leipzig 1938.

evil". Even if many sociologists and economic historians shared the positivist prejudice that archival material and statistical data automatically reveal the truth about the role of the market in the history of art or immediately allow one to generalize or theorize about it,[211] they could not escape the assumption of theoretical premises in their analyses. Raymonde Moulin, for example, faithfully following up the canons of Modernism, conceived of rarity, uniqueness, and originality[212] as the essence of artistic as well as market value: *"Le statut économique particulier de l'œuvre d'art est en relation étroite evec le caractére unique de l'œuvre. Les biens d'art uniques sont le type idéal des biens rares"*, according to Moulin.[213] And consequently *"La rareté du chef-d'œuvre unique de génie unique est la rareté le plus rare"*, according to her.[214] The differentiation between *"art orienté vers le marché"* and *"art orienté vers le musée"* as developed by Moulin in *L'artist, l'institution et le marché*[215] also implies avant-garde axiology i.e. commodification versus the artistic transcendence or utility versus autonomy. As far as the artist/dealer relationship is concerned, Moulin emphasized again the *"artist's creative freedom in contrast to dealers' limited ability to make rational predictions"*,[216] even though acknowledging the importance of the art dealer's role in the artworld.

As a matter of fact, we owe the most pervasive theoretical analysis of the art/market dialectic to Pierre Bourdieu. From a neo-Marxist point of view, he not only demonstrated the social and instrumental class nature of aesthetic values as means of *"power of distinction"*.[217] Challenging the so-called *"ideology*

---

[211] For more about the limits of generalizations concerning the history of Netherlandish art, see MONTIAS 1990 (see note 53), pp. 358-373.

[212] HEINICH, Nathalie: *La sociologie de l'art*. Paris 2001, p. 59, referring to MOULIN, Raymonde: *La valeur de l'art*. Paris 1995: *"… l'importance accordé á la notion de rareté (soit matérielle, avec les œuvres uniques, soit stylistique, avec l'originalité), qui est un facteur constant de renchérissement des œuvres."*

[213] MOULIN 1992 (see note 205), chapter "Le marché et l'histoire 1. La rareté et le jugement de l'histoire: le prix du génie".

[214] Ibid. Moulin's identification of the quality of a work of art with its rarity corresponds with the results of an interview done by Christine und Volker Plagemann among German critics, artists, dealers, and collectors at the beginning of the seventies, see Kunst als Ware, in *Das Kunstwerk*, 24, 1971, No. 2, pp. 3-81. Originality, innovation, invention (*"Erfindung"*), and novelty (sometimes even truth!) were regarded by a majority of interviewed persons as the main preconditions of artistic quality. At the same time, rarity, singularity and scarcity (*"Seltenheit"*) were considered to be the main determinants of market value, i.e. the price of an artwork.

[215] HEINICH 2001 (see note 212), p. 59.

[216] SEIBERLING, Grace: Art market, in *The Encyclopedia of Aesthetics*. Ed. Michael KELLY. New York – Oxford 1998, Vol. 1, p. 144.

[217] BOURDIEU, Pierre: *La distinction. Critique sociale du jugement*. Paris 1979; English translation: *Distinction: A Social Critique of the Judgement of Taste*. London 1984.

of creation,[218] he also demystified *"the modern myths or cult of art"*.[219] According to P. Bourdieu, art has to be regarded as a *"cultural production"* and its products, i.e. works of art, as *"symbolic goods"*.[220] They represent *"a two-faced reality, a commodity and a symbolic object"* i.e. that of *"commercial value"* and *"cultural value"*.[221] Nevertheless, there are *"two modes of production"*, according to P. Bourdieu: *"the production for producers or competitors"* themselves i.e. *"for the restricted public"* on the one hand, and *"the production for non-producers"* or *"for large public"* on the other.[222] The first one governed by *"competion for cultural legitimacy"*[223] and the *"monopoly of a certain class of symbolic goods"*,[224] produces autonomous art (*"art for art's sake"*)[225] and results in *"the incessant explication and redefinition of the foundations"* of the work of art.[226] The second one, aiming at the *"conquest by the market"* and *"public success"* or *"profitability"*[227] produces *"middle-brow art"* where *"works are entirely defined by 'the public at large'"*.[228] Consequently, the (moralizing and we can add romantic or avant-garde) opposition *"art-as-pure-signification"* versus *"art as a commodity"*[229] or *"creative liberty"* versus *"laws of market"*[230] and *"the idealism of devotion to art"* versus *"submission to the market"*[231] or artistic *"mission"* versus a mere *"job"*[232] has been unmasked by Bourdieu as *"defense against the disenchantment produced by the progress of the division of labour"*.[233]

We have seen that the difference between auratic art and that of mass communication was regarded by W. Benjamin as consisting in two successive historical phenomena. In contrast to Benjamin, Adorno juxtaposed autonomous (and critical) art with mass (and trivial) culture conceiving them as hierarchical and axiological antitheses. In comparison, Bourdieu's *"two modes of production"* – for producers and for the large public – resulting in autonomous art on

---

[218] SEIBERLING 1998 (see note 216), p. 143.

[219] FOWLER, Bridget: Pierre Bourdieu, in *Key Writers on Art* (see note 61), p. 56.

[220] BOURDIEU, Pierre: *The Field of Cultural Production. Essays on Art and Literature.* Cambridge – Oxford 1993; French original in *Poetics*, 12, 1983, No. 4-5.

[221] BOURDIEU 1993 (see note 220), chapter on "The Market of Symbolic Goods", p. 113.

[222] Ibid., pp. 112-120, 125-130.

[223] Ibid., p. 117.

[224] Ibid., p. 116.

[225] Ibid., p. 127.

[226] Ibid., p. 118.

[227] Ibid., p. 126.

[228] Ibid., pp. 125, 117.

[229] Ibid., p. 116.

[230] Ibid., p. 127.

[231] Ibid., p. 128.

[232] Ibid., p. 130.

[233] Ibid., p. 127.

the one hand and average art on the other, represent not only opposition but also coexistence or functioning *"within a single universe"*.[234] This coexisting opposition can be regarded as a consequence of the process of division of labour and the division of (social) functions, according to Bourdieu. In addition, the two modes of production represent also *"two (specific) markets"*.[235] Products of both symbolic goods are intended to maintain social distinctions and legitimate *"a form of domination"*.[236] In such a way, as we see, Bourdieu overcomes the dilemma of art versus the market and harmonizes the ideological dimension of art with its commercial dimension, its aesthetic autonomy with its social heteronomy.

Consequent upon the initiatives analysed above, the notion of the art market regarded as a parasitic phenomenon has been gradually replaced by the idea of the commodification of art as an indisputable and important historical fact worth serious and profound examination. In addition, the art market started to be conceived in terms of a logical setting for artworks produced within a commercial society. In Paul Mattick's words: *"Art developed along with the commercialized mode of production that became capitalism, and it is only by understanding art as an aspect of this mode of production that the supposed antagonism between them... can be understood."*[237] Consequently, the commodification of art has started to be seen not only as an unintended and necessary byproduct of commercial society but also, conversely, as a complementary side of art's autonomy. The autonomy of art, therefore, could be interpreted as a function of the (art) market and vice versa: marketing art as the vehicle of art's autonomy. P. Mattick expressed it as follows: *"Thus, it is precisely its distance from market considerations, its 'noneconomic' character, that gives art its social meaning and its market value."*[238]

X.

Since the late eighties and especially in the nineties, art historians joined that trend and started to study the relationship between art and market very intensively. Inspired probably by Baxandall's modell and anticipating case studies by economic historians, art market analysis as a particular research

---

[234] Ibid.

[235] Ibid., p. 130.

[236] Ibid., p. 129.

[237] MATTICK, Paul: Ideology, in *The Encyclopedia of Aesthetics* (see note 216), Vol. 2, p. 460.

[238] Ibid.

theme, focusing on *"how the art market functioned... how pictures were sold and bought"*,[239] was already launched by Lorne Campbell as early as 1976.[240] After Thomas Crow's discussion, in his successfull *Painters and Public Life in Eighteenth-Century Paris*,[241] of the role of salons in giving birth to public art criticism as a catalyst of an independent market, the focus of study shifted gradually to the analysis of the process of marketing art itself. I mention only some of the most stimulating contributions to the current discourse: Patricia Mainardi in *The End of the Salon*[242] distinguished between paintings *"to show"* and paintings *"to sell"* in order to demonstrate the shift from state sponsored and controlled salons to small commercially oriented galleries which became the main agent of art development in the late 19th century. David H. Solkin in *Painting for Money*[243] analyzed *"how 18th century English visual culture came to be shaped by and for the purposes of commerce"* and how painting gained access to market institutions.[244] Robert Jensen in his *Marketing Modernism in Fin-de-siècle Europe*[245], analyzing a competitive and at the same time *"cooperative net of purchases, loans and contracts done by entrepreneurial dealers"*, shows their role in the *"refashioning of the commercial gallery... to rivals of museums"*.[246] In contrast to Raymonde Moulin who regarded artists and dealers in a sense as antipodes, Michael C. Fitzgerald in his *Making Modernism: Picasso and the Creation of the Market for Twentieth-Century Art*[247] argues that some dealers (Paul Rosenberg in Picasso's case) not only shaped the artist's career but also participated in

---

[239] CAMPBELL, Lorne: The Art Market in the Southern Netherlands in the Fifteenth Century, in *The Burlington Magazine*, 118, 1976, p. 188. About Campbell's contribution to the knowledge of *"the production and marketing of art works in the southern Netherlands in the fifteenth century"*, see MONTIAS 1990 (see note 53), p. 369.

[240] Campbell's model was followed up by WILSON, Jean C.: The Participation of Painters in the Bruges "Pandt" Market, 1512 – 1550, in *The Burlington Magazine*, 125, 1983, pp. 476-479; JACOBS, Lynn F.: The Marketing and Standardization of South Netherlandish Carved Altarpieces: Limits on the Role of the Patron, in *The Art Bulletin*, 71, 1989, No. 2, pp. 208-229; or EWING, Dan: Marketing Art in Antwerp, 1460 – 1560: Our Lady's Pand, in *The Art Bulletin*, 72, 1990, No. 4, pp. 558-584.

[241] CROW, Thomas: *Painters and Public Life in Eighteenth-Century Paris*. New Haven – London 1985. See SEIBERLING 1998 (see note 216), p. 143.

[242] MAINARDI, Patricia: *The End of the Salon. Art and the State in the Early Third Republic*. Cambridge 1993.

[243] SOLKIN, David H.: *Painting for Money. The Visual Arts and the Public Sphere in Eighteenth-Century England*. New Haven 1993.

[244] See SEIBERLING 1998 (see note 216), pp. 142-143.

[245] JENSEN, Robert: *Marketing Modernism in Fin-de-siècle Europe*. Princeton 1994.

[246] SEIBERLING 1998 (see note 216), p. 143.

[247] FITZGERALD, Michael C.: *Making Modernism: Picasso and the Creation of the Market for Twentieth-Century Art*. New York 1995.

shaping his work (taking part in the selection process).[248] M. C. Fitzgerald even came to the general conclusion that *"such [commercial; J. B.] calculation... was central to the Avant-garde tradition that began in the middle of the nineteenth century and that still defines the artist as an enterpreneur in modern culture."*[249] Oskar Bätschmann in his *Ausstellungskünstler*[250] discusses how the transformation of the artist's status from courtier to a free exhibiting enterpreneur resulted in dilemmas that artists gradually learned to overcome, having developed highly sophisticated marketing strategies.

Nevertheless, hesitation about the unequivocally positive role of the market still remains among specialists in art market history. Elizabeth Alice Honig, for example, in her *Painting & the Market in Early Modern Antwerp*[251], examining interactions between painters and markets within early burgeoning capitalism, *"as art became increasingly defined as an alluring commodity"* and *"painters tried to produce works that would appeal to the taste of consumers"*[252], did not transcend avant-garde axiology. She not only emphasized the active role of aesthetics in shaping the art market: *"... the roots of collecting and valuing paintings lay within the context of a developing aesthetics of exchange and display"*[253] but also characterized the art market as a negative element: *"The logic of the marketplace is that of trickery, of deceits that may undermine the certainties of 'value' or 'values' formed outside its compass."*[254]

XI.

Challenging the myth of independent and abstract artistic creation while at the same time regarding the art market as *"a driving force"* in the field of modern cultural production can be identified as a common denominator of the majority of those studies. According to Grace Seiberling: *"... the art market is viewed as a participant in a dynamic process of negotiating cultural meaning."*[255] In other words, the art/market relationship is conceived no longer as an antin-

---

[248] Ibid., p. 12.

[249] Ibid., p. 268.

[250] BÄTSCHMANN, Oskar: *Ausstellungskünstler. Kult und Karriere im modernen Kunstsystem*. Köln 1997; English translation: *The Artist in the Modern World*, with its symptomatic subtitle *The Conflict between Market and Self-Expression* (Cologne – Bonn 1998).

[251] HONIG, Elizabeth A.: *Painting & the Market in Early Modern Antwerp*. New Haven – London 1998.

[252] I quote the text on the book wrapper.

[253] Ibid.

[254] Ibid., p. 213.

[255] SEIBERLING 1998 (see note 216), p. 146.

omy nor as a system based on a one-sided exploitation (of artists by dealers) but on a dialectical reciprocity or even regarded as a *"harmonious conjunction"*. In addition, for Michele Bogart, *"the harmonious conjunction of art and commerce would also help society to reach its fullest potential"*.[256]

Due to the acceptance of an affirmative role for the market in the art-world as well as to the belief that no *"cultural subgroup"* (including the community of artists) is able *"to withstand the owerhelming power of capitalism and commercialism"*,[257] the relation between artistic freedom and commercial success has also been radically redefined. Freedom from the market ceased to be regarded as a prerequisite for creativity, and commercial success ceased to be conceived of as an antithesis to artistic quality.[258] According to advocates of postmodern capitalism, the success of avant-garde artists *"owes as much to their complicity with capitalist forces as to their defiance of them"*.[259] Consequently, *"the price for artistic autonomy is dependency on financial power"*.[260] That is why *"the romanticized view of starving artists as creative geniuses who are misunderstood in their lifetime"* has been replaced *"with a realistic picture of artists as producers of goods... for which some are lavishly rewarded"*.[261] For the same reason, the belief in *"the separation between fine and commercial arts"* was revealed as a myth.[262] Consequently, also *"the old myth of the freedom that comes with fine arts was being replaced by"* – we can add, a postmodern – *"myth that freedom comes with commercial success"*.[263] Or in Thierry de Duve's words: *"Yes, artists are free: they are free to exchange and exchange whatever, but only there where exchange takes place, in the market. They are also free to do whatever, but the violence of this freedom is no longer that of revolution, it is merely that of economic competition."*[264]

It was Russian philosopher and art theorist Boris Groys who went a step further towards rehabilitating, in a sense, the worship of money or commodity fetishism. According to him, the *"predominance of money"* can be regarded as an universal religion, *"the new religion of money and the market"*. (*"Vielmehr*

---

[256] BOGART, Michele H.: *Artists, Advertising, and the Borders of Art.* Chicago 1995. Quoted according to SASSOWER, Raphael – CICOTELLO, Louis: *The Golden Avant-gard. Idolatry, Commercialism, and Art.* Charlottesville – London 2000, p. 131.

[257] Ibid., quoted from the book wrapper.

[258] According to SASSOWER – CICOTELLO 2000 (see note 256), p. 53, *"what determines, classifies, and reifies human creation into artworks is the willingness of people to pay for them and extract them from circulation"*. As we can see, the author's anti-Marxist position is unequivocally expressed in their notion of artwork (or artistic value) as substantially dependent on exchange value.

[259] Ibid., quoted from the book wrapper.

[260] Ibid., p. 129.

[261] Ibid., p. 8.

[262] Ibid., p. 130.

[263] Ibid., p. 131.

[264] DUVE, Thierry de: *Kant after Duchamp.* Cambridge – London 1996, p. 350.

leben wir in der Zeit einer neuen Religion des Geldes und des Marktes, welche die alten Religionen vor allem deswegen abgelöst hat, weil sie mit einem noch radikaleren Anspruch auf Universalität aufgetreten ist.")[265] Nevertheless, religion is not here regarded in the Marxist way as *"an opium of mankind"* or a means of brainwashing but as a collective faith or worldview by Groys. For him, *"the cultural omnipotence of the market"* (*"die kulturelle Allmacht des Marktes"*)[266] transforms everything including art into *"the function of the market"* without disgracing it. (*"Die Kunst [ist] in unserer Zeit endgültig zum Teil und zur Funktion des Marktes geworden."*)[267] On the contrary, *"art manifests in a radical way subjective, mental [spiritual] dimension of money, the inner, mysterious connection between number and feeling"* (*"Die Kunst manifestiert zunächst einmal mit einmaliger Radikalität die subjektive, seelische Dimension des Geldes, eine innere, rätselhafte Verknüpfung zwischen Zahl und Gefühl."*),[268] i.e. *"the inner feeling of a hidden presence of money in all things"* (*"das innere Empfinden einer verborgenen Geldpräsenz in allen Dingen"*).[269] The art of Modernism in particular, cannot be understood without *"the new, quasi-Christian mystique of money"* (*"Ohne diese neue, quasi-christliche Mystik des Geldes ist die Kunst der Moderne undenkbar."*), according to Groys.[270] *"Modern art seems to have been a revelation of the depest secret of money"* (*"Die moderne Kunst scheint zur Offenbarung des tiefsten Geheimnisses des Geldes geworden zu sein."*)[271] and the *"modern artist is a money-Saint or... a mystic stock exchange agent".* (*"Der Moderne Künstler ist ein Geldheiliger, oder, anders gesagt, ein mystischer Börsespekulant."*)[272] Mixing justification of the hegemony of the market with the critical unmasking of the commercial orientation of modern artists, Groys also puts in question the Marxist antinomy of art versus the market or aesthetic versus commodity value. According to him, *"the conflict between aesthetics and economy is absolutly fictitious".* (*"Der Konflikt zwischen dem Ästhetischen und dem Ökonomischen ist... volkommen fiktiv."*)[273] Or in other words, there is no longer *"the opposition commerce versus not commerce, market*

---

[265] GROYS, Boris: Die Sprache des Geldes, in *Wiener Slawistischer Almanach*, 50, 2002; reprinted in GROYS, Boris: *Topologie der Kunst.* München – Wien 2003, p. 256.

[266] Ibid., p. 257.

[267] Ibid.

[268] Ibid., p. 258.

[269] Ibid., pp. 258-259.

[270] Ibid., p. 261.

[271] Ibid.

[272] Ibid. The shift from the avant-garde to the post-modern concept of the artist's relationship to the market, or from the critique to the affirmation, is particularly evident when we compare Groy's notion of the modern artist as *"a money Saint"* with Karel Teige's characterization of the artist corrupted by the market as *"aesthetic courtesan".* See note 21.

[273] Ibid., p. 264.

versus not market, or commodity versus truth. (*"Es geht heute nicht mehr wie früher um die Opposition kommerziell vs. nicht-kommerziell oder Markt vs. Nicht-Markt oder die Ware vs. das Wahre, sondern um durchaus unterschiedbare und oft sogar gegensätzliche Marktstrategien."*)[274] The difference between exclusiveness, rarity and singularity on the one and mass commodity production on the other, must be conceived of as a consequence of two simultaneously existing and dialectically linked markets and their different market strategies: the *"closed market"* destined for an élite of insiders or connoisseurs on the one hand and the *"open market"* with products of mass culture for the public at large, on the other.[275] Despite the affinity with Bourdieu's distinction between *"two modes of production"* (i.e. *"production for producers"* and *"production for the public at large"*),[276] Groys's intention seems to be entirely different: not to unmask the strategy of concealed social domination but to justify the postmodern *"harmonious"* status quo. (*"Die innere Einheit zwischen den ästhetischen, ideologischen und ökonomischen Strategien wird hier endgültig manifest."*)[277] As we can see, this prophet, coming from a defeated communist Russia, confirms the final victory of Western global capitalism.

XII.

To conclude this survey, it might be worth mentioning that academic art history itself represents a small wheel of the market megamachine and cannot transcend it. As a matter of fact, within the commercial society everything art historians do is being swallowed up by market calculation, evaluation and pricing. As Grace Seiberling expressed it: *"the 'discovery' and the reconstruction of artist's careers, and especially the authentication of works of art* [and we might add: all art historical writings without any exception] *inevitably affect market values"*[278] (i.e. market prices) directly or indirectly. And so *"a consciousness of the market has involved a challenge* [not only] *to the notion of pure art, but also to that of disinterested scholarship"*.[279] In Charles W. Haxthausen's words: *"However*

---

[274] Ibid., p. 267.

[275] Ibid., pp. 262-264.

[276] See note 220.

[277] GROYS 2003 (see note 265), pp. 266-267.

[278] SEIBERLING 1998 (see note 216), p. 146.

[279] Ibid. Or in Ivan Gaskell's words: *"One of the cornerstones of... art history is the market in art... scholars bolster the market... Even scholars whose writings lead one to believe that they might be inimical to the market can participate within it."* – GASKELL, Ivan: Tradesmen as Scholars: Interdependencies in the Study and Exchange of Art, in *Art History and Its Institutions* (see note 4), pp. 158-159.

removed academics may feel from the marketplace... what they say and write can be deployed to serve the interest of commerce."[280] Therefore, *"historians... who take the art market into accont must recognize... their own involvement in the networks that make them".*[281]

Given that the involvement of art historians in the art market can be considered as indirect or implicit, then the merchandizing role of art critics is entirely explicit and direct. Given that *"artworks are commodities in our culture, high-priced things for sale in the galleries"*[282] and that *"aesthetic judgments directly imply economic judgments"*,[283] then not only can *"contemporary theories of art"* be regarded *"as marketing strategies, as ways of advertising art"*,[284] but also *"the critic's role in the present art world system is to promote artworks, to persuade people to buy them"*,[285] as David Carrier expressed it.

Whether art historians and critics want it or not, art history and art criticism are being included in the process of the perpetuation and recycling of the mass market society. Thus, the painful qestion put by Jutta Held still remains unanswered: can the withdrawal from ideological critique be regarded as a consequence of the fall of all great utopias and an expression of the global victory of capital? Does the fact that our theories are embedded in the present necessarily mean that they are nothing more than obedient vehicles and recycling tools for the ideological justification of the status quo? Is there no other escape from this imprisonment in the market megamachine than a turn to new utopias? Moreover, does critical and selfreflexive analysis represent

---

[280] *The Two Art Histories. The Museum and the University.* Ed. Charles W. HAXTHAUSEN. New Haven – London 2002, Introduction, p. XV. More about that GASKELL, Ivan: Magnanimity and Paranoia in the Big Bad Art World, ibid., pp. 14-24; GASKELL 2002 (see note 279), pp. 146-162.

[281] SEIBERLING 1998 (see note 216), p. 146.

[282] CARRIER, David: Art and Its Market, in *Theories of Contemporary Art.* Ed. Richard HERTZ. Englewood Cliffs 1985, p. 193.

[283] Ibid., p. 202.

[284] Ibid., p. 199.

[285] Ibid., p. 198. Compare it with Timothy J. Clark's moralizing critique: *"I don't propose to discuss the way in which art history became manservant of the art market, checking dates for the dealers, providing pedigrees for rich collectors – though I'm surrounded by evidence of the stupidity, and straightforward corruption, that resulted."* – CLARK 1974 (see note 94) in FERNIE 1995 (see note 94), p. 250. Clark invoked Kurt W. Forster who *"has written elsewhere of the way in which art history became the vehicle for reach-me-down notions of taste, order and the good life, 'compensatory history' for the 'Bildungsbürgertum'".* – Ibid., p. 250. Clark referred to K. W. Forster's paper "Critical History of Art, or Transfiguration of Values?" (quoted in note 9). According to GASKELL 2002 (see note 279), p. 147: *"Social histories of art whether loosely Marxist-inspired or not, or, more recently, motivated by feminist or queer theorizing, largely sidestep or explicitly repudiate concerns that appear to have direct art market application. The same can be said of those recently established theoretical orthodoxies based on linguistics or psychoanalysis."*

a residuum of already falsified avant-garde utopias or a Pontius Pilate-type theatrical ritual of cathartic washing of hands? Whatever the answer, the present is offering not only new rituals but also opening new epistemological perspectives. The challenge should be accepted.

V. IN DEFENCE OF LIBERAL „HUMANISM": GOMBRICH'S STRUGGLE AGAINST METAPHYSICS

> *"The greatest compliment to be paid to Gombrich would be to treat his theories with the seriousness which they deserve, and to examine their ideological and philosophical basis."*
>
> Stephen Bann[*]

"Hypostatized Collective Personalities"

In the German art historical journal *Kritische Berichte* (1937), the twenty-eight years old Ernst Gombrich, who had already immigrated to London, reviewed Ernst von Garger's essay "Über die Wertungsschwierigkeiten bei mittelalterlicher Kunst".[1] Max Dvořák's disciple Ernst von Garger had referred to Alois Riegl's theory of *"Kunstwollen"* in order to improve its vague distinction between *"intention"* and *"achievement"* (*"Wollen"* and *"Können"*). He proposed to estimate the value of a medieval work of art by comparing its original intention and final achievement. But Garger's solution was resolutely rejected by the young Gombrich. He argued that Garger's idea of medieval art understood in terms of intention was in principle wrong.

According to Gombrich, medieval works of art falling within the category of *"primitive mode of image making"* had to be conceived in terms of a *"conceptual image"* and *"pictorial writing"*. Following his teacher Julius von Schlosser's notion of medieval art as rooted in tradition and convention and, as a consequence, based on schemes and stereotypes, Gombrich also implicitly rejected Max Dvořák's and Ernst von Garger's interpretation of medieval art as expression, including *"the widely held assumption that... the so-called transcendentalism of medieval art is a direct reflection of transcendental metaphysics"*.[2] However, neither

---

[*]   BANN, Stephen: How Revolutionary is the New Art History, in *The New Art History*. Eds. Alan L. REES – Frances BORZELLO. London 1986, p. 22.

[1]   GOMBRICH, Ernst H.: *Meditations on a Hobby Horse and Other Essays on the Theory of Art*. London 1963, pp. 70-77. See BAKOŠ, Ján: The Vienna School's Hundred and Sixty-Eighth Graduate: The Vienna School's Ideas Revised by E. H. Gombrich, in *Gombrich on Art and Psychology*. Ed. Richard WOODFIELD. Manchester – New York 1996, pp. 234-261.

[2]   Ibid., p. 75.

the idea of the history of art as the history of intentions nor the notion of art as the expression of a worldview were the only targets of Gombrich's criticism. He also firmly rejected belief in *"hypostatized collective personalities – either of a people or a period"*[3] – regarded as carriers of the history of art, and in styles conceived of as their expressions. Metaphysical collectivism, expressionism and relativism, the three main targets of Gombrich's lifelong polemics against metaphysics in art history, had already been addressed in the review of Garger's essay. In the ensuing polemics, lasting more than six decades, Gombrich developed, enlarged, improved on and reiterated these original arguments. Even in his last posthumously published book *The Preference for the Primitive* (2002), Gombrich repeated his reservations about Riegl's relativistic idea of the history of art as the history of incommensurable intentions and its variant, Dvořák's history of art as the history of worldviews.[4]

In fact, it was not Garger himself, but Riegl and his theory of *"Kunstwollen"* (*"will to form"*), Dvořák's *"Geistesgeschichte"* (*"the history of ideas"*) and Hegel's philosophy of history that were above all the implicit addressees of Gombrich's critique. The importance attached to this early paper was confirmed by Gombrich himself, when he included it under the title "Achievement in Medieval Art" among his *Meditations on a Hobby Horse and Other Essays on the Theory of Art* published sixteen years later in 1963.[5]

"Trugbild einer 'autonomen' logischen Entwicklung"

During World War II, Gombrich was *"largely removed from scholarhip"* since *"he was occupied with the exacting job of radio monitor, listening to and retailing the content of German broadcasts"*.[6] After the War, he resumed the critique of Riegl's theory of art history in the Swiss encyclopedia *Das Atlantisbuch der Kunst*.[7] Explicitly declaring Riegl's belief in the autonomy of the evolution of art to be an abstraction or even a phantom (*"Trugbild"*) and blaming Riegl for neglecting *"ausserkünstlerische Motivierungen politischer oder soziologischer*

---

[3]   Ibid.

[4]   GOMBRICH, Ernst H.: *The Preference for the Primitive. Episodes in the History of Western Taste and Art*. London 2002, pp. 35-37.

[5]   GOMBRICH 1963 (see note 1).

[6]   McGRATH, Elisabeth: E. H. Gombrich (1908 – 2001), in *The Burlington Magazine*, 144, 2002, pp. 111-115.

[7]   GOMBRICH, Ernst H.: Kunstwissenschaft, in *Atlantisbuch der Kunst. Eine Enzyklopädie der bildenden Künste*. Zürich 1952, pp. 653-664.

Natur",[8] Gombrich did not however, reject the idea of the autonomy of the evolution of art as such. According to him, the autonomy could be accepted if understood as a concrete artistic (workshop) tradition instead of as an abstract intention (*"Kunstwollen"*). But Gombrich's critique of Riegl's theory was aimed this time, primarily against its Hegelian inspiration. Following Hegel, Riegl attempted *"diese 'autonome' Entwicklung der Formen... in der Entwicklung des Zeigeistes zu verankern"*, according to Gombrich.[9] Thus, adopting Hegel's holism, he presupposed *a priori,* the unity of all expressions of any particular age while hypostatizing the existence of such entities as *"people"* (*"Volk"*) or *"race"* (*"Rasse"*), regarded as the *"carriers of the evolution"* (*"Träger der Entwicklung"*) of art.[10] As a consequence, Riegl assumed that *"der 'Stil' sei ein Schlüssel zum 'Wesen' einer Zeit oder eines Volkes"*.[11]

"The Intellectual Mousetrap of Dialectical Materialism"

Sharing with Karl Popper his aversion to all forms of Hegelianism, as expressed in Popper's creed: *"I have not the slightest sympathy with these 'spirits', neither with their idealistic prototype nor with their dialectical and materialistic incarnations, and I am in full sympathy with those who treat them with contempt"*,[12] Gombrich made use of the review of Arnold Hauser's *The Social History of Art* to take a strong line against the Marxist version of Hegelianism.[13] According to Gombrich, Hauser, despite his attempt at a materialist social history of art, became stuck *"within the fantasy-world of Hegel's metaphysical system"*. Consequently, *"he has caught himself in the intellectual mousetrat of 'dialectical materialism'... untroubled by the discovery of contradictions"*.[14] Moreover, Hauser as *"a collectivist"* *"believed in nations, races or periods"* and replaced them only with social classes regarded henceforth *"as unified psychological entities"*.[15] As a result, he maintained, according to Gombrich, that the problematic idea of *"style"* in art, understood as an expression of collectives, was now to be interpreted in a Marxist way as *"an expression of the class-situation"* or *"an indication*

---

8   Ibid., p. 661.
9   Ibid., p. 660.
10   Ibid., pp. 661-662.
11   Ibid., p. 661.
12   GOMBRICH, Ernst H.: *Art and Illusion. A Study in the Psychology of Pictorial Representation.* London 2002 (1st ed. London 1960), p. 17.
13   GOMBRICH 1963 (see note 1), pp. 86-94.
14   Ibid., pp. 86, 88, 91.
15   Ibid., p. 91.

of social and intellectual change.[16] Thus Hauser believed in impersonal social determinism rather than realizing that *"what we bundle together under the name of art has"*, according to Gombrich, *"a constantly changing function in the social organism of different periods... because form follows function"*.[17] The idea of the function of art used as an argument against expressionist historicism, articulated by Gombrich two years earlier in the essay "Meditations on a Hobby Horse, or the Roots of Artistic Form" (1951) was reiterated here.

"Style: This Imaginary Super-Artist"

Metaphysical collectivism and expressionism were also targeted by Gombrich in his review of André Malreaux's *The Voices of Silence*.[18] In Malraux's expressionist history of art, Gombrich found *"the neglect of social setting and function of images"*, *"the uncritical faith that the visual arts provided the shortest route to the mentality of civilisations"*, *"the Romantic belief that style – this imaginary super-artist... expressed the 'world view' of a civilisation"* or *"the spirit of the respective age"*, and that *"each style of a period or race directly mirrors its group-mind"*.[19] But the expressionist idea that historical changes in style reflected changes in group mentality must, according to Gombrich, lead to the kind of extreme relativism articulated by Oswald Spengler. Gombrich resolutely rejected Spengler's conclusion that *"each culture represents a different species"* and that, consequently, *"the concept of mankind is empty"*.[20] He also strongly opposed the kind of epistemological relativism according to which *"the historian being immured in his own culture can never understand, only describe"*. Echoing Popper's theory of science as based on the testing/falsifying of hypotheses, Gombrich expressed the conviction that *"critical reason... can... advance towards the truth by testing interpretations, by sifting the evidence... narrowing the scope of myth"*.[21] He also referred to Malreaux's idea of *"le musée imaginaire"* (the *"Museum without Walls"*) characterized sceptically by Gombrich as *"a temple dedicated to a myth"*.

---

16   Ibid., pp. 91, 118.
17   Ibid., p. 91.
18   Ibid., pp. 78-85.
19   Ibid., pp. 79-80, 82.
20   Ibid., p. 83.
21   Ibid., p. 85.

"The Simulacrum of an Explanation Hostile to Scholarship"

Even if there is, according to Gombrich, " *the essential difference... between the role of research in the sciences and in the humanities*" and "*the scientist... is ultimately valued for his discoveries rather than his knowledge*" while "*humanistic education aims first and foremost at knowledge*", he is convinced that "*the study of art can be conducted in a rational way*".[22] Using the clear difference between science and myth, or "*truth*" and "*falsehood*", as his starting point, Gombrich believes that "*where scholarship decays, myth will crowd in.*"[23] In his inaugural lecture *Art and Scholarship* at University College, London in February 1957, Gombrich decided to challenge the most ambitious theories of art history which pretended to scientific status.[24] Riegl's theory and Viennese Structuralism and iconology received particular attention here. According to Gombrich, Riegl's theory of "*Kunstwollen*" is more myth than scientific explanation: "*Riegl's idea that all style is intentional has obscured rather than illuminated the problem*" and, as a consequence, "*this type of explanation is not only hostile to reason; it is also hostile to scholarship because it produces that simulacrum of an explanation which put an end to further research*".[25] Nevertheless, Riegl's scientific ambition failed not only because he "*fell victim to... the fetishism of the single cause*", according to Gombrich, but also because he had found the carrier of "*Kunstwollen*" "*in those Hegelian collectives, the spirit of the age and the spirit of the race*".[26]

In addition, Gombrich came to the conclusion that not only the intellectual variant of Riegl's theory, i.e. the history of art as the history of worldviews, but also the iconology fell victim to Hegel's holism: "*Iconology is subject to the same dangers to which the interpretation of styles had been so prone, the danger of circularity.*"[27]

But neither did the Viennese Structuralists' attempt at a "*new Kunstwissenschaft*" achieve success. Their ambition to base "*rigorous science*" on analysing the structure of a single work of art failed, according to Gombrich, "*for surely it is not scientific to take signs... out of context, and investigate their 'structure'.*"[28] Paradoxically, this structuralist immanent approach resulted in metaphysical essentialism: "*This procedure only leads to... the myth that the system of signs, the*

---

[22] GOMBRICH, Ernst H.: *Ideals and Idols. Essays on Values in History and in Art*. Oxford 1979, pp. 57-58.

[23] GOMBRICH 1963 (see note 1), p. 107.

[24] Ibid., pp. 106-119.

[25] Ibid., pp. 117.

[26] Ibid., pp. 114.

[27] Ibid., p. 116.

[28] Ibid., p. 112.

style, is not a language but an utterance of the collective, in which a nation or an age speaks to us."[29]

"Physiognomic Fallacy"

The art historical models mentioned above share in common *"the tendency to see the past in terms of its typical style"*, known as the *"physiognomic fallacy"*, in Gombrich's own terminology.[30] This tendency *"would be a harmless fallacy"* if it did not result in relativism, according to Gombrich; *"if it did not strengthen the illusion that mankind changed as dramatically and thoroughly as did art"*.[31] However, Gombrich claims to know the way out of all these metaphysical *"pitfalls"*. Besides taking into consideration *"a change of function in the image"*, Gombrich calls for the revival of a "craftsmanship" idea of art as follows: *"We may have to retrace our steps to Vasari and acknowledge the role of skill, of the learning process which is involved."*[32]

"Mythological Explanation Weakens Resistance to Totalitarian Habits of Mind"

In Gombrich's opus magnum *Art and Illusion* (1960), relativism became the main target of his critique. Riegl's attempt *"to account for all stylistic changes by one unitary principle… made him a prey to prescientific habits… the habits of myth-makers"*, according to Gombrich.[33] His *"Kunstwollen"* (*"will to form"*) – a kind of *"a ghost in the machine"* – has its origin in Hegel's philosophy of history as well as in his idea of art as the *"expression of the age… and a symptom… of the World Spirit"*. But *"this reliance of art history on mythological explanations"* is not only *"pre-scientific"*, according to Gombrich, it is even *"dangerous"*. As he put it: *"By inculcating the habit of talking in terms of collectives, of 'mankind', 'races', or 'ages', it weakens resistance to totalitarian habits of mind."*[34] This political radicalization of Gombrich's polemics had surely been inspired by Karl Popper's pillorying of all forms of totalitarianism. But the immediate impulse to come to grips with an extreme relativism followed on from Hans Sedlmayr's interpre-

---

[29]   Ibid.
[30]   Ibid., p. 108.
[31]   Ibid.
[32]   Ibid., p. 117.
[33]   GOMBRICH 1960 (see note 12), p. 16.
[34]   Ibid., p. 17.

tation of Riegls theory.[35] Gombrich professed proudly to *"all those... ideas which Sedlmayr... asked [us]... to discard in favour of a Spenglerian historicism".*[36] He *"passionately believes"* in the idea, that *"only individual human beings are real while groups and spiritual collectives are mere names"*, *"in the unity and immutability of human nature and human reason"*, in the idea that *"nature remains the same and is only represented 'in different modes'"*, and in *"the causal analysis of history"* which *"conceives of historical change merely as a resultant of blind and isolated chains of causation".*[37] Gombrich further believes that: *"There are few historians today, and even fewer anthropologists who believe that mankind has undergone any marked biological change within historical periods... even those who might admit the possibility of some slight oscilation in genetic make-up of mankind would never accept the idea that man has changed as much... as have his art and his style."*[38]

"The History of Preferences"

On the other hand, Gombrich does not, in general, contest the existence of *"attitudes, beliefs, or tastes that are shared by many... as the mentality or outlook dominant in a class, generation, or nation"*. Rejecting only their metaphysical interpretation, he is convinced that *"changes in intellectual climate and changes in fashion or taste"* can be interpreted sociologically as *"symptomatic of social change".*[39] According to Gombrich, styles in art can also be regarded as sociological phenomena, as *"problems arising within a tradition... as instances of such traditions"*. Besides, Gombrich emphasises that the idea of *"styles as symptomatic of something else"* presupposes *"some theory of alternatives"* because *"an act of choice... is expressive of something only if we can reconstruct the choice situation".*[40] Consequently: *"The history of taste and fashion"*, and we can add that the same is true of the history of styles, is not the history of automatic expressions or indexes but *"is the history of preferences, of various acts of choice between given alternatives".*[41] If, on the contrary, changes are conceived of as autonomous (*"change becomes the symptom of change as such"*) and *"this tautology"*

---

[35] SEDLMAYR, Hans: Die Quintessenz der Lehren Riegls (1927), in RIEGL, Alois: *Gesammelte Aufsätze*. Augsburg – Wien 1929 (2nd ed. 1996), pp. XII-XXXIII; English translation in *Framing Formalism, Riegl's Work*. Ed. Richard WOODFIELD. Amsterdam 2001.
[36] GOMBRICH 1960 (see note 12) p. 17.
[37] Ibid., p. 17.
[38] Ibid., p. 18.
[39] Ibid., p. 17.
[40] Ibid., p. 18.
[41] Ibid.

is hidden, then, according to Gombrich, *"some grandiose scheme of evolution has to be called in, as happened not only to Riegl, but to many of his successors"*.[42] In that sense: *"Evolutionism is dead but the facts which gave rise to its myth are still stubbornly there to be accounted for"*, according to Gombrich.[43] Thus *"what is their [i.e. Riegl's and his followers and interpreters] greatest pride is in fact their fatal flaw: by throwing out the idea of skill... they have made it impossible to realize their ambition, a valid psychology of stylistic change"*.[44]

"The Enemies of Reason" and "Mumbo-Jumbo"

However, Gombrich was confronted very early with the fact that neither metaphysical essentialism nor relativism was as dead as he believed them to be. The Festschrift *Kunstgeschichte und Kunsttheorie im 19. Jahrhundert. Probleme der Kunstwissenschaft I* (1963), devoted to Hans Sedlmayr's 65th anniversary by his disciples, provoked Gombrich to utter very *"harsh words against the enemies of reason"* because *"the failure to speak out against them... has caused enough disasters"*.[45] He strongly criticized the essentialist belief in the *"ontological place of Kunstwissenschaft"* or the idea that *"the art historian must for ever stick to the essential last"*. Sedlmayr's claim that the value of Structuralism can be seen *"inter alia in the recognition that 'reason is a variable that changes with history'"* has been resolutely rejected by Gombrich as *"mumbo-jumbo"* from which such nonsense could be deduced as: *"art being both everything and nothing"* or that *"art is not a fit subject for a 'science' or for any discussion, since all statements... will equally apply, as will their contradictions"*.[46]

"The Hegelian Wheel" and "a Circular Reasoning"

The Philipe Maurice Deneke Lecture *In Search of Cultural History* delivered by Gombrich at Lady Margarett Hall, Oxford on November 1967 provided him with an occasion for unmasking the hegemony of Hegelianism in art history. According to Gombrich, Hegelians *"have blocked the emergence of a true*

---

[42] Ibid.

[43] Ibid.

[44] Ibid., p. 17.

[45] GOMBRICH, Ernst H.: [Review of] Kunstgeschichte und Kunsttheorie im 19. Jahrhundert. Probleme der Kunstwissenschaft I. Berlin 1963, in *The Art Bulletin*, 46, 1964, pp. 418-420.

[46] Ibid., pp. 418-419.

cultural history".[47] The true cultural history, according to him, has to avoid metaphysical collectivism as well as *"the belief in the existence of an independent supra-individual collective spirit"* and *"fix its attention firmly on the individual human being"*[48]. Thus, the belief in *"a collective, the supra-individual entities of nations and periods"* must be superseded by the individualist notion of *"movements... started by people"*.[49] Besides, *"the Hegelian Wheel"*, must also be banished i.e. the holistic belief in *"the unity of all manifestations of a civilisation"*, the belief that they were all *"the expression of the same... national spirit"*.[50] The expressionist premise that *"everything must be treated not only as connected with everything else, but as a symptom of something else"*[51] results, according to Gombrich, in a circular reasoning that *"finds in every factural detail the general principle that underlies it"*.[52]

Nevertheless, metaphysical collectivism and holism lead inevitably towards a relativism that represents another obstacle to true cultural history. As Gombrich puts it, since *"the changing styles of art... become the index of changing spirit"* and *"since the individual... could only be thought of as a part of such collective it was quite consistent for Hegelians to assume that 'man' underwent profound changes in the course of history"*.[53] But relativism results not only in the pessimist assumption that *"different species of man could never understand each other"*, but also in the projects of *"the totalitarian philosophies... to create a new man"*. In order to avoid that, the true cultural history has to *"resist the temptation to use changing styles and changing fashions as indicators of profound psychological changes... a radical change in the mental make-up"*.[54]

"Holistic Conviction"

Gombrich's item on "Style" in the *International Encyclopedia of Social Sciences*[55] provided an occasion to return to the critique of Riegl's evolutionism on the one hand and to develop the criticism of Hegel's holism on the other. The way out of metaphysical determinism that was characteristic of art his-

---

[47] GOMBRICH 1979 (see note 22), p. 50.
[48] Ibid.
[49] Ibid.
[50] Ibid., p. 42.
[51] Ibid., p. 46.
[52] Ibid.
[53] Ibid., pp. 34, 50.
[54] Ibid., pp. 50, 51.
[55] GOMBRICH, Ernst H.: Style, in *International Encyclopedia of Social Sciences*. New York 1968, Vol. 15, pp. 352-361.

torical evolutionism can be found, according to Gombrich, only by conceiving of *"the future as open"* and resisting *"the temptation... to regard the outcome... as inevitable"*. In addition, the evolutionary notion of *"a continuous chain of development"* must be regarded, according to Gombrich, as *"the tradition within which the masters concerned operated"*.[56]

As far as the *"holistic conviction"*, i.e. the belief in *"one unitary principle"*, *"one common centre"* or *"central cause from which all the characteristics of a period can be deduced"* is concerned, Gombrich states that such a *"connection is assumed on metaphysical grounds"* because *"there is no necessary connection between one aspect of a group's activities and any other"*.[57] *"What distinguishes all these* [i.e. holistic; J. B.] *theories from a genuintly scientific search for causal connections is their a priori character"* and *"arguing in a circle"*.[58]

"Hegel's 'Giants' and 'Siren Songs'"

Gombrich's lecture on *A Reading of the Lectures on Aesthetics of G. W. F. Hegel,* delivered when he was awarded the Hegel Prize of the City of Stuttgart in February 1977, can be regarded as a summary of Gombrich's critical handling of Hegel.[59] He appreciated Hegel as *"The Father of Art History"*,[60] the founder of universal/world history of art, on the one hand, yet still held him responsible for all the metaphysical confusion and pre-scientific failures of art history on the other. The following metaphysical *"giants"* of Hegel's aesthetics were enumerated by Gombrich: *"aesthetic transcendentalism"*, *"historical collectivism"*, *"historical determinism"*, *"metaphysical optimism"*, and *"dialectical relativism"*. *"The dangerous allures of these siren songs"* ensued, according to him, not only from the deep influence of (Hegel's) philosophy on *"the further course of events"*, but also from *"its temptingly easy applicability"*.[61] And concerning *"the dialectic"*, it justifies the relativistic assertion that *"every method of interpretation can claim success"* since it *"makes [it] all too easy... to find a way out of every contradiction"*.[62]

---

[56]   Ibid., p. 357.

[57]   Ibid., p. 358.

[58]   Ibid., pp. 357-358.

[59]   SUMMERS, David: E. H. Gombrich and the Tradition of Hegel, in *A Companion to Art Theory.* Eds. Paul SMITH – Carolyn WILDE. Oxford 2002, pp. 139-149, here p. 143.

[60]   GOMBRICH, Ernst H.: *Tributes. Interpreters of Our Cultural Tradition.* Oxford 1984.

[61]   Ibid., pp. 62-63.

[62]   Ibid., p. 63.

Despite that, Gombrich does not *"wish to create the impression that he lacks respect for these masters"*, i.e. for Hegel and his followers. As he assures us: *"It cannot be too often repeated that the best tribute that one can pay a scholar is to take him seriously and constantly to reappraise his line of argument."*[63] No doubt, this at least holds true for Gombrich's relationship to Hegel.

"Canon of Excellence"

As a part of the Roman lecture, *Art History and Social Sciences*, delivered by Gombrich at the Sheldonian Theatre, Oxford on 22 November 1973, the topic of cognitive relativism was dealt with as follows: *"There are some who even wish to deprive science of the claim to serve the truth"* and *"even scientific truth has been described as relative to the society that practices it, so that the history of science should really be written not as a story of discoveries and problem solutions but merely as the account of the changing bahaviour of those members of society who call themselves scientists."*[64] But Gombrich has no sympathy with other kinds of relativism either. *"I happen to have no more sympathy for moral relativism than I have for the aesthetic variety."*[65] He accepts neither *"stylistic relativism"* according to which *"different styles resemble different games which have their own yardstics of success"*[66] nor epistemological subjectivism, i.e. the idea that *"the work of art means what it means to us, there is no other criterion"*. Despite the historicity of art, with its implication that *"art is not a game with fixed rules but makes up the rules as it goes along"* which leads to the kind of *"radical relativism"* according to which *"we can only compare performances within the same game"*,[67] Gombrich dares *"to assert that even in the elusive region of aesthetic judgment there are statements which are true and others which are false"*.[68] As a consequence, the critique of relativism is transformed into an *apologia* for the universality of artistic values. Gombrich believes that *"our response to art is rooted in human nature and must therefore be universal"* and that *"there is something universally human in psychological states we have seen embodied in art"*.[69] According to him, *"to insist on this universality is not to ignore the surprising plasticity of 'human nature'"*, since all art forms *"be-*

---

[63]   Ibid., p. 62.
[64]   GOMBRICH 1979 (see note 22), pp. 141.
[65]   Ibid., p. 162.
[66]   Ibid., p. 154.
[67]   Ibid.
[68]   Ibid., p. 144.
[69]   Ibid., p. 158.

long to the common experience of humanity".[70] Thus Gombrich also believes in the *"objective criteria of artistic mastery"* and *"in the objectivity of aesthetic values"*.[71] As a consequence, following his teacher Julius von Schlosser, Gombrich insists on the individualist idea of the history of art: *"The history of art"*, according to him, *"is rightly considered to be the history of masterpieces and of the 'old masters'."*[72] It leads to a transhistorical notion of artistic values. Even if *"invariably rooted in the life and value system of their age and society"*, masterpieces of art *"transcend these situations"* and *"stand the test of time not as formal exercises but as embodiment of a value system which teach us to recognize."*[73] They represent the *"canon of excellence"* which *"plays the real role in any culture"* and *"offers... standards of excellence which we cannot level down without loosing direction"*.[74] *"Canon"* is, according to Gombrich, *"deeply embedded in the totality of our civilisation"* so that *"what we call civilisation may be interpreted as a web of value judgments which are implicit rather than explicit"*.[75] Thus, as we can see, antropological universality has been transformed by Gombrich into the universality of a civilisation, as he puts it in a letter to Quentin Bell: *"We were born into our civilisation and we owe our orientation to that tradition... to the 'canon'."*[76] Despite the fact that the civilisation has not been explicitly specified by Gombrich, this *apologia* for the universality of *"the canon of excellence"* with Michelangello as its peak,[77] leads unequivocaly to the glorification of Western civilisation. In addition, insofar as he takes competitiveness to be an anthropological constant, regarding *"the logic of situation"* of capitalist market competition as a metahistorical principle in his essay "The Logic of Vanity Fair. Alternatives to Historicism in the Study of Fashions, Style and Taste" (1965),[78] it seems that Gombrich's *apologia* refers implicitly to Western neo-liberalism. Expressed in Jonathan Harris's words: *"The canon of great art, and its confirmation in, and by art history, are thus both integral parts of the humanism of western liberal-democratic society."*[79]

---

[70]   Ibid.
[71]   Ibid., p. 164.
[72]   Ibid., p. 152.
[73]   Ibid., p. 162.
[74]   Ibid., p. 163.
[75]   Ibid.
[76]   Ibid., p. 181.
[77]   Ibid., pp. 144-183.
[78]   Ibid., pp. 60-92.
[79]   HARRIS, Jonathan: *The New Art History. A Critical Introduction.* London 2001, p. 37.

"Humbug"

In the first half of the 1970s, Gombrich believed that *"we art historians gener-ally attempt to mitigate or avoid the most radical relativist conclusions"*.[80] Four years later, he had to change his mind admitting that *"I do not think I am too far wrong if I also describe this relativism as the official dogma, so to speak, of the contemporary art historical teaching"*.[81] Moreover, he came to the conclusion that *"the fallacies which tempted art history to adopt cultural relativism"* and which he had relent-lessly attempted to unmask, such as the *"physiognomic fallacy"* and the belief in styles as expressions of an age or a nation or *"the circular reasoning"*, *"also occur in other fields of humanities"*.[82] As a consequence, he decided to extend his polemics against the hegemony of relativism to the whole field of the humani-ties. Nevertheless, there was also, for Gombrich, a very personal reason for focusing on the critique of relativism. Throughout the 1980s, Gombrich, and his idea of a universal *"canon"* in particular, became the target of revisionist criticism by the radical and poststructuralist strand of art history.[83] Gombrich responded to the invasion of relativism with a series of essays against rela-tivism in the humanities, in the history of ideas and in the appreciation of art.[84] In the plenary address given to the VIIth International Congress of Ger-manic Studies in Göttingen in August 1985, Gombrich avowed his allegiance to Goethe's *"belief in the universality of human nature"* as expressed in his belief *"They were all human beings – so much is plain"* in contrast to Hegel's *"cultural relativism"* which *"refuses to acknowledge any constants that would enable us to recognize a permanent nature behind all changing appearances"*.[85] The relativistic assertions that *"every generation has its own truths"* and that *"our concern with testimonies of the past cannot be much more than a clever game that does not serve knowledge but simply the display of intellectual acrobatics"* or that *"any striving for understanding is naive and obsolete"* because *"not only the search for explanations, but even the striving for understanding should be thrown on to the scrap heap"*[86]

---

[80]   GOMBRICH 1979 (see note 22), p. 146.

[81]   GOMBRICH 1984 (see note 60), p. 65.

[82]   GOMBRICH, Ernst H.: *Topics of Our Time. Twentieth-Century Issues in Learning and in Art*. Lon-don 1991, p. 40.

[83]   *The New Art History*. Eds. Alan L. REES – Frances BORZELLO. London 1986, pp. 21-24, 135, 159; BRYSON, Norman: *Vision and Painting. The Logic of the Gaze*. New Haven – London 1983, p. 43; MOXEY, Keith: *The Practice of Persuasion. Paradox & Power in Art History*. Ithaca – Lon-don 2001, pp. 79-80; HARRIS 2001 (see note 79), pp. 37, 41.

[84]   GOMBRICH 1991 (see note 82), pp. 36-46, 47-55, 56-61.

[85]   Ibid., pp. 36-39.

[86]   Ibid., p. 38.

have been declared to be *"humbug"* by Gombrich.[87] In his view, it has *"led to the jettisoning of the most precious heritage of all scholarly work".*[88] *"The negation of all standards"* is, according to him, an *"exageration [that] can only lead ad absurdum".*[89]

Universality as "a Working Hypothesis"

It is worth mentioning that despite his radical critique of subjectivism, Gombrich's polemics against relativism became more cautious and objective throughout the 1980s. He acknowledged that *"no doubt it is fallacious to conclude from the fact that 'they were all human beings' that they must also have thought and felt as we do",*[90] since *"the way in which various cultures try to cope with the insistent clamour of our natural instincts is subject to countless variations".*[91] Admitting the positive role played by cultural relativism in damping down a narcissistic presentism, Gombrich conceded that *"the influence of cultural relativism must certainly be welcomed... where it restrains us in applying our own cultural standards to other societies".*[92] He even goes so far as to admit that belief in the *"universality of human nature"* is only *"a working hypothesis"*. Despite that, *"the hypothesis that there are indeed constants in the psyche of man"* is, anyway, worth testing, according to Gombrich[93]: *"I believe it is always worthwile to make the initial assumption that even in foreign countries and in distant ages we have to do with people who are not all that different from ourselves... even though this assumption may occasionaly fail to stand a further test."*[94] For the biological core of man represents the base of the visual arts, according to Gombrich. As he put it: *"I am convinced that the visual arts also rest... on biological foundations."*[95] That is why great artists *"operate within fields of tensions which derive their energy from the original polarity of universal human reactions",*[96] and why the masterworks represent universal values, in Gombrich's view.

---

87   Ibid., p. 39.
88   Ibid., p. 38.
89   Ibid., p. 39.
90   Ibid.
91   Ibid., p. 41.
92   Ibid., p. 39.
93   Ibid., p. 44.
94   Ibid., p. 41.
95   Ibid., p. 44.
96   Ibid.

"Inhuman Cold Objectivity" and One of Gombrich's "Lacunae"

Despite conceiving of the idea of an anthropological constant as a hypothesis and regardless of the fact that the humanities, including psychology, *"being science... must not submit to any dogma, not even to dogma of the unity of mankind"*,[97] Gombrich reiterates that *"to oppose relativism"* represents the prime task in order *"to prevent it* [i.e. relativism] *from dominanting the entire field"*.[98] Endorsing the substantial difference between science and ideologies and considering science as the main weapon against myth, Gombrich emphasizes that the *"interactions... between ideologies and the development of science"* cannot be studied *"if we give up the belief in the objectivity of certain scientific discoveries"* and *"if we eliminate the notion of error altogether and adopt a wholy relativistic stance"*.[99] At the same time, he claims that *"the humanities... would atrophy and die if they attempted to become 'value free'."*[100] Nevertheless, Gombrich's *"attempt to rest humanism on a 'scientific basis'"*,[101] or, in other words, his *"desire to bring to humanistic studies something of the discipline of scientific method"*[102] can be classified among his "lacunae".[103] Insisting on the substantial difference between rational and mythical approaches, like that between science and ideologies, Gombrich believes that *"the study of art"* and humanistic studies in general *"can be conducted in a rational way"*.[104] Nonetheless, he denies the humanities the status of objective and disinterested, or value-free, research. While *"ideas originate with human beings and affect human beings"*, *"to discuss them with cold objectivity"* seems to Gombrich *"inhuman in the true sense of the word"*.[105] Thus, he invites us to carry on the humanities as a moralizing or ideological activity. Paradoxically, Gombrich involuntarily confirms Maurice Mandelbaum's assertion that *"an insistence on knowledge as value-charged can have only one resultant: relativism"*.[106] Moral responsibility is regarded by Gombrich as a more

---

[97]   Ibid., p. 43.

[98]   Ibid., p. 39.

[99]   Ibid., pp. 48-49.

[100]   Ibid., p. 55.

[101]   HEMINGWAY, Andrew: E. H. Gombrich in 1968: Methodological Individualism and the Contradictions of Conservatism, in *Human Affairs*, 19, 2009, No. 3, pp. 297-303.

[102]   ONIANS, John: Gombrich, Sir Ernst Hans Josef (1909 – 2001), in *Oxford Dictionary of National Biography*, Index No. 101076475.

[103]   HOROWITZ, Gregg: Gombrich, Ernst Hans Josef, in *The Encyclopedia of Aesthetics*. Ed. Michael KELLY. New York – Oxford 1998, Vol. 2, pp. 315-320, here p. 318; BAKOŠ 1996 (see note 1), pp. 247-248, chapter "An uneasy humanist".

[104]   GOMBRICH 1979 (see note 22), p. 165.

[105]   GOMBRICH 1991 (see note 82), p. 55.

[106]   MANDELBAUM, Maurice: *The Problem of Historical Knowledge. An Answer to Relativism*. New York – Evanston – London 1967, p. 36.

important task for the humanities than that of scientific objectivity. And really, his critique of metaphysics, lasting for more than six decades, has served first, to condemn nationalism and racism, then, to warn against all forms of totalitarianism, and finally, to glorify those fundamental values of Western civilization: rationality and individualism. Thus, his plea for humanism has become a concealed *apologia* for liberal democratic society.[107]

---

[107] HARRIS 2001 (see note 79), p. 37; VIDRIH, Rebeka: Gombrichov boj [Gombrich's Fight], in *Zbornik za umetnostno zgodovino* [Art History Proceedings], 40. Ljubljana 2004, pp. 326-346, here p. 346; HEMINGWAY 2009 (see note 101).

Part two

VI. FROM UNIVERSALISM TO NATIONALISM: TRANSFORMATIONSOFTHEVIENNASCHOOL'SIDEAS IN CENTRAL EUROPE

I. Art History as a State Science

First, let us enumerate the well-known facts concerning the Vienna School of Art History: on December 31, 1850, the Central Commission on the Research and Preservation of Historical Monuments ("K. k. Central-Commission für die Erforschung und Erhaltung der Baudenkmale", since 1873 "Zentralkomission für Erforschung und Erhaltung der Kunst-und historischen Denkmale") was established. In 1852, Rudolf von Eitelberger was appointed Extraordinary, and a little later, Ordinary Professor of Art History. On October 20, 1854, the establishment of the Institute for Austrian Historical Studies ("Institut für österreichische Geschichtsforschung") followed. The history of art was part of the curriculum there. This was later turned into a chair and a department of art history. In 1864, a proposal by Rudolf von Eitelberger materialised as the Austrian Museum for Art and Industry ("Österreichisches Museum für Kunst und Industrie").

It is also a fact that the institutionalisation of art history in the Habsburg Monarchy came into existence just after the defeat of the 1848 bourgeois Revolution – a fact that had very serious consequences for the nature of art history in Austria. Austrian art historical institutions did not arise as the realisation of the Enlightenment ideals. On the contrary, they were deliberately established as vehicles for political restoration. Generally speaking, their task was, on the one hand, to legitimise the restored political power of aristocracy by means of history, and on the other to contribute to the centralization of the Empire by means of the idea of a common trans-national cultural heritage. In other words, art historical institutions were expected to help overcome the social as well as the national controversies of the restored multinational Empire. They were intended as instruments of the state ideology of Monarchic patriotism. Alexander von Helfert, Secretary of the Ministry of Education, explicitly demanded the construction of a *"Nationalgeschichte von Großösterreich als Mittel zur Erziehung von Großösterreichischen Patrioten"*.[1] He regarded it as

---

[1] LHOTSKY, Alphons: Das Institut für österreichische Geschichtsforschung, in LHOTSKY, Alphons: *Aufsätze und Vorträge III. Historiographie. Quellenkunde. Wissenschaftsgeschichte.* Wien 1972, pp. 291-296, here p. 293.

the proper task of the historical (and we can add "art historical") institutions of the state. At the same time, Austrian art historical institutions established after 1848 can be regarded as realisations of a post-revolutionary compromise between aristocracy and bourgeoisie. Paraphrasing Carl Schorske's interpretation, one may conclude that art historical institutions represented the post-revolutionary compromise between the aristocratic culture of faith and theatre on the one hand, and the middle class culture of science and learning on the other.[2] Consequently, the history of art was regarded not only as a business of culture, but also as an object of scientific research. In addition, training in art history at Vienna University or at the Institute for Austrian Historical Research did not aim at achieving Humboldt's ideal of a general and autonomous "Bildung", but, on the contrary, at providing its graduates with specialised practical skills.[3] The stress on the method, characteristic of the Vienna School of Art History, can also be regarded as one of the means to develop state professionals, learned specialists for museums, archives or monument care. Art historians were seen as state experts and consequently as members of the main buttress of the Monarchy, i.e. the state bureucracy.[4] Their primary task was thus to protect the state cultural heritage and to maintain state ideology, i.e. trans-national Monarchic patriotism by means of science. It is known that the Monarchy had to cope with two fatal dilemmas: one, resulting from the conflict between the political dominance of the aristocracy and the growing economic power of the bourgeoisie, and the other one, resulting from the multinational nature of the Empire. Consequently, the task of state bureaucracy (including experts in art history) was to protect the interest of the state against all particular and centrifugal tendencies. In that sense, academic

[2]   SCHORSKE, Carl E.: Austrian Aesthetic Culture, 1870 – 1914. A Historian's Reflection, in *Akten des XXV. Internationalen Kongresses für Kunstgeschichte, Wien, 4. – 10. September 1983*. Vols. 1-9. Eds. Hermann FILLITZ – Martina PIPPAL. Wien – Köln – Graz 1984 – 1986, Vol. 9: Eröffnungs- und Plenarvorträge. Arbeitsgruppe "Neue Forschungsergebnisse und Arbeitsvorhaben" (1985), pp. 27-40; SCHORSKE, Carl E.: Grace and the Word: Austria's Two Cultures and Their Modern Fate, in SCHORSKE, Carl E.: *Thinking with History. Explorations in the Passage to Modernism*. Princeton 1998, pp. 125-140. See also SCHORSKE, Carl E.: *Fin-de-siècle Vienna. Politics and Culture*. New York 1981.

[3]   SCHORSKE, Carl E.: History as Vocation in Burckhardt's Basel, in SCHORSKE 1998 (see note 2), pp. 56-70, here p. 58 f.

[4]   JOHNSTON, William M.: *The Austrian Mind. An Intellectual and Social History 1848 – 1938.* Berkeley – Los Angeles – London 1983, pp. 45-75. Margaret Olin was the first to point out the relationship between the ideas of Vienna School of Art History and the state ideology of the Habsburg Monarchy. See OLIN, Margaret: Alois Riegl: The Late Roman Empire in the Late Habsburg Empire, in *The Habsburg Legacy. National Identity in Historical Perspective*. Eds. Ritchie ROBERTSON – Edward TIMMS. Edinburgh 1994, pp. 107-120. At the time of writing the present essay, the author had not the access to Olin's groundbreaking article.

art history represented a state science, *par excellence*. From that point of view, even the stress on the scientific nature of art history and the emphasis on the exact method of art historical research symptomatic for the Vienna School, can be interpreted as an embodiment of the ambition of state experts to be as "objektiv", impartial, and as disinterested as possible.

It is quite evident that the theory of art history as developed by Franz Wickhoff, Alois Riegl, Julius von Schlosser and Max Dvořák was full of contradictions. It can be summarised (or simplified, if you please) into the antinomy, "universalism versus historical relativism". On the one hand, art history was regarded as the universal and continuous evolution of "ars una". In Hans Tietze's words: *"Die Entwicklung der Kunst ist eine allgemeine und umfaßt alle Erscheinungen und Äußerungen, die die betreffende Periode hervorbringt."*[5] According to Riegl, *"erscheint diese universalgeschichtliche Art der Betrachtung gewissermaßen als die eigentliche Krönung der kunstgeschichtlichen Forschung"*.[6] On the other hand, it represented a plurality of *"Kunstwollen"* or permanently changing notions (*"Auffassungen"*) and concepts of art. This theoretical antinomy shared a remarkable similarity to the fatal dilemma faced by the multinational Monarchy who tried to solve it by means of universalist or (later) cosmopolitan ideology. But rather than being a mere projection of the main political dilemma of the Monarchy onto the autonomous theoretical model, the Vienna School's contradictory ideas can be regarded as a token of the indirect or masked participation of its members in the ideological battles of the time, as a sublimation of direct action in the struggle between Monarchy and liberalism on the one hand, and between liberals and their nationalistic opponents on the other. In other words, Viennese professors of art history were not only influenced by those ideological tensions but also took an active, even if concealed, part in it. As the leading experts of the state on the one hand and middle class intellectuals on the other, they did their duty, defending the interest of the Monarchy by means of bourgeois ideas. The position between the Monarchy and the bourgeoisie necessarily resulted in the contradictory nature of their theoretical models. Nevertheless, this antagonism cannot be regarded simply as an unconscious theoretical oversight. On the contrary, it should be considered as an expression of their authors' intention to harmonise and reconcile the different or even contradictory ideological interests. And as specialists in the history, Vienna School art history professors projected

---

[5] TIETZE, Hans: *Die Methode der Kunstgeschichte*. Leipzig 1913, p. 41.

[6] RIEGL, Alois: Kunstgeschichte und Universalgeschichte (1898), in RIEGL, Alois: *Gesammelte Aufsätze* (=Klassische Texte der Wiener Schule der Kunstgeschichte, 5). Wien 1996, pp. 3-9, here p. 7.

the ideological controversies of the present onto the past. They looked, so to speak, for symbolic answers to them. Following the ideal of an impartial "objective" science, they masked the ideological loading of the studied phenomena and presented them as solutions of autonomous art historical problems.

II. Art Historians in Ideological Struggles

The first professor of art history at Vienna University, Rudolf von Eitelberger, played, as is known, an active role in shaping the idea of a universal trans-national cultural heritage of the Monarchy. It functioned as a means of post-revolutionary centralization.[7] Later influenced by Gottfried Semper – as exemplified by the Museum for Art and Industry[8] – Eitelberger forsook his mediaeval revival position in favour of a pragmatic historicism and propagated liberal ideas by means of the Renaissance revival.

His pupil, Moritz Thausing, rejected the revivalist practice of mixing the past with the present, as well as the confusion of art and science. He explicitly formulated the doctrine of art history as a science.[9] He anchored art history as a discipline explicitly located in the liberal value system of reason and rationality. By strictly dividing art history from aesthetics, Thausing not only demarcated a rational approach from an irrational aesthetic evaluation, but also launched the Vienna School crusade against ahistorical normativism. This later resulted in the open crisis of the liberal ideal of progress.[10]

Thausing´s follower, Franz Wickhoff, continued to unfold both elements of his teacher: As far as liberal rationalism was concerned, he strengthened the belief in art history as an exact science. He incorporated Morelli's analytical connoisseurship and Sickel's historical critique into the art historical curriculum and transformed it into an organic part of the research method of art history. Nevertheless, Wickhoff did not regard the liberal ideal of clearly distinguishing the "true" from the "false" as a pragmatic instrument of connoisseurship intended for commercial practice. On the contrary, he conceived

---

[7]   MAROSI, Ernő: Die Anfänge der Denkmalpflege und die Tätigkeit der K. u. k. Zentralkommission in Ungarn, in *Die Ungarische Kunstgeschichte und die Wiener Schule, 1846 – 1930*. Budapest 1983, pp. 3-19, here p. 16 f.

[8]   CHADRABA, Rudolf: Max Dvořák a vídeňská škola dějin umění [Max Dvořák and the Vienna School of Art History], in *Kapitoly z českého dějepisu umění* [Chapters from Czech Historiography of Art]. Vol. 2. Eds. Rudolf CHADRABA – Josef KRÁSA – Rostislav ŠVÁCHA – Anděla HOROVÁ. Praha 1987, pp. 9-70, here p. 16.

[9]   ROSENAUER, Artur: Moritz Thausing und die Wiener Schule der Kunstgeschichte, in *Wiener Jahrbuch für Kunstgeschichte*, 36, 1983, pp. 135-139, here p. 135.

[10]   SCHORSKE 1981 (see note 2), p. 238.

the exact method of art historical research as a means of autonomous scientific knowledge on the one hand and as a tool exclusively in the service of the state (or state institutions), on the other.

As far as the contradiction between universalism and relativism is concerned, Wickhoff unequivocally expressed his belief in a common origin of art: *"Weil alle Kunst eines Ursprungs ist, hat sich in jeder ihrer Verzweigungen so viel des Ursprünglichen erhalten, daß überall ein loszulösender Faden könnte gefunden werden, mit dem dann die hervorgesuchten Reste älterer Perioden an die neue Kunstübung angeknüpft wurden."*[11] Simultaneously, defending Klimt's University paintings, Wickhoff explicitly rejected any universal nature of beauty.[12] Despite that, Wickhoff's project to write a history of Naturalism implied his belief in a common denominator of art history and in a hidden transhistorical norm. Moreover, in his book *Wiener Genesis* (1895), Wickhoff articulated openly the belief in plurality and equality of styles. As is well known, he vindicated Late Roman illusionism and rejected the idea of periods of decline in the history of art. In addition, he acknowledged the experience of contemporary (impressionist) art as a key to the knowledge of a particular past. As a consequence, for the first time, doubts were cast on the concept of art history as a value- free and impartial science.

This first foreshadowing of the crisis of liberal optimism by Wickhoff was developed into an explicit critique of the *"liberal ego"*[13] by Alois Riegl. His conception of art history cannot be regarded solely as a token of the general intellectual and cultural transition from positivism to new idealism, or from impressionism to expressionism, as Julius von Schlosser and Guido von Kaschnitz-Weinberg assumed.[14] Riegl's theory can be understood as a critical reflection on the particular problems of the crisis of Austrian Liberalism and as an attempt to overcome the dilemmas of the *fin de siècle* Habsburg Monarchy in a symbolic way. The central problem of the Vienna School, *"das spätan-*

---

[11] WICKHOFF, Franz: Über die historische Einheitlichkeit der gesamten Kunstentwicklung, in WICKHOFF, Franz: *Abhandlungen. Vorträge und Anzeigen* (=Die Schriften Franz Wickhoffs, 2). Berlin 1913, pp. 81-91, here p. 91.

[12] SCHORSKE 1998 (see note 2), p. 134; HOLLY, Michael Ann: Spirits and Ghosts in the Historiography of Art, in *The Subjects of Art History. Historical Objects in Contemporary Perspectives.* Eds. Mark A. CHEETHAM – Michael Ann HOLLY – Keith MOXEY. Cambridge 1998, pp. 61-64.

[13] SCHORSKE, Carl E.: Gustav Klimt. Painting and the Crisis of the Liberal Ego, in SCHORSKE 1981 (see note 2), pp. 208-278.

[14] SCHLOSSER, Julius von: Die Wiener Schule der Kunstgeschichte. Rückblick auf ein Säkulum deutscher Gelehrtenarbeit in Österreich, in *Mitteilungen des Österreichischen Instituts für Geschichtsforschung*, 13, 1934, No. 2, pp. 141-228; KASCHNITZ-WEINBERG, Guido von: [Review of] Alois Riegl, Die Spätrömische Kunstindustrie, in *Gnomon*, 4-5, 1929, pp. 195-213; reprinted in *Die Neue Wiener Schule.* Ed. Artur ROSENAUER. Wien 1986, pp. 92-101.

tike Problem", i.e. the transition from Antiquity to the Middle Ages, characterised by Riegl as the *"Kardinalfrage der Kulturgeschichte"* and as *"das wichtigste und einschneidendste in der ganzen bisherigen Geschichte der Menschheit"*, can be regarded, in a sense, as a projection of the cultural and intellectual situation of the *fin de siècle* "Donaumonarchie" (Danube Monarchy) into the remote past.[15] The analysis of the process of transition from Antique sensuality to Mediaeval spiritualism, from objectivism to subjectivism, or from rationalism to irrationalism was employed by the Vienna School art historians as a substitution to cope with the crisis of liberal optimism in a symbolic way. Riegl rejected the revivalist, heteronymous notion of art as an instrument of cultural history and replaced it by the modernist idea of the autonomy of art. He also severely criticised materialist determinism (significant for pragmatic historicism), replacing it by a "scientific" version of the new spiritualism, "Vitalism". (It was embodied in his notion of *"Kunstwollen"*, regarded as an immanent motor of history). Moreover, Riegl condemned all forms of historical normativity,[16] including the liberal belief in progress. Advocating an anti-normativist position, he definitively rejected the idea of periods of decline in art history, replacing it with the idea of plurality of equal and incommensurable *"Kunstwollen"*. Nevertheless, Riegl's critique of optimistic liberalism was a moderate one. He never fully exchanged rationalism for irrationalism. He did not defeat normativity by means of the idea of revolution, but, on the contrary, by the idea of evolution, by the belief in continuity and causality. *"Evolution nicht Revolution. Im Kunstleben gibt es keinen Tod, sondern bloss ewig fortschreitende, wechselseitige Durchdringung alles einmal Gewesenen in einem endlos fortlaufenden Wellenlinie."*[17] Riegl's theory of art history can be regarded both as a concealed justification of *fin de siècle* Modernism (committed to the freedom and independence of art, and the idea of art as the expression of subjective truth) and as an indirect advocacy of the ideology of Monarchic universalism. Nevertheless, he transformed normativist and hegemonic universalism into a quantitative, democratic and rationalist one: i.e. into Formalism and Scientism. He never gave up the idea of causality in history, his belief in historical laws, or

---

[15]   RIEGL, Alois: Spätrömisch oder orientalisch, in *Münchner Allgemeine Zeitung*, 1902, No. 93, pp. 153-154; OLIN 1994 (see note 4), pp. 109-112; OLIN, Margaret: Art History and Ideology: Alois Riegl and Josef Strzygowski, in *Cultural Visions: Essays in the History of Culture*. Eds. Penny Schine GOLD – Benjamin C. SAX. Amsterdam – Atlanta (GA) 2000, pp. 151-162; ELSNER, Jaś: The Birth of Late Antiquity: Riegl and Strzygowski in 1901, in *Art History*, 25, 2002, No. 3, pp. 358-379.

[16]   DVOŘÁK, Max: Alois Riegl, in DVOŘÁK, Max: *Gesammelte Aufsätze zur Kunstgeschichte*. München 1929, pp. 279-298.

[17]   RIEGL 1902 (see note 15), p. 154.

the notion of an "objective", value-free, unprejudiced art historical research. The discovery of parallelism between the evolution of art on the one hand, and the evolution of spiritual culture on the other (as expressed in the last chapter of his *Die Spätrömische Kunstindustrie*, 1901, or in his university lectures *Historische Grammatik der bildenden Künste* given in 1897 – 1899[18]) led him to the threshold of epistemological relativism. Despite that, he never fully accepted the idea of the dependence of art historical knowledge on the contemporary *"will to form"*.[19] In other words, we can regard Riegl's theory of art history as an embodiment of the alliance between an official Monarchic ideology and an intellectual critique of Liberalism. Also Riegl's late interest in Baroque art in Rome, on the one hand, and in 17th century Dutch art on the other,[20] can be interpreted as a concealed projection of contemporary political problems onto the remote past: the conflict between Monarchy and bourgeoisie was projected onto the contrast between theatrical illusionism and corporative sobriety. Riegl, attracted by a similarity between baroque spiritualism and modern Vitalism, concentrated here on a typical "Monarchic" theme, i.e. Roman Baroque theatrical representation on the one hand, and on a bourgeois subject matter par excellence, i.e. Dutch liberal corporativism, on the other.

Riegl's successor, Max Dvořák, at first followed Riegl in his epistemological optimism. He unfolded what Hans Tietze called *"genetische Kunstgeschichte"*, i.e. the notion of the immanent nature of the evolution of art (*"die Entwicklung der Kunst ist... in erster Linie eine selbständige und wird von ihrer eigenen Notwendigkeit geregelt"*)[21] and the idea of its continuity based on the principle of causal connection between works of art (*"Die Entwicklung der Kunst ist stetig und ununterbrochen."*).[22] Nevertheless, affected by war experience, Dvořák parted with Riegl's evolutionist, autonomous and formalist theoretical model. He rehabilitated the idea of the irrational nature of the history of art. As a consequence, Riegl's rationalist belief in continuity of evolution of art was replaced by an acknowledgment of the discontinuous nature of the art historical process. At the same time, Dvořák relinquished

---

18   RIEGL, Alois: *Historische Grammatik der bildenden Künste*. Eds. Karl M. SWOBODA – Otto PÄCHT. Graz – Köln 1966, pp. 9-16.

19   RIEGL 1898 (see note 6), pp. 3-9.

20   RIEGL, Alois: *Die Entstehung der Barockkunst in Rom. Vorlesungen aus 1901 – 1902*. Eds. Arthur BURDA – Max DVOŘÁK. Wien 1908; RIEGL, Alois: Das holländische Gruppenporträt, in *Jahrbuch des allerhöchsten Kaiserhauses*, 22, 1902, pp. 71-278; KEMP, Wolfgang: Alois Riegl, in *Altmeister moderner Kunstgeschichte*. Ed. Heinrich DILLY. Berlin 1990, pp. 52-56; KEMP, Wolfgang: Introduction, in RIEGL, Alois: *The Group Portraiture of Holland*. Los Angeles 1999, pp. 1-57.

21   TIETZE 1913 (see note 5), p. 43 f.

22   Ibid., p. 42.

the notion of the autonomy of art, for which he substituted the idea of its heteronomy. As is well known, he started to regard the history of art as affected by spiritual factors, conceiving it as the history of ideas (called *"Geistesgeschichte"* by his pupils)[23]. Consequently, changes of artistic form were considered as expressions of changing ideas of the world. Influenced by avant-garde art (particularly by expressionist painting), Dvořák not only transformed Riegl's "Vitalism" into a spiritual approach, but also drew out his historical relativism: Dvořák's idea of the historical changes of the concept of "art" itself (as articulated in his "Idealismus und Naturalismus in der gotischen Skulptur und Malerei", published 1918)[24] can be regarded as a projection of the Avant-garde casting doubt upon the identity of art itself. Following Wickhoff's projection of contemporary art onto the past, Dvořák discovered Mannerism by means of 20th century Expressionism. Dvořák abandoned Riegl's project of a strict impartiality of art historical knowledge. As a consequence, he relinquished his predecessor's epistemological optimism. In spite of that, Dvořák's fight against misusing the protection of historical monuments for particular nationalist interest (as exemplified e.g. by his engagement in the case of the Wavel castle)[25] clearly showed him following Riegl as a loyal advocate of state interest. The alliance of Monarchic trans-nationalism with an intellectual universalism was transformed by Dvořák into a syncretic association of Monarchic nostalgia with avant-garde transcendental cosmopolitanism.

As we see, the Viennese professors of art history, Franz Wickhoff, Alois Riegl and Max Dvořák, can be regarded as active supporters of Monarchic cosmopolitanism and loyal adherents to the Monarchic policy of centralism. In contrast to that, the head of the other Viennese art history institute, Josef Strzygowski, an inveterate opponent of Wickhoff's and Riegl's Vienna School,[26] can be regarded as a supporter of bourgeois centrifugal particularism. Criticizing Wickhoff's *Wiener Genesis* in his *Orient oder Rom* (1901), Strzygowski not only rejected "Eurocentrism" while rehabilitating the role of the provinces in the history of art, but also symbolically criticised the Vienna

---

[23] DVOŘÁK, Max: *Kunstgeschichte als Geistesgeschichte. Studien zur abendländischen Kunstentwicklung*. Eds. Johannes WILDE – Karl M. SWOBODA. München 1924, pp. IX-XII.

[24] Ibid., p. X.

[25] See FRYCZ, Jerzy: *Restauracja i konserwacja zabytków architektury w Polsce w latach 1795 – 1918* [Restoration and Conservation of Architectural Monuments in Poland in the Years 1795 – 1918]. Warszawa 1975, p. 216.

[26] FRODL-KRAFT, Eva: Eine Aporie und der Versuch ihrer Deutung. Josef Strzygowski – Julius v. Schlosser, in *Wiener Jahrbuch für Kunstgeschichte*, 42, 1989, pp. 7-52; OLIN 2000 (see note 15), pp. 162-170; ELSNER 2002 (see note 15), pp. 371-376.

School's centralism. Moreover, in his *Hellas in des Orients Umarmung* (1902), Strzygowski attacked Riegl's idea of immanent evolution by means of the idea of an external impact regarded as the decisive factor of the historical process (the so-called "Barbarism idea"). Nevertheless, Strzygowski's polemics against hegemonic centralism were not limited to the vindication of an active role for the provinces. He developed his attack against centralism into a pluralist geographical model of art history. The idea of the universal and linear evolution of art was replaced with the model of the global plurality of cultural zones or areas mutually communicating with each other and influencing each other but keeping their own lasting identity. Strzygowski unmasked Humanism, i.e. the dominant tradition of the center (of Rome as well as of Vienna) as a *"Machtkunst"*[27] serving the maintainance of the power of state and church.[28] In contrast to that, he regarded the lasting identity of independent artistic organisms (e.g. Nordic or Slavic art) as derived from *"Volkskunst"* and rooted in the nation or racial identity. As a consequence, Strzygowski not only replaced the historical (or diachronic) pluralism of the Vienna School with a synchronic and geographical one. He also replaced linear and causal explanations of historical phenomena with the hypostasis of a communication between lasting entities (ethnic and racial or national essences) regarded as fundamental elements of the history of art.[29]

III. Mission and Transformations: The Role of the Disciples I

Despite the idea of *"Slavic art"* as a particular phenomenon, it was not Strzygowski but the cosmopolitan Vienna School – especially Riegl's and Dvořák's disciples – who shaped the 20th century national art historiographies in the Slavic countries of Central Europe. It is commonplace to say that the Vienna School played the role of an incubator of experts for museums, galleries, monument protection bodies, and university institutes of art history in the whole Habsburg Monarchy. Vienna School disciples were trained not only to

---

[27] Ibid., p. 26. See also STRZYGOWSKI, Josef: *Europas Machtkunst im Rahmen des Erdkreises*. Wien 1941.

[28] FRODL-KRAFT 1989 (see note 26), p. 37.

[29] About Strzygowski, see also MAROSI, Ernő: Josef Strzygowski als Entwerfer von nationalen Kunstgeschichten, in *Kunstgeschichte im "Dritten Reich": Theorien, Methoden, Praktiken*. Eds. Ruth HEFTRIG – Olaf PETERS – Barbara SCHELLEWALD. Berlin 2008, pp. 103-113; EBERLEIN, Johann K.: Josef Strzygowski. Gedanken über die Zeitlosigkeit eines Typus, in *De re artificiosa. Festschrift für Paul von Naredi-Rainer zu seinem 60. Geburtstag*. Eds. Lukas MADERSBACHER – Thomas STEPPAN. Regensburg 2010, pp. 81-93.

guarantee high expertise in treating a cultural heritage that covered the whole territory of the Empire, but also to disseminate the universalistic approach to the history of art and, consequently, the propagation of the ideology of the unity of the Monarchy. Nevertheless, Vienna School disciples coming from the Slavic parts of the Empire were confronted with a totally new situation after the collapse of the Monarchy. They had to cope with the task of drawing up the history of art of the new national states of Central Europe. Loyal to the universalistic or cosmopolitan doctrine and their strict training, Vienna School graduates regarded their mission as a search for the harmony between universalism and particularism. In other words, they focused their minds on the problem of the relationship between the universal and the national history of art. They aimed at a specification of the particular place or role that the art of a nation played in the universal evolution of art. It is logical that the concept of art as form and the *"genetic art history"* were regarded as the most suitable to this end. Formalist quantification made it possible to compare disparate phenomena and to look for their genetic links. The causal method of explanation offered the opportunity to identify the place of a particular phenomenon in a genetic chain. In addition, the exact method with which the Vienna School disciples were equipped protected them against an easy relapse into romantic nationalism while interpreting the history of art of a nation. Moreover, Formalism when allied with Scientism – thanks to their "disinterestedness" – offered a very good opportunity to replace former Monarchic patriotism with a new national patriotism without relapsing into an irrational and xenophobic nationalism. That was why *"genetic formalism"*, in contrast to *"Geistesgeschichte"*, had the strongest impact on the development of the majority of national historiographies in Central Europe between the two World Wars.

The Viennese universalistic conception was adapted to Czech art history by Wickhoff's and Riegl's pupils, Vincenc Kramář and Vojtěch Birnbaum. Kramář, since 1919 the director of the Rudolfinum Gallery (Obrazárna Společnosti vlasteneckých přátel umění) in Prague, had graduated from the Institute for Austrian Historical Research in 1902, submitting a thesis *Frankreichs Verhältnis zur Gotik in der Neuzeit*.[30] Birnbaum, since 1919 professor and, a little later, head of the department of art history at the Charles University in Prague, graduated from Vienna University in 1904, submitting a thesis *Der altchristiliche Kirchen-*

---

30   KRÁSA, Josef: Vincenc Kramář, in *Kapitoly z českého dějepisu umění* (see note 8), pp. 118-125, here pp. 118-123. See also KRÁSA, Josef: Dílo Vincence Kramáře v českých dějinách umění [The Work of Vincenc Kramář in the Czech History of Art], in KRAMÁŘ, Vincenc: *O obrazech a galeriích* [Of Pictures and Galleries]. Ed. Josef KRÁSA. Praha 1983, pp. 449-477.

bau und sein Verhältnis zur römischen Baukunst.[31] These two, both true cosmopolitans, continued to study world art intensively, even after the establishment of an independent Czechoslovakia (Birnbaum published papers particularly on Early Christian and Romanesque architecture, Kramář on Cubism).[32] Moreover, they regarded Czech art as an organic part of the universal historical evolution. According to Kramář, true national art must be universal.[33] And the specificity of a national art was expected to play its particular role in the universal history of art by Birnbaum. Following Riegl's tracks, Birnbaum attempted to guarantee the particular role of Czech art by means of general historical laws. Inspired by Heinrich Wölfflin, he formulated a *"baroque principle"* and stimulated by Johann Gottfried Herder, defined a so-called *"law of transgression"*. According to Birnbaum, all styles necessarily result in a *"baroque"* phase, and in addition particular nations take turns at playing the leading historical role in the universal historical process. Small and peripheral nations (like the Czechs) play an active role specifically in the late *"subjectivistic"* *"baroque"* periods, according to Birnbaum. (He saw his generalizations confirmed by 14th century Czech Gothic art, as well as by Czech Baroque art.[34])

Despite intensifying the study of the history of art in Bohemia and Moravia, Max Dvořák's Czech disciples, Eugen Dostál (the first professor of art history at Masaryk University in Brno since 1921), Antonín Matějček (since 1927 professor at Charles University and Birnbaum's successor) and Jaromír Pečírka (since 1920 professor at School of Art Industry in Prague), also emphasised the genetic links of Czech art to world art history (particularly with Italian and French art).[35] The passionate dispute over the origin of Czech Gothic painting (known as the Avignon versus the Italian idea) did not represent a battle between nationalists and cosmopolitanists at that time. Dostál, who had graduated from Vienna University in 1914 (submitting a thesis *Die gotische Architektur in Rom*, and a little later, publishing *Problems of Italian Gothic*

---

31   HOŘEJŠÍ, Jiřina: Vojtěch Birnbaum, in *Kapitoly z českého dějepisu umění* (see note 8), pp. 101-117, here pp. 101-116.

32   Ibid., p. 116 f.; KRÁSA 1987 (see note 30), p. 124 f.

33   SRP, Karel: Situace českého dějepisu umění ve dvacátých letech [The Situation of Czech Art History in the Twenties], in *Kapitoly z českého dějepisu umění* (see note 8), pp. 71-94, here p. 73.

34   HLOBIL, Ivo: Vojtěch Birnbaum – život a dílo v dobových souvislostech [Vojtěch Birnbaum – His Life and Work in Historical Context], in BIRNBAUM, Vojtěch: *Vývojové zákonitosti v umění* [Developmental Principles in Art]. Ed. Ivo HLOBIL. Praha 1987, pp. 379-411; HOŘEJŠÍ 1987 (see note 31), pp. 112-115.

35   HLAVÁČEK, Luboš: Antonín Matějček a jeho škola [Antonín Matějček and His School], in *Kapitoly z českého dějepisu umění* (see note 8), pp. 152-160; VACKOVÁ, Jarmila: Eugen Dostál, ibid., pp. 171-178; HLAVÁČEK, Luboš – STEJSKAL, Karel: Jaromír Pečírka, ibid., pp. 179-184; KRÁSA 1987 (see note 30), p. 124 f.

(1923), opposing the ideas of Dvořák and Matějček), not only stressed the Italian source of 14th century Czech painting, but in addition adjusted the Viennese notion of an immanent and continuous evolution of art to the needs of the national (Czech) art history.[36] He developed the idea of a regional or national artistic organism arising from foreign sources but characterised by its own relatively independent development. It is known that Julius von Schlosser (in "Zur Kenntnis der künstlerischen Überlieferung im späten Mittelalter", 1903) and Max Dvořák (in "Les Aliscamps", 1903) started to revise the idea of linear evolution and to recognise the role of tradition. Vincenc Kramář and Vojtěch Birnbaum also contributed to that revision by analyzing revivals as important historical phenomena (i.e. Birnbaum noticed Romanesque revival in the late Middle Ages).[37] Nevertheless, Dvořák's late *"Geistesgeschichte"*, and his explicit acknowledgment of the discontinuous nature of the history of art (regarded as the consequence of changes in the spirit of the age), were scarcely followed by Czech art historians as far as their particular research interests were concerned. Despite growing doubts concerning the belief in the immanent continuity of artistic evolution – especially during the thirties[38] – Czech art history was dominated by Formalism and evolutionist theory for the whole first half of the 20th century. This can be regarded as a consequence of the fact that the idea of continuous evolution of form provided a chance to argue in favour of national patriotism by means of Scientism.[39] In addition, it also fitted very well with the desire to harmonise Czech national patriotism with the cosmopolitan nature of avant-garde art.

The impact of the Vienna School on the development of art history in Poland was not as direct and intensive as in the case of former Czechoslovakia. It had started already in the last quarter of the 19th century and took the shape of an indirect influence.[40] The first ordinary professor of art history at Jagellonian University in Kraków, Marian Sokołowski, mediated Eitelberger's and

---

[36] VACKOVÁ 1987 (see note 35).

[37] KRÁSA 1987 (see note 30), pp. 121-122; HOŘEJŠI 1987 (see note 31), p. 109.

[38] KRÁSA 1983 (see note 30), pp. 465-472.

[39] BAKOŠ, Ján: La Scuola Viennese di Storia dell'Arte e la storiografia dell'arte ceca, in *La Scuola Viennese di Storia dell'Arte. Atti del XX Convegno del Istituto pre gli Incontri Culturali Mitteleuropei*. Ed. Marco POZZETTO. Gorizia 1996, pp. 123-142.

[40] MAŁKIEWICZ, Adam: Die Kunstgeschichte in Polen und die Wiener Schule der Kunstgeschichte, in *Akten des XXV. Internationalen Kongresses für Kunstgeschichte, Wien, 4. – 10. September 1983*. Vols. 1-9. Eds. Hermann FILLITZ – Martina PIPPAL. Wien – Köln – Graz 1984 – 1986, Vol. 1: Wien und die Entwicklung der kunsthistorischen Methode (1984), pp. 157-160; MAŁKIEWICZ, Adam: Historia sztuki w Polsce a "Wiedeńska szkoła historii sztuki" [The History of Art in Poland and the "Vienna School of Art History"], in *Rocznik Historii Sztuki*, 16, 1986, pp. 331-336.

Thausing's ideas (particularly the analysis of the work of art combined with the philological critique). He was followed by Julian Pagaczewski and his mediation of Riegl's and Dvořák's *"genetic method"* of the analysis of style.[41] The first Polish art historian who had graduated from the Vienna School (1913), Max Dvořák's disciple Szczęsny Dettloff, was appointed assistant professor in 1919, associate professor in 1920, and a full professor of art history at Poznań University in 1924.[42] Dettloff focused on the history of Italian art in his lectures and concentrated on the analysis of Polish art in his seminars.[43] Combining the classical tradition with *"patriotic motives"*, Dettloff aimed at *"a teaching... unburdened of the German tradition"*.[44] In spite of stressing *"regional and national artistic styles"* in the classes dealing with artistic topography and geography, *"he himself was totally immune to any 'nationalist' temptations"*.[45] Dettloff's devotion to the Vienna School's scientific legacy, to *"the genetic-comparative method"*, and to the ideal of critical verifiability in particular, prevented him from sinking into romantic nationalism. His attempt to harmonise a universalistic approach to the history of art with patriotism based on belief in evolution, did not allow Dettloff to follow Dvořák's *"Geistesgeschichte"*.

Dvořák's view of the history of art as the history of ideas was adapted to

---

[41] MAŁKIEWICZ 1984 (see note 40), p. 158. See also MAŁKIEWICZ, Adam: Storia dell'arte in Polonia rispetto alla "Scuola di Vienna", in *La Scuola Viennese* (see note 39), pp. 143-150; BOCHNAK, Adam: *Zarys dziejów polskiej historii sztuki* [An Outline of the History of Polish Art History]. Kraków 1948; BOCHNAK, Adam: Historia Sztuki [The History of Art], in *Polska Akademia Umiejętności 1872 – 1952. Nauki humanistyczne i spoleczne* [Polish Academy of Art 1872 – 1952. Humanities and Social Sciences]. Wrocław – Warszawa – Kraków – Gdańsk 1974, pp. 235-248; KALINOWSKI, Lech: *Dzieje i dorobek naukowy Komisji Historii Sztuki Akademii Umiejętności i Polskiej Akademii Nauk 1873 – 1952 oraz powstanie Katedry Historii Sztuki Uniwersytetu Jagiellońskiego 1882* [The History and Scientific Results of the Commission of the History of Art of the Academy of Art and the Polish Academy of Sciences 1873 – 1952 as well as the Rise of the Department of Art History of the Jagellonian University 1882], in *Dzieje historii sztuki w Polsce. Ksztaltowanie sie instytucji naukowych w XIX i XX wieku* [The History of Art History in Poland. The Rise and Development of Academic Institutions in the 19th and 20th Centuries]. Ed. Adam S. LABUDA – Katarzyna ZAWIASA-STANISZEWSKA. Poznań 1996, pp. 22-43.

[42] PIWOCKI, Ksawery: Profesor Szczęsny Dettloff, in PIWOCKI, Ksawery: *Sztuka żywa. Szkice z teorii i metodyki historii sztuki* [Live Art. Sketches from the Theory and the Method of Art History]. Wrocław – Warszawa – Kraków 1970, pp. 179-183; MAŁKIEWICZ 1984 (see note 40), p. 158.

[43] LABUDA, Adam S.: Horyzont wielkopolski, horyzont europejski. Seminarium historii sztuki Uniwersytetu Poznańskiego 1919 – 1939 [Great Polish Perspective, European Perspective. Seminar on the History of Art at the Poznań University], in *Dzieje historii sztuki w Polsce* (see note 41), pp. 176-192.

[44] Ibid., p. 192.

[45] Ibid.

Polish art history by another Vienna School disciple, Karolina Lanckorońska.[46] Supervised by Julius von Schlosser, she graduated from the Vienna School in 1926 and was appointed associated professor at Lwów University in the thirties. Nevertheless, Lanckorońska's cosmopolitan interpretation of the history of ideas did not find a strong echo in Poland except in Lwów art historical circles.[47]

A much deeper impact on Polish art history than Max Dvořák was made by the opponent of the Vienna School, Josef Strzygowski. He had not only been offered a chair at the Warsaw University, but also became a foreign member of the Polish Academy of Sciences.[48] In Poland, Strzygowski's anti-humanistic approach, and his notion of *"Slavic art"* as a particular historical phenomenon, provoked a heated discussion between his opponents (like Tadeusz Szydłowski) and his adherents (represented by Stanisław Gąsiorowski and Michał Walicki) in the twenties.[49] It was an expression of the conflict between "Panslavism" and "Occidentalism" that played an important role in the development of Polish art history.[50] Nevertheless, it is symptomatic that Strzygowski's Slovenian disciple, Wojsław Molè, who had graduated from Strzygowski's Institute in 1912, and had been appointed professor and head of the department of the history of art of Slavic nations at the Jagellonian University in 1926,[51] joined Strzygowski's opponents. Despite appreciating Strzygowski's imagination, he rejected his master's essentialist notion of *"old Slavic art"* and criticised him from the point of view of Vienna School scientism.[52] On the one hand, Molè followed his teacher as far as his specialisation in Byzantine and Russian art were concerned. On the other hand, concerning method, he was much more attracted by Dvořák's *"Geistesgeschichte"* and especially by von Schlosser's distinction between *"Stilgeschichte"* and *"Sprachgeschichte"*, or his idea of great masters regarded as authors of the history of art.[53] Combining Schlosser's and Strzygowski's stimuli, Molè developed the idea of two essentially different kinds of artistic creativeness – the static and the dynamic. Consequently, he distin-

---

46   MAŁKIEWICZ 1984 (see note 40), p. 159.

47   PIWOCKI, Ksawery: Lwowskie środowisko historyków sztuki [Lwów Centre of Art Historians], in PIWOCKI 1970 (see note 42), pp. 166-178; MAŁKIEWICZ, Adam: Historia sztuki na Uniwersytecie Lwowskim 1893 – 1939 [Art History at Lwów University 1893 – 1939], in *Dzieje historii sztuki w Polsce* (see note 41), pp. 58-73, here p. 68.

48   FRODL-KRAFT 1989 (see note 26), p. 44.

49   MAŁKIEWICZ 1984 (see note 40), p. 159 f.

50   MUTHESIUS, Stefan: *Kunst in Polen/Polnische Kunst, 966 – 1990. Eine Einführung.* Königstein im Taunus 1994, p. 5.

51   KALINOWSKI, Lech: Wojsław Molè 1886 – 1973, in *Folia Historiae Artium*, 11, 1975, pp. 5-11; MAŁKIEWICZ 1984 (see note 40), p. 158.

52   MOLÈ, Wojsław: "Sztuka starosłowiańska" Strzygowskiego [Strzygowski's "Old Slavic Art"], in *Przeglad Historii Sztuki*, 1, 1929, pp. 40-47, 94-100.

53   KALINOWSKI 1975 (see note 51), p. 10 f.

guished between two cultures – a stationary culture and a differential one.[54] In addition, Molè also played the role of a bridge between Polish and Slovenien art history. During World War II, Molè was appointed professor of the history of art at Ljubljana University. (In 1949, he returned to Kraków.) It is also worth mentioning that Molè is one of the three founding fathers of the modern art history in Slovenia – along with Izidor Cankar and France Stelé.[55]

Dvořák's pupil Izidor Cankar, the founder of the department of art history and professor at Ljubljana University from 1920 to 1936, was the most ambitious of the three Slovenien Vienna School graduates as far as the theory of art is concerned.[56] Inspired not only by Heinrich Wölfflin but, above all, by Alois Riegl and Max Dvořák, he wrote an ambitious book on the system of styles (*Uvod v likovno umetnost* [An Introduction to Visual Arts], 1926) and attempted to interpret the whole history of West European art from the point of view of his theory.[57] Since 1936, Cankar's successor to the department of art history at the Ljubljana University, Max Dvořák's pupil France Stelé followed Riegl's and Dvořák's conservation doctrine of monument protection – first in his capacity as the regional conservator at Carniola and, since 1920, as the general conservator of the cultural heritage of Slovenia.[58] Confronted with a new patriotic task to define the specific nature of the history of art in Slovenia (as articulated in his book *Oris zgodovine umetnosti na Slovenskem* [An Outline of the History of Art in Slovenia, 1923), Stelé not only rejected romantic and nationalist interpretation but also criticised the opposite idea of art in Slovenia as backward and peripheral.[59] He faithfully followed the Vienna School's ideal of art history as an independent and rational science. Insisting on the concept of *"art in Slovenia"* as opposed to *"Slovenien art"*,[60] Stelé emphasised its international links and European context. In addition, he regarded Riegl's term *"Kunstwollen"* more as a psychological than an ethnic expression. He interpreted it as *"an artistic inclination"* or *"predisposition"*.[61] In order to define the particular place of Slovenia in the history of European art, Stelé even endorsed a geo-

---

54   Ibid.

55   ŠUMI, Nace: Izidor Cankar, fondatore della Scuola Lubianese di Storia dell'Arte, in *La Scuola Viennese* (see note 39), pp. 195-198, here p. 195; CEVC, Emilijan: Gli echi della scuola di Vienna. France Stelé e Vojeslav Molè, ibid., pp. 199-204, here p. 199.

56   ŠUMI 1996 (see note 55), p. 195; CEVC 1996 (see note 55), p. 199.

57   ŠUMI 1996 (see note 55), p. 196; CEVC 1996 (see note 55), p. 199.

58   Ibid., p. 200.

59   Ibid.

60   Ibid.

61   Ibid., p. 201; PRELOVŠEK, Damjan: Il "Kunstwollen" e la storia dell'arte Slovena, in *La Scuola Viennese* (see note 39), pp. 205-210, here p. 207 f.

historical approach to art.[62] Simultaneously with Dvořák's Croatian disciple Ljubo Karaman, Stelé even revised the idea of lasting geographical constants. Without rehabilitating Strzygowski's antihistorical doctrine, both Stelé and Karaman combined a diachronic with a synchronic approach, intending to emphasise the creative character of regional art.

It is well known that Strzygowski's ideas were strongly criticised by all the main representatives of the Vienna School.[63] Many Slavic disciples of the school – among them Vojtěch Birnbaum and Ljubo Karaman – joined that criticism. They rejected Strzygowski's antiscientism, criticised his belief in lasting ethnic or racial "essences", and dismissed his ethnological idea of the origin of art. In 1925, Birnbaum severely criticised Strzygowski's explanation of the origin of Romanesque architecture in Bohemia as the result of an old pagan vernacular tradition.[64] Ljubo Karaman, who had graduated from Vienna School in 1920, also rejected Strzygowski's interpretation of old Croatian art.[65] As is known, Karaman developed the theory of significant differences between the art of centers, provinces, borderline areas and peripheries. His apologetic typology had been articulated already in the thirties (*Iz kolijevke hrvatske prošlosti* [From the Cradle of Croatian History], 1930), but was not fully developed until the sixties (*O djelovanju domaće sredine u umjetnosti hrvatskih krajeva* [The Impact of the Indigenous Environment on the Development of Art in the Croatian Comities, 1963).[66] In contrast to Strzygowski's idea of the essential (ethnic or racial) nature of artistic wholes, Karaman developed the idea of functional differences between particular regions. Paradoxically in a sense, Karaman's theory can be regarded as an implicit apology for the Vienna School's universalist centralism, despite his vindication of the specific and important role of areas situated outside the centers: since the idea of the particular or even creative nature of the art of provinces and peripheries implies the belief in the universal and linear nature of the history of art.

In comparison to Czechoslovakia or Poland, Dvořák's history of art as the history of world views aroused a stronger echo in Hungary, even if only for

---

[62]   CEVC 1996 (see note 55), p. 201.

[63]   FRODL-KRAFT 1989 (see note 26), p. 29 f.

[64]   HOŘEJŠI 1987 (see note 31), p. 107.

[65]   IVANČEVIĆ, Radovan: Ljubo Karaman e la nozione dell'arte provinciale, dell'arte di frontiera e dell'arte periferica, in *La Scuola Viennese* (see note 39), pp. 183-194, here pp. 183-193. See also IVANČEVIĆ, Radovan: Die Wiener Schule der Kunstgeschichte und Zagreb: Einflüsse und Fortsetzung, in *Ambivalenz des Fin de siècle: Wien – Zagreb*. Eds. Damir BARBARIĆ – Michael BENEDIKT. Wien – Köln – Weimar 1998, pp. 239-241.

[66]   The second edition KARAMAN, Ljubo: *Problemi periferijske umjetnosti*. Zagreb 2001. See also BIAŁOSTOCKI, Jan: Langsames und schnelles Geschehen in der Geschichte der Kunst, in *Stil und Epoche. Periodisierungsfragen*. Dresden 1989, pp. 210-217, here p. 213.

a short time and limited to a particular milieu. Dvořák's pupils Frederick Antal (graduated from Vienna University in 1914), Johannes Wilde (coeditor of Dvořák's *Kunstgeschichte als Geistesgeschichte*, graduated in 1918), Júlia Gyárfás (graduated from Vienna University in 1923) and Charles de Tolnay (who had started his university study with Dvořák in 1918 and had graduated in 1924 supervised already by Julius von Schlosser), represented a bridge to the Budapest intellectual circle around Georg Lukács and Lajos Fülep, known as "Sonntagskreis" (Sunday Circle).[67] Possibly, except for Fülep, the members of this circle were not that interested in the problem of the relationship between universal and national dimensions of art.[68] Following Dvořák's cosmopolitan interpretation of the history of ideas, his Budapest pupils contributed rather to the acknowledgment of avant-garde art as a necessary offshoot of European cultural tradition.[69] Later they transformed "*Geistesgeschichte*" into the social history of art on the one hand (by Frederick Antal) and iconology on the other (by Charles de Tolnay). Due to their participation in the Communist Revolution 1918 – 1919, they had to emigrate from Hungary and never returned. In general, the impact of the Vienna School on Hungarian art history was very limited, despite the fact that Pasteiner's and Schmarsow's disciple, László Éber, professor of art history at Budapest University from 1905 to 1919, attempted to teach Viennese "*genetic-comparative method*" and "*Quellenforschung*" relatively early.[70] After having spent one semester attending Dvořák's lectures, another Hungarian art historian, Edith Hoffmann, curator of the Budapest Museum, found herself enabled to resist nationalist interpretations of the history of art in Hungary. She wrote many papers to demonstrate the European genetic links of Hungarian art.[71] However, the attempt of Kálmán Pogány to provide a platform of communication between Hungarian and Viennese art historians in the journal *Ars una*, published in 1923 – 1924, remained only an episode.[72] After the defeated Revolution 1918 – 1919, the key art historical positions at

---

[67]   TIMÁR, Árpád: Kunstgeschichte und Kunstwissenschaft am Anfang des 20. Jhs., in *Die ungarische Kunstgeschichte* (see note 7), pp. 75-77. Lajos Fülep dealt with the problem of the relationship between universal and national art in his book – FÜLEP, Lajos: *Magyar művészet* [Magyar/Hungarian Art]. Budapest 1923.
See to that also WESSELY, Anna: Der Diskurs über die Kunst im Sonntagskreis, in *Wechsel-Wirkungen. Ungarische Avantgarde in der Weimarer Republik*. Ed. Hubertus GAβNER. Marburg 1985, pp. 541-553.

[68]   TIMÁR 1983 (see note 67), p. 75 f.

[69]   MAROSI, Ernő: Die ungarische Kunstgeschichtsschreibung in den 1920-er Jahren und die Wiener Schule, in *Die ungarische Kunstgeschichte* (see note 7), pp. 84-87, here p. 85; SZABÓ, Júlia: Die Zeitschrift Ars Una, ibid., pp. 83-84, here p. 84.

[70]   SZABÓ, Júlia: László Éber, ibid., pp. 69-70.

[71]   WEHLI, Tünde: Edith Hoffmann, ibid., pp. 80-82.

[72]   SZABÓ 1983 (see note 69), p. 83.

Budapest University were occupied by the conservative nationalists Anton Hekler and Tibor Gerevich.[73] As a consequence, official Hungarian art history returned to a neo-romantic and irrational belief in the autochtonous nature of the history of Hungarian art. In Ernő Marosi's words: *"Diese Rückkehr bestand vor allem in der Annahme einer Autochtoneität der ungarischen Kunstentwicklung, im Programm der Erforschung der national bedingten Eigentümlichkeiten."*[74]

IV. The Vienna School as a Source of Nationalism:
The Role of Disciples II

With regard to what has been said up to this point, it is paradoxical that Alois Riegl and Max Dvořák, but not Josef Strzygowski, are held responsible for nationalist interpretations of the history of art. Despite Strzygowski's explicit notion of cultural geographical wholes as ethnic or racial entities, he was not called to acount for the dissemination of nationalist or racist approaches. This can be explained by Strzygowski's scientific inconsequence and lack of exactness, due to which his impact – even if large – was not as deep as Riegl's. In addition, the anti-hegemonic intention of Strzygowski's geographical pluralism did not fit well with xenophobic nationalism or hegemonic racism.

There is a general agreement among art historians that *"Kunstwollen"* and *"Geistesgeschichte"* can be seen as the expressions of latent or implicit (endemic) nationalism.[75] The interpretation of Riegl as a father of nationalism had been launched by Julius von Schlosser in his history of the Vienna School published in 1934. He understood Riegl's central concept of *"Kunstwollen"* as demonstrating his metaphysical and latent nationalism. According to Schlosser, Riegl perceived *"Kunstwollen"* as an expression of the spirit of a nation: *"Tatsächlich bricht in Riegls Geschichtskonstruktion etwas wie ein Neu-Vitalismus hervor, die 'Kunstentwicklung' stellt sich dem 'Volksgeist' entspringend, als Personifikation oder Allegorie eines Begriffes dar, wie ein hypostasierter Organismus."*[76]

---

[73]   MAROSI 1983 (see note 69), p. 86 f.

[74]   Ibid., p. 87.

[75]   HAUSSHERR, Reiner: Kunstgeographie und Kunstlandschaft, in *Kunst in Hessen und am Mittelrhein,* 9. Darmstadt 1969, pp. 38-44, here p. 39; KUTZNER, Marian: Społeczne uwarunkowania rozwoju śląskej architektury w latach 1200 – 1330 [Social Conditions of the Development of Silesian Architecture in the Years 1200 – 1330], in *Sztuka i ideologia XIII wieku* [Art and Ideology of the 13th Century]. Ed. Piotr SKUBISZEWSKI. Wrocław – Warszawa – Kraków – Gdańsk 1974, p. 235; LARSSON, Lars-Olof: Nationalstil und Nationalismus in der Kunstgeschichte der zwanziger und dreißiger Jahre, in *Kategorien und Methoden der deutschen Kunstgeschichte, 1900 – 1930.* Ed. Lorenz DITTMANN. Stuttgart 1985, pp. 169-175, here p. 175.

[76]   SCHLOSSER 1934 (see note 14), p. 190.

However, Schlosser's interpretation of Riegl was accepted by post-war art history without taking its context into consideration. Nobody noticed that Schlosser's reconstruction of the history of the Vienna School came into being thirty years after Riegl's death in the context of rapidly rising xenophobic nationalism and anti-Semitism. Due to that, it can be regarded as a response to the particular historical situation, as a token of a strong susceptibility to the question of nationalism, and, consequently, as a retrospective projection of the political situation of rising Fascism onto the period around 1900.

It is true that Riegl used expressions like the *"nationalste Thema der Holländer"*, *"holländisches Kunstwollen"*, *"das spezifisch nationale Kunstwerk der Holländer"* or *"die nationalholländische Kunst"* in his *Das Holländische Gruppenporträt* (1902).[77] Nevertheless, *"das holländische Kunstwollen"* does not need to be necessarily understood as an expression of nationalism nor as evidence for the belief in a collective spiritual subject. It can easily be seen as a metaphor of Holland as a state, or simply as an indication of provenance. According to Hubert Locher, the need to specify the mover of the history of art, *"die treibende Energie der universalen Stilgeschichte"*[78] and the conception of it as a national *"collective subject"* *"mit einem biologisch bedingten 'nationalen Charakter' und entsprechendem 'Kunstwollen'"*,[79] is the logical consequence of Riegl's teleological notion of history and his metaphorical concept of the autonomy of art.[80] Despite the plausibility of Locher's perspicacious analysis, another interpretation can also be offered of *"Kunstwollen"*. Not the idea of the autonomy of art, but that of *"Kunstwollen"* can be regarded as a metaphor and as an instrument at the same time. Owing to the *fin de siècle* modernist experience on the one hand, and to the ideal of art history as an exact science on the other, the autonomy of art, the immanent nature of its development and the incompatible plurality of notions of art represented Riegl's primary concerns. He used the concept of *"Kunstwollen"* to stress them. At the same time, his notion of the history of art as an (autonomous) *"evolution"* based on the model of the natural sciences did not need the concept of a personalised mover of historical changes. Riegl regarded the movement of history of art as the necessary result of immanent (and autonomous) (art)historical laws. His idea of the history of art had, rather, the shape of a natural organism than that of a spiritual being. Consequently, the term *"holländisches Kunstwollen"* can also be

---

[77]   RIEGL, Alois: *Das holländische Gruppenporträt*. Wien 1931, pp. 3 f., 21, 180.

[78]   LOCHER, Hubert: *Kunstgeschichte als historische Theorie der Kunst*. München 2001, p. 439.

[79]   Ibid., p. 448.

[80]   Ibid., p. 439; LOCHER, Hubert: Stilgeschichte und die Frage der "nationalen Konstante", in *Zeitschrift für Schweizerische Archäologie und Kunstgeschichte*, 53, 1996, pp. 285-294.

interpreted as a geographical localisation and as an indication of the concept of art of a particular (corporative) society. It is true that Riegl spoke about *"a higher third element"* determining social structure as well as art.[81] Nevertheless, he did not specify it explicitly as the spirit of a nation. Even if it is true that a latent nationalist element was implied in the concept of *"Kunstwollen"* which stimulated Riegl's followers to develop a nationalistic or biological-racist interpretation of the history of art, Riegl himself cannot be regarded as a nationalist *par excellence*. His rejection of nationalism as a kind of egoism in contrast to altruism in the protection of historical monuments, as formulated in his polemics against Georg Dehio,[82] can be regarded as explicit evidence of Riegl's preference for universalism.

Riegl's successor as the Austrian general conservator of historical monuments, Max Dvořák, demonstrated his adherence to Monarchic cosmopolitanism unequivocally, too. He fought against all attempts to misuse historical monuments for nationalist or commercial purposes.[83] Even if he used the term *"nationales Ingenium"* while looking for the origin of Dutch painting,[84] or characterised Dürer's "Apocalypse" as *"the first great German work of art of our era"*,[85] Dvořák's conception of the history of art as the history of world-views had an explicitly universalistic nature. He avoided all potential risks of nationalistic interpretation implicit in *"Geistesgeschichte"*. In contrast to Schnaase or Pinder, he regarded art rather as an embodiment of the *"Zeitgeist"* than as an expression of *"Volksgeist"*.[86] Whether intentionally or not, Dvořák avoided the nationalist or racist interpretation of *"Geistesgeschichte"* as replacing the anonymous notion of the history of ideas (*"geistesgeschichtliche 'Kunstgeschichte ohne Namen'"*) with the idea of great masters. He regarded them as creators of the worldview of a particular age or even as prophets.[87] Focusing on the interpretation of the spiritual mission of art by Giotto, Brueghel, El Greco, Tintoretto or Dürer,[88] he anticipated the aristocratic individualism by

---

[81]   RIEGL 1931 (see note 77), p. 3.
[82]   See, for example HUSE, Norbert: *Denkmalpflege. Deutsche Texte aus drei Jahrhunderten*. München 1984, pp. 124-130.
[83]   See note 23.
[84]   DVOŘÁK, Max: Die Anfänge der holländischen Malerei (1918), in DVOŘÁK, Max: *Das Rätsel der Kunst der Brüder van Eyck* (=Klassische Texte der Wiener Schule der Kunstgeschichte, 2/1). Ed. Artur ROSENAUER. Wien 1999, p. 245.
[85]   DVOŘÁK, Max: Dürer's Apokalypse, in DVOŘÁK 1924 (see note 23), pp. 193-202, here p. 197.
[86]   SCHNAASE, Karl: *Geschichte der bildenden Künste*. Vol. 1. Düsseldorf 1866 (2nd ed.), p. 53: *"die Kunst einer jeden Zeit [sei] der vollständigste Ausdruck des jedesmaligen Volksgeistes"*.
[87]   HASKELL, Francis: *History and Its Images. Art and the Interpretation of the Past*. New Haven – London 1993, pp. 411-415.
[88]   DVOŘÁK 1924 (see note 23), pp. 149-202, 217-276.

means of which Schlosser coped with the rise of metaphysical nationalism and racism in the thirties. In addition, Dvořák as a Czech also demonstrated his aristocratic cosmopolitanism by not accepting the offer of a chair of art history at Charles University in Prague after the establishment of an independent Czechoslovakia.

It is known that in the late twenties and at the beginning of the early thirties, the latest cadre of Dvořák's students who had graduated from Vienna University (already under the supervision of Schlosser), came out with a programme of rigorous art science (*"strenge Kunstwissenschaft"*).[89] This initiative was launched by Hans Sedlmayr, Otto Pächt and Guido von Kaschnitz-Weinberg as a critical reaction against the *"Geistesgeschichte"* which had been regarded as an insufficiently exact procedure. They returned to Riegl's Formalism and concentrated on the analysis of the structure of works of art. At the same time, however, intending to establish a rigorous art history in a strictly inductionist way, they also rejected Riegl's ambition to reconstruct art historical development as an abstract construct. In contrast to that, they focused on the analysis of the structure of a single work of art or the structure of a particular style. But Viennese structuralists did not solely aim at establishing art historical research in a strictly inductive way. Their ambition was to synthesise the historical approach with aesthetic evaluation. They believed that they could catch the irrational core of a work of art, i.e. its aesthetic quality by means of rational analysis. In addition, they believed that they could discern the historical uniqueness of a work of art in an unprejudiced, purely empirical way. Owing to its evidently contradictory approach, Viennese structuralism – Hans Sedlmayr above all – resulted in a new ahistorical normativism or even mysticism. As Meyer Schapiro warned very early,[90] the Viennese Structuralists opened the way to the false myth of eternal transhistorical constants and metaphysical collective subjects dominating the history of art by understanding structure as an essence, which may justify the ascription of *"the negativity of Structure analysis"*.[91]

Despite their metaphysical tendency, it was not the Viennese Structuralists but their older colleagues and Dvořák's direct pupils, Karl Maria Swoboda and Dagobert Frey, who transformed Riegl's and Dvořák's legacy into a nationalist

---

89 ROSENAUER, Artur: Zur neuen Wiener Schule der Kunstgeschichte, in *L'Art et les révolutions, 5. Révolution et évolution de l'Histoire de l'Art de Warburg á nos jours. Actes du XXVIIème congrès international d'histoire de l'art, Strasbourg, 1 – 7 septembre 1989*. Strasbourg 1992, pp. 73-84.
90 SCHAPIRO, Meyer: The New Viennese School, in *The Art Bulletin*, 18, 1936, pp. 258-266.
91 WOOD, Christopher S.: Introduction, in *The Vienna School Reader. Politics and Art Historical Method in the 1930s*. Ed. Christopher S. WOOD. New York 2003, pp. 9-71, here p. 42.

or racist one.[92] Not only Riegl's *"Kunstwollen"* but also Dvořák's *"Geistesgeschichte"* were considered as a point of departure for a biologically and racially shaped nationalist interpretation of the history of art. According to Swoboda, the new task of art history was to study *"sogenannten kunsthistorischen Konstanten"*, asking *"Welches ist trotz allem geschichtlichen Wandel der sich gleichbleibende Charakter der Kunst eines Volkes, einer Landschaft, einer Stadt?"*.[93] Paradoxically, it was precisely the transformation of spirituality into biological metaphysics, which was regarded as an unfolding of the Vienna School's ideal of exact art history. As a consequence, not only was *"Geistesgeschichte"* reinterpreted biologically, but also the old Vienna School (Monarchic) universalism was transformed into a new (Pangerman) nationalistic hegemonism. In addition, it is worth mentioning that Strzygowski not only inspired Sedlmayr's idea of two art histories[94] but also stimulated Swoboda's and Frey's belief in transhistorical constants and metaphysical (national and ethnic or racial) collective subjects.[95] Owing to that, Sedlmayr's and Swoboda's or Frey's imperial nationalism can also be regarded as a result of the reinterpretation of the Vienna School ideas by means of Strzygowski's phantasmagorias.

It is significant that after the defeat of Fascism, Swoboda returned penitently to the universalistic conception of the history of art.[96] Dagobert Frey overcame the post-war trauma by means of an anthropological philosophy of art,[97] stressing the role of man in contrast to race or nation on the one hand,

---

[92] KUTZNER, Marian: Sztuka i kolonizacja niemiecka na wschód od Odry [Art and the German Colonisation to the East of the Odra], in *Niemcy – Polska w średniowieczu. Materiały z konferencji naukowej zorganizowanej przez Instytut historii UAM w dniach 14 – 16 XI 1983 roku* [Germany – Poland in the Middle Ages. Materials from the Conference Organized by the Institute of History of the AMU, 14 – 16 November 1983]. Ed. Jerzy STRZELCZYK. Poznań 1986, pp. 343-348. See too, BAKOŠ, Ján: Vienna School Disciples and "The New Tasks" of Art History, in *Ars*, 40, 2007, No. 2, pp. 145-155.

[93] SWOBODA, Karl M.: *Neue Aufgaben der Kunstgeschichte.* Brünn – Prag – Leipzig – Wien 1935, p. 21.

[94] LACHNIT, Edwin: Julius v. Schlosser und die Geschichte der Wiener Schule. Anläßlich zweier fünfzigster Anniversarien in Österreich 1988, in *Kritische Berichte*, 16, 1988, No. 4, pp. 29-35, here p. 35; FRODL-KRAFT 1989 (see note 26), p. 34.

[95] FREY, Dagobert: Bemerkungen zur "Wiener Schule der Kunstwissenschaft", in FREY, Dagobert: *Eine Erinnerungsschrift.* Kiel 1962, pp. 5-15, here p. 15: *"Ich bin sicher ein Dvořák Schüler, aber ich muss zugeben, daß doch da entscheidende Anregungen von Strzygowski gekommen sind."* DEMUS, Otto: K. M. Swoboda als Forscher, in *Festschrift Karl M. Swoboda zum 28. Januar 1958.* Ed. Otto BENESCH. Wien – Wiesbaden 1959, pp. 7-11, here p. 11: *"In der Person eines Gelehrten* [i.e. K. M. Swoboda] *wird der Zwiespalt der beiden Wiener Richtungen überwunden, der 'Wiener Schule' und jener... Josef Strzygowski's."*

[96] DEMUS 1959 (see note 95), p. 11, characterises Swoboda's approach to the history of art in the post-war time as *"Geistesgeschichte des Erdkreises"*.

[97] GENSBAUR-BENDLER, Ulrike: Dagobert Frey – Lebensphilosophische Grundlagen seiner Kunsttheorie, in *Wiener Jahrbuch für Kunstgeschichte*, 42, 1989, pp. 53-79.

and a global art historical comparison on the other,[98] nevertheless insisting on the existence of geographical entities, even if no longer understood as ethnic or racial ones. Moreover, as far as Hans Sedlmayr is concerned, he tried to escape into a retrospectivist clericalism (developing the conception of the history of art as the history of *"epiphany of absolute spirit"*)[99] on the one hand, with an aggressive, hyper-conservative attack on Modernism, on the other.[100]

Nevertheless, the interpretation of Riegl and Dvořák as fathers of nationalism in art history oversimplifies the complexity of their ideas and overlooks the dialectical nature of their theories.[101] Riegl's and Dvořak's contradictory models, in a sense, can be regarded as mirrors of the political and ideological contradictions of the Habsburg Monarchy at the turn of the century and as attempts at their symbolic reconciliation. They can also be perceived as expressions of the dilemmas with which the Austrian middle class intellectuals engaged as state officials, had to cope.

---

[98] FREY, Dagobert: Autobiographie, in *Österreichische Geschichtswissenschaft der Gegenwart in Selbstdarstellungen* (=Schlern-Schriften, 69). Vol. 2. Ed. Nikolaus GRASS. Innsbruck 1951, pp. 47-77.

[99] SEDLMAYR, Hans: Kunstgeschichte als Geistesgeschichte, in *Wort und Wahrheit*, 4, 1949, pp. 264-277; reprinted in SEDLMAYR, Hans: *Kunst und Wahrheit. Zur Theorie und Methode der Kunstgeschichte*. Hamburg 1958, pp. 71-86, here p. 85.

[100] SAUERLÄNDER, Willibald: Hans Sedlmayrs "Verlust der Mitte", in SAUERLANDER, Willibald: *Geschichte der Kunst/Gegenwart der Kritik*. Ed. Werner BUSCH. Köln 1999, pp. 229-238; SCHNEIDER, Norbert: Revolutionskritik und Kritik der Moderne bei Hans Sedlmayr, in *L'Art et les révolutions* (see note 89), pp. 85-92; SCHNEIDER, Norbert: Hans Sedlmayr (1896 – 1984), in *Altmeister moderner Kunstgeschichte*. Ed. Heinrich DILLY. Berlin 1990, pp. 274-281.

[101] On this, see BAKOŠ, Ján: Alois Riegl – otec umeleckohistorického nacionalizmu? [Alois Riegl – the Father of Art Historical Nationalism?], in *Regnum Bohemiae et Sacrum Romanum Imperium. Sborník k poctě Jiřího Kuthana*. Praha 2005, pp. 399-408.

VII. THE REVISION OF A BOURGEOIS IDEA: FROM A NATIONAL TO A DYNASTIC HISTORY OF ART

Hegemonic Nationalism and the Centre-Periphery Problem

The nationalist paradigm of the history of art, which sees the history of styles as the expression of *"national characteristics"* and which dominated continental art history in the 1930s and 1940s, was a hegemonic rather than a pluralist ("Herderian") theory. Competition between nations was regarded as a struggle for superiority and dominance. It was Émile Mâle who had already, in 1914, articulated the idea of the inferiority of German art in comparison with that of France or Italy, which filled the whole German art historical community with indignation.[1] On the other hand, this "inferiority complex" functioned as a catalyst in German art history. In 1913, Kurt Gerstenberg published a book on a specific German version of the Gothic style, *Deutsche Sondergotik*;[2] and Georg Dehio in his *Geschichte der deutschen Kunst*; articulated not only the patriotic credo that the German nation is the true *"hero"* of the history of German art[3] but also responded to the humiliation

---

[1]   LARSSON, Lars-Olof: Nationalstil und Nationalismus in der Kunstgeschichte der zwanziger und dreissiger Jahre, in *Kategorien und Methoden der deutschen Kunstgeschichte, 1900 – 1930.* Ed. Lorenz DITTMANN. Stuttgart 1985, p. 180; LAMBOURNE, Nicola: Production versus Destruction: Art, World War I and Art History, in *Art History*, 22, 1999, pp. 347-363; DILLY, Heinrich: September 1914, in *Revue Germanique Internationale*, 13, 2000, pp. 23-37.

[2]   GERSTENBERG, Kurt: *Deutsche Sondergotik. Eine Untersuchung über das Wesen der deutschen Baukunst im späten Mittelalter.* München 1913 (2nd ed. Darmstadt 1969). See about that in LARSSON 1985 (see note 1), p. 75; BELTING, Hans: *Die Deutschen und ihre Kunst. Ein schwieriges Erbe.* München 1992, p. 23.

[3]   DEHIO, Georg: *Geschichte der deutschen Kunst.* Berlin – Leipzig 1919 – 1926, Vol. 1, p. V (Vorwort, 31. Oktober 1918): *"mein wahrer Held ist das deutsche Volk"*. See to that LOCHER, Hubert: *Kunstgeschichte als historische Theorie der Kunst.* München 2001, p. 201. The same opinion had been expressed already by Dehio in "Deutsche Kunstgeschichte und deutsche Geschichte" in *Historische Zeitschrift*, 100, 1908, pp. 473-485; reprinted in DEHIO, Georg: *Kunsthistorische Aufsätze.* München – Berlin 1914, pp. 61-74. See also DEHIO, Georg: *Kunstgeschichte als Kulturgeschichte.* Berlin 1993, p. 5. Dehio not only regarded the German nation as a collective standard bearer (*"Träger"*) of the history of art, he also regarded art as expressive of the character of a nation: *"Die dieses Buch durchgehend beherrschende Frage lautet nicht: Was erfahren wir durch die Deutschen über das Wesen der Kunst? Sondern was offenbart uns die Kunst vom Wesen der Deutschen?"*, quoted according to DEHIO 1993 (see this note), p. 12. Nevertheless, at the same

with a conception of German art as an active mediator between West and East, transmitting Western models to the Slavic nations,[4] and in 1932, Heinrich Wölfflin built up the theory of two different but equal *"feelings for form"* – Italian and German – in his *Italien und das deutsche Formgefühl*.[5] German response culminated in Wilhelm Pinder's theory of centre and periphery.[6] Pinder's theory consisted of two components: the *"Sonderleistungen"* (*"special achievements"*) and *"Ausstrahlungen"* (*"radiations"*) of German art. The first component was directed against the accusation of German art's lack of independence and represented an effort to set up a list of German inventions and unique contributions to the world history of art (e.g. the winged retable and the woodcut). The second claimed a dominant position for German art in Central Europe and analysed its role as mediator of Western models to the East European nations. Thus it was Pinder who introduced the idea of migration, exchange and hybridization that transcended state borders, as

---

time Dehio regarded art history as an international discipline: *"Die Wissenschaft ist nach ihrem Wesen übernational."* – DEHIO 1919 – 1926 (see in this note), Vol. 1, p. V. See also MUTHESIUS, Stefan: Schlesische Kunst im Lichte der polnischen und deutschen Kunstgeschichte, in *Kunstchronik*, 50, 1997, No. 7, p. 334. On Georg Dehio, see BETTHAUSEN, Peter: *Georg Dehio. Ein deutscher Kunsthistoriker*. München – Berlin 2004.

4   KUTZNER, Marian: Społeczne uwarunkowania rozwoju śląskej architektury w latach 1200 – 1330 [Social Conditions of the Development of Silesian Architecture in the Years 1200 – 1330], in *Sztuka i ideologia XIII wieku* [Art and Ideology of the 13th Century]. Ed. Piotr SKUBISZEWSKI. Wrocław – Warszawa – Kraków – Gdańsk 1974, p. 235; KUTZNER, Marian: Sztuka i kolonizacja niemiecka na wschód od Odry [Art and the German Colonisation to the East of the Odra], in *Niemcy – Polska w średniowieczu. Materiały z konferencji naukowej zorganizowanej przez Instytyt historii UAM w dniach 14 – 16 XI 1983 roku* [Germany – Poland in the Middle Ages. Materials from the Conference Organized by the Institute of History of the AMU, 14 – 16 November 1983]. Ed. Jerzy STRZELCZYK. Poznań 1986, pp. 338, 341; LABUDA, Adam S.: "...eine von sinnvollen Zweckgefühlen erfüllte, herbe und großartige Kolonialkunst..." Zum kunsthistorischen Diskurs über Ostmitteleuropa, in *Zeitschrift für Kunstgeschichte*, 56, 1993, No. 1, p. 4.

5   WÖLFFLIN, Heinrich: *Italien und das deutsche Formgefühl*. München 1931. On this, see LARSSON 1985 (see note 1), p. 174 and BELTING 1992 (see note 2), pp. 24-26.

6   As expressed in the Introduction to PINDER, Wilhelm: *Vom Wesen und Werden deutscher Formen I. Die Kunst der deutschen Kaiserzeit bis zum Ende der staufischen Klassik*. Leipzig 1935 (1940), consisting of the following parts: "Das Verhältnis zum Fremden", "Die Auslandsdeutsche Kunst", "Wesenszüge der deutschen Kunst", "Herkunft und Begegnung". According to HELD, Jutta: Kunstgeschichte im "Dritten Reich". Wilhelm Pinder und Hans Jantzen an der Münchner Universität, in *Kunstgeschichte an den Universitäten im Nationalsozialismus* (=Kunst und Politik, 5). Eds. Jutta HELD – Martin PAPENBROCK. Göttingen 2003, p. 35: *"Pinder entwirft hier eine Kunstgeschichte der Peripherie."* See also LARSSON 1985 (see note 1), pp. 179-180. On Pinder, see especially: HALBERTSMA, Marlite: *Wilhelm Pinder und die Deutsche Kunstgeschichte*. Worms 1992; and DILLY, Heinrich: *Deutsche Kunsthistoriker, 1933 – 1945*. München – Berlin 1988, pp. 51-54.

essential factors in the history of art.[7] Nonetheless, his theory of centre-periphery relationship was formed on, let us say, the premise of the superiority of German art over the art of Slavic nations and represented an explicitly hegemonic nationalist approach. If the special contributions of German art were emphasized in relation to French or Italian art, then the relationship of German art to the art of Eastern Europe was regarded as the relation of a centre to a periphery. According to Pinder, there was a hierarchy in the arts of nations. The art of whole nations rather than particular social organisms (such as cities) was categorized as central or peripheral. As a consequence, the idea of the history of art as an autonomous and impersonal development, applied by Pinder in *Die deutsche Plastik des ausgehenden Mittelalters und der Frührenaissance,*[8] was transformed into an idea of art history as the expression of a collective subject, a people (*"Volk"*), a nation. The German nation was identified by him as the collective carrier (*"Träger"*) of the history of art in Central Europe.

Escape to the "Christian Occident"

The concept of art as the expression of national or ethnic character, together with the belief in nation and *"Volk"* as the collective author and consequently owner of artworks, then prepared the base for the looting of Polish and Czech art collections during World War II and justified it as "repatriation" or "restitution" of German property. It is known that Dagobert Frey was involved in confiscation of works of art from Poland.[9] It is symptomatic that he based his active participation in plundering artworks from Poland on a theory of centre-

---

[7] HELD 2003 (see note 6), p. 35. On *"colonial art"*, see KUTZNER 1986 (see note 4), pp. 337-353; LABUDA 1993 (see note 4), pp. 1-17; HERRMANN, Christofer: Kunstlandschaft, Kunstgeographie und Kolonialkunst. Grundsätzliche und Methodische *Überlegungen*, in HERRMANN, Christofer: *Mittelalterliche Architektur im Preussenland. Untersuchungen zur Frage der Kunstlandschaft und -Geographie.* Petersburg 2007, pp. 25-39, here pp. 33-34.

[8] PINDER, Wilhelm: *Die deutsche Plastik des ausgehenden Mittelalters und der Frührenaissance.* Berlin 1924. See BOERNER, Bruno: Stilgeschichte um 1900 und im 20. Jahrhundert, in *Stilfragen zur Kunst des Mittelalters. Eine Einführung.* Eds. Bruno KLEIN – Bruno BOERNER. Berlin 2006, pp. 66-72.

[9] See MUTHESIUS, Stefan: *Kunst in Polen/Polnische Kunst, 966 – 1990. Eine Einführung.* Königstein im Taunus 1994, p. 11; STÖRKUHL, Beate: Paradigmen und Methoden der kunstgeschichtlichen "Ostforschung" – der "Fall" Dagobert Frey, in *Die Kunsthistoriographien in Ostmitteleuropa und der nationale Diskurs.* Eds. Robert BORN – Alena JANATKOVÁ – Adam S. LABUDA. Berlin 2004, pp. 155-172; DaCOSTA KAUFMANN, Thomas: *Toward a Geography of Art.* Chicago – London 2004, p. 86; BAKOŠ, Ján: Vienna School Disciples and "The New Tasks" of Art History, in *Ars*, 40, 2007, No. 2, pp. 145-155, here pp. 152-154.

periphery relationship, inverse in comparison to Pinder's concept, in that it emphasized the active role of the periphery.[10] As a matter of course, the active role of the periphery was prepared for by the appropriation or nationalization of the regions of East European art , which came to be seen as German "colonial" art.

Nevertheless, the collapse of German hegemonism and expansionism resulted not only in a deep crisis of *"Kunstgeographie"* after World War II[11] but also into the effort to replace hegemonic nationalism with the conception, or *"myth"* in Hans Belting's words, of the *"christliches Abendland"* (*"Christian Occident"*).[12] In this way, the idea of the exceptionality or superiority of national art was replaced with the idea of long established membership of the trans-national and continuous Western Christian tradition.[13]

---

[10] See HERRMANN 2007 (see note 7), p. 27. Herrmann comments on Frey's theory as follows: *"Die Voraussetzungen für eine bodenständige, künstlerische Sonderentwicklung in der deutschen Kunst sei dabei von Osten, von den Kolonisiationsgebieten gerade des Ostseeraums ausgegangen."* In D. Frey's own words: *"Der Osten wird schöpferisch... die bisher herrschende, durch das Kulturgefälle bedingte, westöstliche Kulturströmung schlägt in eine Gegenbewegung von Osten nach Westen um."* Nevertheless, it is worth noting that Frey derives that change from a sociological phenomenon, namely the coming into existence of court art (in Prague and Vienna): *"Der Osten wird schöpferisch. Entscheidend hierfür ist die Entwicklung einer höfischen Kultur..."* See FREY, Dagobert: Die Entwicklung nationaler Stile in der mittelalterlichen Kunst des Abendlandes, in *Deutsche Vierteljahrsschrift für Literaturwissenschaft und Geistesgeschichte*, 16, 1938, pp. 1-74, reprinted in Darmstadt, 1970, p. 62.

[11] FREY, Dagobert: Geschichte und Probleme der Kultur- und Kunstgeographie, in *Archaelogia Geographica*, 4, 1955, pp. 90-105; reprinted in FREY, Dagobert: *Bausteine zu einer Philosophie der Kunst*. Darmstadt 1976, p. 284, speaks about *"das Versagen der Kunstgeographie"* and claims that "Nach dem Zweiten Weltkrieg ist das Interesse an der Kunstgeographie bedauerlicherweise jäh abgesunken". More about that in DaCOSTA KAUFMANN 2004 (see note 9), pp. 89-93.

[12] See SAUERLÄNDER, Willibald: Von der "Sonderleistungen deutscher Kunst" zur "Ars Sacra", in SAUERLANDER, Willibald: *Geschichte der Kunst/Gegenwart der Kritik*. Ed. Werner BUSCH. Köln 1999, pp. 277-292; BELTING 1992 (see note 2), pp. 49-55, chapter "Das 'Abendland' als Ausweg". As examples of that trend, can be mentioned BAUCH, Kurt: *Abendländische Kunst*. Düsseldorf 1952; JANTZEN, Hans: *Die Gotik des Abendlandes*. Köln 1962; or BRAUNFELS, Wolfgang: *Abendländische Klosterbaukunst*. Köln 1969. Hans Jantzen played the role of an initiator of that conception. See his paper "Die Einheit Europas in der Geschichte seiner Kunst" in *Geistige Welt*, 3, 1948 – 1949, pp. 115-117. On this, see HELD 2003 (see note 6), p. 27; PAPENBROCK, Martin: Kurt Bauch in Freiburg 1933 – 1945, in PAPENBROCK – HELD 2003 (see note 6), pp. 201-202; DOLL, Nikola: Der Erste Deutsche Kunsthistorikertag 1948, in *Kunstgeschichte im Nationalsozialismus. Beiträge zur Geschichte einer Wissenschaft zwischen 1930 – 1950*. Eds. Nikola DOLL – Christian FUHRMEISTER – Michael H. SPRENGER. Weimar 2005, pp. 332, 335; PAPENBROCK, Martin: Die Freiburger Kunstgeschichte in der Nachkriegszeit, in *Kunst und Politik. Jahrbuch der Guernica-Gesellschaft*, 8, 2006, Schwerpunkt: Kunstgeschichte an den Universitäten in der Nachkriegszeit, ed. Martin PAPENBROCK, p. 204. On German post-war art history, see DILLY 1988 (see note 6), pp. 77-89.

[13] According to HELD, Jutta: Kunstgeographie, in HELD, Jutta – SCHNEIDER, Norbert: *Grundzüge der Kunstwissenschaft. Gegenstandsbereiche – Institutionen – Problemfelder*. Köln – Weimar – Wien 2007, pp. 130-147, here, p. 143, critically reacting against nationalist or racist Kunst-

Revision of "Kunstgeographie": "Kunstlandschaft" as the Product of Tradition and a Communications System

However, this nationalistic doctrine of the history of art was critically revised not only outside German art history but also by German art historians themselves.[14] Since it was precisely the notion of *"Kunstlandschaft"* that German nationalist *"Kunstgeographie"* misused, critical revision of hegemonic nationalism focused on this concept. Despite its compromised reputation, German art historians were not been prepared to give it up, since the term *"Kunstlandschaft"* enabled them to express the specific situation of the history of German art, namely the fact that the history of art in Germany did not always coincide with state history. In addition, the term also suited very well the pluralist character of the history of art in Germany. Moreover, the notion of *"Kunstlandschaft"* corresponded well to the dialectical nature of the history of art in Germany, characterized by the duality of *"activity and creativity"* on the one hand and *"the peripheral position"* outside great world art centres on the other.[15] That is why critical revision of the concept *"Kunstlandschaft"* was aimed mainly at its nationalist and metaphysical misuse. Reconsidering art geography between 1965 and 1970, Reiner Haussherr[16] came to the conclusion that the idea of *"Kunstlandschaft"* had to be cleansed of all biological, ethnic and metaphysical connotations and could be made acceptable only as a result of regional artistic traditions (established by particular workshops).[17] In 1975, Herbert Beck and Horst Bredekamp unmasked the political and ideological use of the term *"Kunstlandschaft"* and emphasized its historical and anti-metaphysical nature: *"'Kunstlandschaft' [sei] keine überhistorisch gegebene, sondern*

---

geographie, post-war German art history was universalistically oriented: *"Die Kunstgeschichte der Nachkriegszeit strebte... nach einer universalistischen Kunstgeschichte mindestens europäischen Zuschnitts."*

[14] According to DaCOSTA KAUFMANN 2004 (see note 9), p. 93: *"... not until the mid-1960s or even the 1970s did German scholars of a younger generation... revive art geography in the sense that they suggested different directions for its scholarship to take."*

[15] Harald Keller attempted to rehabilitate the concept of *"Kunstlandschaft"* demonstrating its applicability also to the history of art in Italy and France. See KELLER, Harald: *Die Kunstlandschaften Italiens*. München 1960; KELLER, Harald: *Die Kunstlandschaften Frankreichs*. Wiesbaden 1963.

[16] HAUSSHERR, Reiner: Überlegungen zum Stand der Kunstgeographie. Neuerscheinungen, in *Rheinische Vierteljahrsblätter*, 30, 1965, pp. 351-372; HAUSSHERR, Reiner: Kunstgeographie und Kunstlandschaft, in *Kunst in Hessen und am Mittelrhein, 9*. Darmstadt 1969, pp. 38-44; HAUSSHERR, Reiner: Kunstgeographie – Aufgaben, Grenzen, Möglichkeiten, in *Rheinische Vierteljahrsblätter*, 34, 1970, pp. 158-171.

[17] HAUSSHERR 1970 (see note 16), p. 164: *"Wir sollen von regionalen Traditionen sprechen, ohne diesen einen kunstgeschichtlichen Stammesbegriff zu applizieren."*

zeitbedingte und erklärbare Große. Sie ist nicht vom überdauernden Eigenleben eines Kunststiles oder dem 'Wesen' des Menschen in einer geographischen Region abzuleiten, sondern vielmehr aus konkreten historischen Verhältnissen."[18] A little later, Wolfgang Braunfels also replaced the ethnic notion of a territory with the idea of a region resulting from a tradition and now applied to a mega-region.[19] According to Hans Belting's comment: *"Hier gibt es keine Stammmesmerkmale mehr, geschweige denn eine nationale Eigenart deutscher Kunst, sondern nur noch ein buntes Mosaik von gewachsenen Traditionen in regionalen und lokalen Rahmen."*[20] In addition, the idea of *"Kunstlandschaft"* as a temporary communications system, was developed in the 1980s.[21]

---

[18] BECK, Herbert – BREDEKAMP, Horst: Der Mittelrhein als Kunstlandschaft, in *Kunst um 1400 am Mittelrhein.* [Exhib. Cat.] Frankfurt am Main 1975, p. 40.

[19] BRAUNFELS, Wolfgang: *Die Kunst im Heiligen Römischen Reich Deutscher Nation.* München 1979 – 1989.

[20] See the comment by BELTING 1992 (see note 2), p. 54. A similar opinion was expressed later by Heinrich Klotz, even if not unequivocally: *"Es liegt allzu nahe, ethnische Besonderheiten erkennen zu wollen, obwohl es doch überwiegend künstlerische Traditionen sind, die bestimmte ästhetische Vorlieben entstehen liessen."* – KLOTZ, Heinrich: *Geschichte der Deutschen Kunst.* Vol. 1. München 1998, p. 12.

[21] STAMM, Lieselotte E.: Zur Verwendung des Begriffs Kunstlandschaft am Beispiel des Oberrheins im 14. und frühen 15. Jahrhundert, in *Zeitschrift für Schweizerische Archäologie und Kunstgeschichte,* 41, 1984, No. 2, pp. 85-91. According to Stamm, p. 85: *"Der Versuch einer Definition des Begriffs Kunstlandschaft geht von einem Modell aus, in dem sich die Kommunikation auf drei verschiedenen Ebenen abspielt: Zunächst die primäre, d.h. geographische Kommunikation, die sich im engsten lokalen Raum ereignet... In der Kunst benennen wir diese Ebene mit dem Begriff 'Lokalstil'... Die zweite Ebene würde die gesellschaftlich-wirtschaftliche Kommunikation umfassen, die sich als 'Regionalstil' bezeichnen möchte. In der dritten Ebene... spielt sich die politisch-religiöse Kommunikation ab... die sich mit dem Begriff 'Territorialstil' umschreiben mochte."* Stamm, p. 89, emphasized the importance of the third level of communication, namely *"political-territorial communication"* which implies *"adaptation of trans-regional influences"* (*"Adaptation überregionaler Einflüsse"*) and the temporary nature of the art region (*"eine Kunstlandschaft sozusagen auf Zeit"*). In 1994, Wolfgang Schmid (SCHMID, Wolfgang: Kunstlandschaft – Absatzgebiet – Zentralraum. Zur Brauchbarkeit unterschiedlicher Raumkonzepte in der kunstgeographischen Forschung vornehmlich an rheinischen Beispielen, in *Figur und Raum. Mittelalterliche Holzbildwerke im historischen und kunstgeographischen Kontext.* Eds. Uwe ALBRECHT – Jan von BONSDORF. Berlin 1994, pp. 21-34) argued that the *"mobility of persons and objects"* which resulted from commissions and the art market, falsified the idea of a static *"Kunstlandschaft"*. This had to be replaced by a notion of a dynamic and hierarchical network of centres (*"System von Ober-, Mittel- und Unterzentren... und den Gesamtraum strukturierendes Netz"*). On the concept of *"Kunstlandschaft"*, see recently HERRMANN 2007 (see note 7), pp. 25-34; GRÖTECKE, Iris: Mittelalterforschung und wissenschaftliche Reform nach 1968. Kunstgeographie zwischen Kontinuität, Umkodierung und Auflösung, in *Kunst und Politik. Jahrbuch der Guernica-Gesellschaft,* 12, 2010, Schwerpunkt: Kunstgeschichte nach 1968, eds. Martin PAPENBROCK – Norbert SCHNEIDER, pp. 99-116.

Nation-State Centred Patriotism: The Étatiste Conception

Thus, biological and metaphysical nationalism, based on the equation of a nation with a territory and art style, seemed definitely to have been overcome by the end of the 1960s. The history of art was no longer regarded as an expression of an ethnic group or embodiment of a national collective psychology, but as a product of individual artists and great artistic centres. On the other hand, a radical nationalism was replaced by an implicit and nation-centred patriotism, and the ethnic art geography paradigm by an *étatiste* conception of the history of art. As a result, the history of art in (Central) Europe was conceived of as the history of nation-states and that model was supported by belief in the autonomy of art. In other words, the nation-state was regarded as an artistic organism with its identity rooted in the artistic tradition of its territory. As a consequence, the great majority of art historical syntheses in East Central Europe in the second half of the 20th century were based on the *étatiste* model, making the history of art identical with that of a nation-state.[22]

Since the end of the 1960s, patriotic nation-state-centred art history also began to use the idea of royal courts as centres of art.[23] Royal courts were regarded as birthplaces of style and centres for the radiation of taste (*"Austrahlungszentren des vorherschenden Geschmacks"*).[24] Seen thus, the dynastic *topos* incorporated into the patriotic model was still interpreted in terms of artistic au-

---

[22] See for example KUTAL, Albert: *České gotické sochařství, 1350 – 1450* [Czech Gothic Sculpture, 1350 – 1450]. Praha 1962; RADOCSAY, Dénes: *Gotische Tafelmalerei in Ungarn.* Budapest 1963; KUTAL, Albert: *Gotik in Böhmen.* Praha 1971; PEŠINA, Jaroslav: *Česká gotická desková malba* [Czech Gothic Table Painting]. Praha 1976. The long survival of the *étatiste* paradigm is documented by collective compendia such as e.g. *Dějiny českého výtvarného umění* [The History of Czech Art]. Eds. Rudolf CHADRABA et al. Praha 1984 – 2007; *Magyarországi művészet 1300 – 1470 körül* [Hungarian Art 1300 – 1470]. Ed. Ernő MAROSI. Budapest 1987; *Geschichte der bildenden Kunst in Österreich.* Vols. 1-6. Eds. Hermann FILLITZ – Günter BRUCHER – Artur RO-SENAUER – Hellmut LORENZ – Gerbert FRODL – Wieland SCHMIED. München 1998 – 2002.

[23] RECHT, Roland: Einleitung, in *Sigismundus Rex et Imperator. Kunst und Kultur zur Zeit Sigismunds von Luxemburg, 1387 – 1437.* [Exhib. Cat.] Ed. Imre TAKÁCS. Budapest – Luxemburg 2006, p. 1: *"Seit Ende der sechziger Jahre des 20. Jahrhunderts wurden zahlreiche Ausstellungen mittelalterlichen Herrschern gewidmet, bei denen mehr oder weniger umfassend die Kunst der Zeit Karls des Großen. Ludwigs IX. (des Heiligen) oder Karls V. von Frankreich präsentiert wurde."* See e.g. *Saint Louis/Saint Chapelle.* Paris 1960; *Karl der Große: Lebenswerk und Nachleben.* Vols. 1-5. Ed. Wolfgang BRAUNFELS. Düsseldorf 1965 – 1968; *La France de Saint Louis, exposition nationale du septiéme centenaire de la mort de Saint Louis.* Paris 1970; *L'art et la cour: France et Angleterre 1259 – 1328.* Ottawa 1972; *Die Zeitalter der Staufer: Geschichte, Kunst, Kultur.* Stuttgart 1977; *Transformations of the Court Style. Gothic Art in Europe 1270 – 1300.* Providence 1977; *Les fastes du Gothique. Le siécle de Charles V.* Paris 1980 – 1981; *L'art au temps des rois maudits. Philippe le Bel et ses fils 1285 – 1328.* Paris 1998.

[24] RECHT 2006 (see note 23), p. 1.

tonomy. Owing to that *"die Akzente lagen jeweils auf herausragenden Werken"*.[25] Only later, in the 1990s, did the trans-national character of royal courts and the cultural and even political nature of their art, start to be emphasized.

Artistic Mega-Region: The European Art Domain

Nevertheless, another trend was launched simultaneously, namely, an attempt to overcome nationalist hegemonism through the discovery of mega-regions that transcended the borders of nation states. Such mega-regions were regarded first, as arising from the autonomy of art and only later, as the effect of a common socio-economic structure. In the first instance, a mega-region was considered to result from an internal artistic communication or exchange between artists; later, it came to be seen as a token of a social and economic organism. Theodor Müller's reconstruction of the history of 15th century sculpture in Northern Europe represents a symptomatic example of the first kind.[26] In a sense, he returned to John Roosval's notion of an *"arte dominium"*, namely an autonomous artistic organism that transcended national borders, developing the idea of *"a vast domain"* or *"the great unity of European sculpture* (art) *north of the Alps"* which was based on *"the common bond between the sculptors"*.[27]

Mega-Region as a Sociological Organism

An important role as far as the articulation of the idea of a mega-region is concerned, was played by Jan Białostocki. In 1976, he formulated the idea of a multi-national artistic organism *"stretching across national borders"* called by

---

[25]   Ibid.

[26]   MÜLLER, Theodor: *Sculpture in the Netherlands, Germany, France, Spain: 1400 – 1500.* Baltimore 1966. See a very detailed review by HOMOLKA, Jaromír: K některým otázkám středoevropské plastiky 15. století [On Some Questions about 15th Century Central European Sculpture], in *Umění*, 17, 1969, pp. 539-569. The idea of interaction between an autonomous idea of art and the notion of an international, i.e. Pan-European artistic context had already been articulated by PÄCHT, Otto: Die Gotik der Zeit um 1400 als gesamteuropäische Kunstsprache, in *Europäische Kunst um 1400. Achte Austellung unter den Auspizien des Europarates.* [Exhib. Cat.] Wien 1962, pp. 64-65. The coming into existence of the autonomy of art around 1400 was regarded by Pächt as a result of international court patronage. According to Pächt, *"wir stehen hier dem Phänomenon einer weitgehenden Autonomisierung der bildkunstlerischen Sphäre gegenüber"* enabled by *"das leidenschaftliche höfische Mäzenatentum der Zeit"* which *"hat die Welle dieser Künstlerwanderung recht eigentlich in Bewegung gesetzt"*.

[27]   MÜLLER 1966 (see note 26), p. XV.

Erich Kubach *"Großlandschaft"*[28] that shared *"common artistic features... specific for no other area"*.[29] *"The specific* [artistic] *character"*, and *"the common features* [of art] *of this multi-national region"*, was not a consequence of *"a common national background"*, according to Białostocki,[30] but the result of *"common points of departure... common ideological crisis... common artistic sources in some centres and workshops... the common natural... [and]... the common social background"*.[31] In other words, a multi-national artistic organism was built up on the common history, common artistic tradition, common natural conditions and common social structure (e.g. rich Protestant patrons and their commissions in the case of the Baltic area). As we can see, Białostocki's interpretation relied on Jacob Burckhardt's and Aby Warburg's cultural/historical and commercial theory on the one hand and Erwin Panofsky's iconological and ideological model on the other: *"History is not made by spirits and tendencies but by the people who decided about commissions, who gave money, but who also believed in ideas and their beliefs were sometimes more decisive factors in artistic developments than economic and geographic reasons."*[32] Thus, art is here regarded, neither as the product of a collective subject nor an immanent artistic communication, but as the result of a commission by a particular patron, the work of art being conceived of as the fulfilment of a particular social task rather than the expression of a national spirit.

Mega-Region and Nation-Dynastic History

At the same time, Jan Białostocki came up with the idea of another mega-region, namely that of *"Eastern Europe"* as an artistic organism consisting of Hungary, Bohemia and Poland.[33] The political intentions of that concept were obvious: Białostocki's idea of a multi-national region in Eastern Europe represented not only an open criticism of German nationalist hegemonism (the idea of Central Europe as dominated by German art), but also an implicit polemic against Russian communist hegemonism, masked with feigned in-

---

28   BIAŁOSTOCKI, Jan: The Baltic Area as an Artistic Region in the Sixteenth Century, in *Hafnia. Copenhagen Papers in the Theory of Art*, 1976, pp. 11-23.

29   Ibid., p. 14. The idea of Baltic area as an artistic organism had already been articulated by ROOSVAL, John: Das baltisch-nordische Kunstgebiet, in *Nordelbingen*, 6, 1927, 270-290. See DaCOSTA KAUFMANN 2004 (see note 9), p. 73.

30   BIAŁOSTOCKI 1976 (see note 28), pp. 14, 15, 20.

31   Ibid., p. 20.

32   Ibid., p. 15.

33   BIAŁOSTOCKI, Jan: *The Art of the Renaissance in Eastern Europe. Hungary, Bohemia, Poland.* Ithaca 1976.

ternationalism.[34] The role of a connecting force within the East European artistic multi-national region was attributed again to patrons of art. This time[35] however, in contrast to the Baltic area as an artistic whole, it was not wealthy merchants but the royal dynasties themselves, namely *"the reign of the Jagellonian dynasty"* or Matthias Corvinus, who were regarded as the common denominator of the trans-national artistic organism. As a consequence, the idea of the history of art as the history of a nation has been replaced by the concept of the history of art as the history of a dynasty.[36] The bourgeois, abstract, constructed concept of "national history" was thus renounced and instead, the history of art began to be interpreted according to pre-modern political and administrative structures. In addition, the history of art as the history of expression was transformed into the history of patronage. Following on Jacob Burckhardt's track, the history of art was conceived of as the history of *"Aufgaben"* or tasks by Jan Białostocki. Works of art were analysed according to their particular genres and specific functions (*"the castle"*, *"the chapel"*, *"the tomb"*, *"the town"*). Consequently, the character of a work of art and its style were mainly considered to result from a very particular commission and the fulfilment of an intended social function, such as political representation or the articulation of a particular social status.

Attempts at Internationalism

Even if Białostocki's concept of Eastern Europe as an artistic whole still implied Polish patriotism (as documented by the focus on the national and, at the same time, imperial Jagellonian dynasty), the door had been opened both to overcoming such national particularisms and to the search for multi-

---

[34] About the ideological background and Białostocki's inherent Polish nationalism, see the review of Białostocki's Renaissance book by DaCOSTA KAUFMANN, Thomas: [Review of] Jan Białostocki, The Art of the Renaissance in Eastern Europe, Ithaca 1976, in *The Art Bulletin*, 58, 1978, pp. 164-169. See also CIULISOVÁ, Ingrid: Against Hegemony: Jacob Burckhardt, Jan Białostocki and the Renaissance, in *Renaissance Theory*. Eds. James ELKINS – Robert WILLIAMS. New York – London 2008, pp. 309-313, 460-461.

[35] BIAŁOSTOCKI 1976 (see note 33), pp. 4-9.

[36] On Jan Białostocki's idea of dynastic art, see MICHALSKI, Sergiusz: Jan Białostocki a evolucja historii sztuki po roku 1945 [Jan Białostocki and the Evolution of Art History after 1945], in *Ars longa. Prace dedykowane pamięci profesora Jana Białostockiego*. Ed. Maria POPRZÉCKA. Warszawa 1999, pp. 53-68, here p. 60. The dynastic premise of Białostocki's conception was emphasized also by CIULISOVÁ, Ingrid: Humanizmus a renesancia. Mestá, umenie a idey Erazma Rotterdamského [Humanism and Renaissance. Cities, Art and the Ideas of Erasmus of Rotterdam], in *Problémy dejín výtvarného umenia Slovenska* [Problems of Art History of Slovakia]. Ed. Ján BAKOŠ. Bratislava 2002, pp. 120-122.

national artistic organisms such as East Central Europe and Central Europe, or to a pan-European conception of the history of art. Interest in the study of trans-national art historical phenomena such as the international style around 1400, in imperial or royal court art, and in the art of international Church organizations such as the Orders of Franciscans or Cistercians, increased very rapidly.[37] The Parler-project arranged by Anton Legner can be regarded as a symptomatic example of this combination of belief in the autonomy of art, which is to say the history of art still conceived of as the result of immanent artistic influences or exchange, with the new idea of a trans-national European artistic whole. Moreover, the European artistic organism started to be thought of as having its base in a dynastic structure (the sub-heading of the project was as follows: "Europäische Kunst unter den Luxemburgen").[38]

An attempt to find a compromise between the national and trans-national approach and to overcome the ethno-nationalist model by means of a pre-industrial political structure, was undertaken already by Wolfgang Braunfels.[39] Here, an abstract ethnic and hegemonic construct transcending state borders (*"German art"*) was replaced with a model based on the historical administrative and political body (*"The Holy Roman Empire"*). As a consequence, the history of art regarded as the history of a polyphonic political (super state) organism was substituted for the history of art conceived of as the history of a nation.[40] Consequently, the historical development of art was regarded as an interplay between the immanent evolution of regional artistic traditions

---

[37] See e.g. *Europäische Kunst um 1400* (see note 26); *Internationale Gotik in Mitteleuropa*. Eds. Götz POCHAT – Brigitte WAGNER. Graz 1991; *The Courts of Europe: Politics, Patronage and Royalty 1400 – 1800*. Ed. Arthur G. DICKENS. London 1977; *Art, Patronage and Ideology at Fifteenth Century Italian Courts*. Ed. Joanna WOODS-MARSDEN. Modena 1991; *Courts and Regions in Medieval Europe*. Eds. Sarah-Rees JONES – Richard MARKS – Alastair MINNIS. York 2000; SCHENKLUHN, Wolfgang: *Architektur der Bettelorden: die Baukunst der Dominikaner und Franziskaner in Europa*. Darmstadt 2000. See also publications cited in note 43.

[38] *Die Parler und der schöne Stil, 1350 – 1400. Europäische Kunst unter den Luxemburger*. Vols. 1-5. [Exhib. Cat.] Ed. Anton LEGNER. Köln 1978 – 1980. The study of the relationship between *"Parler art"* (*"Parlerkunst"*) and *"the art of Parlertime"* (*"Kunst der Parlerzeit"*) was defined as the main goal of the project. See the introduction to the first volume by Anton Legner ("Zum Handbuch und zur Ausstellung", pp. XVIII-XXVI). See on that recently GRÖTECKE 2010 (see note 21), pp. 105-108.

[39] BRAUNFELS 1979 – 1989 (see note 19).

[40] Braunfels' theory was based on belief in the primacy of political bodies (*"politische Korperschaften"*) over ethnic or national ones since *"gesellschaftlichen, religiösen, politischen Verhältnisse, nicht irrationale Bezüge formen die Geschichte"*. In his words: *"Wir möchten von Staatsgebilden ausgehen, nicht vom 'Volk'"* because art territories (*"Kunsträume"*) represented irrational constructs (*"ein Vorrationales, zu dem sich Volkscharakter und Landschaftsstruktur verbinden"*) and had never existed in the past (*"diese Länder [haben] in der historischen Wirklichkeit nie gegeben"*). – BRAUNFELS 1979 – 1989 (see note 19), pp. 15-16.

and patronage by social institutions.[41] Nevertheless, the way was open[42] for the transformation of a national history of art into a polyphonic dynastic one together with the replacement of an abstract ethnic construct with pre-industrial social structures. But this conception of the history of art as the history of dynasties, based on the patronage model of art, was still regarded either as a culture historical project within which art played no more than a documentary role, or it was still interpreted as an autonomous artistic world.[43]

Court Art and Dynastic History

Referring to the French Gothic architecture of the age of St Louis, Robert Branner had already introduced the concept of *"court style"* in 1965.[44] Nev-

---

[41] According to Braunfels, art was characterized by an interplay between artistic (genetic) autonomy (i.e. dependency of a work of art on its model) on the one hand, and patronage by social institutions such as courts, monasteries and cities on the other. See BRAUNFELS 1979 – 1989 (see note 19), pp. 14-15. Without explicitly quoting Braunfels, KUTZNER 1986 (see note 4), p. 353, shared with Braunfels, not only the idea of Holy Roman Empire as the general frame of Central European art but also the opinion that art was determined sociologically since it mainly served the power elite and not ethnic groups.

[42] Hans Belting characterized Braunfels' approach as follows: *"Versuch, die Kleinstaatenwelt... als Masstab für die geographische Streuung und lokale Vielfalt... zu wählen. Hier gibt es keine Stammesmerkmale mehr, geschweige denn eine nationale Eigenart... sondern nur noch ein buntes Mosaik von gewachsenen Traditionen in regionalen und lokalen Rahmen, also die Eigenart der weltlichen und geistlichen Fürstentümer, Grafschaften, Reichskloster und Reichstädte."* – BELTING 1992 (see note 2), pp. 54-55. See also KLOTZ 1998 (see note 20), p. 15. HELD 2007 (see note 13), p. 143, took note of the fact that Braunfels had anticipated the return to pre-modern i.e. historical political structures: *"Braunfels... [geht] jedoch nicht von modernen Nationalstaatsgrenzen, sondern von den historischen Grenzen und Regionen des Alten Reichs aus."*

[43] See e.g. *Kaiser Karl IV. Staatsmann und Mäzen.* Ed. Ferdinand SEIBT. Nürnberg – Köln 1978, catalogue München 1978; *Sigismund von Luxemburg. Kaiser und König in Mittelalter.* Eds. Josef MACEK – Ernő MAROSI – Ferdinand SEIBT. Warendorf 1994, as examples of the cultural/historical approach. In contrast to that *Művészet Zsigmond Király Korában 1387 – 1437* [Art in the Times of King Sigismund 1387 – 1437]. Eds. László BEKE – Ernő MAROSI – Tünde WEHLI. Budapest 1987, represents a conception based on the notion of the art of the royal court as an autonomous phenomenon.

[44] BRANNER, Robert: *St. Louis and the Court Style in Gothic Architecture.* London 1965. Otherwise the notion of *"court style"* had commonly referred to the art around 1400, known as *"international Gothic"*. According to PÄCHT 1962 (see note 26), p. 55: *"So wird es verständlich, daß sich in der Kunstgeschichte die Bezeichnung 'höfischer Stil von 1400' geradezu als Synonym von 'internationaler Gotik' eingebürgert hat."* Nevertheless, referring to Jagiellonians the notion of *"court art"* has already been introduced by Jiřina Hořejší, Jarmila Vacková and Viktor Kotrba at the end of the 1960s and the beginning of the 1970s. See HOŘEJŠÍ, Jiřina: Hofkunst um 1500 in Böhmen, in *Alte und moderne Kunst*, 13, 1968, No. 97, pp. 2-12; KOTRBA, Viktor: Baukunst und Baumeister der Spätgotik am Prager Hof, in *Zeitschrift für Kunstgeschichte*, 31, 1968, pp. 181-215; KOTRBA, Viktor: Zwei Meister der Jagiellonischen Hofkunst. Meister Hanns

ertheless, the term has not been generally accepted and other terms such as *"Paris taste"* or *"St Denis style"* were preferred instead.[45] In order to challenge the nation state *étatiste* model and the belief in artistic autonomy, Michael Viktor Schwarz resumed the term *"court art"* in his work on court sculpture in the 14th century, in 1986.[46] He followed Walter Paatz's and Anton Legner's emphasis on the international nature of late Gothic art on the one hand, but refused to regard *"Parler's art"* as an autonomous phenomenon and the business of one artistic family, on the other.[47] According to him, 14th century European art was dominated by one centre, namely the royal court in Paris and its *"court culture"*.[48] Central Europe played the role of a periphery.

Despite the fact that Branner's and Schwarz's theory implied the concept of style conceived of as *"a tool of the self-representation of patrons"* and *"the history of style as a function of the representation of domination and political influence"*,[49]

(Hanusch) Spiess von Frankfurt und Meister Hanns (Hanusch) Schoecher von Nürnberg, in *Umění*, 20, 1972, pp. 248-267; HOŘEJŠÍ, Jiřina – VACKOVÁ, Jarmila: Některé aspekty jaggelonského dvorského umění v Čechách [Some Aspects of Jagiellonian Court Art in Bohemia], in *Umění*, 21, 1973, pp. 496-511; HOŘEJŠÍ, Jiřina – VACKOVÁ, Jarmila: Die Hofkunst zur Zeit der Jagiellonen-Herrschaft in Böhmen, in *Die Kunst der Ranaissance und des Manierismus in Böhmen*. Eds. Jiřina HOŘEJŠÍ et al. Hanau 1979.
On *"court art"*, see CARQUÉ, Bernd: *Stil und Erinnerung. Französische Hofkunst im Jahrhundert Karls V. und im Zeitalter ihrer Deutung*. Göttingen 2004, pp. 367-398, especially chapter IV. "Höfe und Hofkunst: Eine interdisziplinäre Mesalliance". Carqué criticizes art historians for their dualist notion of *"court art"* interpreting *"court art"* as an autonomous style on the one hand, and the matter of commissions by individual patrons and their taste, on the other. According to him (p. 398), in art history *"Der Begriff 'Hofkunst' ist zu einem nichtssagenden Klischee geronnen, da die auf historischer Seite gewonnene Einsichten in die Funktions- und Bedeutungszusammenhänge des Hofes nicht zu einem bestimmenden Moment des Werkverständnisses werden"*. Concerning the *"court milieu and its aesthetics"*, see also Hans Belting in BELTING, Hans – KRUSE, Christiane: *Die Erfindung des Gemäldes. Das erste Jahrhundert der niederländischen Malerei*. München 1994, pp. 36-39.

45 BRÜCKLE, Wolfgang: Revision der Hofkunst. Zur Frage historischer Phänomene in der ausgehenden Kapetingerzeit und zum Problem des höfischen Pariser Stils, in *Zeitschrift für Kunstgeschichte*, 3, 2000, pp. 404-434, here p. 432. According to Brückle, pp. 433-434, in spite of all reservations concerning the notion of *"court style"*, the term can be used as a heuristic tool (*"heuristisches Hilfsmittel"*).

46 SCHWARZ, Michael Viktor: *Höfische Skulptur im 14. Jahrhundert. Entwicklungsphasen und Vermittlungswege im Vorfeld des weichen Stils*. Worms 1986.

47 Ibid., pp. 6-9.

48 Ibid., p. 9. Referring to the art around 1400, an opposite opinion was expressed by PÄCHT 1962 (see note 26), p. 55: *"Daß die französische Kultur in der Ausbildung der spätmittelalterlichen Profankunst zeitweilig die Initiative innehatte, ist unbestreitbar und doch sind... die treibenden Kräfte nicht ausschliesslich in einem einzigen Lande zu suchen."*

49 BRÜCKLE, Wolfgang: Stil als Politikum: Inwiefern, in *Stilfragen zur Kunst des Mittelalters* (see note 8), p. 30. According to Brückle, Branner had regarded style as *"Mittel zur Selbstdarstellung von Auftraggebern"* and *"Stilgeschichte als Funktion von Herrschaftsrepräsentation und politischen Einfluss"*.

they had not explicitly articulated it.[50] It was Robert Suckale who realized the interdependence of the project of the history of art as the history of a dynasty and an anti-expressionist and anti-autonomist concept of style. In his book on the court art of Emperor Ludwig of Bavaria, he developed not only a project of the history of art regarded as the history of a royal dynasty, replacing Białostocki's mega-regional idea of dynastic art with the art of one regional imperial court.[51] He, moreover, explicitly expressed the belief that the idea of *"court art"* and the dynastic conception of art history necessarily implied a notion of art radically different from the premises of the nationalist and immanent art historical model.[52] Both the idea of art as an expression of (the spirit) of a nation and the notion of art as an autonomous phenomenon had to be replaced with the notion of art as the fulfilment of a task demanded by a concrete patron.[53] Or, in other words, the metaphysical, romantic idea of art as the expression of truth together with the modernist idea of art as an autonomous world, had to give way to an instrumental craft idea of art production as the result of commissions. That was why Suckale formulated a rhetorical notion of style as *"genera dicendi"*.[54] However, the revision of the

---

[50] According to CARQUÉ 2004 (see note 44), pp. 149-150, *"der dritte Paradigmawechsel in der Geschichte der Stilinterpretation"* that replaced the notion of style, regarded as an unconscious expression, with the idea of style as an intentional, pragmatic and functional tool of patron's demands, has been launched in the 1980s by Robert Suckale, Willibald Sauerländer, Lieselotte E. Stamm and Karl Clausberg.

[51] SUCKALE, Robert: *Die Hofkunst Kaiser Ludwigs des Bayern.* München 1993. Simultaneously with Robert Suckale, Jiří Kuthan introduced the notion of *"court style"* in his book on Přemysl Otakar II. Moreover, Kuthan also pleaded for the idea of the history of art regarded as the history of dynasties. – KUTHAN, Jiří: *Přemysl Otakar II. Král železný a zlatý, král zakladatel a mecenáš* [Přemysl Otakar II. King Iron and Golden, King Founder and Patron]. Vimperk 1993, p. 293. See also KUTHAN, Jiří: *Přemysl Otakar II. König, Bauherr und Mäzen. Höfische Kunst im 13. Jahrhundert.* Wien – Köln – Weimar 1996.

[52] Suckale summarized his criticism of the old history of styles as follows: *"Das Bewusste der Stilbildung und Formung wird ebenso vernachlässigt wie die vielfältige Bindung des künstlerischen Schaffens an die Darstellung, an Aufgabe und Funktion, aber auch an den Bestimmungsort, die Adressaten, das Material usw."* – SUCKALE, Robert: Stilgeschichte zu Beginn des 21. Jahrhunderts, in *Stilfragen zur Kunst des Mittelalters* (see note 8), p. 274.

[53] Following Günther Bandmann, Ulrike Bergmann (BERGMANN, Ulrike: Prior omnibus autor – an höchsten Stelle aber steht der Stifter, in *Ornamenta Ecclesiae. Kunst und Künstler der Romanik.* Ed. Anton LEGNER. Köln 1985, p. 117) came to the conclusion that *"der Bau* [and we can say art; J. B.] *ist... immer auch und besonders Ausdruck der Intentionen seines Auftraggebers"*. Nevertheless, she referred only to the art of the Middle Ages: *"Mittelalterliche Kunst ist wesentlich dadurch bestimmt, daß es sich um Auftragskunst handelt."* For more about the patronage idea of art, i.e. art regarded as a token of the intentions of patrons as developed by adherents to iconology (R. Krautheimer and G. Bandmann before all), see CROSSLEY, Paul: Medieval Architecture and Meaning: the Limits of Iconography, in *The Burlington Magazine*, 130, 1988, pp. 116-121, here pp. 116-117.

[54] SUCKALE 1993 (see note 51), see the chapter "Stilbegriffe und Stil um 1370. Versuch einer

metaphysical idea of style as expression had already been launched in 1960 – 1961 by Jan Białostocki.[55] Robert Suckale himself had articulated a rhetorical notion of style namely *"nach der gewählten Stillage bzw. nach dem Rang der Aufgabe, des Ortes und des Autraggebers"* in 1979,[56] reviving Białostocki's idea.[57] Introducing the dynastic model into the history of art, Suckale emphasized not only the instrumental, functional nature of art but also considered style as resulting from social norms and fashions.[58] Consequently, *"the court style"* has been elevated by Suckale to one of the key phenomena of the history of art of the Middle Ages.[59]

The Imperial Dynastic History of Art

One year later, in 1994, implicitly following Białostocki's model,[60] Robert Suckale enlarged the idea of the dynastic history of art to a mega-region, when he launched his Jagellonian research project *Die Jagiellonen in der Kunst und Kultur Mitteleuropas 1454 – 1572.*[61] Suckale's original idea of dynastic art history as *"court art"*[62] was extended and transformed into an imperial and

---

Grundlegung", pp. 48-70. Suckale had already articulated the new notion of style in his paper "Peter Parler und das Problem der Stillagen" in *Die Parler und der schöne Stil* (see note 38), Vol. 4 (Internationales Colloquium, 5 – 12 March 1979), pp. 175-184.

[55] BIAŁOSTOCKI, Jan: Das Modusproblem in den bildenden Künsten, in *Zeitschrift für Kunstgeschichte*, 24, 1961, pp. 128-141; reprinted in BIAŁOSTOCKI, Jan: *Stil und Ikonographie. Studien zur Kunstwissenschaft*. Dresden 1966, pp. 9-35; originally published in Polish in *Estetyka*, 2, 1961. Nevertheless, the rhetorical notion of style had already been introduced by Meyer Schapiro in 1941. See his review of *Early Christian Art* by Charles R. Morey in *The Review of Religion*, 8, 1943 – 1944, pp. 165-186. See CARQUÉ 2004 (see note 44), p. 147.

[56] SUCKALE, Robert: Peter Parler und das Problem der Stillagen, in *Die Parler und der schöne Stil* (see note 38), Vol. 4 (Internationales Colloquium, 5 – 12 March 1979), pp. 175-184.

[57] SUCKALE, Robert: *Stil und Funktion*. München – Berlin, Nachschrift, s. 280.

[58] SUCKALE 2006 (see note 52), p. 277: *"Da die Lehre von den Stillagen gerade die Unterschiedlichkeit der Funktionen der Kunstwerke thematisiert, greifen Stil- und Funktionsgeschichte an diesem Punkt ineinander."* *"Fast alle Fürstenhöfe kodifizierten ihre Gewohnheiten, Normen und Vorschriften... die so etwas wie einen 'Hofstil' ergaben."*

[59] More on that, see CARQUÉ 2004 (see note 44), pp. 367-383, 383-398.

[60] MICHALSKI 1999 (see note 36).

[61] See *Die Jagiellonen. Kunst und Kultur einer europäischen Dynastie an der Wende zur Neuzeit*. Eds. Dietmar POPP – Robert SUCKALE. Nürnberg 2002. See about that: *Künstlerische Wechselwirkungen in Mitteleuropa* (=Studia Jagellonica Lipsiensia, 1). Eds. Jiří FAJT – Markus HÖRSCH. Ostfildern 2006, pp. 7-10.

[62] According to Suckale's followers FAJT – HÖRSCH 2006 (see note 61), p. 9: *"... der Begriff einer 'Hofkunst', der... eine zentrale Rolle spielen wird, ist dann nicht zu unrecht gewählt, wenn man bereit ist, das Höfische in jenem weiteren Sinne zu verstehen, der dem vielfältigen Bild der spätmittelalterlichen Adels- und Bürgergesellschaft entspricht, und nicht in der Verengengung eines rückprojizierten absolutistischen Modells von Hof."*

European conception.[63] Simultaneously, the theoretical foundation of the dynastic model, namely the functional patronage notion of the work of art, i.e. the artwork regarded as the tool of a patron,[64] resulted in the idea of art as a cultural/historical document, as *"Zeitzeuge"*.[65] Thus, the dynastic conception of the history of art was conceived of in terms of a multi-disciplinary cultural/historical approach, as exemplified by many books published by the Geisteswissenschaftliches Zentrum Geschichte und Kultur Ostmitteleuropas (GWZO) in Leipzig. Such projects as *Karl IV. Kaiser von Gottes Gnaden*[66] or *Sigismund von Luxemburg: ein Kaiser in Europa* and *Sigismundus Rex et Imperator. Art and Culture during the Time of Sigismund of Luxemburg, 1387 – 1437*[67] reveal that the imperial dynastic idea has been largely accepted as a new paradigm for art history in Central Europe. It had been explicitly declared by Winfried Eberhard, the director of the GWZO at that time, in the "Geleitwort" to the collective book *Die Jagiellonen. Kunst und Kultur einer europäischen Dynastie an der Wende zur Neuzeit* in 2002. Here, he characterized the field of work (*"Arbeitsgebiet"*) of the GWZO as *"die kulturwissenschaftliche Forschung"* based on *"der Einbeziehung und Kooperation unterschiedlicher Disziplinen im Rahmen einer gemeinsamen Fragestellung"* and defined *"die kulturelle Vernetzung auf Basis dynastischer und ökonomischer Verbindungen"* as one of the main axioms of the project.[68] Moreover, following and transforming in a sense, Dehio's and Frey's ideas, Eberhard introduced *"die Prozesse des Kulturtransfers zwischen dem Süden und Norden, Osten und Westen Europas"* together with the rehabilitation of the active historical and cultural role of the Eastern part of Central Europe as the main aims of the GWZO.[69]

---

[63] In 1999, in his "Eröffnungsrede" to Nuremberg Colloquium, *Die Jagiellonen* (see note 61), Robert Suckale explicitly expressed the political intention of the Jagiellonian project as follows: *"Wir wollen zur Erweiterung Westeuropas zum ganzen Kontinent, zu Einheit und gegenseitigen Verständnis beitragen."* Following Suckale and referring to Jagiellonian project, Jiří Fajt (*Karl IV. Kaiser von Gottes Gnaden. Kunst und Representation des Hauses Luxemburg, 1310 – 1437*. Ed. Jiří FAJT. München 2006, pp. 7, 9) speaks about *"eine neue Ideologie des vereinigten Europas"* as *"ein Zusammenschluss von Nationalstaaten"* and demarcate the mega-region as *"ein die heutigen Nationen übergreifendes Herrschaftsgebiet von der Ostsee bis Ungarn"*.

[64] FAJT – HÖRSCH 2006 (see note 61), p. 9, characterize it as *"den Einsatz von Stilsprachen und Bildinhalten im Dienst herrscherlicher, höfischer und bürgerlicher Gruppen"*.

[65] SUCKALE, Robert: *Das mittelalterliche Bild als Zeitzeuge*. Berlin 2002.

[66] *Karl IV. Kaiser von Gottes Gnaden* (see note 63).

[67] *Sigismund von Luxemburg: ein Kaiser in Europa*. Ed. Michel PAULY – François REINERT. Mainz am Rhein, 2006; *Sigismundus Rex et Imperator* (see note 23). See MAROSI, Ernő: [Review of] Sigismundus Rex et Imperator. Kunst und Kultur zur Zeit Sigismunds von Luxemburg, 1387 – 1437, in *Bulletin du Musée hongrois des beaux-arts*, 105, 2006, pp. 131-138.

[68] We can add that the rhetorical or functional model of style enabled art historians to take part in that interdisciplinary project.

[69] According to Eberhardt: *"Dabei geht es vor allem um Prozesse des Kulturtransfers zwischen dem*

Thus, by means of the patronage model of art, the particularism and abstract generalizations of the old nation-centred paradigm have been replaced by a cosmopolitan idea of a common European artistic organism based on pre-modern historical structures. Nevertheless, the crucial question whether old national hegemonism has been definitively eliminated or rather masked by the cosmopolitan imperial model still remains open.

The Central European Mega-Region and the Polyphony of Centres

The dynastic idea of history, the patronage notion of art production and the cultural/historical approach have also been carefully treated by Thomas DaCosta Kaufmann in 1995.[70] Revising Białostocki's excessively narrow idea of Eastern Europe, excluding especially the Habsburg Empire from Central Europe art as a whole and rejecting Białostocki's implicit nation-centred patriotism, Kaufmann developed a very broad idea of Central Europe as a large region embracing the territories of the Holy Roman Empire, Respublica Poloniae, and the former Kingdom of Hungary.[71] Simultaneously, Kaufmann emphasized the sociological identity of art, deriving the idea of style from the role of art in particular social milieu and those tasks commissioned by patrons. At the same time, Kaufmann stressed social stratification, particular demands put by different social milieu and the plurality of centres (i.e. court, monasteries and cities).[72] That was why Kaufmann[73] later expressed his dissatisfaction with the socio-economic model of the nature of the metropolis,

---

Süden und Norden, Osten und Westen Europas sowie um die kulturelle Vernetzung auf Basis dynastischer und ökonomischer Verbindungen innerhalb der ostmitteleuropäischen Länder. In diesen Bezügen werden kulturelle Verdichtungen angesprochen, in denen der Entwicklungsausgleich, ja zuweilen Vorsprung des ostlichen gegenüber dem westlichen Mitteleuropa deutlich werden kann. Dieser seit dem 14. Jahrhundert zu beobachtende Ausgleich des jüngeren mit dem älteren Europa widerspricht eklatant der verbreiteten westlichen Vorstellung von der ständigen Entwicklungsverspätung des sogenannten Ostens." See *Die Jagiellonen* (see note 61), p. 11.

[70] DaCOSTA KAUFMANN, Thomas: *Court, Cloister & City. The Art and Culture of Central Europe, 1450 – 1800.* London 1995.

[71] See DaCOSTA KAUFMANN 1978 (see note 34), pp. 164-169; DaCOSTA KAUFMANN 1995 (see note 70), pp. 13-25. See also review of Kaufmann's book by Ivo Hlobil in *Umění*, 46, 1998, pp. 489-490.

[72] DaCosta Kaufmann not only revived, in a sense, Braunfels' idea of a superstate ("Holy Roman Empire") as an artistic organism but also combined this with Białostocki's idea of a mega-region. He followed also Braunfels' patronage approach to art. As already mentioned, Braunfels divided the history of art according to different classes of patrons regarding them as institutions, i.e. *"Höfe"*, *"Fürstentümer"*, *"Reichsstädte"*, *"Reichsklöster"*, represented by *"Kaiser"*, *"Bischöfe"*, *"Bürger"*. See BRAUNFELS 1979 – 1989 (see note 19), pp. 11-19.

[73] DaCOSTA KAUFMANN 2004 (see note 9), pp. 154-158.

seen as arriving mostly from competition and preference for urban centres at the expense of courts or Church (ideological) centres. This scepticism concerning the monopoly of centres based on capitalist competition, is a logical consequence of the interpretation of history according to pre-industrial historical structures, which is to say, the dynastic model of the history of art.

In addition, the concept of *"metropolis"* took a really important place in the critical revision of the nationalist theory of the history of art. Regarded as a concrete sociological phenomenon, the city or metropolis replaced the notion of the nation or state regarded as a dominant centre. Since the 1980s, cultural and social historians started to study intensively such phenomena as *"the residence"*, *"the capital"*, *"the metropolis"* emphasizing their multi-social and multi-ethnic nature.[74] It is as a logical consequence that the research project *Metropolen und Zentren* has been launched within the GWZO in Leipzig and that art historians have also been invited to take part in it.[75]

Dynastic versus National Approach

In his latest compendium on the geography of art,[76] DaCosta Kaufmann claimed that *"national or ethnic identity [came into] opposition to dynastic identity"* in the early modern period and *"the conflict"* between *"dynastic identities and those of national origin"* also played an important role in the history of art, especially from the 19th century onward.[77] Kaufmann also noticed that *"the dynastic identity"* was characterized by a cosmopolitan or supranational approach in contrast to the particularism and *"imaginary constructions"* of nationalism. It

---

[74] See ENGEL, Evamaria – LAMBRECHT, Karen: Hauptstadt – Residenz – Residenzstadt – Metropole – Zentraler Ort, in *Metropolen im Wandel. Zentralität in Ostmitteleuropa an der Wende vom Mittelalter zur Neuzeit.* Eds. Evamaria ENGEL – Karen LAMBRECHT – Hanna NOGOSSEK. Berlin 1995; DaCOSTA KAUFMANN 2004 (see note 9), p. 416.

[75] See ENGEL – LAMBRECHT – NOGOSSEK 1995 (see note 74); *Krakau, Prag und Wien. Funktionen von Metropolen im frühmodernen Staat.* Eds. Marina DMITRIEVA – Karen LAMBRECHT. Stuttgart 2000. The idea of big international cities and metropolises as artistic centres had already been articulated by CLARK, Kenneth: *Provincialism.* London 1962, pp. 3-12; and KUBLER, George: *The Shape of Time. Remarks on the History of Things.* New Haven – London 1962, pp. 93-96; KUBLER, George: Introduction to "Metropolitan Schools in Latin American archaeology and Colonial Art", in *Studies in Western Art.* Vol. 3. Princeton 1963, pp. 145-147. This represented a critical revision of the hegemonic-nationalistic concept of the centre-periphery problem. On this see BAKOŠ, Ján: Jan Białostocki and Center-Periphery Problem, in *Białostocki. Materiały z Seminarium Metodologicznego Stowarzyszenia Historyków Sztuku "Jan Białostocki – między tradycją a inovacją".* Ed. Magdalena WRÓBLEWSKA. Warszawa 2009, pp. 65, 67-68.

[76] DaCOSTA KAUFMANN 2004 (see note 9).

[77] Ibid., pp. 107-114, 135-153.

is worth noticing, that the opposite shift namely from the nationalist to the dynastic approach has been characteristic of art history in recent decades. We saw that in order to avoid the consequences of chauvinist nationalism, art historians in Central Europe started to replace national particularism with internationalism and, by implication, the notion of art as expression (of truth or essence) came to be superseded by the patronage (functional) model of art production. It is evident that the return of art historical interpretations to pre-industrial and pre-bourgeois historical structures represents the radical revision of the bourgeois nation-centred ideology. The fact that it has come into existence just at the time of the unification of Europe and economic globalization, has its ideological implications. Nevertheless, the question still persists as to whether the contrast between the national and dynastic models of the history of art can be regarded as a purely epistemological difference, i.e. as the difference between an abstract construction on the one hand and a model more adequate to the historical reality on the other,[78] rather than as the difference between two interpretative matrices or screens based on different concepts of art and different ideological backgrounds.[79] Art history seems unable to escape from its instrumental and notoriously affirmative role as far as its relationship to politics and ideology is concerned.[80] Thus art historians

---

[78] According to KAUFMANN 1995 (see note 70), p. 18: *"In treating the culture of the ancien régime, this book will propose that the old regimes of the early modern era as they existed before the nineteenth century... supply not only a convenient but also an appropriate geographical definition."*

[79] Some reviewers question the absolute validity of an extra-artistic socio-cultural notion of art, emphasizing instead, the role of fashion or taste. Thus, they stress the important role of a sphere, situated between direct social instrumentality and artistic autonomy on the one hand, and between a concrete commission and anonymous collective force on the other. Addressing Kaufmann's theory of a Central European artistic region regarded as the result of social stratification and social commissions, Marcin Fabiański claimed: *"Here again, the question of fashion and taste seem to provide the decisive stimulus and make the borderline... elusive."* – FABIAŃSKI, Marcin: How Can an Artistic Region Be Defined? The Case of Early-Modern Central Europe, in *Borders in Art. Revisiting Kunstgeographie*. Ed. Katarzyna MURAWSKA-MUTHESIUS. Warszawa 2000, pp. 35-42, here p. 41. Referring to Bernd Carqué's preference for the *"intentional and functional dimension of style"* and the notion of style as the fulfilment of *"Bedürfnisse der Auftraggeber"*, Michaela Krieger came to the conclusion, that even if the intentional and instrumental idea of style *"erweitert... Erklärungsmodelle... um einen bedeutenden Interpretationsansatz"*, it does not falsify *"die Bedeutung gewisser Geschmacksvorlieben oder individueller Kreativität als ausschlaggebende Faktoren künstlerischer Produktion"*. – KRIEGER, Michaela: [Review of] Bernd Carqué: Stil und Erinnerung. Französische Hofkunst im Jahrhundert Karls V. und im Zeitlater ihrer Deutung, in *Journal für Kunstgeschichte*, 11, 2007, No. 3, pp. 210-219, here p. 219.

[80] Jiří Fajt and Markus Hörsch explicitly acknowledged the instrumental role of art historians and the allegiance of the new dynastic art historical project to present European policy: *"Kunsthistoriker, Historiker oder Kulturwissenschatler können Material liefern... für eine neue Ideologie des vereinigten Europas."* See FAJT – HÖRSCH 2006 (see note 61), p. 7.

have always legitimized the status quo: first nationalism, than Modernism, liberalism, hegemonism and expansionism, and economic globalization at the present.[81] The commemoration and even propagation of feudal dynasties in the history of art seems to echo the present-day domination of trans-national economic and financial corporations.

---

[81] James Elkins expressed it as follows: *"Senses of nationalism or ethnicity have been the sometimes explicit impetus behind art historical research from its origins in Vasari and Winckelmann. The current interest in transnationality, multi-culturalism, and postcolonial theory has not altered that basic impetus but only obscured it by making it appear that art historians are now free to consider themes that embrace various cultures or all cultures in general."* – *Is Art History Global?* Ed. James ELKINS. New York 2007, p. 9.

VIII. PATHS AND STRATEGIES
OF THE HISTORIOGRAPHY OF ART
IN CENTRAL EUROPE

From the Local to the Universal

The thematization of the history of art in Central Europe as a specific art historical phenomenon is a fascinating, and at the same time quite dramatic, story, and as such merits serious study.[1] This essay, however, does not have the slightest ambition to be a history of the historiography/historiographies of Central European art. It is rather an attempt to outline the main trends, which shaped research into the history of art in the region.

In the 18th century, the plurality of local histories cultivated by local patriotic chroniclers was replaced by the conception of one universal history.[2]

---

[1] The statement of Heinrich Klotz and Martin Warnke concerning the history of German art also applies to this process: *"Die Geschichte der Historiographie ist immer auch eine Geschichte kulturgeschichtlicher Machtansprüche, also eine Geschichte kultureller Propaganda."* – KLOTZ, Heinrich: *Geschichte der Deutschen Kunst.* Vol. 1. München 1998, p. 9. In other words, the history of the historiography of art, at least in Central Europe, can be regarded as a symbolic struggle over territory. Moreover, as Warnke expressed it: *"Alle entsprechende Versuche seien zeitbedingte Konstrukte."* – WARNKE, Martin: *Geschichte der Deutschen Kunst.* Vol. 2. München 1999, p. 10. What are called *"constructs"* today in order to express the arbitrary and ideological nature of our interpretation of the past, were labelled *"conceptions"* in the 1980s and *"models"* in the 1990s. See BAKOŠ, Ján: *Dejiny a koncepcie stredovekého umenia na Slovensku* [History and Conceptions of Medieval Art in Slovakia]. Bratislava 1984; MAROSI, Ernő: Modelle Mitteleuropas in der Historiographie zur Kunst des Mittelalters, in *Westmitteleuropa, Ostmitteleuropa. Vergleiche und Beziehungen. Festschrift für Ferdinand Seibt zum 65. Geburtstag.* Eds. Winfried EBERHARD – Hans LEMBERG – Heinz-Dieter HEIMANN – Robert LUFT. München 1992, pp. 59-69. For more about constructivism in cultural history, see BURKE, Peter: *What is Cultural History?* Cambridge 2004; German translation: *Was ist Kulturgeschichte?* Frankfurt am Main 2005, pp. 111-133.

[2] KOSELLECK, Reinhart: Geschichte, in *Geschichtliche Grundbegriffe. Historisches Lexikon zur politisch-sozialen Sprache in Deutschland.* Eds. Otto BRUNNER – Werner CONZE – Reinhart KOSELLECK. Stuttgart 1998 (1st ed. 1975), Vol. 2, pp. 593-770, particularly p. 647 ff.; KOSELLECK, Reinhart: Historia Magistra Vitae. Über die Auflösung des Topos im Horizont neuzeitlich bewegter Geschichte, in KOSELLECK, Reinhart: *Vergangene Zukunft. Zur Semantik geschichtlicher Zeiten.* Frankfurt am Main 1989 (1st ed. 1979), pp. 38-66. See also LOCHER, Hubert: *Kunstgeschichte als historische Theorie der Kunst.* München 2001, pp. 203-204.
In Bickendorf's words: *"... in der zweiten Hälfte des 18. Jahrhunderts... [wurde] aus der Vielzahl der Künste und der Künstler die eine 'Kunst', wie auch die vielfältigen Geschichten abgelöst wurden*

At the same time, Johann Joachim Winckelmann conceived the idea of art as having a single true essence. In this way, the previous history of a plurality of artefacts and artists was transformed into a universal history of art with a capital A.[3] Many local histories were subordinated to one universal history of the classical norms of art.[4] However, the idea of the plurality of specific local histories did not disappear for ever. For example, it was Italian patriotism that motivated Luigi Lanzi's conception of Italian art as a plurality of geographically located schools.[5] The plurality of specific local histories was, however, already subordinated to the universal ideal. Nevertheless, the way to the pluralism of nationalities had been opened.[6]

---

von der Vorstellung der 'einen Geschichte', die sich nun linear und kontinuierlich im Verlauf der Zeit entfaltet haben sollte... Erst aus der Zusammensetzung der beiden Kollektivsingulare entstand die Idee der 'einen Kunstgeschichte' in der sich das Abstraktum 'Kunst' im Laufe der Zeit verändert und eine eigene Geschichte erhält." – BICKENDORF, Gabriele: Die ersten Überblickswerke zur "Kunstgeschichte", in *Klassiker der Kunstgeschichte I. Von Winckelmann bis Warburg.* Ed. Ulrich PFISTERER. München 2007, pp. 32-33.

[3] *"Erst aus der Zusammensetzung der beiden Kollektivsingulare entstand die Idee der 'einen Kunstgeschichte', in der das Abstraktum 'Kunst' im Laufe der Zeit verändert und eine eigene Geschichte erhält. [...] ...seine prägnanteste Formulierung fand der Begriff der 'Kunstgeschichte' bei Johann Joachim Winckelmann. [...] Die gemeinsame Grundlage sowohl der neu errichteten oder neu geordneten Sammlungen als auch der Überblickswerke zur Kunstgeschichte war das Konzept der 'einen Geschichte' der 'einen Kunst', das die älteren Formen der Kunsthistoriographie mit ihrer Vielzahl von 'Geschichten' einer Vielzahl von Küstlern ablöste."* – BICKENDORF 2007 (see note 2), pp. 29-30, 33. See also LOCHER 2001 (see note 2), p. 204.

[4] *"Am Anfang steht der Gegensatz lokal – universal. Vor dem späten 18. Jahrhundert... herrschte eine strikte Hierarchie, von den wenigen Spitzen der europäischen Kunst herunter zum engsten lokalen Kunstgeschehen."* – MUTHESIUS, Stefan: Universal, lokal – europäisch, national: Fragestellungen der frühen Kunstgeographie im späten 19. und frühen 20. Jahrhundert, in *Die Kunsthistoriographien in Ostmitteleuropa und der nationale Diskurs.* Eds. Robert BORN – Alena JANATKOVÁ – Adam S. LABUDA. Berlin 2004, p. 69.

[5] LANZI, Luigi: *Storia pittorica della Italia dal risorgimento delle belle arti fin presso al fine del XVIII secolo.* Bassano 1809.

[6] Lanzi followed Vasari's identification of the local (in Vasari's case Florentine) with the universal, but related this to Italy as a whole. As a consequence, the universal was regarded as national. *"Das Resultat war die erste nationale Malereigeschichte, die... die Einheit der Nation kunsthistorisch abbildete."* – BICKENDORF, Gabriele: "Kunstgeschichte" als Geschichte der künstlerischen Schulen und als Gattungsgeschichte, in PFISTERER 2007 (see note 2), pp. 33-34. According to LOCHER 2001 (see note 2), p. 197, in spite of the idea of Italian painting as a whole, *"ein gemeinsames Wesen der italienischen Kunst ist nicht Gegenstand der Darstellung"* of Lanzi's *"Storia"*. More about Lanzi, see BICKENDORF, Gabriele: Luigi Lanzis *"Storia pittorica della Italia"* und das Entstehen der historisch-kritischen Kunstgeschichtsschreibung, in *Jahrbuch des Zentralinstituts für Kunstgeschichte,* 2, 1986, pp. 231-294; BICKENDORF, Gabriele: Luigi Lanzi, in *Hauptwerke der Kunstgeschichtsschreibung.* Ed. Paul von NAREDI-RAINER. Stuttgart 2010, pp. 269-271.

In the era of Napoleon, the idea of the universal character of history became an instrument of global imperialism.[7] French political and cultural hegemony provoked as a reaction, a critical revision of the Enlightenment belief in a universal civilisation. German thinkers, especially the Romantics, emphasized particularity in opposition to universality, replacing the idea of humanity or the universal man with the idea of the nation or ethnic group.[8] Instead of emphasising the idea of natural rights as underpinning the equality of peoples, they used arguments regarding historical rights in support of the historical equality of *nations*.[9] At the same time, they cast doubt on the universal validity of the classical canon and sought to validate anti-classical national styles of art.[10] Thus, it was only logical that the idea of universal history came to be reformulated in a fundamentally new way. J. G. Herder conceived the history of humanity as a relay race of nations, a sequence of historic initiatives by individual nations.[11] Herder's emphasis on the pluralistic character of history, which did not reject faith in the common basis of humanity, was radically developed by the German historicism of the "Prussian historical school".[12] History was understood as the plurality of incom-

---

[7] Jean-Dominique Vivant Denon's arrangement of the Louvre (the Musée Napoléon) on the principle of national schools can also be understood as displaying the symbolic seizure of the world, or as a world-dominating museum. On this, see POMMIER, Édouard: *Les Musées en Europe a la veille de l'ouverture du Louvre*. Paris 1995; McCLELLAN, Andrew: *Inventing Louvre. Art, Politics, and the Origins of the Modern Museum in Eighteenth-Century Paris*. Berkeley – Los Angeles – London 1994, pp. 124-154, particularly pp. 147-148; GAEHTGENS, Thomas W.: Le musée Napoléon et son influence sur l'histoire de l'art, in *L'Histoire de l'histoire de l'art II. XVIIIe et XIXe siécles*. Ed. Édouard POMMIER. Paris 1997, pp. 89-110. See also SHEEHAN, James J.: *Museums in the German Art World. From the End of the Old Regime to the Rise of Modernism*. Oxford 2000, pp. 50-52.

[8] As Stefan Muthesius expressed it, in German culture "'*Volk*'... *wurde Synonym für 'die Nation'*". – MUTHESIUS 2004 (see note 4), pp. 73, 75. According to Reinhart Koselleck: "'*Volk' wird... ein spezifisch deutscher Kompensationsbegriff, der einlösen sollte, was der französische Nachbar mit 'nation'... verwirklicht zu haben schien." "'Volk' [rück]... zum Oberbegriff [auf], der alle Stände oder Klassen, Regierenden und Regierten einschliesst."* Thus, "*scheinbar vorpolitische 'Sprachnation'... [gerichtet] gegen die französische (Staats-)Nation, das... deutsche Volk zur Einheit aufrufend*". – KOSELLECK, Reinhart: Volk, Nation, Nationalism, Masse, in *Geschichtliche Grundbegriffe*. Stuttgart 1997 (1st ed. 1978), Vol. 7, pp. 142-151, here pp. 147-149. Generally speaking, the German notion of "*Volk*" emphasized ethnic origin, unlike French sociological notion of "*la nation*".

[9] See IGGERS, Georg G.: *The German Conception of History. The National Tradition of Historical Thought from Herder to the Present*. Middletown (Conn.) 1968, pp. 3-28.

[10] As is well known, they thought they had found it in medieval art. On this, see FRANKL, Paul: *The Gothic. Literary Sources and Interpretations through Eight Centuries*. Princeton (NJ) 1960, pp. 415-488; KULTERMANN, Udo: Histoire de l'art et identité nationale, in POMMIER 1997 (see note 7), pp. 223-247.

[11] "*Herder's nationalism was still cosmopolitan in spirit. Each nation contributes to the richness of human life.*" – IGGERS 1968 (see note 9), p. 41. See also LOCHER 2001 (see note 2), p. 205.

[12] IGGERS 1968 (see note 9), pp. 28-43 (chapter "The Origins of German Historicism. The Trans-

patible unique phenomena with their own mutually incomparable criteria. The representatives of the German historical school also connected the new philosophy of history with a new understanding of historiography as a science based on the presentation of facts and the historical criticism of sources. It was precisely these dimensions of the German historical school – the new pluralist, relativist paradigm of history and the conception of historiography as an empirical and critical science – that created the conditions for the new, institutionalised historiography of art.

It is generally accepted that art history as an institution was born at Berlin University in the first half of the 19th century.[13] One of the most important contributions of the so-called Berlin School of Art History was the conception of the history of art as the history of world art.[14] However, this was not derived from Winckelmann's adherence to one universal norm, but rather from two other, different, sources. The first was Herder's pluralist idea of history, the second, G. W. F. Hegel, the *"father of the world history of art"*.[15] He constructed a speculative dialectic of artistic development – a three-phase conception that

---

formation of German Historical Thought from Herder's Cosmopolitan Culture-Oriented Nationalism to the State-Centered Exclusive Nationalism of the Wars of Liberation").

[13] DILLY, Heinrich: *Kunstgeschichte als Institution. Studien zur Geschichte einer Disziplin.* Frankfurt am Main 1979; BEYRODT, Wolfgang: Kunstgeschichte als Universitätsfach, in *Kunst und Kunsttheorie 1400 – 1900* (=Wolfenbütteler Forschungen, 48). Eds. Peter GANZ – Martin GOSEBRUCH – Nikolaus MEIER – Martin WARNKE. Wiesbaden 1991, pp. 313-333; BICKENDORF, Gabriele: Die Anfänge der historisch-kritischen Kunstgeschichtsschreibung, ibid., pp. 359-374; KROUPA, Jiří: *Školy dějin umění. Metodologie dějin umění I* [Schools of Art History. Methodology of Art History I]. Brno 1996, pp. 123-144. On Berlin School of Art History, see recently BREDEKAMP, Horst – LABUDA, Adam S.: Kunstgeschichte, Universität, Museum und die Mitte Berlins, 1810 – 1873, in *Geschichte der Universität Unter den Linden, 1810 – 2010. Genese der Disziplinen. Die Konstitution der Universität.* Eds. Heinz-Elmar TENORTH – Volker HESS – Dieter HOFFMANN. Berlin 2010, pp. 25-54.

[14] BICKENDORF, Gabriele: Die Berliner Schule, in PFISTERER 2007 (see note 2), p. 55. See also LOCHER 2001 (see note 2), pp. 238-240, 244-254.

[15] GOMBRICH, Ernst H.: The Father of Art History, in GOMBRICH, Ernst H.: *Tributes. Interpreters of Our Cultural Tradition.* Oxford 1984, pp. 51-70. On the relationship between the Berlin School of Art History and Hegel, see LOCHER 2001 (see note 2), pp. 205-212; PRANGE, Regine: *Die Geburt der Kunstgeschichte. Philosophische Ästhetik und empirische Wissenschaft.* Köln 2004, pp. 137-147. In the latest writings, Hegel's impact on the Berlin School has been minimized. Despite that fact, the characterization of Hegel as the father of universal art history is still valid. LOCHER, Hubert: Eine neue Wissenschaft der Kunst. Kunstpublizistik und Kunstgeschichte, in *Vom Biedermeier zum Impressionismus. Geschichte der bildenden Kunst in Deutschland.* Vol. 7. Ed. Hubertus KOHLE. München – Berlin – London – New York 2008, s. 566, acknowleges Hegel's impact on Schnaase as follows: *"Indem Schnaase die historische Entwicklung der Kunst auf die Entwicklung der menschlichen Geistes bezieht, folgt er im Prinzip die Vorstellung G. W. F. Hegels."* Similarly, KARLHOLM, Dan: *Art of Illusion. The Representation of Art History in Nineteenth-Century Germany and Beyond.* Bern 2004, p. 49, empasizes Kugler's indebtedness to Hegel concerning the concept of art.

was the first pluralist, but at the same time, global conception of the history of art. Franz Kugler and Carl Schnaase took over the idea of a world history of art, not only replacing the speculative nature of Hegel's project with the concrete presentation of art historical facts, but also putting forward the concept of the succession of period styles as a continuing process, in place of Hegel's three-phase construction of history. What is worth noticing, however, is the fact that those representing the Berlin School of Art History, while clearly inspired by the methodology, did not take over from the "Prussian historical school" the state-oriented model of history. They followed instead, Herder's idea of world history as a relay race of nations. They combined this with the historical relativist idea of the sequence of stylistic forms and the idea that art is an expression of the period (*"Zeitgeist"*) and nation (*"Volksgeist"*).[16] In spite of this orientation to nationhood, a nationalistic understanding of the history of art did not prevail over the idea of universal art inherited from the Enlightenment.[17] Schnaase applied Herder's Enlightenment idea of the division of labour among nations (*"Arbeitsteilung der Nationen"*) to his writing of the universal history of art.[18] When interpreting the global plurality of art,

---

[16]   KARGE, Henrik: Arbeitsteilung der Nationen. Karl Schnaases Entwurf eines historisch gewachsenen Systems der Künste, in *Zeitschrift für Schweizerische Archäologie und Kunstgeschichte*, 53, 1996, No. 4, pp. 300-301, emphasizes Schnaase's indebtedness to Herder concerning the idea of *"Volksgeist"*. Similarly, according to Gabriele Bickendorf, members of the Berlin School followed Herder's notion of *"Volksgeist"* and not its Hegelian version. – BICKENDORF 2007 (see note 14), p. 53. See also KARLHOLM 2004 (see note 15), p. 50. According to Wilhelm Schlink, the belief that *"Bildende Kunst ist Ausdruck des Volksgeistes… war gegen 1840 allgemeine Maxime"*. – SCHLINK, Wilhelm: Der Charakter ganzer Nationen in den Künsten. Jacob Burckhardt über das Verhältnis von Volk und Nation zur Kunst, in *Zeitschrift für Schweizerische Archäologie und Kunstgeschichte*, 53, 1996, No. 4, p. 308.
Concerning the notion of art history as a succession of styles, Schnaase speaks of a continuous history of art (*"fortlaufende Kunstgeschichte"*). – SCHNAASE, Karl: *Geschichte der bildenden Künste*. Vols. 1-8. Düsseldorf 1843 – 1864, Vol. 1, p. 87. According to Karge, Schnaase revised Winckelmann's *"herrschende lineare Modell der Stilgeschichte"*. See KARGE, Henrik: Karl (auch Carl) Schnaase: Geschichte der bildenden Künste, in NAREDI-RAINER 2010 (see note 6), p. 398.

[17]   *"Schnaase, der die Geschichte der Kunst unter der globalen Perspektive der Entwicklung des menschlichen Geistes sah, in der die einzelnen Völker ihre wechselnden Rollen spielen, hat aus der Vorstellung, daß die Kunst der Ausdruck des Volksgeistes sei, kein nazionalistisches Konzept entwickelt."* – LARSSON, Lars-Olof: Nationalstil und Nationalismus in der Kunstgeschichte der zwanziger und dreissiger Jahre, in *Kategorien und Methoden der deutschen Kunstgeschichte, 1900 – 1930*. Ed. Lorenz DITTMANN. Stuttgart 1985, p. 171. *"In der 'Berliner Schule' kristalisierten sich die Italien- und Niederlandeforschung… heraus. Die deutsche Kunst fand daneben vergleichsweise geringe Aufmerksamkeit. Im Zeitalter der Nationenbildung wurde zwar eine nationale Kunstgeschichte ausgebildet, der Akzent darin aber nicht auf die nationale Kunst gelegt."* – BICKENDORF 2007 (see note 14), p. 58. *"Gerade die deutsche Kunstgeschichte erlangte ihren frühen Weltrang vor allem durch ihre internationale Orientierung…"* – MUTHESIUS 2004 (see note 4), p. 70.

[18]   KARGE 1996 (see note 16), pp. 301-303.

Kugler did not accept the idea of *"diffusionism"*,[19] but rather replaced it with the principle of *"polygeneticism"*.[20]

The Inauguration of National Histories of Art

The nationalistic interpretation of art history only entered the German historiography of art after the unification of Germany in 1871.[21] German art as a specific and autochthonous historical phenomenon was first systematically thematized in the collective synthetic work, *Geschichte der deutschen Kunst* (1886 – 1890).[22] This can rightly be regarded as both the expression and ideo-

---

[19]   This means the dissemination of an idea or a form from one center to another. See KUBLER, George: *The Art and Architecture of Ancient America* (=The Pelican History of Art, 21). Bungay [a.o.] 1962, pp. 11-12. More about Kugler's idea of world art history, see EHRINGHAUS, Sibylle: *Germanenmythos und deutsche Identität. Die Frühmittelalter-Rezeption in Deutschland 1842 – 1933*. Weimar 1966, pp. 25-33; KARGE, Henrik: Welt-Geschichte: Franz Kugler und die geographische Fundierung der Kunsthistoriographie in der Mitte des 19. Jahrhunderts, in *Kunsttopographie. Theorie und Methode in der Kunstwissenschaft und Archäologie seit Winckelmann*. Stendal 2003, pp. 19-31; KARLHOLM 2004 (see note 15).

[20]   This means the simultaneous origin of a phenomenon, independently, in different places. See KUBLER 1962 (see note 19). According to the findings of Wilhelm Schlink, Kugler's pupil and co-author of the second edition of the *Handbuch der Kunstgeschichte*, Jacob Burckhardt also consistently avoided nationalist interpretations. *"Der direkten Frage, ob es eine nationale Kunst gebe, ist Jacob Burckhardt zeitlebens ausgewichen. Die Werke der 'großen Künstler' galten ihm als zeitlos und universal, als ewiger Besitz der ganzen Menschheit. Auf der anderen Seite ordnete er Kunst nach Epochen, Regionen und Stilen, so wie er es bei Franz Kugler in Berlin gelernt hatte."* – SCHLINK 1996 (see note 16), p. 312.

[21]   TSCHUDI, Hugo von: Hubert Janitschek [Obituary], in *Repertorium für Kunstwissenschaft*, 17, 1894, pp. 1-7. Hugo von Tschudi considered *Geschichte der deutschen Kunst* as a manifestation of *"der nationale Zug"* that *"die deutsche Kunstgeschichtsschreibung ergriffen [hatte]"* with a delay. – Ibid., p. 5.
According to GEBHARDT, Volker: *Das Deutsche in der deutschen Kunst*. Köln 2004, p. 29: *"Das Interesse am Nationalen bekam erst mit der Reichsgründung 1870/71 etwas Zwangshaftes."* Wolfgang Schenkluhn speaks of two phases *"der Nationalisierung von Kunst mit den Daten 1870/71 und 1914/18… [die] in engem Zusammenhang stehen"*. – SCHENKLUHN, Wolfgang: Bemerkungen zum "Nationalstil" in der Kunstgeschichte, in JANTZEN, Hans: *Ottonische Kunst*. Berlin 1990 (new ed.), pp. 167-168.
According to LOCHER 2001 (see note 2), pp. 198-199, Johann Dominicus FIORILLO (*Geschichte der zeichnenden Künste in Deutschland und den vereinigten Niederlanden, 1815 – 1820*) was the *"Pionier der nationalen Kunstgeschichtsschreibung in Deutschland"*. Fiorillo's *Geschichte* was followed by FÖRSTER, Ernst: *Geschichte der deutschen Kunst*. Vols. 1-5. Leipzig 1851 – 1863.

[22]   BODE, Wilhelm von: *Geschichte der deutschen Plastik*. Berlin 1886; DOHME, Robert: *Geschichte der deutschen Baukunst*. Berlin 1887; FALKE, Jacob von: *Geschichte des deutschen Kunstgewerbes*. Berlin 1888; JANITSCHEK, Hubert: *Geschichte der deutschen Malerei*. Berlin 1890; LÜTZOV, Karl von: *Geschichte des deutschen Kupferstiches*. Berlin 1891.
Simultaneously, Wilhelm LÜBKE published *Geschichte der deutschen Kunst von den frühesten Zeiten bis zur Gegenwart* (Stuttgart 1890). About the historiography of the history of German

logical instrument of German national patriotism.[23] In the volume devoted to German painting,[24] Hubert Janitschek, a native of Opava (Troppau) in Moravia and professor of art history, first at Prague and then at Strasbourg University, formulated the conception of ethnic nationalism. The history of German painting, in his view, reached beyond the history of the state, which started with the Treaty of Verdun in 843. *"The beginnings of German painting"* go back to the *"twilight of the tribal past"*.[25] Therefore, it is the history of the *"artistic sense of form... of the German Volk"*.[26] This purist ethno-national approach considered the art of all German-speaking countries including Austria, as well as the German art of multi-national regions such as Bohemia and Silesia and even the work of German artists abroad, such as Veit Stoss in Kraków and Raffael Donner in Bratislava (Pressburg). It is noteworthy that the authors of the *Geschichte der deutschen Kunst* had close educational and professional links with Vienna,[27] and that the majority of them hold to a universalising

---

art, see MÜLLER, Marcus: *Geschichte, Kunst, Nation. Die sprachliche Konstituierung einer "deutschen" Kunstgeschichte aus diskusrsanalytischer Sicht*. Berlin – New York 2007, pp. 37-45.

[23] SPRINGER, Anton: Geschichte der deutschen Kunst [Review], in *Repertorium für Kunstwissenschaft*, 13, 1890, p. 311, characterized the *Geschichte der deutschen Kunst* as a critical response to *"die mindere Wertschätzung unserer Kunst"*. See also *Metzler Kunsthistoriker Lexikon. Zweihundert Porträts deutschsprachiger Autoren aus vier Jahrhunderten*. Eds. Peter BETTHAUSEN – Peter H. FEIST – Christiane FORK. Stuttgart – Weimar 1999, p. 191. GEBHARDT 2004 (see note 21), p. 29, points out that national patriotism had also another intention: *"Jetzt ging es darum, den... Imperialismus jeweils national zu begründen."*

[24] JANITSCHEK 1890 (see note 22).

[25] *"... die Anfänge der deutschen Malerei"* go back to the *"Dunkel der Stammeszeit"*. – Ibid., p. 3. Like Janitschek, Lübke's *Geschichte der deutschen Kunst* – LÜBKE 1890 (see note 22) – also represented an attempt to reconstruct *"ur-deutsche Kunst"*. He believed in *"einen selbstständig germanischen Kunstsinn"* that had existed since the time of *"der älteren Germanen"*, thus, in *"die Erbfolgreihe 'Germanen'-'Deutschen'"*. In other words, he believed in *"nationale Rückverlängerung des Deutschen in die Stammesgeschichte der Germanen"*. See MÜLLER 2007 (see note 22), p. 137.

[26] *"... künstlerischen Formensinnes... des deutschen Volkes"*. – Ibid., p. 4. Anton Springer accepted Janitschek's conception and supported the autochthonous origin of German art. He derived it from *"Rassen- und Stammesphantasie"* and identified a vital relationship to the *"deutschen Boden"* (German Soil). *"Im tiefsten Grunde wurzelt unsere Kunst in nationalem Boden."* – SPRINGER 1890 (see note 23), p. 319. The romantic roots of this interpretation are obvious, as is the anticipation of the later ethno-nationalism of the 20th century based on *"Blut und Boden"* doctrine. The idea of *"deutsches Volk"* as *"Kollektivsubjekt"* of the history of art had been articulated already by Wilhelm LÜBKE in *Geschichte der deutschen Renaissance* (1873). See on this LOCHER 2001 (see note 2), p. 197.

[27] Bode was actually a graduate of the Vienna School (*Metzler Kunsthistoriker Lexikon* (see note 23), pp. 31-32). From 1863, Lützow taught history and archaeology at Vienna University (Ibid., pp. 254-255), Janitschek cooperated with the director of the Österreichisches Museum für Kunst und Industrie Rudolf Eitelberger, and qualified as a lecturer at Vienna University in 1878 (Ibid., pp. 191-192). Falke was Eitelberger's successor in the function of director of the Österreichisches Museum für Kunst und Industrie from 1885 (Ibid., p. 83).

approach to art that also stressed the autonomous development of style. In contrast to Janitschek, they did not follow the romantic way of seeking the *"national style"*.[28] Hence, the pan-Germanic implications of Janitschek's ethno-nationalist conception were in harmony with the hegemonic ideology of the German Empire, but not with the cosmopolitan ideology of the multi-national Habsburg Monarchy.[29]

---

[28] On Janitschek, see VYBÍRAL, Jindřich: Hubert Janitschek. Zum 100. Todesjahr des Kunsthistorikers, in *Kunstchronik*, 47, 1994, pp. 237-244; *Metzler Kunsthistoriker Lexikon* (see note 23), pp. 190-192. On Janitschek's pan-Germanic and anti-Habsburg position, see OLIN, Margaret: Nationalism, the Jews, and Art History, in *Judaism*, 45, 1996, No. 4, p. 465; OLIN, Margaret: Art History and Ideology: Alois Riegl and Josef Strzygowski, in *Cultural Visions: Essays in the History of Culture*. Eds. Penny Schine GOLD – Benjamin C. SAX. Amsterdam – Atlanta (GA) 2000, p. 157.

[29] After 1871, an explicit idea of German cultural superiority in Central Europe was developed simultaneously with a pan-Germanic hegemonism implied in ethnic nationalism. In 1876, Alfred Woltmann claimed that art in Prague was a true German art (WOLTMANN, Alfred: *Deutsche Kunst in Prague*. Leipzig 1877). See about this VYBÍRAL, Jindřich: What Is "Czech" in Art in Bohemia? Alfred Woltmann and Defensive Mechanisms of Czech Artistic Historiography, in *Kunstchronik*, 59, 2006, No. 1, pp. 1-7. Cornelius Gurlitt joined Woltmann's pan-German idea (GURLITT, Cornelius: *Geschichte des Barockstiles und des Rococo in Deutschland*. Stuttgart 1889, p. 16): *"Eine slawische Kunst gibt es in Böhmen so wenig wie in Polen."* See De MEYER, Dirk: Writing Architectural History and Building a Czechoslovak Nation, 1887 – 1918, in *Nation, Style, Modernism*. Eds. Jacek PURCHLA – Wolf TEGETHOFF. Cracow – Munich 2006, pp. 82-87; RAMPLEY, Matthew: For the Love of the Fatherland: Patriotic Art History and the "Kronprinzenwerk" in Austria-Hungary, in *Centropa*, 9, 2009, No. 3, pp. 160-175, here pp. 170, 174. Hegemonic pan-German interpretation of medieval art in Bohemia was developed by NEUWIRTH Josef: *Geschichte der christlichen Kunst in Böhmen bis zum Aussterben der Přemysliden*. Prag 1888; NEUWIRTH Josef: *Geschichte der bildenden Kunst in Böhmen vom Tode Wenzels III. bis zu den Husitenkriegen I.* Prag 1892. Neuwirth regarded art in Bohemia as an offshoot of German art. See about this BENEŠOVSKÁ Klára: Neuwirth, in *Nová encyklopedie českého výtvarného umění* [New Encyclopedia of Czech Visual Art]. Praha 1995, s. 566. Referring to the history of art in Poland, EHRENBERG, Hermann: *Geschichte der Kunst im Gebiete der Provinz Posen*. Berlin 1893, spoke about *"geringe Entwicklung der Kunst in Polen"* and *"Abhängigkeit Polens in künstlerischer und gewerblicher Beziehung von Deutschland"*. Moreover, he regarded art of the Poznań region as a part of so called *"Ostmark"* and a product of German impact. See about this BRYL, Mariusz: Königliche Akademie w Poznaniu 1903 – 1918, in *Dzieje historii sztuki w Polsce. Kształtowanie sie instytucji naukowych w XIX i XX wieku* [The History of Art History in Poland. The Rise and Development of Academic Institutions in the 19th and 20th Centuries]. Eds. Adam S. LABUDA – Katarzyna ZAWIASA-STANISZEWSKA. Poznań 1996, p. 139. According to Marian Kutzner, the idea of German art as a motor for art in East Central Europe had been articulated already by Franz Kugler (KUGLER, Franz: *Pommersche Kunstgeschichte*. Stettin 1840). See KUTZNER, Marian: Sztuka i kolonizacja niemiecka na wschód od Odry [Art and the German Colonisation to the East of the Odra], in *Niemcy – Polska w średniowieczu. Materiały z konferencji naukowej zorganizowanej przez Instityt historii UAM w dniach 14 – 16 XI 1983 roku* [Germany – Poland in the Middle Ages. Materials from the Conference Organized by the Institute of History of the AMU, 14 – 16 November 1983]. Ed. Jerzy STRZELCZYK. Poznań 1986, p. 341. Art historians of non-German countries responded in two following ways to the hegemonic

The Contradictions of Multi-Nationalism

As is well-known, the historiography of art was institutionalized in Vienna immediately after the unsuccessful bourgeois revolution of 1848.[30] Art historians became first of all official state experts. The prime task of their professional mission was to secure state tasks such as caring for state art property, including its cultural heritage and, not least, to strengthen the legitimising political and cultural ideologies of the state.[31] It is understandable that the ideology of a multi-national Monarchy, if it was not going to be internally subverted or changed into the hegemony of one nation, could not be that of nationalism. Therefore, the official ideological platform of the Habsburg Empire became internationalism or cosmopolitanism, the ideology of a multi-national solidarity and cooperation between its different peoples. It goes without saying that the historiography of art played an important role in promoting and strengthening this vision.[32]

After the unsuccessful bourgeois revolution, the first professor of art history at Vienna University, Rudolf Eitelberger, abandoned his youthful sym-

---

idea of German art as the leading force of the history of art in Central Europe and to the related contention that the art of non-German nations was a backward one: either the particular national art was seen to be genetically derived directly from West- or South European artistic centers (Imre Henszlman, Károly Pulszky), or the Romantic belief in the autochthonous origin of folk art was modernized in search of a specific and authentic character of the art of a nation or a country (Karel Chytil, Karel B. Mádl). See on that *Die ungarische Kunstgeschichte und die Wiener Schule, 1846 – 1930*. Budapest 1983, pp. 20-21, 40; *Kapitoly z českého dějepisu umění* [Chapters from Czech Historiography of Art]. Vol. 2. Eds. Rudolf CHADRABA – Josef KRÁSA – Rostislav ŠVÁCHA – Anděla HOROVÁ. Praha 1987, pp. 158, 175; RAMPLEY 2009 (see in this note), pp. 170-172; FILIPOVÁ, Marta: The Construction of a National Identity in Czech Art History, in *Centropa*, 8, 2008, No. 3, pp. 257-271.

30 See SCHLOSSER, Julius von: Die Wiener Schule der Kunstgeschichte. Rückblick auf ein Säkulum deutscher Gelehrtenarbeit in Österreich, in *Mitteilungen des Österreichischen Instituts für Geschichtsforschung*, 13, 1934, No. 2, pp. 145-210. Art historical institutions as state bodies were established at that time: 1850, K. k. Central-Commission für die Erforschung und Erhaltung der Baudenkmale; 1852, Lehrstuhl für Kunstgeschichte an der Universität Wien; 1854, Institut für österreichische Geschichtsforschung; 1864, Österreichisches Museum für Kunst und Industrie.

31 OLIN 2000 (see note 28), p. 156; BAKOŠ, Ján: From Universalism to Nationalism. Transformation of Vienna School Ideas in Central Europe, in *Die Kunsthistoriographien in Ostmitteleuropa und der nationale Diskurs* (see note 4), p. 80; in this volume pp. 125-147.

32 Margaret Olin emphasizes *"the ability of Denkmalpflege to contribute to a unified state"*. – OLIN, Margaret: The Cult of Monuments as a State Religion in Late 19th Century Austria, in *Wiener Jahrbuch für Kunstgeschichte*, 33, 1985, p. 184. Referring to Riegl, she states: *"Riegl's conception of late Roman art exemplifies the way in which an art historian can help construct and intervene in an ideology not of nationalism, but of an official internationalism, specifically, the embattled internationalism of the Habsburg empire..."* – OLIN 2000 (see note 28), s. 155. See also BAKOŠ 2004 (see note 31), pp. 80-81.

pathy for German nationalism.[33] Holding the position of one of the chief representatives of the Central Commission on the Research and Preservation of Historical Monuments ("K. k. Central-Commission für die Erforschung und Erhaltung der Baudenkmale"), he promoted the idea of the polyphonic multinational cultural unity of Central Europe,[34] identifying it with the Habsburg Monarchy.[35] By emphasizing the organic inclusion of the cultural heritage of individual nations of the Monarchy in a common art historical whole, he intended to confront the centrifugal thrust of the ideologues of the national bourgeoisies, who emphasized the autochthonous nature of national art, or in a more sophisticated way, stressed the direct connection of their specific national cultures to other, Western European centres.[36] On the other hand,

---

[33] OLIN 1985 (see note 32), p. 183; OLIN, Margaret: Alois Riegl: The Late Roman Empire in the Late Habsburg Empire, in *The Habsburg Legacy. National Identity in Historical Perspective*. Eds. Ritchie ROBERTSON – Edward TIMMS. Edinburgh 1994, p. 111.

[34] According to Olin: *"Eitelberger... rejected the nationalistic elements"* but *"emphasized the importance of monuments in fostering the national identities of individual states in the Empire"*. – OLIN 1985 (see note 32), p. 184. See also MAROSI, Ernő: Die Anfänge der Denkmalpflege und die Tätigkeit der K. u. k. Zentralkommission in Ungarn, in *Die ungarische Kunstgeschichte und die Wiener Schule, 1846 – 1930*. Budapest 1983, p. 16.

[35] Thus, Eitelberger formulated not only the idea of Central Europe as identical with the Habsburg Monarchy but also the trans-national *étatiste* one of the history of art. According to this, the history of art is identical with the history of the multi-national state. On the typology of the idea of *"Mitteleuropa"*, see BAKOŠ, Ján: The Idea of East Central Europe as an Artistic Region and 14th-Century Painting and Sculpture in Slovakia, in *Künstlerischer Austausch/Artistic Exchange. Akten des XXVIII. Internationalen Kongresses für Kunstgeschichte, Berlin, 15. – 20. Juli 1992*. Ed. Thomas W. GAEHTGENS. Berlin 1993, Vol. 2, pp. 53-54. DaCOSTA KAUFMANN, Thomas: *Court, Cloister & City. The Art and Culture of Central Europe, 1450 – 1800*. London 1995, p. 17: *"For others 'Central Europe' has suggested the lands of one of the empires that comprised the region before 1918 – the dual monarchy of Austria-Hungary."*

[36] MAROSI 1992 (see note 1), p. 62. According to Ernő Marosi: *"Dem national gefärbten kunstgeschichtlichen Separatismus hielt in Österreich-Ungarn ein gesamtmonarchisches Konzept die Waage."* One of the most active separatists was the Hungarian art historian Imre Henszlmann. He emphasized the idea of the *"national character"* of art on the one side and the direct connection of Hungarian Gothic to French Gothic on the other. See ZÁDOR, Anna: A magyar művészettudomány történetének vázlata 1945-ig [An Outline of the History of Magyar/Hungarian Historiography of Art till 1945], in *A magyar művészettörténeti munkakozosség évkönyve, 1951*. Budapest 1952, pp. 12-13; TIMÁR, Árpád: Der Auftritt Imre Henszlmann's, in *Die ungarische Kunstgeschichte und die Wiener Schule, 1846 –1930*. Budapest 1983, pp. 11-12, 20-21; MAROSI 1983 (see note 34), pp. 20-21. In Bohemia, the 19th century Czech patriotic art historians, Karel Chytil or Karel B. Mádl, attempted to define Czech specificity of Gothic art in Bohemia. See on this *Kapitoly z českého dějepisu umění* [Chapters from Czech Historiography of Art]. Vol. 1. Eds. Rudolf CHADRABA – Josef KRÁSA – Rostislav ŠVÁCHA – Anděla HOROVÁ. Praha 1986, pp. 158, 175. See also BARTLOVÁ, Milena: *Naše, národní umění. Studie z dějin dějepisu umění* [Our, National Art. Studies from the History of Art Historiography]. Brno 2009, pp. 21-38; FILIPOVÁ 2008 (see note 29).
E. Marosi expressed the view that the effort of Central European art historians to search for direct connections between the national art and the European centres continues until

Eitelberger did not give up a commitment to the hegemonic place of Western Europe and its central role in the diffusion of art.[37] He was convinced that the historical development of art was based on the *"migration of art from the West to the East"*.[38]

The need for new ways to shape the conception of the Monarchy as a polyphonic multi-national cultural unit became especially urgent at the end of the 19th century. This was not only owing to the recent establishment of the dual state of Austria-Hungary, which meant a new balance of forces after the Austro-Hungarian Compromise of 1867, but also to the constantly growing centrifugal pull of nationalism.[39] The prime task of this polyphonic conception was thus to propagate the official doctrine of multi-national harmony, unity in diversity, solidarity based on respect for the separate identities of all the national cultures under the Monarchy. It also intended to express simultaneously, the internal hierarchy ruling this multi-national unit.[40] Crown Prince Rudolf attempted to solve this dilemma by initiating the monumental multi-volume work: *Dic Österreichisch-Ungarische Monarchie in Wort und Bild* (Wien 1886, Vol. 1). That is why the publication was conceived of as a polyphonic

---

today and results in the petrification of national isolationism. *"... die verschiedenen kunsthistorischen Schulen Mitteleuropas [haben]... die Beziehungen ihrer Kunst vor allem zu den primären normgebenden Zentren, womöglich zu Italien und Frankreich, gesucht. Dies ist in Spiegelbild der zersplitterten Nationalstaaten Mitteleuropas, die Schutz bei den Großmächten der Zeit suchten. [...] Unsere Nationalschulen der Kunstgeschichte tragen bis heute dieses Erbe, das ihnen eine Zusammenschau ihrer Beziehungen verbietet, und die Kunstgeschichte zu einem Mittel der historischen Rückprojizierung der Kultur der Nationalstaaten macht."* – MAROSI, Ernő: Die Domskulpturen von Pécs. Kunsthistorische Einordnung und Inszenierung als ein Paradigma ungarischen Selbstverständnisse, in *Die Kunsthistoriographien in Ostmitteleuropa und der nationale Diskurs* (see note 4), p. 244.

[37] As articulated in: Bericht über einen archäologischen Ausflug nach Ungarn in den Jahren 1854 und 1855, in *Jahrbuch der K. k. Central-Commission für die Erforschung und Erhaltung der Baudenkmale*, 1, 1856, p. 95.

[38] For example, he attributed only secondary participation to the art of Hungary in the process of the spread of impulses from the West to the East. – MAROSI 1983 (see note 34), p. 16. On Eitelberger recently, see RAMPLEY, Matthew: Art History and the Politics of Empire: Rethinking the Vienna School, in *Art Bulletin*, 91, 2009, No. 4, pp. 449-454 (part "Eitelberger, Dalmatia, and the South Slav Question in Art History"); RAMPLEY, Matthew: The Idea of Scientific Discipline: Rudolf von Eitelberger and the Emergence of Art History in Vienna, 1847 – 1873, in *Art History*, February 2011, pp. 55-79.

[39] For further information, see BELLER, Steven: *A Concise History of Austria*. Cambridge 2006, pp. 151-177.

[40] According to Matthew Rampley, Eitelberger was convinced that *"German culture was the superior culture of the Empire"*. Quoted in a private letter. Eitelberger's disciple Albert Ilg attempted to eliminate the contradiction mentioned above by means of the following compromise: *"Alle wahre und große Kunst ist kosmopolitisch in Zweck, Wirkung und Bedeutung, aber national in der Erscheinung, national in den Mitteln, welche zu solchen Zwecken führen."* Quoted according to MUTHESIUS 2004 (see note 4), p. 73.

aggregate, as a collective work, thoroughly incorporating the work of authors from all the nationalities of the Monarchy.[41]

Cosmopolitanism as Science

The professors of art history at Vienna University and the Institute for Austrian Historical Studies ("Institut für österreichische Geschichtsforschung") found a different way of fulfilling their role as propagators of the cosmopolitan ideology of the Monarchy. They absorbed and transposed the ideology of cosmopolitanism into a universalist philosophy of the history of art, which included the idea of the formal autonomy of art and the scientific or causal *"genetic"* method of the historiography of art.[42] This new conception of art history was most systematically formulated by Alois Riegl.[43] It is possible to say that Riegl radicalised and completed the historical-pluralist and relativist conception of the universal history of art of the Berlin School. He freed it from the remnants of Enlightenment normativism[44] and, with the help of the concept of *"Kunstwollen"*, combined it with the modernist idea of the autonomy of art. Thus, the universal history of art became an immanent, evolutionary, continuous process. However, the idea of immanence was also combined with the idea of causality, which led to the genetic method of explaining the history of

---

[41] Beginning with such experts from the Vienna centre as Jacob von Falke, Karl von Lützow and Albert Ilg, through the leading Hungarian writer Mór Jókai, to professors at universities in Kraków and Prague Marian Sokołowski, Karel Chytil and Josef Neuwirth, among many others. For further details, see RAMPLEY 2009 (see note 29), pp. 160-175; RAMPLEY 2009 (see note 38), pp. 446-462.

[42] On the scientism of the Vienna School as an instrument of Monarchic ideology, see BAKOŠ 2004 (see note 31), p. 80-81.

[43] KEMP, Wolfgang: Alois Riegl, in *Altmeister moderner Kunstgeschichte*. Ed. Heinrich DILLY. Berlin 1990, pp. 37-60; OLIN, Margaret: *Form of Representation in Alois Riegl's Theory of Art.* University Park (Penn.) 1992; IVERSEN, Margaret: *Alois Riegl: Art History and Theory.* Cambridge – London 1993; *Framing Formalism, Riegl's Work.* Ed. Richard WOODFIELD. Amsterdam 2001; RAMPLEY, Matthew: Zwischen nomologischer und hermenutischer Kunstwissenschaft: Alois Riegl und das Problem des Kunstwollens, in *Kritische Berichte*, 31, 2003, pp. 5-19; RAMPLEY, Matthew: Alois Riegl, in *Klassiker der Kunstgeschichte I* (see note 2), pp. 153-162; VASOLD, Georg: *Alois Riegl und die Kunstgeschichte als Kulturgeschichte.* Freiburg im Breisgau 2004.

[44] DVOŘÁK, Max: Alois Riegl, in DVOŘÁK, Max: *Gesammelte Aufsätze zur Kunstgeschichte.* München 1929, pp. 279-298. See to that BAKOŠ, Ján: Max Dvořák – a Neglected Re-Visionist, in *Wiener Schule. Erinnerung und Perspektiven* (=Wiener Jahrbuch für Kunstgeschichte, 53). Wien – Köln – Weimar 2004, pp. 56-59. On Dvořák, see RAMPLEY, Matthew: Max Dvořák: Art History and the Crisis of Modernity, in *Art History*, 26, April 2003, pp. 214-237; AURENHAMMER, Hans: Max Dvořák, in *Klassiker der Kunstgeschichte I* (see note 2), pp. 214-226.

art.[45] This excluded from the explanation of art romantic irrational elements to do with art as the emanation of the essence of a nation and polygenetic ideas of artistic origin. The universal history of art became a rationally explainable, monocausal and so, linear genetic development.[46]

As is well known, Riegl explained his philosophy of art history mainly in the field of Late Roman and Early Medieval art, an area previously considered decadent.[47] Not only did he rehabilitate it and, in this way, support his anti-normative relativist conception, but, in addition, he found in the art of Late Antiquity and the Early Middle Ages an historical analogy with the situation of his own time around the turn of the 19th century. On the basis of this historical projection,[48] he conceived an immanent *apologia* for the Habsburg Monarchy and its important historical role between two epochs – that of traditional liberal rationality and that of an up and coming irrational subjectivity, the transition from historicism to modernism.

The Universal History of Art as a Form of Racism

However, it was precisely the idea of a rational, causal linearity of the universal history of art that became the subject of merciless radical criticism. Riegl was accused by the professor of art history at Graz and, later, Vienna Universities, Josef Strzygowski, of Eurocentrism, holding Mediterranean artistic development to be absolutely valid and glorifying in the central role of Rome.[49] Strzygowski himself also designed a universal conception of art

---

[45] Works of art were understood as mutually conditioned links in an evolutionary series.

[46] The idea of the linear causality of the universal history of art was not contradicted even by Riegl's assumption that the universal development of art occurred on the basis of human psychological perception, allegedly between its two poles – haptic and optic.

[47] RIEGL, Alois: *Spätrömische Kunstindustrie*. Wien 1901.

[48] OLIN, Margaret: Alois Riegl: The Late Roman Empire in the Late Habsburg Empire, in *The Habsburg Legacy. National Identity in Historical Perspective*. Eds. Ritchie ROBERTSON – Edward TIMMS. Edinburgh 1994, pp. 107-119; BAKOŠ 2004 (see note 31), p. 83.

[49] STRZYGOWSKI, Josef: *Orient oder Rom. Beiträge zur Geschichte der spätantiken und frühchristlichen Kunst*. Leipzig 1901. See on this SCHOLZ, Piotr O.: Wanderer zwischen den Welten. Josef Strzygowski und seine immer nocht aktuelle Frage: Orient oder Rom, in *100 Jahre Kunstgeschichte an der Universität Graz*. Eds. Walter HÖFLECHNER – Götz POCHAT. Graz 1992, pp. 243-265; recently EBERLEIN, Johann K.: Josef Strzygowski. Gedanken über die Zeitlosigkeit eines Typus, in *De re artificiosa. Festschrift für Paul von Naredi-Rainer zu seinem 60. Geburtstag*. Eds. Lukas MADERSBACHER – Thomas STEPPAN. Regensburg 2010, pp. 81-93. On the polemics Strzygowski versus Riegl, see OLIN 2000 (see note 28), pp. 152-153, 162-170; ELSNER, Jaś: The Birth of Late Antiquity: Riegl and Strzygowski in 1901, in *Art History*, 25, 2002, No. 3, pp. 358-379; VASOLD, Georg: Riegl, Strzygowski und die Entwicklung der Kunst, in *Ars*, 41, 2008, No. 1, pp. 95-111. RAMPLEY 2009 (see note 29), pp. 456-459.

history, but based on substantially different principles. His conception of art history was global, anti-Eurocentric and anti-centralist.[50] He understood the art of the world as a polyphony of simultaneously existing and constant artistic circles. Riegl's linear developmental, diachronic history was replaced by a synchronic artistic geography. In place of the premise of causal linearity, Strzygowski's conception put forward a romantic faith in emanation and poly-genesis. He understood artistic circles as entities that arise simultaneously and independently, and materialize their inner essence, which Strzygowski saw in ethnic or racial terms.[51] World art history became a polyphony of ethnic or racial entities. Since these collective racial entities in the history of art were situated spatially, they formed geographical artistic regions. From this point of view Strzygowski's approach was actually an early application of what would later be known as the *"Blut und Boden"* (Blood and Soil) doctrine, to art history.[52]

If Riegl's universalist theory can be regarded as an implicit *apologia* for the ideology of cosmopolitanism, then Strzygowski's model can be considered as an expression of bourgeois nationalism.[53] The conflict of the time between cosmopolitan monarchism and centrifugal nationalism was symbolically carried on in the polemic between the two Vienna University professors of art history. And both of them had their committed followers. Strzygowski's essentially romantic theory of the endogenous origin and autochthonous nature of the art of individual ethnic groups or races was most appreciated among the representatives of national historiographies of art.[54] His idea of early Slavic art,

---

[50] See FRODL-KRAFT, Eva: Eine Aporie und der Versuch ihrer Deutung. Josef Strzygowski – Julius v. Schlosser, in *Wiener Jahrbuch für Kunstgeschichte*, 42, 1989, pp. 15-50. See also VASOLD 2008 (see note 49).

[51] FRODL-KRAFT 1989 (see note 50), pp. 37-38; MARANCI, Christina: Basilicas and Black Holes: The Legacy of Josef Strzygowski and the Case of Armenian Architecture, in *Acta Historiae Artium*, 47, 2006, pp. 313-320. According to Christina Maranci, Strzygowski believed that *"architectural form was the function of race"*.

[52] FRODL-KRAFT 1989 (see note 50), p. 27. According to Thomas DaCosta Kaufmann: *"As Strzygowski first indicated in his works on south Slavic art and stated finally in his last work on Machtkunst, 'Lage, Blut, und Boden' – place, blood, and soil – are determinants of art."* – DaCOSTA KAUFMANN, Thomas: *Toward a Geography of Art.* Chicago – London 2004, p. 72.

[53] According to Margaret Olin, Strzygowski's theory represented *"A Nationalist Art History"*. – OLIN 2000 (see note 28), p. 162. See also MAROSI, Ernő: Josef Strzygowski als Entwerfer von nationalen Kunstgeschichten, in *Kunstgeschichte im "Dritten Reich": Theorien, Methoden, Praktiken.* Eds. Ruth HEFTRIG – Olaf PETERS – Barbara SCHELLEWALD. Berlin 2008, pp. 103-113.

[54] *"Die Aufwertung dieser volkstümlichen Kunst durch Strzygowski und seine Forderung, die slawische Kunst in ihren verschiedenen Heimgebieten in ihrer volkstümlichen Art vergleichend zu untersuchen, musste daher fast zwangsläufig die Kunstforschung vor allem in den südslawischen Ländern, aber auch in Polen stimulieren und – in Übereinstimmung mit den herrschenden nationalistischen Strö-*

for example, which he identified in medieval Croatian art as an autochthonous entity developed from domestic folk tradition rather than from external influences, was favoured especially by Slavic and Rumanian art historians.[55] However, it provoked serious criticism by some of the disciples of Alois Riegl and Max Dvořák.[56]

---

mungen – ihr Selbstgefühl steigern. [...] Das sind wohl die Gründe, weshalb Strzygowski gerade in den slawischen Ländern die nachhaltigste Wirkung beschieden war..." – FRODL-KRAFT 1989 (see note 50), p. 28. Strzygowski's influence was emphasized also by E. Marosi: "*... Josef Strzygowski, dessen Theorien einen ungemein großen Einfluss auf die nationalen Kunstgeschichtskonstruktionen der Zwischenkriegszeit ausgeübt haben.*" – MAROSI 1992 (see note 1), p. 63.

[55] Strzygowski's influence was dominant in inter-war art historiography in Rumania. The spreaders of his ideas included, in particular, his direct pupils Coriolan Petranu and Virgil Vătăşianu. For details, see BORN, Robert: Die Wiener Schule der Kunstgeschichte und die Kunsthistoriographie in Rumänien der Zwischenkriegszeit, in *Ars*, 41, 2008, No. 1, pp. 112-136; SABĂU, Nicolae: Coriolan Petranu (1893 – 1945). Erforscher der Kunst Transylvaniens (Siebenbürgens), in *Die Kunsthistoriographien in Ostmitteleuropa und der nationale Diskurs* (see note 4), pp. 381-395. The statement of Coriolan Petranu at the XIVth International Congress of the History of Art in Switzerland in September 1936 was entirely in harmony with Strzygowski's ethno-nationalist conception: "*... wir dürfen nicht den politischen Staat, sondern das Völkische als naturgegebene Einheit zum Ausgangspunkt wählen.*" – PETRANU, Coriolan: Begriff und Erforschung der nationalen Kunst, in *Actes du XIVe congrès international d'histoire de l'art.* Basel 1936, Vol. 1, p. 173.
In contrast, Strzygowski's impact on Polish art history was evident, but contradictory. "*... many of the Polish art historians were fascinated with Strzygowski's controversial views.*" – MAŁKIEWICZ, Adam: The History of Art History at Jagiellonian University, in *Historia sztuki na Uniwersytecie Jagiellońskim, 1882 – 2007.* Kraków 2007, s. 11. "*The result of his [Strzygowski's] work and his scientific personality roused contradictory estimations: from enthusiastic notion by Stanisław Gąsiorowski, through Molè's moderate criticism, to total rejection by Tadeusz Szydłowski, who characterized him as a murderer of humanism.*" – MAŁKIEWICZ, Adam: Historia sztuki w Polsce a "Wiedeńska szkoła historii sztuki" [The History of Art in Poland and the "Vienna School of Art History"], in *Rocznik Historii Sztuki*, 16, 1986, p. 334. "*Tadeusz Szydłowski... entered into sharp polemic with the Vienna professor Josef Strzygowski.*" – MAŁKIEWICZ 2007 (see note 55), s. 11. See also MAŁKIEWICZ, Adam: Die Kunstgeschichte in Polen und die Wiener Schule der Kunstgeschichte, in *Akten des XXV. Internationalen Kongresses für Kunstgeschichte, Wien, 4. – 10. September 1983.* Vols. 1-9. Eds. Hermann FILLITZ – Martina PIPPAL. Wien – Köln – Graz 1984 – 1986, Vol. 1: Wien und die Entwicklung der kunsthistorischen Methode (1984), pp. 158, 160 (note 5); MAŁKIEWICZ, Adam: Z dziejów polskiej historii sztuki. Studia i skice [From the History of Polish Art History. Studies and Outlines]. Kraków 2005, pp. 45, 47, 51, 60. Strzygowski's disciples also included Slovene art historians Augustin Stegenšek, August Žigon and above all Wojsław Molè. – *La Scuola Viennese di Storia dell'Arte. Atti del XX Convegno del Istituto pre gli Incontri Culturali Mitteleuropei.* Ed. Marco POZZETTO. Gorizia 1996, pp. 283-284.
[56] BAKOŠ 2004 (see note 31), pp. 86-92.

Between Cosmopolitanism and National Patriotism

The pupils of the so-called Vienna School of Art History were educated to be state officials, representing the interests of the Monarchy and supporters of its ideology. They were led towards universalism or cosmopolitanism and scientism by Franz Wickhoff, Alois Riegl and Max Dvořák. Therefore, the graduates of the Vienna School who became affiliated with the art historical institutions of the newly established independent nation-states, were confronted with a difficult task: how to balance national patriotism with a continuing commitment to their teachers' ideas of a universal or cosmopolitan history of art. In response, they made great efforts to harmonize Viennese art historical rationalism and scientism with the demand to identify specific national artistic traits,[57] and they devised various solutions to this dilemma. Thus, the professor at Prague University and pupil of Riegl, Vojtěch Birnbaum, sought universal art historical laws, following the example of his teacher, but was mainly concerned with finding patterns that could be considered characteristic of *"peripheral"* artistic regions. He found one of them in the so-called *"baroque principle"* associated with the spatial migration of a developmental shift he termed the *"law of transgression"*. In the concluding phases of development of a style, which, according to Birnbaum, are marked by subjectivism, the key developments in art no longer take place in the traditional centres. Late, so-called *"baroque"* phases appear to be just specific products of the initiative of provincial artistic regions, such as Bohemia.[58]

The transformation of the idea of the continuity of artistic development was another more sophisticated effort to harmonize belief in the universal history of art with national regionalism. If, in the hands of the Viennese professors, the idea of the continuity of development was evidence of the universality of the history of art and support for its rational explanation, their pupils from the outlying crown lands regarded it as evidence of the relative independence of the regional and national artistic units.[59] This was the case with

---

[57] Ibid., chapter "3. Mission and transformations: The role of the disciples I".

[58] This is the so-called *"baroque principle"* originally published in 1924. Reprinted in BIRNBAUM, Vojtěch: *Vývojové zákonitosti v umění* [Developmental Principles in Art]. Ed. Ivo HLOBIL. Praha 1987, pp. 24-46. On this, see SRP, Karel: Situace českého dějepisu umění ve dvacátých letech [The State of Czech Art Historiography in the 1920s], in *Kapitoly z českého dějepisu umění* (see note 29), p. 77; HOŘEJŠÍ, Jiřina: Vojtěch Birnbaum, ibid., pp. 112-114; HLOBIL, Ivo: Vojtěch Birnbaum – život a dílo v dobových souvislostech [Vojtěch Birnbaum – His Life and Work in the Context of the Age], in BIRNBAUM 1987 (see note 58), p. 398.

[59] See BAKOŠ, Ján: La Scuola Viennese di Storia dell'Arte e la storiografia dell'arte ceca, in *La Scuola Viennese* (see note 55), pp. 123-142; BAKOŠ, Ján.: Viedenská škola dejín umenia a český dejepis umenia [Vienna School of Art History and Czech Historiography of Art], in *Bulletin*

Eugen Dostál, Brno University professor and pupil of Dvořák, and later on also the case of Vincenc Kramář, Riegl's graduate and fellow-pupil of Dvořák. Both art historians demonstrated their ideas in relation to Bohemian art in the 14th century.[60]

However, perhaps the most prevalent way in which art historians of the time sought to harmonize universalism and patriotism was in seeking to identify the connections between regional or national art and what was going on elsewhere in Europe, as well as placing regional or national art in the context of universal development. The starting point was still the premise of art's universal and autonomous development. The aim was, however, to identify regional transformations of this universal development and specific regional and national contributions. Thus, regional or national development was seen as a concretisation of universal development.[61]

Moravské galerie v Brně, 54, 1998, pp. 5-11; BAKOŠ, Ján: *Štyri trasy metodológie dejín umenia: Viedenská škola dejín umenia – Česko-slovenský štrukturalizmus – Ruská historiografia umenia – Ikonológia a semiotika* [Four Routes for the Methodology of Art History: Vienna School of Art History – Czecho-Slovak Structuralism – Russian Historiography of Art – Iconology & Semiotics]. Bratislava 2000, pp. 41-66.

[60] SRP 1987 (see note 58), pp. 80-81; VACKOVÁ, Jarmila: Eugen Dostál, in *Kapitoly z českého dějepisu umění* (see note 29), pp. 171-178; KRÁSA, Josef: Vincenc Kramář, ibid., pp. 118-125; KRÁSA, Josef: Dílo Vincence Kramáře v českých dějinách umění [Vincenc Kramář's Work in Czech History of Art], in KRAMÁŘ, Vincenc: *O obrazech a galeriích* [About Paintings and Galleries]. Praha 1983, pp. 452-453. See also the catalogue *Vincenc Kramář: od starých mistrů k Picassovi* [Vincenc Kramář: From Old Masters to Picasso]. Praha 2000.

[61] As far as the relationship between European and regional development in the Polish historiography of art is concerned, see MAŁKIEWICZ 2007 (see note 55), pp. 3-21. The representatives of this approach in Polish art historiography included the professors at Kraków University, Marian Sokołowski and Julian Pagaczewski. Sokołowski, who were influenced by the older Vienna School, *"whereas conducting research on Polish art"*, he saw it *"through the perspective of the vast European context"*. His successor at Kraków University Julian Pagaczewski *"likewise his master... laid emphasis on the study of Polish art (and more precisely: on the study of art in Poland) which was treated as part of European art"*. – Ibid., pp. 4-11. On this, see also MUTHESIUS, Stefan: *Kunst in Polen/Polnische Kunst, 966 – 1990. Eine Einführung.* Königstein im Taunus 1994, pp. 3-8. At Poznań University, Szczęsny Dettloff, a pupil of Max Dvořák, combined the European approach with regional patriotism. On this, see LABUDA, Adam S.: Seminar on the History of Art in the Poznań University, 1919 – 1939, in *Dzieje historii sztuki w Polsce* (see note 29), p. 192. When searching for the *"deserved position [of Polish art] in the European artistic tradition"*, Dettloff relied on Viennese methods (*"genetic-comparative method"* and causal explanation with the help of terms such as *"radiation"* and *"influence"*). See Ibid.
It can be regarded as symptomatic that already Izidor Kršnjavi, the first Croatian pupil of the Vienna School, in applying the idea of continuity of development and its causal explanation, derived the origin of South Slavonic ornament from Antiquity, in much the same way to Alois Riegl. See JIRSAK, Libuše: *Izidor Kršnjavi und die Wiener Schule der Kunstgeschichte.* Zagreb 2008, pp. 226-247. About I. Kršnjavi, see also DAMJANOVIĆ, Dragan: Bishop Juraj Strossmayer, Izidor Kršnjavi and the Foundation of the Chairs in Art History and Ancient Classical Archeology of Zagreb University, in *Centropa,* 9, 2009, No. 3, pp. 176-184.

Combining the principle of continuous universal evolution with the idea of autochthonous origins, Max Dvořák's Croatian pupil Ljubo Karaman thought up an especially noteworthy synthesis of universalism and regionalism.[62] He developed his causal explanation of regional distinctiveness precisely on the basis of a polemic against Strzygowski. He rejected Strzygowski's thesis concerning the autochthonous and continuous domestic or *"barbarian"* origin of Early Medieval architecture in Croatia,[63] which he regarded it as an unscientific denial of the principle of causality in that it ignored, first Classical external influences and later Italian ones. However, Karaman also defended the distinctive character of marginal regions, replacing Strzygowski's essentialist arguments with causal and rational considerations. He did not deny the de-

---

The art historians striving to harmonize universalism and regionalism, also included the Slovene scholar France Stelé, a pupil of Max Dvořák. See CEVC, Emilijan: Gli echi della Scuola di Vienna: France Stelé e Vojeslav Molè, in *La Scuola Viennese* (see note 55), pp. 199-204; PRELOVŠEK, Damjan: Památková péče a slovinské dějiny umění [Monument Preservation and Slovene Art History], in *Regnum Bohemiae et Sacrum Romanum Imperium. Sborník k poctě Jiřího Kuthana*. Praha 2005, pp. 413-420. In contrast to Izidor Cankar, another of Dvořák's Slovenian pupils, Stelé, who concentrated on European art, attempted to articulate the specificity of local art by means of combining Riegl's *"Kunstwollen"* with Strzygowski's *"Kunstgeographie"*. In this way, his work paralleled the project of the Croat, Ljubo Karaman. See PRELOVŠEK, Damjan: Il *"Kunstwollen"* e la storia dell'arte Slovena, in *La Scuola Viennese* (see note 55), pp. 205-209; ŠUMI, Nace: Izidor Cankar, fondatore della Scuola Lubianese di Storia dell'Arte, ibid., pp. 195-198; BAKOŠ 2004 (see note 31), pp. 90-91. On Slovene historiography of art, see also STELÉ, France: Slovenija razvoj historije umjetnosti [The Development of Slovene Art History], in *Enciklopedija likovnih umjetnosti*. Vol. 4. Zagreb 1966, p. 342 ff.
According to Lajos Vayer, it is necessary to understand *"das Universale und das Regionale"* *"als einander gegenseitig ergänzende, korrelative Kategorien"*. – VAYER, Lajos: Allgemeine Entwicklung und regionale Entwicklungen in der Kunstgeschichte – Situation des Problems in "Mitteleuropa". Plenary lecture at the XXIInd International Congress of the History of Art, Budapest, 1969, in *Évolution génerale et dévelopment régionaux en histoire de l'art*. Budapest 1972, Vol. 1, pp. 20-21. However, according to Vayer, the absolutization of universal, in comparison with regional, development, often led to the underestimation of regional phenomena which tended to be seen as peripheral and developmentally backward. As a consequence, this provoked the nationalist idea of autochthonicity. – Ibid., pp. 25-26.

[62] IVANČEVIĆ, Radovan: Ljubo Karaman e la nozione dell'arte provinciale, dell'arte di frontiera e dell'arte periferica, in *La Scuola Viennese* (see note 55), pp. 183-194. According to Radovan Ivančević, Ljubo Karaman was not only Dvořák's but also Strzygowski's student. – IVANČEVIĆ, Radovan: Die Wiener Schule der Kunstgeschichte und Zagreb: Einflüsse und Fortsetzung, in *Ambivalenz des Fin de siècle: Wien – Zagreb*. Eds. Damir BARBARIĆ – Michael BENEDIKT. Wien – Köln – Weimar 1998, pp. 231, 239; SCHERKE, Katharina: Der formale Ansatz Alois Riegls und die Entwicklung nationaler Kunsthistoriographien in der Österreich-Ungarischen Monarchie – dargestellt am Beispiel Ljubo Karamans, in *Die Kunsthistoriographien in Ostmitteleuropa und der nationale Diskurs* (see note 4), pp. 109-115.

[63] *Ambivalenz des Fin de siècle* (see note 62), pp. 239-240, 250-260. See also GOSS, Vladimir P.: Josef Strzygowski and Early Medieval Art in Croatia, in *Acta Historiae Artium*, 47, 2006, pp. 335-343.

cisive role of external influences as evidence of the diffusion of universal development, but regarded insufficient intensity and *lack* of influences, as what mainly characterized marginal regions (in border zones, provinces, peripheries). Moreover, he conceived of peripheries as a specific kind of art historical region, which displayed special creativity and originality precisely because of their geographical remoteness.[64]

Strzygowski's irrational and essentialist approach was rejected not only by the Czech and Croatian pupils of Riegl and Dvořák such as Birnbaum[65] and Karaman, but also by those Vienna graduates, who strove to defend the specific creativity of regional art and to harmonize Riegl's diachronic and Strzygowski's synchronic approaches.[66] Nor were Strzygowski's theories accepted by Europe-oriented national patriots.[67] Even some of Strzygowski's own pupils, who took up his typological oppositions – *"persistence versus development"* and *"folk art versus individual artistic personality"*[68] – ultimately joined the camp of his critics.[69]

Nationalists versus Cosmopolitans

The quarrel between the two Vienna schools, Riegl's and Strzygowski's, was, therefore, a conflict between two camps: causalists and cosmopolitans versus essentialists and nationalists. It continued in the Central European national historiographies of art after the break up of the Austro-Hungarian Monarchy in the 1920s and 1930s. While Czech inter-war art historiography was

---

[64]   IVANČEVIĆ 1998 (see note 62), pp. 250-253. According to Matthew Rampley, Karaman *"highlighted the local character… of Dalmatian art and architecture"* so that *"most of his work was dedicated to rebutting many of its* [the Vienna School's] *central assumptions"*. – RAMPLEY, Matthew: Dalmatia is Italian! The Politics of Art History in Austria-Hungary and South-Eastern Europe, 1862 – 1930, in *Études Balkaniques*, 44, 2008, No. 4, p. 145.
By means of Riegl's notion of *"Kunstwollen"*, also the Lwów (Ľviv) art historian Władysław Podlacha attempted to find *"the true criteria for evaluating the works of peripheral art… the criteria that will enable us to grasp their originality"*. – MAŁKIEWICZ, Adam: Historia sztuki na Uniwersytecie Lwówskim, 1893 – 1939 [The History of Art at Lwów University, 1893 – 1939], in *Dzieje historii sztuki w Polsce* (see note 29), p. 67.

[65]   Birnbaum argued against the vernacular interpretation of the origin of Romanesque architecture in Bohemia. See HOŘEJŠÍ 1987 (see note 58), pp. 384, 397.

[66]   BAKOŠ 2004 (see note 31), pp. 90-91.

[67]   MAŁKIEWICZ 1984 (see note 55), pp. 158, 160 (note 5); MAŁKIEWICZ 1986 (see note 55), p. 334. See also MAŁKIEWICZ 2007 (see note 55), p. 11.

[68]   See to that GLÜCK, Heinrich: Beharrung und Entwicklung. Volkskunst und Persönlichkeit, in *Studien zur Kunst des Ostens*. Wien 1923, pp. 177-181.

[69]   It refers to Wojsław Molè before all. See MAŁKIEWICZ 1984 (see note 55), p. 158; MAŁKIEWICZ 1986 (see note 55), p. 334; BAKOŠ 2004 (see note 31), p. 90.

unambiguously dominated by the outlook of Riegl, Wickhoff and Dvořák, with patriotic themes treated as problems of universal development,[70] Hungarian art historiography saw a radical polarization after the defeat of the Hungarian Soviet Republic in 1919. On the one side were the supporters of the idea of the autochthonous, specifically Hungarian or Magyar, character of art in Hungary.[71] On the other side were those who emphasized the connection of national developments with the wider universal history of art, and who sought to define the specific contribution of national art to the general development of European art.[72] Through polemics against the supporters of

---

[70] See SRP 1987 (see note 58), pp. 71-94; HOROVÁ, Anděla: Náznaky nové orientace ve třicátých letech [Indications of a New Orientation in the Thirties], in *Kapitoly z českého dějepisu umění* (see note 29), pp. 265-272. Nevertheless, there were also nationalists in the camp of the cosmopolitans. In the view of Dvořák's protégé Antonín Matějček *"all our art is national"*. See *Hlasy světa a domova* [Voices of the World and the Home]. Praha 1931. Quoted according to VYBÍRAL, Jindřich: Co je českého na umění v Čechách? [What is Bohemian in Art in Bohemia?], in *Dějiny umění v české společnosti: otázky, problémy, výzvy* [Art History in Czech Society: Questions, Problems, Chalenges]. Ed. Milena BARTLOVÁ. Praha 2004, p. 201.

[71] The nationalistically oriented art historians, Tibor Gerevich and Anton Hekler, dominated official Hungarian art historiography. See ZÁDOR 1952 (see note 36), pp. 28-30; MAROSI 1983 (see note 34), p. 87. See also GEREVICH, Tibor: A régi magyar művészet európai helyzete [The European Position of the Old Magyar/Hungarian Art], 1923; GEREVICH, Tibor: A magyar művészet jelentősége [The Meaning of Magyar/Hungarian Art], 1927; GEREVICH, Tibor: L'art national de la Hongrie, in *Actes du XIIIe congrès international d'histoire de l'art*. Stockholm 1933, pp. 49-52. T. Gerevich not only emphasized the distinctness of Hungarian art and its role in mediating European art towards the East. He was also convinced that there was *"l'art nationale de la Hongrie"* in the sense of a transhistorical *"l'art national hongrois"*, which expressed *"l'ame nationale"* or the *"propre genius nationale"*. This was a nationalist-hegemonist position, which identified the nation with the *"state"* or so-called ruling nation (*"state nation"*). Anton Hekler also based the history of art in Hungary on the identification of the state with the *"state nation"*. – HEKLER, Anton: *A magyar művészet története* [The History of Magyar/Hungarian Art]. Budapest 1935. In the German version (*Ungarische Kunstgeschichte*. Berlin 1937, p. 4), he replaced the nationalistic conception (the history of Hungarian or Magyar art) with an *étatiste* idea (the history of the art of the great Kingdom of Hungary). Nevertheless, he still treated it in a nationalist-hegemonic way as the history of the *"ungarische Nation"*. Similarly, István Genthon identified the history of art in Hungary with ethnic Hungarian or Magyar art and explicitly regarded it as the history of *"Magyar masters"* (*"magyar mesterek"*). – GENTHON, István: *A régi magyar festőművészet* [Old Magyar/Hungarian Painting]. Vác 1932.

[72] It is revealing that the internationalist camp included mostly those art historians who had some connection with the Vienna School. See about that ZÁDOR 1952 (see note 36), p. 26; MAROSI 1983 (see note 34), pp. 75-76. According to Lajos Fülep, one of the members of the so-called "Sonntagskreis" (led by Georg Lukács): *"Das Nationale ist eine spezielle nationale Sendung innerhalb der großen Universalität und Totalität der Kunst..."* – FÜLEP, Lajos: *Európai művészet és magyar művészet* [European Art and Magyar/Hungarian Art], 1918. Fülep in *Magyar művészet* [Magyar/Hungarian Art] (1923) spoke about *"eine Korrelation zwischen Universalem und Nationalem... Die Synthese dieser beiden Korrelationen ergibt die Universalgeschichte der Künste"*. Quoted according to MAROSI 1983 (see note 34), p. 76. See also SÁRMÁNY--PARSONS, Ilona: Constructing the Canon of Modern Hungarian Painting, 1890 – 1918, in

the essentialist autochthonous Hungarian or Magyar art, they endeavoured to demonstrate its European connections and inspirations.[73]

Where Polish art historiography is concerned, nationalists did not predominate in the inter-war period, and the polarity between local patriotism and cosmopolitanism did not have the form of an irreconcilable conflict.[74] However, supporters of the national interpretation were not lacking here (e.g. Michał Walicki, Juliusz Starzyński), and by the end of the 1930s, their position was shaped in response to the wider radicalisation of national politics in Europe.[75] In spite of this, due to the influence of Riegl, Wickhoff and their heirs, art in Poland or Polish art was still understood as part of European art, even in the art historical centres, especially Kraków, where local art was the primary subject of research.[76]

Centropa, 8, 2008, No. 3, p. 238. Sármány-Parsons quotes from the introductory chapter of *Hungarian Art* ("European Art and Hungarian Art") as follows: *"In other words: transcending its local significance, has Hungarian art a special mission within the community of European art, or within the art of the World? [...] the artistic mission of a nation is expressed through the solution of certain formal and aesthetic problems; this mission is national insofar as the solution of these artistic problems was originally vouchsafed only to that nation."*

[73] It refers especially to Edith Hoffmann, the student of Max Dvořák. See ZÁDOR 1952 (see note 36), p. 25; MAROSI 1983 (see note 34), p. 82.

[74] The situation from around 1900, when the supporters of an autochthonous national Polish art (mainly critics of art and architecture) sharply criticized art historians for their international, pro-Western orientation, was not repeated. At the turn of the century, the anti-nationalist approach to Veit Stoss by Kraków art historian Tadeusz Szydłowski was one of the main targets of severe nationalist criticism. Nevertheless, Szydłowski also later endorsed a nationalist approach. See MUTHESIUS 1994 (see note 61), pp. 4-6, 8-10; MUTHESIUS 2004 (see note 4), p. 76.

[75] In Adam Bochnak's words, the *"Romantic"* Michał WALICKI and his paper "Z badań nad problemem narodowości w polskim malarstwie gotyckim" ["From the Research into the Problem of Nationality in Polish Gothic Painting"] in *Życie sztuki*, 1, 1931, pp. 67-100, can be cited as an instance of the nationalist approach. See KUTZNER 1986 (see note 29), s. 347. In the collective book *Dzieje sztuki polskiej* [The History of Polish Art]. Warszawa 1935, pp. 911-912, by Warsaw University professors Michał WALICKI and Juliusz STARZYŃSKI, *"the original Polish characteristics"* were regarded as *"determined by the social situation"*. Nevertheless, at the end of the 1930s, Polish art historians focused on *"the survey of the 'Polish element'"*. See WALICKI, Michał: *Malarstwo polskie XV wieku* [Polish Painting of the 15th Century]. Warszawa 1938, p. 1.

[76] *"In Polen, d.h. in... Kraków... schien sich... die dringendere Aufgabe zu stellen, zunächst einmal eine Geschichte der Kunst in Polen zu etablieren. Wesentlich dabei aber war, daß diese Erforschung der polnischen Kunst innerhalb des gesamteuropäischen Zusammenhangs... betrieben werden sollte."* – MUTHESIUS 2004 (see note 4), p. 70. *"In the twenty-year period between the wars... what predominated was... a tradition of examining local art in the vast European context."* – MAŁKIEWICZ 2007 (see note 55), p. 13. It is also revealing that the book *Dzieje malarstwa w Polsce* [The History of Painting in Poland]. Kraków 1925 – 1929, by the director of the National Museum in Kraków and specialist in Polish art history Feliks KOPERA, was considered as charting French, Cologne, Czech and Hungarian influences.

From Modernism to Nationalism

It is known that the ideology of cosmopolitanism underlay pressure on the Monarchy's officials to side with artistic Modernism.[77] The international outlooks of artistic Modernism and its demand for the independence of art also harmonized with the universalist and autonomist conception of art of Riegl's school.[78] However, in the middle of the First World War, the internationalist agenda of artistic Modernism could not resist the imperialist struggle for hegemony.[79] The historiography of art also participated in the conflict between xenophobic nationalisms.[80] In France, Émile Mâle deliberately aimed at the German inferiority complex, when he declared that German art was uncreative and had contributed nothing to the universal history of art.[81] The response was a sharp reaction from leading representatives of German art historiography,[82] and an intensive search for the specific historical contributions of German art.[83] Xenophobic nationalism also led to the articulation of a new national-hegemonic conception of the history of German art. This drew on Friedrich Naumann's idea of a pan-Germanic *"Mitteleuropa"*, which was the ideological fruit of the military struggle for hegemony.[84] Georg

---

[77] *"Within this framework of supra-national policy, state encouragement of the Secessionist movement made complete sense. Its artists were as truly cosmopolitan in spirit as the bureaucracy and the Viennese upper middle class. At the time when nationalist groups were developing separate ethnic arts, the Secession had taken the opposite road. Deliberately opening Austria to European currents, it had reaffirmed in a modern spirit the traditional universalism of the Empire."* – SCHORSKE, Carl E.: *Fin-de-siècle Vienna. Politics and Culture.* New York 1981, p. 237.

[78] The Vienna School's approach provided the implicit *apologia* for modern art by means of historical projection. Support for Gustav Klimt from the side of the Vienna professors of art history, especially Franz Wickhoff, in the so-called university quarrel, harmonize with their generally cosmopolitan approach. See SCHORSKE 1981 (see note 77), pp. 234-235; LACHNIT, Edwin: Neuentdeckte Dokumente zum Professorenstreit um Klimts "Philosophie", in *Wiener Jahrbuch für Kunstgeschichte*, 39, 1986, pp. 205-220.

[79] On the relationship between modernism and nationalism, see *Nation, Style, Modernism* (see note 29).

[80] LAMBOURNE, Nicola: Production versus Destruction: Art, World War I and Art History, in *Art History*, 22, 1999, pp. 347-363; KOTT, Christina: Histoire de l'art et propagande pendant la Première guerre mondiale, in *Revue germanique internationale*, 13, 2000, pp. 201-221.

[81] MÂLE, Émile: Studien über die deutsche Kunst, in *Monatshefte für Kunstwissenschaft*, 9, 1916, pp. 387, 403, 429-447; 10, 1917, pp. 43-64 (originally published in *Revue de Paris*, 1916). See DILLY, Heinrich: September 1914, in *Revue germanique internationale*, 13, 2000, pp. 23-37.

[82] German art historians Paul Clemen, Kurt Gerstenberg, Adolf Gotze, Cornelius Gurlitt, Arthur Haseloff, Rudolf Kautzsch, Heinrich A. Schmid, Josef Strzygowski, Geza Supka, Oskar Wulff replied to Mâle in *Monatshefte für Kunstwissenschaft*, 10, 1917, pp. 127-173.

[83] See for example GERSTENBERG, Kurt: *Deutsche Sondergotik. Eine Untersuchung über das Wesen der deutschen Baukunst im späten Mittelalter.* München 1913 (2nd ed. Darmstadt 1969); WÖLFFLIN, Heinrich: *Italien und das deutsche Formgefühl.* München 1931.

[84] NAUMANN, Friedrich: *Mitteleuropa.* Berlin 1915. About the application of Naumann's con-

Dehio, who hailed from Tallinn (Reval) on the Baltic and who succeeded Janitschek at Strasbourg University in 1892, wrote the well-known *Handbuch der Deutschen Kunst* (published since 1901),[85] in which he formulated its first version. Dehio's originally international position[86] was replaced in his three-volume *Geschichte der deutschen Kunst*[87] with a national-patriotic conception that implicitly assumed the hegemony of German art and culture.[88]

Dehio distinguished between scholarship and education. He considered the first to be international, but he ascribed a patriotic mission to the second.[89] In his view, the history of German art was not just a history of art, but a process through which the constant spiritual identity of the German nation shows itself.[90] It was a document of the history of the nation or *"Volk"*.[91] Therefore, in his view the main task of the historiography of art was to create and strengthen national self-consciousness.[92]

However, the ethno-national conception of the history of art as the history of a nation or ethnic group implied that German art reached beyond the state frontiers of Germany.[93] Thus, the topic of the spread, dissemination and export of German art formed an integral part of this history. In connection with this, Dehio formulated his thesis concerning the historic role of German art, seeing

---

cept to art history, see BAKOŠ 1993 (see note 35), p. 53; DaCOSTA KAUFMANN 1995 (see note 35), p. 17.

[85] About Dehio, see *Metzler Kunsthistoriker Lexikon* (see note 23), pp. 54-57; BETTHAUSEN, Peter: *Georg Dehio. Ein deutscher Kunsthistoriker.* München – Berlin 2004.

[86] See DEHIO, Georg – BEZOLD, Gustav von: *Die kirchliche Baukunst des Abendlandes.* Stuttgart et al. 1887 – 1901. In the lecture held in Paris in 1900, Dehio professed *"l'idée de l'unité de la civilisation européenne"*. See MUTHESIUS 2004 (see note 4), pp. 75, 78.

[87] Published in Berlin – Leipzig 1919 – 1929.

[88] Dehio had articulated that idea already in the paper "Deutsche Kunstgeschichte und deutsche Geschichte" written in 1907 and published in *Historische Zeitschrift*, 100, 1908, pp. 473-485.

[89] *"Die Wissenschaft ist nach ihrem Wesen übernational; Bildung entsteht nur auf dem Boden... der Nation."* – DEHIO, Georg: *Geschichte der deutschen Kunst.* Berlin – Leipzig 1919 – 1926, Vol. 1, p. V.

[90] *"Die dieses Buch durchgehend beherrschende Frage lautet nicht: Was erfahren wir durch die Deutschen über das Wesen der Kunst? Sondern was offenbart uns die Kunst vom Wesen der Deutschen?"* Quoted from DEHIO, Georg: *Kunstgeschichte als Kulturgeschichte.* Berlin 1993, p. 12.

[91] *"Mein wahrer Held ist das deutsche Volk. Ich gebe deutsche Geschichte im Spiegel der Kunst."* – DEHIO 1919 – 1926 (see note 89), Vol. 1, p. V. Relying on the identification of nation with people (*"Volk"*), Dehio articulated *"Kunstgeschichte 'des deutschen Volkes' "*. See MUTHESIUS 2004 (see note 4), pp. 73, 75; LOCHER 2001 (see note 2), pp. 201-202.

[92] *"Als seine aktuelle Aufgabe sieht Dehio jedoch massgeblich die Pflege des Patriotismus mit den Mitteln der historischen Darstellung, durch Erinnern des nationalen Erbes."* – LOCHER 2001 (see note 2), p. 202.

[93] According to Wolfgang Schenkluhn, Dehio's theory cannot be regarded as a purely ethnic nationalist one. It was based on the idea of *"völklicher und staatlicher Einheit"*. – SCHENKLUHN 1990 (see note 21), p. 159.

it in the role of mediator between West and East.[94] Moreover, he combined this role of mediator with the hegemonic premise of the superiority of the West, the so-called *"West-Ost-Gefälle"*,[95] attributing to German art the mission of spreading Western culture towards the East. The result of this cultural transfer was the so-called *"Kolonialkunst"*, a term he devised to describe German art in the eastern part of Central Europe.[96]

Nationalism as the General Consensus

An important change occured in European art historiography at the beginning of the 1930s. Art historians abandoned the modernist platform, replacing cosmopolitanism with nationalism. They ceased to be interested primarily in defining the relationship between universal and national development, concentrating instead, on the search for *"national character"* in art.[97] As a consequence, the diachronic dimension of art receded into the background. Research concentrated mainly on historic synchronies or the search for national and geographical constants. If a residue of Modernism was still preserved, in terms of the history of art as the history of stylistic forms, it was nonetheless, deprived of the premise of autonomy. It was precisely modern expressionism that facilitated this transformation of the history of forms into the history of expression, prompting the effort to identify its standard bearers.[98] However,

---

[94] KUTZNER, Marian: Społeczne uwarunkowania rozwoju śląskej architektury w latach 1200 – 1330 [Social Conditions of the Development of Silesian Architecture in the Years 1200 – 1330], in *Sztuka i ideologia XIII wieku* [Art and Ideology of the 13th Century]. Ed. Piotr SKUBISZEWSKI. Wrocław – Warszawa – Kraków – Gdańsk 1974, p. 235.

[95] MUTHESIUS 2004 (see note 4), p. 76.

[96] DEHIO 1919 – 1926 (see note 89), Vol. 2, pp. 57-73. See on that KUTZNER 1986 (see note 29), pp. 337-353; LABUDA, Adam S.: "...eine von sinnvollen Zweckgefühlen erfüllte, herbe und großartige Kolonialkunst..." Zum kunsthistorischen Diskurs über Ostmitteleuropa, in *Zeitschrift für Kunstgeschichte*, 56, 1993, No. 1, pp.1-17; KĘBŁOWSKI, Janusz: Zur Frage der Bewertung der sog. "Kolonisation" und "Germanisierung" Schlesiens unter den Aspekten der Politik, Kultur und Kunst, in *Wanderungen: Künstler – Kunstwerk – Motiv – Stifter*. Warszawa 2005, pp. 257-261.

[97] *"Ohne Zweifel wurden in der Zwischenkriegszeit die nationalen Definitionen der Kunst... zum Hauptthema."* – MUTHESIUS 2004 (see note 4), p. 77.
Heinrich Wölfflin joined this trend in his *Italien und das deutsche Formgefühl* (1931). Wölfflin spoke about *"nationale Typen der Phantasie"* already in his *Kunstgeschichtliche Grundbegriffe* (1915). Nevertheless, he regarded it as *"eine notwendige Hilfskonstruktion"* at that time. – WÖLFFLIN, Heinrich: *Kunstgeschichtliche Grundbegriffe*. München 1929 (7th ed.), p. 254.

[98] BELTING, Hans: *Die Deutschen und ihre Kunst. Ein schwieriges Erbe*. München 1992; HALBERTSMA, Marlite: *Wilhelm Pinder und die Deutsche Kunstgeschichte*. Worms 1992; BUSHART, Magdalena: *Geist der Gotik und expressionistische Kunst*. München 1990; MUTHESIUS 1994 (see note 61), p. 8.

in contrast to modern expressionism, the standard bearers (*"Träger"*) of the history of art were not considered to be individual artists, nor was the history of art itself treated as the history of the expressions of individual artists.[99] Anonymous collective entities, namely nations (*"Völker"*) or races, were regarded as the standard bearers of the development of art. Consequently, the history of art was understood as the history of the expression of the constant psychic natures of these entities.[100]

This ethno-nationalist conception was not an exclusive feature of German art history, however. In the 1930s, it became a general European phenomenon. At the XIIIth International Congress of the History of Art in Stockholm in September 1933, the search for *"national character"* and geographical constants in the history of art was officially *"codified"* as the most topical task for art history.[101] What was specific to German art historiography with regard to this question was the extraordinary intensity with which the German art historians attempted to solve such *"new tasks"* of art history.[102] They treated national history as biological history: the history of

---

[99] Max Dvořák articulated the idea of genii as creators of the world view of their age, in his interpretations of Albrecht Dürer, Pieter Brueghel, Jacopo Tintoretto and El Greco. See DVOŘÁK, Max: *Kunstgeschichte als Geistesgeschichte. Studien zur abendländischen Kunstentwicklung.* Eds. Johannes WILDE – Karl M. SWOBODA. München 1924. On expressionist art history, see KULTERMANN, Udo: *Geschichte der Kunstgeschichte. Der Weg einer Wissenschaft.* Wien – Düsseldorf 1966, pp. 350-373.

[100] According to Christopher S. Wood: *"'Expressionist' art history was too smoothly blended with German nationalist sentiment and with* völkisch ..." – *The Vienna School Reader. Politics and Art Historical Method in the 1930s.* Ed. Christopher S. WOOD. New York 2003, p. 30. Individual artists were understood solely as "spokesmen" for abstract national communities. On artists as agents of nations, see LABUDA, Adam S.: Die Künstler im Osten um 1500. Ansichten und Forschungsmodelle, in *Die Jagiellonen. Kunst und Kultur einer europäischen Dynastie an der Wende zur Neuzeit.* Eds. Dietmar POPP – Robert SUCKALE. Nürnberg 2002, pp. 19-20.

[101] See LARSSON 1985 (see note 17), pp. 169-170. The following papers were read at the Stockholm Congress: "L'art gothique: ses origines françaises" (Marcel AUBERT), "Der nationale Charakter in der deutschen Kunst des 18. Jahrhunderts" (Albert E. BRINCKMANN), "Le style nationale norvègien" (Harry FETT), "L'art nationale de la Hongrie" (Tibor GEREVICH), or "L'art moderne finlandais et son caractére national" (Nils-Gustav HAHL). It was significant that Wickhoff's and Riegl's disciple Hans Tietze preferred *étatiste* to the nationalist approach. He read about "Die Stellung Österreichs in der bildenden Kunst" emphasizing *"eine durchgängige Spannung zwischen einem Streben ins Übernationale... und einer eindringlichen Betonung des Bodenständigen".* – *Actes du XIIIe congrès international d'histoire de l'art.* Stockholm 1933, p. 24. About the agenda of the Stockholm Congress, see SCHMIDT, Gerhard: Die Internationalen Kongresse für Kunstgeschichte, in *Wiener Jahrbuch für Kunstgeschichte,* 36, 1983, p. 47.

[102] On the phenomenon "Neue Aufgaben der Kunstgeschichte", see HALBERTSMA 1992 (see note 98), pp. 96-99, 112; DILLY, Heinrich: *Deutsche Kunsthistoriker, 1933 – 1945.* München – Berlin 1988, pp. 43-54; BAKOŠ, Ján: Vienna School Disciples and "The New Tasks" of Art History, in *Ars,* 40, 2007, No. 2, pp. 145-155.

the ethnic group ("*Volk*") or the history of the race. Moreover, they combined racial history with artistic geography,[103] as expressed in the so-called "*Blut und Boden*" doctrine. In addition, they regarded art history as a direct ideological instrument of politics. The combination of the idea of art as the expression of the spiritual essence of an ethnic group ("*Stamm*") or nation ("*Volk*") with the belief in geographical stylistic constants, enabled them to transcend state frontiers and follow an extensive ethno-territorial conception of the history of art. The first step in justifying territorial claims was thus taken.[104]

From Nationalism to Expansionism

In the mid 1930s, Dehio's conception of the history of German art was developed by the distinguished German art historian and professor at the most prestigious universities in Munich and Berlin, Wilhelm Pinder.[105] Pinder abandoned the impersonal form-genetic conception of art history, based on the avant-gard premise of artistic autonomy, which he originally shared with Riegl's school.[106] He also abandoned his internationally oriented theory

---

[103] For more on that, see HAUSSHERR, Reiner: Kunstgeographie und Kunstlandschaft, in *Kunst in Hessen und am Mittelrhein, 9*. Darmstadt 1969; HAUSSHERR, Reiner: Kunstgeographie – Aufgaben, Grenzen, Möglichkeiten, in *Rheinische Vierteljahrsblätter, 34*, 1970, pp. 158-171; HALBERTSMA 1992 (see note 98), p. 109 ff. See also DaCOSTA KAUFMANN 2004 (see note 52), pp. 43-104.

[104] It refers to the so-called "*Ostforschung*". On this, see KUTZNER 1986 (see note 29); LABUDA 1993 (see note 96); MUTHESIUS 1994 (see note 61), pp. 10-13 (chapter "Deutsch-polnische Auseinandersetzung II: Der kunsthistorische Angriff auf Polen und die Folgen"); MUTHESIUS, Stefan: Schlesische Kunst im Lichte der polnischen und deutschen Kunstgeschichte, in *Kunstchronik, 50*, 1997, pp. 337-341; SKUBISZEWSKI, Piotr: Polen und die deutsche Kunstgeschichte. Aus persönlicher Sicht, in *Zeitschrift des deutschen Vereins für Kunstwissenschaft, 62*, 2008, pp. 195-219. Apart from works on art in Bohemia or Poland, the publications *Deutsche Kunst in der Zips* (Brünn – Wien 1938) by Oskar SCHÜRER – Erich WIESE or *Die deutsche Kunst in Siebenbürgen* (Berlin 1934) by Victor ROTH can also be regarded as symbolic annexations of territory.

[105] See HALBERTSMA 1992 (see note 98); HALBERTSMA, Marlite: Wilhelm Pinder, 1878 – 1947, in *Altmeister moderner Kunstgeschichte* (see note 43), pp. 235-248; SUCKALE, Robert: Wilhelm Pinder und die deutsche Kunstwissenschaft nach 1945, in *Kritische Berichte, 14*, 1986, No. 4, pp. 113-117; DILLY 1988 (see note 102); Pinder, Wilhelm, in *Metzler Kunsthistoriker Lexikon* (see note 23), pp. 309-312; HELD, Jutta: Kunstgeschichte im "Dritten Reich". Wilhelm Pinder und Hans Jantzen an der Münchner Universität, in *Kunstgeschichte an den Universitäten im Nationalsozialismus* (=Kunst und Politik, 5). Eds. Jutta HELD – Martin PAPENBROCK. Göttingen 2003, pp. 17-59.

[106] This applied particularly to Pinder's work *Die deutsche Plastik vom ausgehenden Mittelalter bis zum Ende der Renaissance* (Berlin – Neubabelsberg 1924 – 1928). It was based on the form-

of artistic generations as the standard bearers of art historical change.[107] Instead, he accepted the ethno-nationalist version of the expressionist doctrine[108] and identified the German *"Volk"* as the standard bearer (*"Träger"*) of the history of German art.[109] However, he understood *"Volk"* as an historically changing ethno-social collective entity. Thus, the history of German art became, in his view, a process of the alternating initiatives of social classes, starting with German ruling dynasties, continuing through German burghers, to the great creative individuals of German art such as Albrecht Dürer or Hans Holbein.[110] This history was manifested in changing artistic forms, genres and types.

Pinder still believed in visual form as a basis for the history of the fine arts.[111] However, he now interpreted the history of German art trans-historically as the history of a specific timeless essence of German art – the *"being"* and *"becoming"* of *"German forms"*.[112] Pinder also perfected Dehio's conception of the mediating role of German art between West and East, eliminating the inferiority complex that motivated it.[113] Consequently, he distinguished be-

---

genetic paradigm and the premise of the impersonal autonomy of art. For more details, see BOERNER, Bruno: Stilgeschichte um 1900 und im 20. Jahrhundert, in *Stilfragen zur Kunst des Mittelalters. Eine Einführung*. Eds. Bruno KLEIN – Bruno BOERNER. Berlin 2006, pp. 66-69.

[107] Pinder articulated it in his work *Das Problem der Generation in der Kunstgeschichte Europas* (Berlin 1926). See HELD 2003 (see note 105), pp. 28-29. See also HALBERTSMA 1992 (see note 98), pp. 61-81; HALBERTSMA 1990 (see note 105), pp. 238-240.

[108] See *The Vienna School Reader* (see note 100), p. 30. On Pinder's affirmative relationship to expressionism, see SUCKALE, Robert: Wilhelm Pinder und die deutsche Kunstwissenschaft nach 1945, in *Kritische Berichte*, 14, 1986, No. 1, p. 9; HELD 2003 (see note 105), pp. 19-20. U. Kulterman classifies Pinder among *"Kunstgeschichte des Expressionismus"*. – KULTERMANN 1966 (see note 99), pp. 370-372. Marlite Halbertsma emphasizes Pinder's relationship to *"Kunstgeschichte als Geistesgeschichte"*. – HALBERTSMA 1992 (see note 98), p. 49. See also HALBERTSMA 1990 (see note 105), p. 243.

[109] HELD 2003 (see note 105), p. 31.

[110] Suckale speaks of a shift (*"Akzentverschiebung"*) in Pinder's approach to the history of German art from *"der Dominanz des Staatlich-Politischen"* to *"auf das Gesellschaftliche"* *"um zuletzt… zu zeigen, daß nie zuvor in Deutschland der Künstler so nah der Autonomie gewesen ist"*. – SUCKALE 1986 (see note 108), p. 15.

[111] Jutta Held claims that Pinder maintained to keep to *"eine Autonomie der Kunstgeschichte… als den kunstgeschichtlichen Rahmen seiner Interpretationen"*. – HELD 2003 (see note 105), pp. 26-27.

[112] PINDER, Wilhelm: *Vom Wesen und Werden deutscher Formen. Geschichtliche Betrachtungen*. Vols. 1-4. Leipzig – Köln 1937 – 1951. Marlite Halbertsma characterizes Pinder's effort to integrate a transhistorical approach with historicism as follows: *"… das Wesentliche und das Historische werden miteinander verknüpft und auf einen gemeinsamen Nenner gebracht; Ausganspunkt aller Betrachtungen ist die Form."* – HALBERTSMA 1990 (see note 105), p. 241.

[113] According to Jutta Held, Pinder introduced into art historical research, the concepts of *"Hybridisierung"*, *"künstlerischer Austausch"* and *"Migrationen"*, and outlined *"eine Kunstgeschichte der Peripherie, deren innovatives Potential disziplingeschichtlich nicht zu leugnen ist"*. – HELD 2003 (see note 105), p. 35. However, apart from clarifying the relations between centre and

tween the contribution of German art to the global, universal history of art ("*Sonderleistungen*"), and the radiating effect ("*Ausstrahlungen*") of German art on foreign countries. Understandably, he emphasized in particular, the activity in the East, which was the basis for its dominant position in Central Europe.[114]

Graduates of the Vienna School also played a significant role in formulating this hegemonic conception of German art in Central Europe. It was no coincidence that pupils of both Max Dvořák and Josef Strzygowski, such as Hans Sedlmayr and Dagobert Frey, contributed a great deal,[115] combining Dvořák's nostalgia for the Habsburg Monarchy with Strzygowski's racial understanding of "*Kunstgeographie*". The concept of "*Großösterreich*" was replaced with the idea of a pan-Germanic Central Europe. For instance, Sedlmayr[116] researched "*the role of Austria in the history of German art*"[117] and emphasized the idea of the "*Reichsstil*".[118] Frey,[119] head of the Institute of Art

---

periphery, Pinder also took an important step towards rehabilitating the art of the periphery. He regarded German "*Kolonisationskunst*" as a significant and unique phenomenon, "*... eine von sinnvollem Zweckgefühle erfüllte herbe und großartige Kolonialkunst... wie sie kein anderes Volk der Welt kennt*". – PINDER, Wilhelm: *Vom Wesen und Werden deutscher Formen. Geschichtliche Betrachtungen II. Die Kunst der ersten Bürgerzeit bis zur Mitte des 15. Jahrhundert.* Leipzig 1937, p. 139. On Pinder's notion of the periphery-centre relationship, see also MICHALSKI, Sergiusz: The Concept of National Art. Problems of Artistic Periphery and Questions of Artistic Exchange in Early Modern Europe, in *Ars,* 40, 2007, No. 2, pp. 208-209.

[114] See PINDER, Wilhelm: *Vom Wesen und Werden deutscher Formen. Geschichtliche Betrachtungen I. Die Kunst der deutschen Kaiserzeit bis zum Ende der staufischen Klassik.* Leipzig 1937, pp. 9-57. According to Marlite Halbertsma: "*Die politische Wünsche der damaligen Zeit, Deutschland als 'Führer Mitteleuropas' zu erweisen, werden hier von Pinder kunsthistorisch eingekleidet.*" – HALBERTSMA 1990 (see note 105), p. 241. On German art history during the "Third Reich", see DILLY 1988 (see note 102); HELD 2003 (see note 105); *Kunstgeschichte im "Dritten Reich"* (see note 53).

[115] Dvořák's former assistant Karl Maria Swoboda also actively participated in this process. By means of the idea of a specific "*Kunstlandschaft*", the so-called "*Sudetenländer*", the art of which, in his view, was clearly dominated by the German element, he endeavoured to formulate the concept of a harmonious synthesis of German and Slavic art. – SWOBODA, Karl M.: *Zum deutschen Anteil an der Kunst der Sudetenländer.* Brünn – München 1938; SWOBODA, Karl M.: Die deutsche bildende Kunst als gestaltende Kraft im böhmisch-mährischen Raum, in *Forschungen und Fortschritte,* 15, 1939, pp. 416-418. See CANZ, Sigrid: Karl Maria Swoboda (1889 – 1977). Kunsthistoriker: Wissenschaftler zwischen Wien und Prag, in *Prager Professoren, 1938 – 1948. Zwischen Wissenschaft und Politik.* Eds. Monika GLETTER – Alena MIŠÍKOVÁ. Essen 2001, pp. 186-188. See also BAKOŠ 2007 (see note 102), pp. 151-152.

[116] AURENHAMMER, Hans: Hans Sedlmayr und die Kunstgeschichte an der Universität Wien, 1938 – 1945, in *Kunst und Politik,* 5, 2003, pp. 161-193. See also BAKOŠ 2007 (see note 102), pp. 150-151.

[117] Published in *Forschungen und Fortschritte,* 13, 1937, pp. 418-419.

[118] LORENZ, Hellmut: Der habsburgische "Reichstil" – Mythos und Realität, in *Künstlerischer Austausch/Artistic Exchange* (see note 35), Vol. 2, pp. 163-172.

[119] STÖRKUHL, Beate: Paradigmen und Methoden der kunstgeschichtlichen "Ostforschung" – der "Fall" Dagobert Frey, in *Die Kunsthistoriographien in Ostmitteleuropa und der nationale Dis-*

History in Wrocław (Breslau), transformed Dehio's and Pinder's conceptions of centre and periphery, rehabilitating the role of the eastern part of Central Europe. According to Frey, in some stages of history, the spread of artistic initiatives from the West to the East was reversed, and the art of eastern Central Europe took the initiative.[120] However, in his view, it was already a Germanized *"Ost-Mitteleuropa"*.[121]

If, in Riegl's and Dvořák's school, the lingering universalism of Habsburg historiography was replaced with pan-Germanic hegemonism, Strzygowski's nationalist school accepted the idea of Austria as one of the *"Kunstlandschaften"* of *"Großdeutschland"*. It was then quite logical that the first history of fine art in Austria[122] was not a product of the pupils of Riegl's and Dvořák's cosmopolitan school. It came rather from Strzygowski's nationalist geographical workshop[123] using his *"anthropologically"* (that is national-ethnologically) treated idea of the geography of art.[124]

From Nationalism to *Étatisme*

After the Second World War, the reaction of Polish or Czech art historians to the aggressive nationalism of the German historiography of art had a simi-

---

 kurs (see note 4), pp. 155-172. See also BAKOŠ 2007 (see note 102), pp. 152-154; FEIST, Peter H.: Frey, Dagobert, in *Metzler Kunsthistoriker Lexikon* (see note 23), pp. 100-101.

[120] According to Dagobert Frey: *"... die bisher herrschende, durch das Kulturgefälle bedingte, westöstliche Kulturströmung schlägt in eine Gegenbewegung von Ost nach West um."* – FREY, Dagobert: Die Entwicklung nationaler Stile in der mittelalterlichen Kunst des Abendlandes, in *Deutsche Vierteljahrsschrift für Literaturwissenschaft und Geistesgeschichte*, 16, 1938, pp. 1-74, reprinted in Darmstadt, 1970, p. 62.

[121] MUTHESIUS 2004 (see note 4), p. 76; HERRMANN, Christofer: *Mittelalterliche Architektur im Preussenland. Untersuchungen zur Frage der Kunstlandschaft und -Geographie.* Petersburg 2007, p. 27; BAKOŠ, Ján: From National to Dynastic History of Art. A Path of Art History in Central Europe, in *Prag und die grossen Kulturzentren Europas in der Zeit der Luxemburger (1310 – 1437)*. Eds. Markéta JAROŠOVÁ – Jiří KUTHAN – Stefan SCHOLZ. Praha 2008, p. 765; in this volume 148-167.

[122] *Die bildende Kunst in Österreich.* Vols. 1-6. Ed. Karl GINHART. Wien 1936 – 1943.

[123] It grew from lectures given by Strzygowski and his pupils at the Society for Comparative Art Research in Vienna ("Gesellschaft für vergleichende Kunstforschung in Wien") in 1934/1935.

[124] It is symptomatic that it was not regarded as the history of the art of a state, i.e. of the Austrian Republic, but as the *"Kunstgeschichte eines Landes"*, the history of a specific artistic territory, the so-called *"Ostalpenraum"*. That territory was regarded as part of a German artistic whole (*"Teil des gesamtdeutschen Kunstschaffens"*), and its specific character was characterized as a spiritual expression (*"geistige Antlitz"*) of the people of the given living space (*"Lebensraum"*). Consequently, Austrian art was regarded as German art (*"die österreichische Kunst ist seit mehr als einem Jahrtausend rein deutsch... hat ihre deutsche Eigenart immerzu gewahrt"*). – *Die bildende Kunst in Österreich* (see note 122), Vol. 1, pp. 5-8.

larly Romantic spiritual nationalist character.[125] They considered the ethnic nation, personified as a *"Super-artist"*, as the basic subject of art history.[126] Regarding art as an expression of national character, they searched for specific and constant national characteristics.[127]

This nationalist interpretation of art history was not eliminated even after the export of Soviet Marxism to Central and Eastern Europe in the 1950s.

---

[125] KUTZNER 1986 (see note 29), pp. 347-348; MUTHESIUS 1994 (see note 61), pp. 13-17; CHRZANOWSKI, Tadeusz: Die Lage der Kunstgeschichte in Polen nach dem Zweiten Weltkrieg. Versuch eines Überblicks, in *Kunstchronik*, 44, 1991, pp. 677-686. In contrast to that, Piotr Skubiszewski is convinced that *"die nationalistische Tendenzen in der Kunstbetrachtung in Polen... nur in der populärwissenschaftlichen Literatur zum Ausdruck gekommen sind. Ganz besonders nach dem Zweiten Weltkrieg... Diesem Weg sind einige Publizisten, aber keine bedeutenden Kunsthistoriker gefolgt."* – SKUBISZEWSKI 2008 (see note 104), p. 190.

[126] In Ernő Marosi's words, *"die Nation (erscheint) als eine unmittelbar erlebbare kollektive Persönlichkeit"*. – MAROSI 1992 (see note 1), p. 63.

[127] *"We sought for every trace of 'Slavonic' lyricism or formal simplicity in Polish and Czech medieval painting."* – KUTZNER 1986 (see note 29), p. 348. On the idea of *"lyricism"* and *"poetism"* as the specific feature of Slavic (Czech) art and expression of *"the peaceful and domestic character of the [Slavic] people"*, see FILIPOVÁ 2008 (see note 29), pp. 262-263. A symptomatic example of the ethno-nationalist approach is the publication MENCL, Václav: *Česká architektura doby Lucemburské* [Czech Architecture of the Luxembourg Period]. Praha 1948. On p. 15, the author states: *"We are concerned here with Czech Gothic and its meaning... the specifically Czech features, which mean a special Czech contribution... the constant, timeless, and already historically invariable Czechness, because it was shaped by the physical and spiritual essence of the nation and flavoured by the typical scent of our soil."* On this, see VYBÍRAL 2004 (see note 70), p. 204. In a similar way, Jaroslav Pešina speaks of the *"traditional Czech inclination to lyricism, which appears again and again through the whole course of development"*. – PEŠINA, Jaroslav: *Česká malba pozdní gotiky a renesance. Deskové malířství, 1450 – 1550* [Czech Painting of the Late Gothic and Renaissance. Panel Painting, 1450 – 1550]. Praha 1950, p. 13.
This ethno-nationalist interpretation persisted for a relatively long time. A typical example is the work WALICKI, Michał: *Malarstwo polskie. Gotyk, Renesans, Wczesny manieryzm* [Polish Painting. Gothic, Renaissance, Early Manierism]. Warszawa 1961. In it, pp. 8-9, the author still aimed at *"making visible the Polish ingenium"*. Similarly, in 1971, Jaroslav Pešina still believes in *"die tschechische Spezifizität"*. Even if he speaks of a *"schwer greifbaren Ausdrucksqualitäten"*, he regards *"Lyrismus, der Hang zum Poetischen, süsse Sinnlichkeit und große Gefühlsnote"* as specific and constant characteristics of Czech Gothic art. See PEŠINA, Jaroslav: Gotik in Böhmen [Review], in *Umění*, 14, 1971, p. 361. On this, see BARTLOVÁ, Milena: "Slavonic features" of Bohemian Medieval Painting from the Point of View of Racist and Marxist-Leninist Theories, in *Die Kunsthistoriographien in Ostmitteleuropa und der nationale Diskurs* (see note 4), pp. 173-179; BARTLOVÁ 2009 (see note 36), pp. 17, 21-28.
The idea that national specificity does not lie in particular formal features but in the ability to transform foreign impulses in a creative way represents a more sophisticated version of the nationalist interpretation. Jaromír Neumann's characterization of the specific nature of Czech Baroque art as *"its extraordinary ability to assimilate and transform which was connected with the inclination to synthesize diverse and often even contradictory stimuli in a quick and organic way"* can be mentioned as an example of that approach. – NEUMANN, Jaromír: *Český barok* [Czech Baroque]. Praha 1974, p. 11; German edition: *Das böhmische Barock*. Hannover 1970. See to this VYBÍRAL 2004 (see note 70), p. 203.

The originally international program of Marxism was soon pushed into the background by post-war Great Russian imperialism. This was masked by the doctrine of the official art of Socialist Realism, which expressed the slogan: *"Socialist content, national form"*.[128] However, it was especially in reaction to this imposition of Soviet hegemony that East Central European art historians came to emphasize European art historical connections. This resulted in the decline of extreme ethno-nationalism. It can be said that in the course of the 1960s, the ethnic approach was gradually replaced by the territorial or political conception of the history of art.[129] The history of art ceased to be understood as the history of nations and began to be treated as the history of states or state territories.[130] However, the identification of art history with the his-

---

[128] MUTHESIUS 1994 (see note 61), p. 17. The historiography of art was employed as an explicit instrument for the ideological legitimization of the cultural policy of the time. *"Für die Entwicklung der neuen, in ihrem Inhalt sozialistischen, in der Form nationalen, polnischen Kunst sind von erstrangiger Bedeutung die Kenntnisse der Entwicklungsgeschichte der Kunst in ihren reifsten realistischen Erscheinungen sowie das aus dieser Quelle strömende Bewusstsein von dem Bestehen eines lebendigen Zusammenhanges mit dem fortschrittlichen Erbe unserer Kultur."* – STARZYŃSKI, Juliusz: *Piec wieków malarstwa polskiego*. Warszawa 1953; German edition: *Fünf Jahrhunderte polnischer Malerei*. Warszawa 1953, p. 5. Another example of the openly presentist political instrumentalization of the history of art is the publication NEUMANN, Jaromír: *Malířství XVII. století v Čechách* [17th Century Painting in Bohemia]. Praha 1951, in which, pp. 7-9, so-called *"Baroque realism"* was interpreted as an historical preparation for Socialist Realism. Ewa Chojecka speaks appropriately in this context about *"einer fast surrealistichen Symbiose zweier scheinbar unvereinbarer heterogener ideologischer Elemente...: dem marxistischen Programm internationalistischer klassenloser Gesellschaft"* and *"radikal nationalistischen... Konzept eines national homogenen Staates, das... in Allianz mit dem russischen Zaren stand"*. – CHOJECKA, Ewa: Polnische *"Westforschung"* und das Syndrom des Eisernen Vorhangs, in *Kunsthistoriographien in Ostmitteleuropa und der nationale Diskurs* (see note 4), p. 412.

[129] As an example, it is possible to mention the introduction to the collective publication *Historia sztuki polskiej w zarysie* [The History of Polish Art in Outline]. Eds. Tadeusz DOBROWOL-SKI – Władysław TATARKIEWICZ. Kraków 1962, p. 9, where its authors state: *"The ethnic and national criterion... could not be applied. [...] It was necessary to turn attention to the territorial criterion."* The territorial approach was also applied by Tadeusz DOBROWOLSKI in the publication *Życie, twórczość i znaczenie społeczne artystów polskich i w Polsce pracujących w okresie późnego gotyku (1440 – 1520)* [Life, Creativity, and Social Importance of Polish Artists or Artists Working in Poland in the Late Gothic Period (1440 – 1520)]. Wrocław [a.o.] 1965.

[130] On the *étatiste* premise in Hungarian and Slovak art historiography, see BAKOŠ, Ján: Koncepcie dejín stredovekého dreveného sochárstva Slovenska do polovice 15. storočia [Conceptions of the History of Medieval Wooden Sculpture in Slovakia till the Middle of the 15th Century], in *Umění*, 27, 1979, pp. 322-345, 427-452; BAKOŠ 1984 (see note 1), pp. 20-52. The author distinguished four conceptions of the history of art as follows: 1. the history of art regarded as the history of the nation; 2. the history of art as the history of the state; 3. the history of art as the history of the territory; 4. the history of art as the history of art. – Ibid., pp. 266-282. BAKOŠ, Ján: Rekonstruieren oder konstruieren wir die Geschichte der Kunst? Beispiel: Die Kunst der Slowakei, in *Kunstchronik*, 55, 2002, pp. 122-130. DaCosta Kaufmann called that approach *"a kind of restrictive regionalism"*. According to him, transformation of ethnic nationalism to patriotic *étatism* had started immediately after the Second World War: *"... histories and*

tory of a state did not mean the definitive elimination of nationalism.[131] The *étatiste* conception was essentially still highly patriotic and represented in many ways merely a more sophisticated version of the nationalist approach. It was open to nationalistic readings in the form of the identification of the state with the nation-state or state nation (dominating nation).[132] It also implied two forms of projection: on the one hand, the projection of the modern state onto the history of art, a projection of the present onto the past that might be termed the myth of the eternal present;[133] on the other hand, the historicist projection, i.e. the illusionary reconstructed historic state considered as still present, which can be regarded as the nostalgic myth of the eternal

---

    histories of art since 1945 have tended to follow national borders." – DaCOSTA KAUFMANN 1995 (see note 35), p. 18.

[131] The authors of the publication *Historia sztuki polskiej w zarysie* (see note 129), pp. 9-10, state that the *"territorial criterion"* of the history of art needs to be combined with the *"purely ethnic criterion"*. *"The psychic properties of the nation... the psychic character of Polish society"* were regarded as the proper object of art historical research.

[132] *"Nach dem zweiten Weltkrieg blieben solche kunstgeschichtlichen Konstruktionen... bestimmende Teile der Kunstgeschichtsschreibung dieser Staaten... beinhalten sie zwei absurde Elemente: die offizielle Geschichte der Staatsnation als Strukturprinzip und... das irrationale Element der nationalen Eigenart."* – MAROSI 1992 (see note 1), p. 63.

[133] The presentist projection of modern state frontiers onto the past was nevertheless, already criticized by Tibor Gerevich and Dagobert Frey, from a position of ethno-nationalism. See GEREVICH 1933 (see note 71); FREY 1938 (see note 120). According to T. Gerevich: *"Il serait faux d'identifier l'idée de l'art national dans la passé avec l'idée actuelle de la nation, et l'extension de celle-là avec les formations politique du présent."* – GEREVICH 1933 (see note 71), p. 51. Gerevich's criticism was motivated by the *apologia* for the Great Hungary conception of art history, while the intention of Frey's criticism was a legitimization of pan-German expansionism.
From the point of view of the revision of a nationalist approach, Reiner Haussherr and Wolfgang Braunfels criticized the presentist projection in the late 1960s and 1970s. See HAUSSHERR 1969 (see note 103), p. 39. According to Wolfgang Braunfels: *"... nationale Grenzen der Gegenwart (wurden meist) als Grenzen von Kunstprovinzen in die Vergangenheit projiziert."* – BRAUNFELS, Wolfgang: *Die Kunst im Heiligen Römischen Reich Deutscher Nation.* München 1979 – 1989, Vol. 1, p. 12.
Presentist projection, described as *"Historisierung"*, has been repeatedly criticized also by Ernő Marosi. See MAROSI 1992 (see note 1), pp. 59-69; MAROSI, Ernő: Zwischen Kunstgeographie und historischer Geographie. Das Königreich und der Ständestaat Ungarn im Mittelalter, in *Ars*, 40, 2007, No. 2, pp. 135-143, here p. 135. Marosi's criticism seems to be prompted by the effort to defend the idea of the Kingdom of Hungary as an artistic unit and as the only historically justified interpretation of the history of art on its territory.
On the problem of the projection of the present onto the past, see recently also SUCKALE, Robert: Über die Hinfälliget einiger historiographischer Konzepte und Begriffe zur Deutung der Kunst Böhmens, in *Kunst als Herrschaftsinstrument. Böhmen und das Heilige Römische Reich unter Luxemburgern im europäischen Kontext.* Eds. Jiří FAJT – Andreas LANGER. Berlin – München 2009, p. 27-28. Referring to *"Rückprojizierung der heutigen Verhältnisse"*, Robert Suckale points out: *"Man hält sich dabei meist an die heutigen Staatsgrenzen, von denen man angenommen wird, sie seien identisch mit den Volks- bzw. Sprachgrenzen."*

past.[134] In both cases, however, art history assisted in the symbolic justification of the territorial claims of the present or past state.

From *Étatisme* to the Trans-National History of Art

The national-patriotic dimension of *étatisme* was restrained by the premise of artistic autonomy. The ethno-nationalist idea of a specific national expression was attenuated by the idea of the universal development of art regarded as an autonomous process. The history of art was treated as the development of universal stylistic currents in the framework of the territory of the state. In the art of a nation-state regarded as artistic organism, historians sought links to European art, analysed the relationship between the acceptance of external stimuli and their transformations, and examined participation in the general development of European art. The ideal goal was to identify and reconstruct the continuous development of local and regional art in terms of a creative transformation of internationl (European) stimuli. If this could be identified, it would provide proof of a relatively self-governing artistic organism within the European artistic whole.[135] The idea of artistic autonomy facilitated the transformation of the ethno-nationalist or racial interpretation of territorialism into the state-territorial conception.[136]

---

[134] According to Ernő Marosi, *"historicizing"* means the opposite approach, the projection of the present political and geographical order onto the past. – MAROSI 1992 (see note 1).

[135] The construction of the history of Czech Gothic sculpture by Albert KUTAL (*České gotické sochařství, 1350 – 1450* [Czech Gothic Sculpture, 1350 – 1450]. Praha 1962) can be regarded as the outstanding example of this approach. Kutal understood *"Bohemian Gothic sculpture"* as a territorial and relatively autonomous developmental organism. He based the synthesis *České gotické umění* [Czech Gothic Art]. Praha 1970 (German edition: *Gotische Kunst in Böhmen.* Praha 1971) on the territorial *étatiste* premise, that there was a territorial Czech artistic tradition, which was expressed in the ability *"to absorb foreign stimuli and transform them into a locally conditioned specific shape"*. *"This process of active assimilation"* led to the *"creation of particular values"*, which, according to Kutal's conviction, entitle us to speak of a territorially specific *"Bohemian Gothic art"* rather than of *"Gothic art in Bohemia"*. – Ibid., p. 8. Kutal's approach can be characterized as territorial patriotism in contrast to ethnic nationalism.
The conception of Czech Gothic art as an organism *"with its internal developmental logic, organic growth and own dynamics"*, which was not only *"able to keep up with European developments"*, but was *"dominant in the broader Central European region"*, was also the basis for the collective synthesis *České umění gotické, 1350 – 1420* [Czech Gothic Art, 1350 – 1420]. Praha 1970; see PEŠINA, Jaroslav – HOMOLKA, Jaromír: České země a Evropa [Czech Lands and Europe], ibid., pp. 19-55.

[136] An example is the collective synthesis by German and Austrian art historians *Gotik in Böhmen*. Ed. Karl M. SWOBODA. München 1969, which followed the publication *Barock in Böhmen*. Ed. Karl M. SWOBODA. München 1964. The latter was reviewed by the Czech researchers – BLAŽÍČEK, Jakub – BLAŽKOVÁ, Jarmila – PREISS, Pavel: Německý obraz českého baroku

The history of art understood as the history of the dominant nation presupposed an idea of the multi-ethnic state as a united, centralized organism.[137] The idea of the autonomy of universal artistic development opened this organism to the international artworld, enabling it to be understood as part of the European artistic polyphony while not casting doubt on the premise of the main determinant of art history. This keystone was the nation in the ethno-nationalist conception. In the state and territorial definition of the history of art, it was either the administrative centre, the centrally organized state or the royal court.[138]

The idea of a centralized state and the notion of the developmental continuity of regional and local art supported each other. That kind of argument together with the nationalist residue still implicitly present in the state conception of the history of art, stepped aside when the sociological approach to art history gradually displaced belief in the autonomy of art. This tendency strengthened in the East Central European historiography of art from the 1980s onwards.[139] Historians gradually stopped treating art as the expression

---

[A German Image of Czech Baroque], in *Umění*, 15, 1967, pp. 381-409. The pupils of K. M. Swoboda transformed his former concept of the art of Bohemia as a specific, racially based *"Kunstlandschaft"*, as expressed by Swoboda in his works on Sudeten art (see note 115), into the notion of an artistically autonomous organism. The conception of this collective synthesis by German and Austrian authors was accurately described by Jaroslav Pešina as *"die Auffassung der Entwicklung der böhmischen Kunst als eines territorial vollkommen unbegrenzten autonomen Prozesses, in dem die Geschichte der Kunst Böhmens schliesslich ganz in der Geschichte der europäischen Kunst aufgeht"*. – PEŠINA 1971 (see note 127), p. 361. See also the critical review by BAXANDALL, Michael: Gothic Art in Bohemia: Architecture, Sculpture and Painting, ed. E. Bachmann, Phaidon Press, Oxford, in *The Burlington Magazine*, 119, 1977, p. 781.

[137] On the centralist premise in Hungarian art historiography, see BAKOŠ 1984 (see note 1), pp. 20-52.

[138] Marosi corrects the centralist *étatism* of the former Hungarian art historiography with the concept of the state as a socially stratified and polyphonic organism. See, e.g., MAROSI, Ernő: Zentrifugale Kräfte als zentripetales Deutungsschema der Geschichte der Kunst in Ungarn am Ende des Mittelalters, in *Metropolen im Wandel. Zentralität in Ostmitteleuropa an der Wende vom Mittelalter zur Neuzeit*. Eds. Evamaria ENGEL – Karen LAMBRECHT – Hanna NOGOSSEK. Berlin 1995, pp. 173-184; MAROSI 2007 (see note 133), pp. 135-143.

[139] Such synthetic publications as *Dějiny českého výtvarného umění* [The History of Czech Art]. Eds. Rudolf CHADRABA et al. Praha 1984 – 2007 (for a critical comment on this from an anti-national point of view, see BARTLOVÁ 2009 (see note 36), pp. 10-13); *A művészet története Magyarországon. A honfoglalástól napjainkig* [The History of Art in Hungary. From Hungarian Conquest to the Present]. Eds. Nóra ARADI et al. Budapest 1983; *A magyarországi művészet története* [Magyar/Hungarian History of Art]. Eds. Anna ZÁDOR et al. Budapest 1970; *Magyarországi művészet 1300 – 1470 körül* [Magyar/Hungarian Art 1300 – 1470]. Ed. Ernő MAROSI. Budapest 1987, can be seen in the perspective of the gradual shift away from the national-*étatiste* model anchored in the idea of artistic autonomy, towards a polyphonic cultural/sociological model of *étatism*. The series *Dzieje sztuki polskiej* [The History of Polish Art]: MIŁOBĘDZKI, Adam: *Architektura polska XVII wieku* [Polish Architecture of the 17th Century].

of a collective entity and its history as the autonomous development of the art of a state.[140] Instead, they started to interpret art as a sociological phenomenon, i.e. as a product of its social environment, a function of the taste of patrons and a means of satisfying their social demands. Initially, this turn towards the cultural and social history of art was hampered by the axiom of the aesthetic autonomy of art and belief in the state as a relatively independent artistic unit. Later on, however, it led gradually to the art history of a state being regarded as a geographically and sociologically stratified, polyphonic whole.[141] The role of catalyst in this gradual transition from a formalist to a sociologically stratified and polyphonic art history was played by iconology, which influenced the historiography of art in East Central Europe, particularly in the 1960s.[142]

Vols. 1-2. Warszawa 1980; *Architektura gotycka w Polsce* [Gothic Architecture in Poland]. Eds. Teresa MROCZKO – Marian ARSZYŃSKI. Warszawa 1995, and *Malarstwo gotyckie w Polsce* [Gothic Painting in Poland]. Eds. Adam S. LABUDA – Krystyna SECOMSKA. Warszawa 2004, also belong to this line of transition from the autonomist to the sociological treatment of territorial *étatism*. The introductory essay of the above mentioned synthesis of the Gothic painting in Poland by Adam S. Labuda can be regarded as symptomatic of the shift toward a sociological approach. – LABUDA, Adam S.: Malarstwo – zleceniodawca – malarz. Gatunek, funkcje, konteksty twórczości artystycznej [Painting – Customer – Painter. Genre, Function, Contexts of Artistic Production], in *Malarstwo gotyckie w Polsce* (see above), pp. 17-68. See also MOSSAKOWSKI, Stanisław: Introduction, ibid., pp. 9-10.

[140] Art historical studies of smaller geographical, administrative or regional units represent an important phenomenon. They continue the tradition of local patriotism on the one hand, but implicitly imply a critical scepticism towards the great abstract constructions, such as the history of art of a nation or a state, on the other. For example, GADOMSKI, Jerzy: *Gotyckie malarstwo tablicowe Małopolski, 1420 – 1470* [Gothic Panel Painting in Little Poland, 1420 – 1470]. Warszawa 1981; GADOMSKI, Jerzy: *Gotyckie malarstwo tablicowe Małopolski, 1460 – 1500* [Gothic Panel Painting in Little Poland, 1460 – 1500]. Warszawa 1988; *Malarstwo gotyckie w Wielkopolsce: studia o dziełach i ludziach* [Gothic Painting in Great Poland: Studies into Works and People]. Ed. Adam S. LABUDA. Poznań 1994; *Umění baroka na Moravě a ve Slezsku* [Art of Baroque in Moravia nad Silesia]. Eds. Ivo KRSEK – Zdeněk KUDĚLKA et al. Praha 1996; or the series *Od gotiky k renesanci. Výtvarná kultura Moravy a Slezska, 1400 – 1550* [From Gothic to Renaissance. Visual Culture of Moravia and Silesia, 1440 – 1550]. Vols. 1-4. Eds. Ivo HLOBIL – Kaliopi CHAMONIKOLA. Brno – Olomouc – Opava 1999 – 2002.
HOMOLKA, Jaromír: *Gotická plastika na Slovensku* [Gothic Sculpture in Slovakia]. Bratislava 1972 or *Malarstwo gotyckie w Polsce* (see note 139) are examples of the combination of the *étatiste*-territorial and local-geographical approaches. The artistic organism is defined here on the basis of the present state territory, but internally differentiated according to historical geographical-administrative regions.
Radical scepticism towards abstract art historical constructions is represented by works that regard a specific locality as the only natural art historical unit. They conceive the history of a locality as the *"geological"* or *"archeological"* stratification of its historical layers. *Raněstředověká Olomouc* [Olomouc in Early Middle Ages] by Václav RICHTER (Praha – Brno 1959) can serve as an example of systematic scepticism of this type.

[141] In relation to research on the art of Slovakia or Hungary, this trend is analysed in BAKOŠ 1984 (see note 1), p. 98 ff.; BAKOŠ 2002 (see note 130), pp. 128-129.

[142] The concept of the work of art as a cryptogram, bearing hidden conceptual meanings, was

Eventually, however, this research trend also contributed to a gradual overcoming of explicit nationalism and to an internationalisation of the image of the history of art in the state.[143] The history of art ceased to be regarded as the history of the ethnic nation or the history of artistic autonomy – the history of styles, formal influences or form developmental series. The door was consequently open to art history conceived in terms of the history of the taste of patrons and customers and not least, that of the ruling dynasties, their international courts and trans-national connections.[144]

From "*Abendland*" to an International Perspective

The reaction of post-war West German historiography of art to the defeat of aggressive, expansionist ethno-nationalism, was an escape into the phenomenological interpretation of art[145] and the idea of the "*Abendland*".[146]

---

a step towards the sociological understanding of art, regarded as instrument of the representations of the customer. The initiator of the iconological method in post-war Poland was Lech Kalinowski and its main protagonist in East-Central Europe was Jan Białostocki. See MAŁKIEWICZ, Adam: Początki metody ikonologicznej w polskiej historii sztuki [Beginnings of Iconological Method in Polish Art History], in MAŁKIEWICZ 2005 (see note 55), pp. 79-91. On iconology in former Czechoslovakia, see Rostislav ŠVÁCHA, in *Kapitoly z českého dějepisu umění* (see note 29), pp. 359-362, 369; BAKOŠ 2000 (see note 59), pp. 350-353.

[143] Marosi underlines the international character of the royal courts of Central Europe. He also emphasizes the role of scholars, some monastic orders, especially mendicants and the commercial links of the towns as standard bearers of universalist tendencies ("*als Träger universalistischer Tendenzen*"). – MAROSI 1992 (see note 1), pp. 64-67. However, international interpretations of the history of art of a state can also become the instrument of a sophisticated crypto-nationalism or crypto-hegemonism!

[144] Adam S. Labuda refers this change of the paradigm of the notion of art regarded as "*eine Antwort auf die Erwartungen der Auftraggeber*" to Thomas DaCOSTA KAUFMANN's publication *Court, Cloister & City. The Art and Culture of Central Europe, 1450 – 1800* (London 1995). – LABUDA 2002 (see note 100), pp. 22-23. In contrast to that, Bernd Carqué underlines the contribution of Robert Suckale. See CARQUÉ, Bernd: *Stil und Erinnerung. Französische Hofkunst im Jahrhundert Karls V. und im Zeitalter ihrer Deutung*. Göttingen 2004, pp. 148-149. In both cases, the initiative of Lajos Vayer, Wolfgang Brauenfels and Jan Białostocki has been disregarded. See on this BAKOŠ 2008 (see note 121), pp. 763-783; in this volume pp. 148-167.

[145] See SAUERLÄNDER, Willibald: Zersplitterte Errinnerung, in *Kunsthistoriker in eigener Sache*. Ed. Martina SITT. Berlin 1990, pp. 310-311; DILLY 1988 (see note 102), pp. 81-89.

[146] SAUERLÄNDER, Willibald: Von der "Sonderleistungen deutscher Kunst" zur "Ars Sacra", in SAUERLÄNDER, Willibald: *Geschichte der Kunst/Gegenwart der Kritik*. Ed. Werner BUSCH. Köln 1999, pp. 277-292; BELTING 1992 (see note 98), pp. 49-55, chapter "Das 'Abendland' als Ausweg".
PAPENBROCK, Martin: Kurt Bauch in Freiburg 1933 – 1945, in PAPENBROCK – HELD 2003 (see note 105), pp. 201-202; DOLL, Nikola: Der Erste Deutsche Kunsthistorikertag 1948, in *Kunstgeschichte im Nationalsozialismus. Beiträge zur Geschichte einer Wissenschaft zwischen 1930 –*

In place of the focus on its ethnic identity, the inclusion of German art in Western European Christendom was emphasized.[147] After 1945, however, the interest of the majority of younger German art historians shifted to the universal or European history of art.[148] In the second half of the 1960s, German art history returned to the theme of the geography of art, but this time in order to undertake a critical revision of its irrational foundations. The central concept of "*Kunstlandschaft*" was freed from its metaphysical, essentialist meaning, and the idea of the "*Kunstlandschaft*" as a time-limited regional tradition began to be reconsidered.[149] Some ten years later, German art history

---

1950. Eds. Nikola DOLL – Christian FUHRMEISTER – Michael H. SPRENGER. Weimar 2005, pp. 332, 335; PAPENBROCK, Martin: Die Freiburger Kunstgeschichte in der Nachkriegszeit, in *Kunst und Politik. Jahrbuch der Guernica-Gesellschaft*, 8, 2006, Schwerpunkt: Kunstgeschichte an den Universitäten in der Nachkriegszeit, ed. Martin PAPENBROCK, p. 204.

[147] The initiative was taken by Hans Jantzen. See JANTZEN, Hans: Die Einheit Europas in der Geschichte seiner Kunst, in *Geistige Welt*, 3, 1948 – 1949, pp. 115-117; DILLY 1988 (see note 102), pp. 82-83. According to Jutta Held, Jantzen promoted the occidental perspective from 1940 onwards: "*Es fällt ferner auf, daß Jantzen seit 1940 nicht mehr die Künste der Nationen einzeln oder vergleichend thematisierte... sondern die abendlädische oder europäische Perspektive... hervorhebt.*" – HELD 2003 (see note 105), p. 27. See also SCHENKLUHN 1990 (see note 21), pp. 157-171. Interpreting "*Ottonian Art*" as the first German national style, Jantzen identified the ethnic (nation) with the state (empire, dynasty) and Christian religion (spirituality). Due to that, he harmonized German art with Western Christianity. In Schenkluhn's words, Jantzen can be regarded as "*der Vater der Ottonischen Kunst als Nationalstil der Deutschen*". – Ibid., p.162. In the first post-war history of German art, the so-called Bruckmann's *Deutsche Kunstgeschichte.* Eds. Eberhard HEMPEL – Adolf FEULNER – Theodor MÜLLER – Otto FISCHER – Heinrich KOHLHAUSEN – Victor ROTH. München 1949 – 1958, the nationalist concept of German art regarded as "*unmittelbaren Ausdruck des Wesens des Volkstums*" (Vol. 1, p. 7) was gradually replaced by the spiritualist idea of its history conceived of as "*geschlossene Geschichte der Entwicklung des deutschen Geistes*" (Vol. 2, p. 7) and finally synthesized with the interpretation of German art "*im Rahmen der Kunst des Abendlandes*" (Vol. 2, p. 7). According to A. Feulner and Th. Müller (Vol. 2, p. 7), Germany was not only an organic part of Christian Occident but also situated in its centre ("*das Land der Mitte*"). During the history of Western art, it played the key role of a creative mediator ("*Mittlerrolle*"): "*Seitdem es eine kulturelle Einheit des Abendlandes gibt, [...] war das Land der Mitte durch Wirkung und Gegenwirkung mit den anderen Kulturländern verbunden. In allen Epochen hat Deutschland anderen Nationen gegeben und zu allen Zeiten hat es von anderen Kulturvölkern empfangen, um das Empfangene schöpferisch zu verwerten.*"

[148] HELD, Jutta – SCHNEIDER, Norbert: *Grundzüge der Kunstwissenschaft. Gegenstandsbereiche – Institutionen – Problemfelder*. Köln – Weimar – Wien 2007, p. 143. On German post-war art history, see also *Kunstgeschichte nach 1945. Kontinuität und Neubeginn in Deutschland.* Eds. Nikola DOLL – Ruth HEFTRIG – Olaf PETERS – Ulrich REHM. Köln – Weimar – Wien 2006.

[149] HAUSSHERR, Reiner: Überlegungen zum Stand der Kunstgeographie. Neuerscheinungen, in *Rheinische Vierteljahrsblätter*, 30, 1965, pp. 351-372; HAUSSHERR 1969 (see note 103), pp. 38-44; HAUSSHERR 1970 (see note 103), pp. 158-171; BECK, Herbert – BREDEKAMP, Horst: Der Mittelrhein als Kunstlandschaft, in *Kunst um 1400 am Mittelrhein*. [Exhib. Cat.] Frankfurt am Main 1975; STAMM, Lieselotte E.: Zur Verwendung des Begriffs Kunstlandschaft am Beispiel des Oberrheins im 14. und frühen 15. Jahrhundert, in *Zeitschrift für Schweizerische Archäologie und Kunstgeschichte*, 41, 1984, No. 2, pp. 85-91; MÖBIUS, Friedrich: Von der Kunstgeographie

attempted to replace the ethno-national expansionist territorial conception of the history of German art with a new territorial state oriented model. Thus, the history of German art ceased to be regarded as the history of the nation or *"Volk"*, giving way to a conception of the history of a polyphonic political-administrative organism, a sort of megastate – the Holy Roman Empire.[150] Thus, a very important step towards a trans-national, pluralist, but also socially instrumental or institutional conception of the history of art in Central Europe, was taken.[151]

However, the particular national and state conception of the history of art of Central Europe was overcome by other routes, too. They were especially stimulated by multi-volume syntheses of the universal history of art, such as *The Pelican History of Art*[152] and the new series, *Propyläen Kunstgeschichte*.[153] The authors of passages devoted to the art of Central Europe searched for international artistic links and considered trans-national macro-regional artistic units. One example is Eberhard Hempel's conception of Baroque art in Central Europe as an organism comprising the German lands including Silesia,

---

zur kunstwissenschaftlichen Territorienforschung, in *Regionale, nationale und internationale Kunstprozesse*. Jena 1983, pp. 21-42. See also DaCOSTA KAUFMANN 2004 (see note 52), pp. 89-95; GRÖTECKE, Iris: Mittelalterforschung und wissenschaftliche Reform nach 1968. Kunstgeographie zwischen Kontinuität, Umkodierung und Auflösung, in *Kunst und Politik. Jahrbuch der Guernica-Gesellschaft*, 12, 2010, Schwerpunkt: Kunstgeschichte nach 1968, eds. Martin PAPENBROCK – Norbert SCHNEIDER, pp. 99-116.

[150] BRAUNFELS 1979 – 1989 (see note 133). According to Sigrid Esche: *"... die ersten fünf Bände [schildern] den unlösslichen Zusammenhang der Werke der Künstler mit den territorial und institutionell bedingten Herrschaftsformen und Idealen ihrer Auftraggeber in der Reihenfolge der Standesordnung, in der diese auf dem Regensburger Reichstag vertreten waren."* – ESCHE, Sigrid: Vorwort, ibid., Vol. 6, p. 5. Thus, Braunfels regarded political, religious, administrative, and social institutions (*"Fürstentümer"*, *"Reichsstädte"*, *"Grafschaften"*, *"Reichsklöster"*) as determining factors in the history of art. He structured the history of German art according to the social stratification of patrons (*"Kaiser"*, *"Höfe"*, *"Bischofe"*, *"Äbte"*, *"Bürger"*) and combined sociological and administrative structuring with geographical one.

[151] According to Christiane Fork, Braunfels structured the history of art of the Holy Roman Empire *"nach politischen Institutionen und Ordnungseinheiten... gemäss seiner Maxime, Kunstgeschichte von den Auftraggebern her zu schreiben"*. – FORK, Christiane: Braunfels, Wolfgang, in *Metzler Kunsthistoriker Lexikon* (see note 23), p. 37. DaCosta Kaufmann states that Braunfels did not succeed in getting rid of ethnic-nationalist interpretation in spite of introducing a sociological aproach. – DaCOSTA KAUFMANN, Thomas: *Höfe, Klöster und Städte. Kunst und Kultur im Mitteleuropa, 1450 – 1800.* Köln 1998, p. 520. As a matter of fact, Braunfels speaks of *"deutsche und slawische Kultur"* and puts *"deutsche Handwerkskultur"* in contrast to *"slawisches Empfinden"* or *"slawisches Willen zum Unbegrenzten"*. – BRAUNFELS 1979 – 1989 (see note 133), Vol. 5, p. 73.

[152] *The Pelican History of Art*, edited by Nicolaus PEVSNER, published by Penguin Books.

[153] *Propyläen Kunstgeschichte in achtzehn Bänden.* Eds. Kurt BITTEL – Harald KELLER – Fritz NOVOTNY – Otto von SIMSON – Fritz VOLBACH – Stephan WAETZOLD – Rudolf ZEITLER. Berlin 1967 and later.

as well as Austria, Switzerland, Hungary, Bohemia, Moravia and Poland.[154] Another is Theodor Müller's idea of *"European sculpture of the 15ᵗʰ century north of the Alps"*, conceived of as a *"vast domain"* or *"great unity"* based on the *"common bond between the sculptors"*.[155] Regardless of whether a residue of the national hegemonistic understanding survives in these approaches,[156] the argument in favour of trans-national artistic organisms was still based mainly on the modernistic premise of the autonomy of art and its immanent development.[157]

Another project, that on the Parler family, conceived by Anton Legner in the late 1970s, displayed a related type of internationalisation of art history in Central Europe.[158] The history of art in Central Europe also appeared here as a process that transcended national and state frontiers. The interaction of artists as well as supra-personal artistic currents were regarded not only as a motor of the historic dynamic of art but also as an important factor of trans-national, European artistic communication. Thus, the migration of artists, especially the great internationally active artistic families, became a topic of art historical research. Despite the fact that international contacts were still regarded as a result of autonomous artistic communication, the social dimension of the history of art and particularly the study of the role of patrons and dynasties started to attract the interest of Central European art historians. The sociological approach to the trans-national, European conception of art history was launched as a consequence of this approach.[159]

---

[154] HEMPEL, Eberhard: *Baroque Art and Architecture in Central Europe: Germany/Austria/Switzerland/Hungary/Czechoslovakia/Polen.* Hamondsworth 1965. *"Mitteleuropa"* was defined in a very similar way by VAYER 1972 (see note 61), pp. 21-22. See also note 169.

[155] MÜLLER, Theodor: *Sculpture in the Netherlands, Germany, France and Spain, 1400 – 1500.* Baltimore 1966, p. XV.

[156] For example, Müller's premise of the identity of *"Germany"* with the whole of Central Europe, based on the interaction of the *"main centres"* and *"remoter provinces"* (MÜLLER 1966 (see note 155), p. XVII) and Hempel's belief in the constant specifics and initiative of German art, or the idea of the irrational *"genius loci"* regarded as the keystone of Central European art as a specific unit (HEMPEL 1965 (see note 154), pp. 1-8). In contrast to Hempel, Müller understands the common core of the trans-national artistic organism realistically as *"a common reservoir of sources"*, and so as a common tradition. – MÜLLER 1966 (see note 155), p. XVI.

[157] This means the dialectics of individual artists and impersonal regional currents of artistic development: *"I have always tried to show the personalities of various artists and the peculiarities of regional developments."* – MÜLLER 1966 (see note 155), p. XVI.

[158] *Die Parler und der schöne Stil, 1350 – 1400. Europäische Kunst unter den Luxemburger.* Vols. 1-5. [Exhib. Cat.] Ed. Anton LEGNER. Köln 1978 – 1980, Vol. 1, pp. XVII-XXIII. See on that GRÖTECKE 2010 (see note 149), pp. 105-108.

[159] BAKOŠ 2008 (see note 121), pp. 769-775.

The Idea of Macro-Regions: From Eastern to Central Europe

The isolationist national or nation-state approach was not just overcome by means of intensive research into international artistic communication and the cross-frontier migration of artists. The premise of the national or nation-state structure of the art of Central Europe was revised not least by the search for trans-national artistic units and artistic macro-regions that transcended state frontiers. A good example was Białostocki's proposal to consider the *"Baltic area"* as an artistic organism.[160] However, this way of overcoming nationalism implied a revision of the idea of artistic autonomy. Białostocki's model of a trans-national artistic region was based on the sociological concept of art. Following Jacob Burckhardt[161] and Aby Warburg, he combined their ideas with those of Gregor Paulsson, emphasizing a functional understanding of art in terms of the fulfilment of social roles and the specific demands of patrons.[162] The common socio-economic structure of the region was regarded as an integrating factor of the *"Baltic area"* as a trans-national artistic organism.[163] Belief in the importance of social tasks and functions, as well as the role of patrons, led to an emphasis on the role of ruling dynasties in the history of art. Białostocki's second attempt at conceiving a trans-national artistic unit, namely, the idea of *"Eastern Europe"* as an art historical entity, was regarded as a reflection of the state-political structure of the region and a product of dynastic strategies.[164]

---

[160] BIAŁOSTOCKI, Jan: The Baltic Area as an Artistic Region in Sixteenth Century, in *Hafnia. Copenhagen Papers in the Theory of Art*, 1976, pp. 11-23. Białostocki followed John Roosval's idea of *"arte dominium"* regarded as a trans-national artistic whole. – ROOSVAL, John: Le nord Baltique comme domaine artistique homogénne et sa situation dans le block Saxon-Baltique, in *Actes du XIIIᵉ congrès international d'histoire de l'art*. Stockholm 1933, pp. 96-97.

[161] Ingrid Ciulisová has pointed out the political affinity of J. Białostocki and J. Burckhardt. – CIULISOVÁ, Ingrid: Against Hegemony: Jacob Burckhardt, Jan Białostocki and the Renaissance, in *Renaissance Theory*. Eds. James ELKINS – Robert WILLIAMS. New York – London 2008, pp. 309-314.

[162] Białostocki referred to Paulsson's credo: *"Erst die Funktion, also sein Platz in einem sozialen Zusammenhang und einem von einer gewissen Gesellschaft entwickelten Stufenbau der Werte macht das Kunstwerk zum Kunstwerk."* – *Die Kunst des Mittelalters II. Spätmittelalter und beginnende Neuzeit* (=Propyläen Kunstgeschichte, 7). Berlin 1972, p. 21.

[163] John Roosval regarded *"arte dominium"* as *"un territoire d'un commun gout"*. – ROOSVAL 1933 (see note 160).

[164] BIAŁOSTOCKI, Jan: *The Art of the Renaissance in Eastern Europe. Hungary, Bohemia, Poland.* Ithaca 1976. On Białostocki's initiative concerning the idea of the dynastic history of art, see MICHALSKI, Sergiusz: Jan Białostocki a evolucja historii sztuki po roku 1945 [Jan Białostocki and the Evolution of Art History after 1945], in *Ars longa. Prace dedykowane pamiéci profesora Jana Białostockiego*. Ed. Maria POPRZÉCKA. Warszawa 1999, pp. 53-68. On Białostocki's combination of national and dynastic ideas regarded as an expression of the critical reaction

The notion of Central or East-Central Europe as a specific art historical entity gradually crystallized from the 1960s onwards.[165] Its leading methodological advocates included Lajos Vayer, who had argued as early as 1969 for the study of regional Central European artistic development as superior to national histories of art.[166] According to Vayer, the *"national characteristics of*

---

against Soviet hegemony, see CIULISOVÁ, Ingrid: Notes on the History of Renaissance Scholarship in Central Europe: Białostocki, Schlosser and Panofsky, in *Renaissance? Perception of Continuity and Discontinuity in Europe, c. 1300 – c. 1550.* Eds. Alexander LEE – Pit PÉPORTÉ – Harry SCHNITKER. Leiden – Boston 2010, pp. 349-357.

[165] According to Born, Janatková and Labuda (Vorwort der Herausgeber, in *Kunsthistoriographien in Ostmitteleuropa und der nationale Diskurs* (see note 4), pp. 15-19), the following meetings represented the main steps in the process of crystalizing the idea of (East-)Central Europe as an artistic organism: Colloque Les problémes du gothique et de la renaissance et l'art de l'Europe Centrale in Budapest (1965, published in *Acta Historiae Artium*, 13, 1967); XXIInd, XXVth and XXVIIIth International Congresses of the History of Art in Budapest (1969), Vienna (1983) and Berlin (1992), and last but not least the so-called Niedzica-Seminars (see *Proceedings I-VII*. Kraków 1981 – 1992). It dealt with *"the specificity of art in Central European countries"* and aimed at a *"synthetic approach to artistic phenomena in Poland, Bohemia, Slovakia, and Hungary"*. See KALINOWSKI, Lech: Przemówienie na otwarciu obrad I Seminarium Niedzieckiego [Introduction to the First Niedzica Seminar], in *Seminaria Niedziecke I*. Kraków 1981, pp. 10-11. See also KARŁOWSKA-KAMZOWA, Alicja: *Malarstwo gotyckie Europy środkowo-wschodniej. Zagadnienia odrębności regionu* [Gothic Painting in East-Central Europe. Questions of the Specificity of the Region]. Warszawa – Poznań 1982. According to Karłowska-Kamzowa, East-Central Europe consists of *"Bohemian and Hungarian Kingdoms including Lausitz, the Principality of Austria, Piastów and Jagiellonian Empires, as well as territories of Crusaders' domination"*. – Ibid., pp. 5, 106.
The concept of East-Central Europe had already been applied to Romanesque architecture by Anežka Merhautová and Andrzej Tomaszewski. – MERHAUTOVÁ, Anežka: *Romanische Kunst in Polen, Tschechoslowakei, Ungarn, Rumänien, Jugoslawien.* Praha 1974; TOMASZEWSKI, Andrzej: *Romańskie kościoly z emporami zachodnimi na obsztarze Polski, Czech i Wengier* [Romanesque Churches with Westworks in the Region of Poland, Bohemia and Hungary]. Wrocław 1974. In 1975, a conferrence devoted to Gothic art in East-Central Europe took place at Poznań University. East-Central Europe was regarded as consisting not only of Bohemia, Hungary and Poland, but also Saxony, Thuringia, and Austria. See *Gotyckie malarstwo ścienne w Europie środkowo-wschodniej* [Gothic Mural Painting in East-Central Europe]. Ed. Alicja KARŁOWSKA-KAMZOWA. Poznań 1977. See on that BAKOŠ 1993 (see note 35), pp. 55, 60. On the concept of East-Central Europe (*"Ostmitteleuropa"*) as an *"art historical region"*, see also DMITRIEVA-EINHORN, Marina: Gibt es eine Kunstlandschaft Ostmitteleuropa? Forschungsprobleme der Kunstgeographie, in *Die Kunsthistoriographien in Ostmitteleuropa und der nationale Diskurs* (see note 4), pp. 121-137. On the concept of *"East-Central Europe"* and its art historical research, see recently LABUDA, Adam S.: Ostmitteleuropa. Schicksalsgemeinschaft, Forschungsfeld, Kunstregion, in *kunsttexte.de*, 2010, No. 1, pp. 1-12.
[166] VAYER 1972 (see note 61), p. 19-29. According to Vayer, the historiography of art in Central Europe went through the following three stages: 1. universalism, leading to an underestimation of regional development; 2. nationalism, resulting in irrationalism; and 3. internationally oriented Central European regionalism, which represents the most developed and topical approach. – Ibid., pp. 26-29. See on this also BAKOŠ, Ján: Peripherie und kunsthistorische Entwicklung, in *Ars*, 24, 1991, No. 1, pp. 1-2.

art" had to be understood as elements in the regional development of Central Europe.[167] Vayer was also well aware of the connection between the international or Europe-oriented Central European regionalism on the one hand, and the sociological approach to art on the other.[168] At the same time, Vayer did not limit the concept of Central Europe to the former Soviet Bloc.[169]

In contrast, Białostocki's idea of *"Eastern Europe"* included only three Central European political or state units: Hungary, Bohemia and Poland. In this regard, Białostocki was following the model of Central Europe articulated by Halecki,[170] which echoed the situation after the Second World War. His notion of *"Eastern Europe"* represented a critical rejection of both pan-Germanic and Soviet visions of cultural hegemony.[171] The political motivation of Białostocki's model was reflected not only in its implicit Polish nationalism, but also in its territorial definition.[172] It was precisely his restriction of the Cen-

---

[167] According to Vayer: *"... wir (betrachten) als wichtigstes methodisches Prinzip sogar in der Analyse des Nationalen die Verfolgung eben der regionalen kunsthistorischen Entwicklungsprozesse..."* – VAYER 1972 (see note 61), p. 24.

[168] *"Und hier sehen wir uns auch jener in unserer Forschungstätigkeit mit immer dringlicherer Zwangsläufigkeit auftrenden Problematik gegenüber, die in der Analyse der kunsthistorischen Prozesse dem Fragenkomplex jener Erscheinungen entgegenführt, die mit dem Stifter, dem Auftraggeber, dem Ankäufer, dem Kunstverständigen und Kunstliebhaber, oder mit anderen Worten mit dem Mäzen, dem Kritiker und dem Publikum zusammenhängen."* – Ibid., p. 25.

[169] *"Gewiss bildet dieses seiner Ausdehnung nach nur unscharf umrissene Mitteleuropa... nur einen relativen Begriff, unter dem man herkömmlicherweise die zwischen zwei imaginären Vertikalen liegenden Gebiete versteht, deren westliche vom Ostrand der Friesieschen Inseln bis zum Golf von Genua reicht, während sich die östliche vom Rigaschen Meerbusen bis zur Ostküste der Adria erstreckt. Unter Zugrundelegung der gegenwärtigen Staatsgrenzen bilden diesen Großraum der Nordostzipfel der Niederlande und die westlichen Sowjetrepubliken im Norden, italienische und rumänische Staatsteile im Süden und in ihrer vollen teritorialen Ausdehnung die Deutsche Bundesrepublik und die Deutsche Demokratische Republik, die Schweiz, Österreich, die Tschechoslowakei, Ungarn, Jugoslawien und Polen."* – Ibid., pp. 21-22.

[170] HALECKI, Oskar: *The Limits and Divisions of European History.* London – New York 1950. DaCosta Kaufmann speaks of *"Halecki's Auffassung von Ostmitteleuropa als östlicher Hälfte Mitteleuropas"*. – DaCOSTA KAUFMANN, Thomas: (Ost)Mitteleuropa als Kunstgeschichtsregion?, in *Oskar-Halecki-Vorlesung, 2005.* Leipzig 2006, pp. 8-9. Marian Kutzner pleads for a similar idea: *"All that urges us to study once more the history of art of the specific artistic macro-region that was represented in the Middle Ages by Europe of West Slavs, namely Bohemia, Hungary with Slovakia, Poland with Lithuania, Coast Regions, and Prussia."* – KUTZNER 1986 (see note 29), p. 350.

[171] BAKOŠ 1993 (see note 35), p. 55. According to DaCosta Kaufmann: *"Die Differenzierung zwischen Ostmitteleuropa und Mitteleuropa als Entität scheint eine Folge des Zweiten Weltkrieges und der Zeit des kalten Krieges gewesen zu sein."* – DaCOSTA KAUFMANN, Thomas: Die Geschichte der Kunst Ostmitteleuropas als Herausforderung für die Historiographie der Kunst Europas, in *Kunsthistoriographien in Ostmitteleuropa und der nationale Diskurs* (see note 4), p. 55.

[172] Later Białostocki stated that he had used the notion *"Eastern Europe"* in the sense of *"Ostmitteleuropa"*. – BIAŁOSTOCKI, Jan: Rinascimento pollaco e rinascimento europeo, in *Poloniae – Italia. Relazioni artistiche dal medioevo al XVIII secolo. Atti del convegno termtosi a Roma, 21 – 22 Maggio 1975.* Wrocław – Warszawa – Kraków – Gdańsk 1979, pp. 21-58. See about that

tral European artistic unit to the eastern part of Central Europe that evoked criticism and provoked a fundamentally new formulation of Central Europe as an artistic entity.[173]

In the context of both uniting Europe and explicitly contributing to this, the American scholar Thomas DaCosta Kaufmann took the initiative in reviving the idea of a larger Central Europe as an art historical organism. For Kaufmann, Central Europe included not only the Czech state, the historic Kingdom of Hungary and the Polish "Commonwealth", but also the whole of the Holy Roman Empire.[174] Criticizing both explicit and implicit nationalism, he vehemently promoted the trans-national approach to the history of art of Central Europe. Taking up, but also reworking the ideas of Wolfgang Braunfels and Jan Białostocki, Kaufmann based his vision of a territorially extensive Central Europe on a sociologically stratified model of art. In this model, the art of Central Europe is a polyphonic organism, internally structured according to a variety of demands, tasks, and functions required by three different social milieus, "*Court, Cloister and City*".[175]

When reformulating the concept of Central Europe, Kaufmann modified another of Białostocki's stimuli: the idea of East-Central Europe as an "*artistic periphery*". Białostocki formulated this on the basis of encouragement from

---

DaCOSTA KAUFMANN 1998 (see note 151), p. 518. On the notion "*East-Central Europe*", see JAWORSKI, Rudolf: Ostmitteleuropa. Zur Tauglichkeit und Akzeptanz eines historischen Hilfsbegriffs, in *Westmitteleuropa, Ostmitteleuropa. Vergleiche und Beziehungen* (see note 36), pp. 37-45; BAHLCKE, Joachim: Ostmitteleuropa, in *Studienhandbuch östliches Europa I. Geschichte Ostmittel- und Südosteuropas*. Ed. Harald ROTH. Köln – Weimar – Wien 1999, pp. 59-72.

[173] See review of Białostocki's book by Thomas DaCOSTA KAUFMANN in *The Art Bulletin*, 58, 1978, pp. 164-169. According to DaCosta Kaufmann: "*... the concept of East Europe, as it was utilized until recently, is and will in future historiography be regarded largely as a construct of the second half of twentieth century. As a result of what is now revealed as the temporary division of Europe into two camps, East Europe was the part considered to fall under the Soviet sphere of influence.*" – DaCOSTA KAUFMANN 1995 (see note 35), p. 16.

[174] DaCosta Kaufmann claims: "*This essay represents an effort to consider Central Europe as a cultural entity, an attempt to contribute to its reintegration into a unified notion of European culture.*" – DaCOSTA KAUFMANN 1995 (see note 35), p. 15. His definition of the terrritory of Central Europe conforms to that of Hempel and Vayer: see footnotes 154 and 169. Like DaCosta Kaufmann, Vayer emphasized historically variable character of "*Central Europe*". – VAYER 1972 (see note 61), p. 21.

[175] Christiane Fork states that already Braunfels structured the history of art in the Holy Roman Empire "*nach politischen Institutionen und Ordnungseinheiten... gemäss seiner Maxime, Kunstgeschichte von den Auftraggebern her zu schreiben*". – FORK, Christiane: Braunfels, Wolfgang, in *Metzler Kunsthistoriker Lexikon* (see note 23), p. 37. As mentioned before, Adam S. Labuda credited DaCosta Kaufmann with changing the paradigm of the notion of art as the expression of an artist to the notion of art as the tool of a patron. – LABUDA 2002 (see note 100), pp. 22-23.

George Kubler, Ljubo Karaman, Enrico Castelnuovo and Carlo Ginzburg,[176] in order to articulate the specific status of this art historical phenomenon.[177] Kaufmann took over Białostocki's interpretation of Central Europe as an innovative artistic territory, situated outside the world centres, but still sometimes able to contribute creatively to European art. However, he also emphasized international cultural communication and the mobility of artists and considered the Central European area as an organic part of European culture.[178]

National History as Multi-Cultural Communication

The unification of Germany after the fall of the "Iron Curtain" in 1989 made the history of German art topical again. The subsequent process of the unification of Europe, and especially its doctrine of unity in diversity, together with the conception of a united Europe as a polyphony of nation-states, encouraged German art historians to make renewed attempts to conceive the history of German art as the history of a specific phenomenon.[179] However, after the de-

---

[176] Białostocki borrowed the notion of *"replication"* from Kubler, the idea of periphery as a creative region from Karaman, and belief in competition as a characteristics of centres, from Castelnuovo and Ginzburg. On this, see BAKOŠ, Ján: Jan Białostocki and Center-Periphery Problem, in *Białostocki. Materiały z Seminarium Metodologicznego Stowarzyszenia Historyków Sztuku "Jan Białostocki – między tradycja a inovacja"*. Ed. Magdalena WRÓBLEWSKA. Warszawa 2009, pp. 63-75.

[177] BIAŁOSTOCKI, Jan: Some Values of Artistic Periphery, in *World Art. Themes of Unity in Diversity. Acts of the XXVIth International Congress of the History of Art, Washington, D.C., 1986*. Ed. Irving LAVIN. University Park [a.o.] (Penn.) 1989, Vol. 1, pp. 49-54. On this, see BAKOŠ 1991 (see note 166), pp. 2-3; BAKOŠ 2009 (see note 176), pp. 63-75.

[178] DaCOSTA KAUFMANN 2004 (see note 52), before all, the chapter "Artistic Regions and the Problem of Artistic Metropolises: Questions of (East)-Central Europe", pp. 154-186.

[179] According to Heinrich Klotz: *"In Zeiten der europäischen Einigung ist kaum noch die Frage aktuell, was die einzelnen Nationen auf dem Feld der Künste an Besponderem hervorgebracht haben. Mehr als das Nationale interessiert uns heute im Konzert der europäischen Länder das Verbindende. Dennoch ist uns darüber die Geschichte der einzelnen Nation nicht gleichgültig geworden."* – KLOTZ 1998 (see note 1), p. 8. And he continues: *"Alle Künste und Stile haben in den unterschiedlichen Nationen und Regionen Europas... unterscheidbare Ausprägungen gefunden, ja, Besonderheit und Eigenart der nationalen und regionalen Kunstentwicklungen machen letzlich das gesamte europäische Kunstgeschichte aus."* – KLOTZ 1998 (see note 1), p. 13. See on this also MÜLLER 2007 (see note 22), pp. 42-43: *"Erst nach der deutschen Wiedervereinigung entsteht wieder ein allgemeines Bedürfnis nach kulturhistorischer Fundierung einer nationalen Identität, diesmal aber unter den weltanschaulichen Prämissen des demokratischen Rechtsstaates und vor dem Hintergrund der fortschreitenden Einigung Europas."*
Comments on the study of the history of art in Germany are to be found recently in ENGEL-BERG, Meinrad von: "Deutscher Barock" oder "Barock in Deutschland". Nur ein Streit um Worte, in *Die deutsche Nation im frühzeitlichen Europa*. Eds. Lothar GALL – Georg SCHMIDT – Elisabeth MÜLLER-LUCKNER. Oldenbourg 2010, pp. 307-334.

finitive discrediting of expansionist nationalism, the idea of the history of art as the history of the ethnic nation and the expression of its timeless mental nature was not acceptable. Therefore, for understandable reasons, German art historians at the end of the 1990s rather inclined to an *étatiste* regionalist conception, which was already widespread, as we have seen, in post-war Central European national historiographies.[180] Wolfgang Braunfels and, a little later, East German art historians of the 1980s, had already treated the *Geschichte der deutschen Kunst* on a state basis, *"within the historic frontiers of the German Empire"*.[181] This geographical conception also became the basis for a non-nationalistically defined history of German art at the end of the 1990s. It was defined as the *"history of art in a geographical space"*.[182] However, this territorial unit was not defined ethnically. It was conceived as a historically changing phenomenon, *"without fixed boundaries"*, and as a linguistically defined space, characterized by a specific artistic culture, which made it a *"Kunst- und Kulturlandschaft"*.[183]

Therefore, if the art historical unit in Klotz and Warnke's history of German art, namely German art understood as a *"Kunstlandschaft"*, was finally borne out by the art itself, in the synthesis of Robert Suckale, which appeared at the same time, then the historical subject was no longer art as an autonomous phenomenon, but rather, as formed by the social demands of the patrons. At the same time, the content of the history of art conceived of in this way was again that of the relationship between universal (European) art and regional development. Thus, the history of German art was transformed into the historical destiny of universal art in Germany.[184] According to Suckale, the historical framework was the territory of *"Deutschland"*. As in the work

---

[180] MÜLLER 2007 (see note 22), pp. 43-44: *"Das 'deutsche Volk' als historisches Entwicklungsprinzip ist in den neu entstehenden Texten jedoch nicht mehr akzeptabel. Vielmehr wird versucht, die deutsche Kunst als Kunst in Deutschland zu verstehen… als Ergebnis und Teil einer größeren, internationalen Gesamtentwicklung."* The need to define their historic identity in the European polyphony also seems to have stimulated the genesis of the multi-volume *Geschichte der bildenden Kunst in Österreich*. Vols. 1-6. Eds. Hermann FILLITZ – Günter BRUCHER – Artur ROSENAUER – Hellmut LORENZ – Gerbert FRODL – Wieland SCHMIED. München 1998 – 2002.

[181] *"… innerhalb der jeweiligen historischen Grenzen des deutschen Reiches"*. – *Geschichte der deutschen Kunst, 1350 – 1470*. Ed. Ernst ULLMANN. Leipzig 1981, p. 7. In addition, *"Gebrauch von Kunst in der Not des Alltags"* was regarded by the authors of the book as the proper content of the history of art, assuming the dialectics of art and society that they studied with its historical functioning and social communication of aesthetic phenomena. See *Geschichte der deutschen Kunst, 1200 – 1350*. Eds. Friedrich MÖBIUS – Helga SCIURIE. Leipzig 1989, pp. 10-11. See on that FEIST, Peter H.: Die Kunstwissenschaft in der DDR, in *Kunst und Politik. Jahrbuch der Guernica-Gesellschaft*, 8, 2006, Schwerpunkt: Kunstgeschichte an den Universitäten in der Nachkriegszeit, ed. Martin PAPENBROCK, pp. 29-30.

[182] *"… Geschichte der Kunst in einem geographischen Raum"*. – WARNKE 1999 (see note 1), p. 8-13.

[183] *"… Kunst-und Kulturlandschaft [...] ohne fixen Grenzen"*. – Ibid.

[184] SUCKALE, Robert: *Kunst in Deutschland. Von Karl dem Großen bis Heute*. Köln 1998.

of Klotz and Warnke, *"Deutschland"* is defined by Suckale as the *"German linguistic space"*, which basically coincided with the Holy Roman Empire,[185] but had historically changeable dimensions.[186] At the same time, according to Suckale, the history of art occurring in this region was based on the *"polarity between local patriotism and cosmopolitanism"*,[187] and can be regarded as an interaction between the local and the universal. Therefore, *"at least before 1800, art in Germany must be understood as European art"*.[188] The externally conditioned international nature of art in Germany in this account is also confirmed by its immanent multinationality, i.e. the fact that: *"The Germans themselves are really multinational and they were also multicultural for a large part of their history."*[189] A critical revision of ethno-nationalist purism is evident here.

Similarly, the most recent *Geschichte der bildenden Kunst in Österreich*,[190] which is based on the conception of the contemporary Austrian state while being explicitly distanced from a narrow nationalism,[191] underlines its participation in European artistic communication[192] and accentuates the *"openness of frontiers"* and the *"supra-regional, ultimately pan-European context"*.[193]

---

[185] Limitation to *"den deutschen Sprachraum"* is regarded by Suckale as a practical *"compromise with the modern idea of a nation"*. – Ibid., p. 9. The territorial borders of the history of German art were already demarcated in a similar way by Hans WEIGERT in the second edition of his *Geschichte der deutschen Kunst* (Frankfurt am Main 1963, p. 5): *"Da der Bereich der deutschen Geistesgeschichte nicht von den jeweiligen politischen Grenzen, sondern von der Sprachgrenze bestimmt war, sind Österreich, Böhmen vor Hus, die Schweiz und das Elsass einbezogen, zumal da ihre Kunst größtenteils entstand, als sie noch Teile des Reiches waren."* In contrast to that, Adolf FEULNER and Theodor MÜLLER, the authors of the first post-war *Geschichte der deutschen Plastik* published in München in 1953 (=*Deutsche Kunstgeschichte* (see note 147), Vol. 2, p. 7), maintained that *"die Geschichte der deutschen Stämme ist unsere Geschichte"* and regarded the history of German sculpture *"als geschlossene Geschichte der Entwicklung des deutschen Geistes"*.

[186] *"Die Grenzen der Betrachtung sind in jeder Epoche entsprechend den jeweiligen historischen Realitäten neu zu ziehen."* – SUCKALE 1998 (see note 184), p. 9.
ENGELBERG, Meinrad von: Wie deutsch ist der deutsche Barock? Vorüberlegungen zu einer neuen "Geschichte der bildenden Kunst in Deutschland", in *Zeitschrift für Kunstgeschichte*, 69, 2006, No. 4, pp. 509-510, 530, shares Braunfels's and Suckale's political/territorial conception of the history of art in Germany as the history of the art of the Holy Roman Empire.

[187] *"... Polarität zwischen Lokalpatriotismus und Kosmopolitismus"*. – Ibid., p. 9.

[188] *"... die Kunst in Deutschland, zumindest vor 1800, [muss] als europäisch gemeinte Kunst verstanden werden"*. – Ibid.

[189] *"Die Deutschen selbst sind letzlich 'multinational', und sie verhielten sich über lange Strecken ihrer Geschichte auch 'multikulturell'."* – Ibid.

[190] *Geschichte der bildenden Kunst in Österreich* (see note 180).

[191] According to Hermann Fillitz: *"[Man kann] nicht von einer österreichischen Kunst sprechen..."* *"Die Publikation konzentriert sich auf den Bereich des heutigen Österreich."* – Ibid., Vol. 1, p. 7.

[192] *"Österreich hat sich immer mit bestimmenden Strömungen Italiens, Frankreichs oder Deutschlands auseinandegesetzt."* – Ibid.

[193] Artur Rosenauer emphasizes *"Offenheit der Grenzen"*. – ROSENAUER, Artur: *Spätmittelalter und Renaissance. Geschichte der bildenden Kunst in Österreich*. Vol. 3. München 2003, p. 15. Gün-

Thus, internationally postulated histories of art in Germany and Austria have opened the door to a more extensive, not only Central European but trans-national, pan-European art historical approach.

"Kulturtransfer" and East-Central Europe

Another important initiative introduced as a deliberate contribution to the process of uniting Europe and overcoming nationalism in Central European art history was the so-called Jagiellonian project. It was started with the conference *Jagiellonen. Kunst und Kultur einer europäischen Dynastie an der Wende der Neuzeit*, held in Nuremberg in 1999.[194] The theoretical foundations of the project were laid by Robert Suckale. He revived the rhetorical understanding of style and connected it with Białostocki's dynastic conception of the history of art.[195]

At the same time as Suckale, a number of Central European art historians made an effort to launch a conception of the history of art in Central Europe based on the dynastic principle, on the idea of the history of art conceived as the history of royal courts and dynasties.[196] The intention of this trend

---

ther Brucher speaks of *"überregionalen, letzlich gesamteuropäischen Kontext"*. – BRUCHER, Günter: *Gotik. Geschichte der bildenden Kunst in Österreich*. Vol. 2. München 2000, p. 7.

[194] *Die Jagiellonen* 2002 (see note 100). The project was supported by the Geisteswissenschaftliches Zentrum Geschichte und Kultur Ostmitteleuropas in Leipzig (GWZO). The political intention of the project was explicitly articulated by R. Suckale as follows: *"Wir wollen zu Erweiterung Westeuropas zum ganzen Kontinent, zu Einheit und gegenseitigem Verständnis beitragen."* – Ibid., p. 15.

[195] Suckale reintroduced the rhetorical approach to style by means of the notion *"genera dicendi"* or *"Stillagen"*. See SUCKALE, Robert: Peter Parler und das Problem der Stillagen, in *Die Parler und der schöne Stil* (see note 158), Vol. 4, pp. 173-184; SUCKALE, Robert: Stilbegriffe und Stil um 1330. Versuch einer Grundlegung, in SUCKALE, Robert: *Die Hofkunst Kaiser Ludwigs des Bayern*. München 1993, pp. 48-70. Suckale could rely on BIAŁOSTOCKI, Jan: Das Modusproblem in den bildenden Künsten, in *Zeitschrift für Kunstgeschichte*, 24, 1961, pp. 128-141; reprinted in BIAŁOSTOCKI, Jan: *Stil und Ikonographie. Studien zur Kunstwissenschaft*. Dresden 1966, pp. 9-35; originally published in Polish in *Estetyka*, 2, 1961; BIAŁOSTOCKI, Jan: Zeit, Stil und Aufgaben, in *Die Kunst des Mittelalters II. Spätmittelalter und beginnende Neuzeit* (=Propyläen Kunstgeschichte, 7). Berlin 1972, pp. 21-23.

[196] HOŘEJŠÍ, Jiřina – VACKOVÁ, Jarmila: Die Hofkunst zur Zeit der Jagiellonen-Herrschaft in Böhmen, in *Die Kunst der Ranaissance und des Manierismus in Böhmen*. Eds. Jiřina HOŘEJŠÍ et al. Hanau 1979; SCHWARZ, Michael Viktor: *Höfische Skulptur im 14. Jahrhundert. Entwicklungsphasen und Vermittlungswege im Vorfeld des weichen Stils*. Worms 1986; MAROSI, Ernő: Mitteleuropäische Herrscherhäuser des 13. Jahrhunderts und die Kunst, in *Künstlerischer Austausch/Artistic Exchange* (see note 35), Vol. 2, pp. 15-25; KUTHAN, Jiří: *Přemysl Otakar II. Král železný a zlatý, král zakladatel a mecenáš* [Přemysl Otakar II. King Iron and Golden, King Founder and Patron]. Vimperk 1993; German edition: *Přemysl Otakar II. König, Bauherr und*

was especially to overcome narrow nationalist accounts. The ruling dynasties and their courts were no longer seen as representatives or agents of their nations,[197] but as cosmopolitan patrons, mediating international relations and contacts.[198] The theoretical basis of this cultural/historical approach was to promote the functional and instrumental understanding of the style of art. It entails a definitive departure from the formalist idea of the autonomy of art.[199]

However, apart from historiographic and methodological components, there is a third idea that the authors, sympathizers, and adherents of this model share. It is the conviction that the art historical process in Central Europe has the character of *"Kulturtransfer"*,[200] according to which the history of art is not a one-sided process, based on the dominance of centre over periphery, but an interactive and trans-national *"exchange"*.[201]

Mäzen. Höfische Kunst im 13. Jahrhundert. Wien – Köln – Weimar 1996. According to Kuthan: *"Die Charakterisierung einzelner Epochen nach Herrscherpersönlichkeiten oder Herrscherdynastien... hat auch in unserer Disziplin eine lange Tradition... die Herrscherhöfe [waren] nicht nur bestimmte Machtzentren, sondern auch Zentren für die Schöpfung ästhetischer Modelle... Und so wurden Mäzene und Auftraggeber ebenso zum Gegenstand künstlerischer Forschungen... das Mäzenatentum bedeutender Angehörigen von Herrrscherhäusern oder ganzen Dynastien [nimmt] einen besonderen Platz ein."* – Ibid., p. 363-364.

[197] Royal dynasties were regarded as the embodiment of the nation by nationalist art historians like Pinder or Jantzen. On this, see HELD 2003 (see note 105), p. 27. W. Schenkluhn clearly differentiates between Pinder's ethno-nacionalist and Jantzen's *étatiste*-national notion of royal dynasties. – SCHENKLUHN 1990 (see note 21), pp. 158-162.

[198] E. Marosi underlines the leading role of *"intellectuals"* (men of letters) in internationl cultural communication. – MAROSI 1992 (see note 1), pp. 64-65.

[199] See on this SUCKALE, Robert: Stilgeschichte zu Beginn des 21. Jahrhunderts. Probleme und Möglichkeiten, in *Stilfragen zur Kunst des Mittelalters* (see note 106), pp. 271-281.

[200] In Winfried Eberhard's words: *"... es geht vor allem um Prozesse des Kulturtransfers zwischen dem Süden und Norden, Osten und Westen Europas sowie um die kulturelle Vernetzung auf Basis dynastischer und ökonomischer Verbindungen innerhalb der ostmitteleuropäischen Länder. In diesen Bezugen werden kulturelle Verdichtungen angesprochen, in denen der Entwicklungsausgleich, ja zuweilen Vorsprung des östlichen gegenüber den westlichen Mitteleuropa deutlich werden kann. Dieser seit dem 14. Jahrhundert zu beobachtenden Ausgleich des jüngeren mit dem älteren Europa widerspricht eklatant der verbreiteten westlichen Vorstellung von der ständigen Entwicklungsverspätung des sogenannten Osten."* – EBERHARD, Winfried: Geleitwort, in *Die Jagiellonen* 2002 (see note 100), p. 11. It is worth mentioning that the idea of the historical initiative of the Eastern part of Central Europe is reminiscent of D. Frey's reversal of *"West-Ost Gefälle"*. In contrast to D. Frey, W. Eberhard does not regard the active Eastern Europe any longer as a Germanized East. On the concept of *"Kulturtransfer"*, see DMITRIEVA, Marina: *Italien in Sarmatien. Studien zum Kulturtransfer im östlichen Europa in der Zeit der Renaissance.* Stuttgart 2008, pp. 31-34. See also CARQUÉ, Bernd: Aporien des Kulturtranfers. Bau- und Bildkünstlerische Zeichen von Herrschersakralität in Prag und Paris, in *Böhmen und das Deutsche Reich. Ideen- und Kulturtransfer im Vergleich (13. – 16. Jahrhundert).* Eds. Eva SCHLOTHEUBER – Hubertus SEIBERT. München 2009, pp. 35-62.

[201] According to Suckale: *"... die ganze mitteleuropäische Kunstgeschichte [ist] nicht nach den modernen Nationenverständnis und den heutigen politischen Grenzen zu beurteilen, sondern übernational*

Thanks to the initiative of the Geisteswissenschaftliches Zentrum Geschichte und Kultur Ostmitteleuropas in Leipzig, this cultural/historical and trans-nationally oriented model has established itself as the mainstream of East-Central European art historiography in the first decade of the third millennium.[202] It has also thematized the concept of the history of art, conceived of as the history of European dynasties.[203] However, in spite of its trans-national orientation and intention to understand the history of art as international, pan-European cultural communication, this model still implies an effort to plead for acceptance of the idea of East-Central Europe as an active and creative region. It deliberately limits its range to the territory of the Eastern part of Central Europe and pre-supposes *"Ostmitteleuropa"* as a specific art historical entity.[204]

What is noteworthy, however, is the fact that the nation-state model of the history of art still survives alongside the trans-national project. In the new context of an already united Europe, the state centred interpretation does not appear any longer as a regressive attempt at national isolation. It is rather, a reflection of the polyphonic doctrine of European Union and even a response to ongoing globalisation. A good example is the collective synthesis on the history of Gothic painting in Poland. It is based on a combination of historicizing and presentist state territorialism,[205] which underlines the integrity of the present Polish state. On the other hand, the latest *Geschichte der bildenden*

---

    und überregional." – SUCKALE, Robert: Über die Hinfälligkeit einiger historiographischer Konzepte und Begriffen zur Deutung der Kunst Böhmens, in *Kunst als Herrschaftsinstrument* (see note 133), p. 41.

[202] Jagiellonian project has been further developed by Jiří Fajt, Markus Hörsch and Evelin Wetter. See *Die Länder der böhmischen Krone und ihre Nachbarn zur Zeit der Jagiellonenkönige (1471 – 1526). Kunst, Kultur, Geschichte* (=Studia Jagellonica Lipsiensia, 2). Ed. Evelin WETTER. Ostfildern 2004; *Künstlerische Wechselwirkungen in Mitteleuropa* (=Studia Jagellonica Lipsiensia, 1). Eds. Jiří FAJT – Markus HÖRSCH. Ostfildern 2006; *Kunst als Herrschaftsinstrument* (see note 201).

[203] See, e.g., *Karl IV. Kaiser von Gottes Gnaden. Kunst und Representation des Hauses Luxemburg, 1310 – 1437*. Ed. Jiří FAJT. München 2006; *Sigismundus Rex et Imperator. Kunst und Kultur zur Zeit Sigismunds von Luxemburg, 1387 – 1437*. [Exhib. Cat.] Ed. Imre TAKÁCS. Budapest – Luxemburg 2006; *Sigismund von Luxemburg: ein Kaiser in Europa*. Eds. Michel PAULY – François REINERT. Mainz am Rhein 2006. The dynastic interpretation of the history of art has been launched as a critical revision of nationalist art history. Nevertheless, it can also be misused as a mask for crypto-nationalism or crypto-hegemonism. See on that BAKOŠ 2008 (see note 121), pp. 763-783; in this volume pp. 148-167.

[204] At the moment, a multi-volume *Handbuch der Geschichte der bildenden Kunst und Architektur in Ostmitteleuropa* is in progress at the GWZO in Leipzig.

[205] *Malarstwo gotyckie w Polsce* (see note 139). According to the editors, A. S. Labuda, K. Secomska, p. 12, *"territorial demarcation of the work"* covers *"not only historical regions of the Polish Kingdom... and Great Lithuanian Principality... but also the lands of the present Polish Republic"*. See also MOSSAKOWSKI, Stanisław: Foreword, ibid., pp. 9-10.

Kunst in Deutschland, which is generally held to be a history of media, social functioning of art, and visual communication,[206] can also be considered as an acceleration of the above mentioned trend towards an international, cosmopolitan and pan-European understanding. The history of art in Germany is thus understood as *"international exchange and accelerated communication".*[207] What is, however, still challenging is the idea of an extensive Central Europe[208] as an organic part of the European art historical organism promoted today, especially by DaCosta Kaufmann.[209] Nevertheless, it would seem that the study of the history of art in Central Europe as a system of exchange and communication, will be impossible to manage without such concepts as dissemination, migration, transfer, exchange, acculturation, and even province and periphery.[210]

---

[206] See *Gotik. Geschichte der bildenden Kunst in Deutschland*. Vol. 3. Ed. Bruno KLEIN. München – Berlin – London – New York 2007. Bruno Klein qualifies *"Medienwandel"* and *"Weiterentwicklung der Medien generell und speziell des Bildes in allen seinen Erscheinungsformen"* as the main object of the history of art in Germany. – Ibid., p. 8. According to Susanne Wittekind: *"Ziel dieses Bandes ist es, den Handlungs- und Sinnzusammenhang der Kunstwerke aufzuzeigen und ihre Rolle als visuelle Kommunikationsmittel herauszuarbeiten."* – WITTEKIND, Susanne: *Romanik. Geschichte der bildenden Kunst in Deutschland*. Vol. 2. München – Berlin – London – New York 2009, p. 7.

[207] *Gotik* (see note 206), pp. 8-9. See also KLEIN, Bruno: Internationaler Kunstaustausch, in *Prag und die grossen Kulturzentren Europas...* (see note 121), pp. 137-143. In Klein's words: *"Dennoch dürfte längst feststehen, daß künstlerischer Austausch... [ist] ein wichtiges, künstlerische Prozesse determinierendes Element, dessen Erforschung dringend geboten ist."* – Ibid., p. 142.

[208] Central Europe is reaching beyond, not only the East-Central Europe of Białostocki, but also the Danubian *"Habsburg"* Central Europe of Eitelberger and the pan-German *"Mitteleuropa"* of Naumann.

[209] See DaCOSTA KAUFMANN 1995 (see note 35), pp. 13-27; and DaCOSTA KAUFMANN 2004 (see note 171), pp. 51-64. According to him: *"... westliches und östliches Mitteleuropa bilden zwei Teile eines Ganzen"*. Ibid., p. 55. That is why *"die Betrachtung Mitteleuropas – nicht nur Ostmitteleuropas – [konnte] ein Anreiz sein, die Grundlage der Geschichte der europäischen Kunst... neu zu überdenken"*. – Ibid., p. 53. He believes: *"... es wäre verfehlt, Ostmitteleuropa bzw. besser Mitteleuropa als Sondergebiet zu behandeln. Die Kunstgeschichte Mitteleuropas sollte vielmehr unseren Blick auf Europa als Ganzes lenken... Mitteleuropa darf nicht isoliert von der übrigen Welt betrachtet werden, sondern sollte in das Konzept einer europäischen, westlichen Kunstgeschichte eingegliedert werden."* – Ibid., p. 62.

[210] See DaCOSTA KAUFMANN 2004 (see note 171), p. 62. For more on this, see BURKE, Peter: *Kultureller Austausch*. Frankfurt am Main 2000, pp. 9-40.

BIBLIOGRAPHICAL NOTE

Details of the previous publications of essays in this volume are as follows:

"Humanists" versus "Relativists": Methodological Visions and Revisions within the Vienna School. Paper read at the conference "Etablierung und Entwicklung des Faches Kunstgeschichte in Deutschland, Polen und Mittel-europa", Kraków, 26 – 30 September 2007. Published under the title "'Nominalists' versus 'Realists' or 'Humanists' versus 'Relativists' (Methodological Visions and Revisions within the Vienna School)" in *Die Etablierung und Entwicklung des Faches Kunstgeschichte in Deutschland, Polen und Mitteleuropa*. Eds. Wojciech BAŁUS – Joanna WOLAŃSKA. Warszawa 2010, pp. 315-346.

The Depth of the Historicity of Art and Walter Benjamin. Paper delivered at the international conference "Umelecké dielo v epoche mediálnych výziev" (Work of Art in the Age of Media Challenges), Bratislava, 5 – 6 October 2006. Slovak original "Walter Benjamin a hĺbka historicity (Benjamin a Viedenská škola dejín umenia)", published in *Slovak Review of World Literature Research*, 16, 2007, No. 1, pp. 27-36.

Between Task and Function: Metamorphoses of Jacob Burckhardt's Legacy. Published under the title "Metamorphoses of Jacob Burckhardt's Legacy" in *Horizons. Essays on Art and Art Research. 50 Years Swiss Institute for Art Research.* Eds. Juerg ALBRECHT – Kornelia IMESCH. Ostfildern-Ruit 2001, pp. 345-352.

From the Ideological Critique to the Apologia for the Market. Introduction to the international colloquium "Artwork through the Market", Bratislava, 11 – 13 December 2003. Published in *Artwork through the Market. The Past and the Present.* Ed. Ján BAKOŠ. Bratislava 2004, pp. 13-51.

In Defence of Liberal "Humanism": Gombrich's Struggle against Metaphysics. Introduction to the special issue of the journal *Human Affairs* devoted to "Relativism versus Universalism & Ernst Hans Gombrich". Published in *Human Affairs. A Postdisciplinary Journal for Humanities and Social Sciences*, 19, 2009, No. 3, pp. 239-250.

From Universalism to Nationalism: Transformations of the Vienna School's Ideas in Central Europe. Contribution to the conference "Die ostmitteleuropäischen Kunsthistoriographien und der nationale Diskurs", Humboldt-Universität Berlin, 28 – 30 June 2001. Published in *Die Kunsthistoriographien in Ostmitteleuropa und der nationale Diskurs*. Eds. Robert BORN – Alena JANATKOVÁ – Adam S. LABUDA. Berlin 2004, pp. 79-101.

The Revision of a Bourgeois Idea: From a National to a Dynastic History of Art. Paper read at the international conference "Prague and Great Cultural Centres of Europe in The Luxembourgeois Era (1310 – 1437)", Prague, 31 March – 5 April 2008, and published as "From National to Dynastic History of Art. A Path of Art History in Central Europe" in conference proceedings *Prag und die grossen Kulturzentren Europas in der Zeit der Luxemburger* (1310 – 1437). Eds. Markéta JAROŠOVÁ – Jiří KUTHAN – Stefan SCHOLZ. Praha 2008, pp. 763-783.

Paths and Strategies of the Historiography of Art in Central Europe, in *Ars*, 43, 2010, No. 1, pp. 85-118.

INDEX OF NAMES

Vasari, Giorgio, 112, 167, 169
Vasold, Georg, 11, 19, 179-181
Vătăşianu, Virgil, 182
Vayer, Lajos, 185, 203, 206, 208-210
Veltruský, Jiří, 61
Vermeylen, Filip, 95
Verspohl, Franz-Joachim, 87
Vezér, Erzsébet, 77
Vidrih, Rebeka, 122
Vlnas, Vít, 27
Volbach, Fritz, 205
Volkelt, Johannes, 47
Vossler, Karl, 17
Vries, Jan de, 96
Vybíral, Jindřich, 175, 187, 197

W
Waagen, Gustav Friedrich, 69
Wackernagel, Martin, 96
Waetzold, Stephan, 205
Wagner, Brigitte, 158
Walicki, Michał, 138, 188, 197
Wallach, Alan, 82
Wallis, Brian, 76
Walsh, Philip Hotchkiss, 70
Warburg, Aby, 11, 28, 29, 43, 44, 53, 59-61, 65, 71, 81, 87, 145, 156, 169, 207
Warnke, Martin, 56, 65, 69, 72, 74, 86, 87, 92, 93, 168, 171, 212, 213
Wehli, Tünde, 141, 159
Weigert, Hans, 213
Werckmeister, Otto Karl, 93
Wessely, Anna, 28, 77, 78, 141
Westermann, Mariët, 95
Wetter, Evelin, 216

Whyte, Lancelot L., 32
Wickhoff, Franz, 12, 16, 27, 45, 127-129, 132, 134, 183, 187-189, 192
Wiese, Erich, 193
Wilde, Carolyn, 116
Wilde, Johannes, 12, 13, 44, 60, 77, 132, 141, 192
Williams, Robert, 157, 207
Wilson, Jean C., 100
Winckelmann, Johann Joachim, 167, 169, 171-173
Witkin, Robert W., 79, 82, 84
Wittekind, Susanne, 217
Witteveen, Frans J., 77, 78, 80, 81, 84, 85, 87, 96
Wittkower, Rudolf, 63
Wölfflin, Heinrich, 25, 56-59, 63, 67, 70, 135, 139, 149, 189, 191
Woltmann, Alfred, 175
Wood, Christopher S., 19, 21, 34, 36, 145, 192
Woodfield, Richard, 31, 41, 107, 113, 179
Woods-Marsden, Joanna, 158
Wróblewska, Magdalena, 165, 211
Wulff, Oskar, 189
Wyss, Beat, 17, 58

Z
Zádor, Anna, 177, 187, 188, 201
Zaunschirm, Thomas, 11
Zawiasa-Staniszewska, Katarzyna, 137, 175
Zeitler, Rudolf, 205
Zerner, Henri, 52
Žigon, August, 182
Zijlmans, Kitty, 77
Zima, Petr V., 62, 85
Zohn, Harry, 45